D0864293

HERMES AND ATHENA

University of Notre Dame Studies
in the Philosophy of Religion

Number 7

Hermes and Athena:

Biblical Exegesis and Philosophical Theology

Edited by
Eleonore Stump
and Thomas P. Flint

University of Notre Dame Press • Notre Dame, Indiana

Library of Congress Cataloging-in-Publication Data

Hermes and Athena : biblical exegesis and philosophical theology / edited
by Eleonore Stump and Thomas P. Flint.
    p.   cm. — (University of Notre Dame studies in the philosophy
of religion : no. 7)
    Includes bibliographical references.
    ISBN 0-268-01099-4 (alk. paper)
    1. Bible—Criticism, interpretation, etc.   2. Philosophical theology.
I. Stump, Eleonore, 1947-   . II. Flint, Thomas P.
III. Series.
BS511.2.H47 1993
220.6'01–dc20   92-53750
                                                                      CIP

To

ALVIN PLANTINGA

There is one story
that Virtue dwells above rock walls hard to climb
with an attendant grave chorus of light-footed
    nymphs,
and is not to be looked upon by the eyes of every
    mortal,
only by one who with sweat, with clenched
    concentration
and courage, climbs to break the peak.

Simonides, 37

(Adapted from a translation by Richmond
Lattimore in his *Greek Lyrics*
[Chicago: University of Chicago Press, 1960],
p. 55)

Contents

Contributors

MARILYN McCORD ADAMS (Professor of Philosophy, UCLA) is one of the country's foremost historians of medieval philosophy and noted for her work in philosophical theology. Among her publications are *Ockham's Treatise on Predestination, God's Foreknowledge, and Future Contingents* and the two-volume *William Ockham*.

HAROLD W. ATTRIDGE (Professor of Theology and Dean of the College of Arts and Letters, University of Notre Dame) is known for his work on the Gnostic texts from Nag Hammadi (*Nag Hammadi Codex I [The Jung Codex]*), for his commentary on the book of Hebrews, and for various other books and papers.

ADELA YARBRO COLLINS (Professor of Biblical Studies, Divinity School, University of Chicago) is known for her studies of early Christian apocalypticism in general and the book of Revelation in particular. The editor of *Feminist Perspectives on Biblical Scholarship*, she is the author of *Crisis and Catharsis: The Power of the Apocalypse* and numerous books and essays.

JOHN J. COLLINS (Professor of Biblical Studies, Divinity School, University of Chicago) is an expert on the intertestamental period who has written extensively on the book of Daniel, Hellensitic Judaism, and Jewish apocalypticism. His books include *The Apocalyptic Imagination* and *Between Athens and Jerusalem: Jewish Identity in the Hellenistic Diaspora*.

STEPHEN T. DAVIS (Professor of Philosophy and Religion, Claremont McKenna College) has written extensively on those issues in the philosophy of religion which have a close connection with biblical studies, including biblical authority and the scriptural basis for the doctrine of the Resurrection. He is the author of *Logic and the Nature of God*, *Encountering Jesus: A Debate on Christology*, and many other books and articles.

JOHN R. DONAHUE, S.J. (Professor of New Testament, Jesuit School of Theology at Berkeley) is one of the leading scholars in this country on Gospel criticism, especially with regard to the parables. His recent work includes *The Gospel in Parable: Metaphor, Narrative and Theology in the Synoptic Gospels* and *The Gospel of Mark: A Commentary*.

MICHAEL DUMMETT (Wykeham Professor of Logic, Oxford University) is widely known for his work in metaphysics and philosophy of language; he has also written on the methodology of biblical criticism and its philosophical presuppositions. His works include *Frege: Philosophy of Language* and *Truth and Other Enigmas*.

RONALD J. FEENSTRA (Associate Professor of Theology, Calvin Theological Seminary) is a specialist in philosophical theology who has written on a number of distinctively Christian topics. The author of *Pre-existence, Kenosis and the Incarnation of Jesus Christ*, he is the co-editor (with Cornelius Plantinga) of *Trinity, Incarnation and Atonement: Philosophical and Theological Essays*.

NORMAN KRETZMANN (Susan Linn Sage Professor of Philosophy at Cornell University) is perhaps the leading scholar in this country in medieval philosophy. He served as the principal editor of *The Cambridge History of Later Medieval Philosophy* and has authored, co-authored, or edited eleven other books in medieval philosophy. He is also widely known for his work in philosophy of religion. He has published articles on such subjects as faith, Trinity, and eternity.

WAYNE A. MEEKS (Woolsey Professor of Biblical Studies, Yale University) is renowned for his pioneering work in social-historical studies of Paul and the Gospel of John. Among his recent works are *The Moral World of the First Christians* and *The First Urban Christians: The Social World of the Apostle Paul*.

CORNELIUS PLANTINGA, JR. (Professor of Theology, Calvin Theological Seminary) is a specialist in systematic and philosophical theology. He has written on social theories of the Trinity and on the Cappadocian Fathers. With Ronald Feenstra, he edited *Trinity, Incarnation and Atonement: Philosophical and Theological Essays*.

ELEONORE STUMP (Robert J. Henle Professor of Philosophy, St. Louis University) is widely known for her work in medieval philosophy and philosophy of religion. She is the author or editor of numerous books, including most recently *Dialectic and Its Place in the Development of Medieval Logic*, and she has written articles on such subjects as atonement, faith, sanctification, and free will.

RICHARD SWINBURNE (Nolloth Professor of Philosophy of the Christian Religion, Oxford University) is widely regarded as one of the leading figures in contemporary philosophy of religion. His recent books include *The Evolution of the Soul, Responsibility and Atonement*, and *Revelation: From Metaphor to Analogy*.

THOMAS H. TOBIN, S.J. (Professor of Theology, Loyola University of Chicago) is a widely respected biblical scholar whose work has focused on such figures as Philo, Timaios of Locri, and St. Paul. The author of *The Spirituality of Paul*, he co-edited (with John Collins and Harold Attridge) *Of Scribes and Scrolls: Studies on the Hebrew Bible, Intertestamental Judaism, and Christian Origins*.

BAS VAN FRAASSEN (Professor of Philosophy, Princeton University) is at the forefront of current work in metaphysics and the philosophy of science. He has composed influential essays on space, time, and realism with respect to the interpretations of theories. Among his recent works are *Laws and Symmetry* and *Quantum Mechanics: An Empiricist View*.

PETER VAN INWAGEN (Professor of Philosophy, Syracuse University) is recognized as a leading figure in metaphysics and the philosophy of mind. He has also been prominent in the philosophy of religion and has addressed such issues as the doctrine of the Trinity and its philosophical implications. His published works include *An Essay on Free Will* and *Material Beings*.

Introduction

Historical Background

In recent years, there has been a growing tendency for philosophers to know about and to interact closely with their correlative disciplines. So, for example, besides generic philosophers of science, there are now philosophers of biology and philosophers of physics who enmesh themselves in the science they philosophize about and whose work is of interest to scientists as well as to their colleagues in philosophy. Similarly, philosophers of mind have increasingly interested themselves in neurobiology, psychology, or computer science. Their competence in those areas has enriched their philosophical work in philosophy of mind, and their discussions of the correlative disciplines has been of interest to people working in those disciplines as well as to philosophers.

This trend in philosophy has also been felt in philosophy of religion, where it has manifested itself in an increasing interest in the details of religion. The main correlative discipline for philosophers of religion in recent years has been theology. There have been a number of interdisciplinary conferences in theology and philosophy of religion, and recent work by philosophers of religion has included considerable focus on issues which would once have been thought to be the province of theologians alone, issues such as atonement, justification by faith, Trinity, and Incarnation.

In this environment, open to interdisciplinary approaches, we thought that the time was ripe for philosophy of religion to pay attention also to another of its correlative disciplines, namely, biblical studies. We supposed that such interdisciplinary work would benefit philosophy of religion and also biblical studies, as has been the case in other interdisciplinary ventures between philosophy and its correlative disciplines. And so we conceived a conference on philosophy of religion and biblical studies, a conference which, under the aegis of the Notre Dame Center for Philosophy of Religion, was held at Notre Dame in March 1990. Our title for the conference was "Philosophical Theology and Biblical Exegesis," and the conference was intended to be interdisciplinary between the two fields.

Our plan was to divide the conference papers equally between biblical scholars and philosophers of religion and then to have each paper commented on by someone from the other discipline. For the sake of some thematic unity, we decided to limit the topic to issues in the New Testament. For the sake of balance, we also wanted the program to include a mix of men and women, liberals and conservatives, and (for those with a religious commitment to the New Testament) Catholics and Protestants. (In case it makes a difference to anyone, readers may note that the two editors of this volume between them embody virtually all, or maybe just all, of these categories in one combination or another.) In the event, we found that balance hard to achieve, and some groups remained seriously underrepresented. For example, we did not have as many women as we had hoped we would; conservative Catholics also had little representation.

When those who had agreed to be speakers determined the topics for their papers, we looked for any commonality among the topics, and on the basis of that commonality divided the eight speakers into four pairs, each pair consisting of one philosopher and one biblical scholar. We asked both scholars in a pair to exchange papers well before the conference and to send written comments on the exchanged papers before the papers were put in final form to be sent to commentators. By this means we hoped to achieve as much interdisciplinary reflection as possible. Each paper would have been commented on by a speaker from the other discipline before the conference even began, and during the conference the papers would receive comments from the officially designated commentators as well as discussion generated by the audience. Finally, the conference concluded with an interdisciplinary panel which reflected on the exchanges during the conference and, more generally, on the project of bringing the two fields together. The papers published in this volume were rewritten in the light of all these interdisciplinary discussions. We are very grateful to the speakers who agreed to put up with these conditions, which involved them in substantially more work than is common to conference participation.

We expected our project to generate lively exchange, since we were bringing together two disciplines which normally have nothing to do with each other. As it turned out, the exchanges were not only lively but often heated or even hostile. The controversy manifested itself even before the conference began, and it was tumultuous enough to warrant some last-minute rearrangements among the commentators. Although we did approve of those peace-keeping rearrangements, they had the unfortunate result for one session of pairing a conservative Protestant philosopher among the speakers with a conservative Protestant theologian as commentator. In the end, it turned out that there were other pairings as well in which the commentator and the speaker were less far apart than we had supposed at the outset. But in all such cases we were relieved to find that there was still sufficient disagreement to produce an interesting and worthwhile exchange.

The controversy which preceded the conference continued during it and afterward as well. The details are not particularly edifying, in our view, and so we omit them here, except to say that they account for one peculiar feature of this volume. Since this foray into interdisciplinary work between the two fields occasioned so much disagreement, some of it passionate, we thought it appropriate to allow speakers an opportunity to respond to their commentators in print if they wished to do so. Some of the speakers did and others did not. For this reason some of the papers in the volume are accompanied by comments and response, others only by comments.

At this point, especially with the recurrent mention of heated controversy, it may occur to readers to wonder whether this attempt to build bridges between two disciplines was a success. There is one sense in which the answer to that question is obvious and consists in a resounding affirmative. Philosophers attending the conference or otherwise reviewing the material from the conference have been voluble in their praise of the philosophers' papers and comments; and the same sort of intradisciplinary praise for the work of the biblical scholars has also been evident. So there is good reason to believe that the papers and comments in this volume are excellent. But the question remains whether our project was a success as far as bridge building goes. The answer to that question, in our view, depends in good part on how one thinks of controversy. There are, of course, those who idealize conflict and think of it as essential to human progress. Without wanting to give a nod in that direction, we do suppose that in new interdisciplinary ventures it is precisely controversy which signals whether anything innovative is occurring. The start of interdisciplinary work requires breaching the boundaries delimiting the disciplines being brought together. When boundaries have been in place for some time, not everyone accustomed to those boundaries finds it delightful to break them down. As the history of science in the twentieth century makes clear, for example in the marriage of biology and chemistry which made the study of molecular biology possible, sometimes the progress made in interdisciplinary endeavors seems directly proportional to the degree of controversy engendered in the process. So while we definitely prefer peace to conflict, we take the controversy which accompanied the conference and which we feel sure will also attend the publication of this volume to be a sign of the fact that our interdisciplinary efforts were a success.

Finally, the order of the papers in this volume is the order in which the papers were given at the conference, and papers by philosophers alternate with papers by biblical scholars. We received a number of excellent suggestions about how we might reorder the conference papers for this volume to bring out helpful or interesting points, but we felt that such reordering might be interpreted polemically by one group or another. So we took the route of caution and left the papers in their original order.

The Papers

I. Faith and Philosophy: A Challenge to Contemporary Biblical Studies

"The Impact of Scriptural Studies on the Content of Catholic Belief," by Michael Dummett, is an attack on contemporary historically oriented biblical scholarship from the point of view of conservative Catholicism. Dummett raises an epistemological

question. If the claims of some historically oriented biblical scholars about the nature and mission of Jesus is correct, claims which
Dummett holds to be influential and widely believed, what
grounds can there be for the traditional doctrines of the Catholic
Church? This question takes two forms for him, a historical form
and a theological one. If, for example, Jesus never claimed to
be God, how can we explain its ever occurring to his disciples
to think that he was God? And if he himself never made such a
claim, then what warrant does the Church have for supposing that
that claim is true, as it has traditionally taught? Dummett argues
that the stand of historically oriented biblical scholarship requires
those who accept the claims of the Church to be fideists, acknowl-
edging that they have no evidence of any sort for their beliefs, and
he maintains that their stand also undermines the Church's claim
that the biblical texts constitute a divine revelation. His points
are of interest beyond the circle of Catholic scholars inasmuch
as they constitute a charge of inconsistency against those biblical
scholars who are themselves committed to the common doctrines
of Christianity.

In his comments, John Collins is concerned to call in question
Dummett's general approach to the questions Dummett raises.
Collins maintains that Dummett both insists on founding Christian belief on evidence, or even certainty, rather than faith, and
also inconsistently relies on a position which seems to embody the
Tertullian dictum "*credo quia absurdum.*" What perhaps concerns
Collins the most is what he takes to be Dummett's insensitivity
to the historical context of the biblical texts. Collins argues that
Dummett's conclusions are founded on ignorance of the historical
variety of meanings behind expressions such as 'son of God'
and on uninformed views of the nature of literary genres in the
New Testament period. Collins concludes by reflecting on the
philosophical presuppositions of Dummett's stance, arguing that
Dummett's arguments require valuing certainty in theology over
freedom of inquiry. A short response by Dummett to Collins's
views is included here.

II. Biblical Studies: Knowledge and Morality in Colossians

Wayne Meeks's paper, " 'To Walk Worthily of the Lord':
Moral Formation in the Pauline School Exemplified by the Letter

to the Colossians," is an examination of the Letter to the Colossians. According to Meeks, previous work on Colossians has focused on the heresy that the letter warns against. Meeks thinks that this approach has not been successful, and he suggests approaching the letter in a different way. On his view, the letter makes a strong connection between knowledge and moral behavior. He takes the letter to have been written by a disciple of Paul shortly after Paul's death, and he argues that the letter-writer's main point was the moral edification and exhortation of the Colossians. The writer calls attention to a number of theological claims about the nature and mission of Christ, and he makes a number of claims, some historical and some not, about Paul's ministry and relations to individual Christians. These claims about Christ and Paul are intended to stimulate the Colossians to a certain kind of moral behavior. The idealized picture of the apostle and the mythic figure of Christ, Meeks says, present the Colossians with a picture of the world in which the behavior to which they are exhorted receives intelligibility and value. The knowledge which the letter-writer communicates to the Colossians, on Meeks's view, shows the Colossians a picture, made more vivid by rituals such as baptism, of a specifically Christian and caring society. Thus, Meeks argues, the letter ties the knowledge it conveys to the moral behavior it wants to stimulate in the Colossians.

Meeks's commentator, Eleonore Stump, raises a question about the consistency of his views. She asks whether Meeks's conclusions about the letter's nature are consistent with his presupposition that the letter is pseudonymous. According to Stump, a moral belief acquired on testimony will be warranted only in case the person on whose testimony it was acquired is in fact a recognized moral authority. Since on Meeks's account it is false that the letter is written by Paul, it is also false, Stump says, that the moral beliefs of the Colossians are in fact warranted in the way Meeks's connection between knowledge and moral exhortation supposes. Therefore, there is not the connection between knowledge and moral exhortation which Meeks ascribes to the letter if it is also true, as Meeks holds, that the letter is pseudonymous. A short response by Meeks to Stump's views is included here.

III. Philosophy and Biblical Studies on the Empty Tomb

Stephen Davis's paper "Was the Tomb Empty?" examines the position of some contemporary scholars who apparently assent to the claim that Jesus was raised from the dead but who deny that the tomb was empty. He assumes that if the tomb was empty, that state of affairs is historical and can be investigated by historical means, and he takes the empty tomb to be a necessary but not a sufficient condition for the bodily resurrection of Jesus. There are five main arguments against the claim that Jesus's tomb was empty, according to Davis. They are these: (1) the empty tomb tradition is unreliable because the Gospels give contradictory accounts of it; (2) the story of the empty tomb is a late development and so unreliable; (3) the story was invented for apologetic purposes and so is not true; (4) the tradition of the empty tomb is seriously undermined by the fact that Paul, who is the most reliable source, does not mention it; and (5) the story of the empty tomb played no significant role in the faith of the earliest believers and so is not likely to be significant for faith. Davis calls into question the premises of these arguments. He then discusses two arguments which he thinks count in favor of the claim that the tomb was empty: first, that the story has broad support in the New Testament and, second, that Christian proclamation of the resurrection would have been impossible without the evidence of the empty tomb. He concludes by considering whether the story of the empty tomb is important for Christian doctrine, and he argues that it is.

In his comments, Cornelius Plantinga shows himself in sympathy with Davis's general conclusion, but he points out and calls in question some of Davis's presuppositions. He argues, for example, that Davis is mistaken to accept the common correlation of lateness with unreliability when it comes to Christian traditions; he gives reasons for supposing that sometimes later accounts of historical events are more likely to be accurate than earlier ones. Plantinga then questions the theological presuppositions of those who try to combine belief in the resurrection of Jesus with a denial that the tomb was empty. Finally, he examines Davis's claim that the doctrine of the bodily resurrection of Jesus is important to Christian doctrine. Arguing that Davis is mistaken to put all the emphasis on bodily resurrection alone, he considers the difference between the bodily resurrection attributed to Lazarus in Christian tradition and the bodily resurrection of Jesus, and he concludes with some theological reflections on the significance of that difference.

Adela Collins's paper, "The Empty Tomb in the Gospel According to Mark," also is devoted to discussion of the empty tomb, especially as reported in the Gospel of Mark. She begins with some perspectives on the resurrection of Jesus, presenting and criticizing common reasons given for accepting or denying the resurrection of Jesus. Then she considers the oldest text which mentions the resurrection of Jesus, Paul's first letter to the Corinthians, and she argues that Paul's understanding of the resurrection does not involve the revival of Jesus' corpse and thus does not imply that his tomb was empty. According to Collins, the earliest text attesting to the tradition of the empty tomb is found in Mark. She argues against the claim that the author of Mark used a preexisting passion narrative; she maintains instead that the author of Mark interpreted the early Christian proclamation of the resurrection of Jesus by composing a narrative about the empty tomb. Presenting various ancient sources in which a human being is translated to immortality, she suggests that the focus on the tomb in Mark may have been inspired by such stories of Greco-Roman heroes. Another notion of resurrection current at the time Mark was written, on her view, was the Jewish notion of bodily resurrection. In the light of these notions of resurrection, according to Collins, the author of Mark constructed the story of the empty tomb in order to account, in the best way he could, for the tradition that Jesus had been raised. She concludes with some reflections on the theological views which accompanied the view of resurrection the author of Mark was apparently espousing.

Her commentator, Norman Kretzmann, lays out in ten steps what he takes to be Collins's argument for the claim that Mark originated the story of the empty tomb. He finds the argument valid, but he calls in question some of its premises. In particular, he finds doubtful the following claims which are, in his view, crucial to her argument: Paul's account of the resurrection of Jesus did not imply that the tomb was empty; the summaries of the Gospel in Acts do not mention the empty tomb; and the Markan account of the empty tomb is not dependent on any earlier source. Examining the way in which Collins presents the first of these claims, he concludes that she has not given enough evidence to make the claim plausible; and he argues that the second of these claims is simply false. As for the last of the three crucial claims, Kretzmann argues that the evidence given for it by Collins in fact lend it no support at all. He concludes by reviewing and rejecting Collins's narrative development of her interpretation of the Markan story of the empty tomb. A short response by Collins to Kretzmann's views is presented here.

IV. Faith and Philosophy: A Reaction
to Contemporary Biblical Studies

Peter van Inwagen's paper, "Critical Studies of the New Testament and the User of the New Testament," is one connected argument for the conclusion that ordinary churchgoers, their pastors, and theologians who regard the New Testament as divinely revealed need not take account of the results of what he calls 'critical studies', historical biblical studies which are not based on recognition of the text as divinely revealed. His argument depends crucially on the claims that there are grounds for believing that whatever the Church has presupposed is true and that critical studies do not undermine these grounds. The bulk of van Inwagen's paper is a defense of his argument and its premises. In the process he also gives careful and elaborate explanations of historical reliability. In the end he takes the historical reliability of the New Testament texts to be compatible with a good deal of inaccuracy in what they report, provided that the inaccuracies do no harm to those who believe them true. His claim that religious believers have grounds for believing in the historical reliability of the texts is based on the more general claim that there are good reasons for religious faith, even if those reasons are difficult to articulate or consist in something less than a demonstrative argument for the propositions believed in faith. And he supports his claim that critical studies do not undermine the view that the New Testament texts are reliable by pointing to the great diversity of opinions on virtually every subject in contemporary biblical studies. This diversity, he holds, is reason to doubt whether critical studies has succeeded in establishing clearly any conclusions of much importance about the New Testament.

The commentator, Ronald Feenstra, challenges van Inwagen's rejection of the value of critical studies for religious believers. Feenstra is willing to grant the general thrust of van Inwagen's argument as it applies to ordinary believers and perhaps even to certain pastors, but he balks at granting it with regard to theologians. Critical studies often shed light, Feenstra claims, on the meaning of texts, such as the distinctive messages of the four Gospels, and Feenstra finds it misguided to suppose that theologians need not avail themselves of such useful helps. Furthermore, Feenstra holds that the formation of the canon itself was based on a type of critical studies. Since the canon is something that ordinary believers do need to know about, Feenstra questions whether van Inwagen's claim will in fact apply even to ordinary believers or whether van Inwagen means his definition of critical studies somehow to exclude the sort of historical study which was engaged in by those who helped to determine the canon of New Testament texts. He concludes by reflecting on the issue of methodological neutrality in biblical studies.

V. Biblical Studies and Philosophy on Christology

In his paper, "Calling Jesus Christ," Harold Attridge has as his purpose illustrating the methods of contemporary biblical studies by focusing on Christology in the New Testament. In the process he argues for two claims: first, that there is diversity within the New Testament on theologically important issues and, second, that early Christian documents are heavily influenced by the environment in which they arose. These claims and the results of employing the methods of contemporary biblical studies lead, in his view, to serious but not insurmountable challenges to faith. Attridge argues that the diversity of opinions about Jesus in the early Christian period suggests that Christian confessional affirmations are not dictated by the texts but are rather expressive of values or commitments which believers hold. Even passages in the New Testament texts which seem to ascribe to Jesus some clear statement about his status or mission cannot be taken at face value, since they represent not the views of Jesus himself but only the views of some later Christian community. Attridge explores four different models according to which it might seem appropriate to call the historical Jesus 'Christ', and he concludes by pointing out the ways in which these models influence theological understanding.

In his comments, Richard Swinburne addresses the methodological issues he finds in and underlying Attridge's paper. He argues that biblical scholars tend to make three mistakes in approaching biblical texts. The first is to assume that it is rational to investigate the texts without any assumptions about whether or not there is a God and whether or not God is likely to intervene in human history. The second is to fail to distinguish the role of the biblical books in providing evidence about what was done in, say, first-century Palestine from their role as part of the content of divine revelation. And the third is to suppose that there is just one plain meaning of the biblical texts. In connection with what he takes to be the third mistake Swinburne argues for a certain approach to interpreting texts, which takes the meaning of a sentence to be a function of the context in which it is set. He concludes by arguing that Attridge's four models of Christology are different but altogether consistent with one another, particularly if read in the contextual way he recommends.

Marilyn Adams's paper, "The Role of Miracles in the Structure of Luke-Acts," also addresses the issue of Christology. The thrust of her paper is that the way miracles are understood in Luke and Acts affects their Christology and soteriology. In her view, the author of Luke and Acts ("Luke," for short) uses miracles to vindicate the life and mission of a Christian leader in a way which imitates the story of Jesus' life and mission. In particular, Paul's mission and his insistence on bringing Gentiles into the Church are shown to be legitimate by miracles and visions. She then considers whether this emphasis on miracle reflects the concern with magic in the surrounding Hellenistic community. She makes important distinctions between magic and miracle, in the process stressing Luke's own understanding of the distinction, and she argues that Luke does not present Jesus and Christian leaders as magicians. Other scholars have argued that Luke presents Jesus and the apostles as instances of the divine hero (*theios aner*) common in Hellenistic culture. Adams argues against this conclusion by examining the methodology of the scholarly arguments supporting it. Her own view is that Luke uses miracles to support a soteriology which combines confidence in divine victory with realism about the costs of Christian commitment. She concludes with some reflections on apocalyptic themes and themes of judgment in Luke and Acts.

Her commentator, Thomas Tobin, agrees with Adams's general approach as well as some of her conclusions; but he is concerned to present his own interpretation of the distinction between magic and miracle, and he does not entirely share Adams's understanding of the nature of miracles in Luke and Acts. He argues that there are different ways to understand magic. In one way, 'magic' is a term used to express disapproval of the motivation behind the activities of one's religious opponents; in another way, magic is appropriately described as a technique for imposing human will on nature, without regard for the motivation underlying the use of that technique. Similarly, he holds, there were diverse attitudes toward miracles in the early Christian community. Some of the miracles in Luke and Acts do bear a resemblance to magic, understood in the sense of technique for control over nature, even if not all miracles in those books fit this pattern. He concludes with some general reflections about our epistemic attitudes toward reports of miracles.

VI. Overview of Biblical Studies

In the last paper in this volume, "Between Jerusalem and Athens: The Changing Shape of Catholic Biblical Scholarship," John Donahue presents an overview of the state of biblical scholarship. He begins by laying down a challenge: any dialogue between philosophical theology and biblical studies will have to take account of the current acceptance of historical biblical scholarship both by biblical scholars and by theologians, in particular by Roman Catholic theologians. He holds that historical biblical criticism has its roots in the Renaissance and that it proliferated during the Enlightenment, and he goes on to catalogue the somewhat rocky rise of this style of biblical criticism among Catholics during the twentieth century, culminating finally in its vindication by Vatican II. The bulk of his paper is devoted to the reception of the council's attitude toward biblical scholarship and the subsequent changes and developments in Catholic biblical studies. Two movements characterize the postconciliar period, on his view. One is the increasing acceptance of historical biblical scholarship by the vast majority of biblical scholars, and the other is the attempt to relate the results of this scholarship to theology. He then reflects on criticism of the historical method which has arisen in the past couple of decades and describes new approaches to the texts now gaining currency—in particular, social scientific criticism and literary criticism. He himself opts for a species of the latter sort of criticism, namely, rhetorical criticism, as offering the most promise for future interaction between biblical studies and theology.

In his comments, Bas van Fraassen elects not to respond to the details of Donahue's paper but instead to give his own over-view, a philosopher's overview, of biblical studies, particularly as it relates to philosophical theology. Citing the current tendency in philosophy to draw near to its correlative fields (a tendency to which this volume of papers itself bears witness), van Fraassen approves of the desire on the part of biblical scholars to be part of the general enterprise in the neighboring disciplines of history or literary criticism. But then he asks a number of questions about biblical studies as that discipline is currently studied. For example, is biblical studies science and is it secular? Secondly, why is it interesting? He answers the first, conjoint question as a philosopher, and his answer is decidedly against the view that contemporary biblical studies constitutes a secular science. He responds to the second question personally, as a Christian, and his answer here is much more tentative. Is it possible, he wonders, that biblical scholarship might uncover something which would destroy Christianity as we now know it? What is the relationship between faith and historically oriented biblical studies? His final answer, and the concluding line of his paper, is "I don't know."

Conclusion

In our view, though these papers and comments do comprise useful and important interdisciplinary exchanges between the two fields, in another sense they simply constitute the necessary preliminaries for dialogue. As the material published here makes abundantly clear, the two disciplines operate with different pre-suppositions, different attitudes toward methodology, and perhaps even different values. Readers who reflect on the papers, comments, and responses will see that the two disciplines can have varying understandings, for example, of the nature of knowledge, the appropriate methods for determining the meanings of texts, and even the desirability of separating one's religious convictions from one's work on the biblical texts. One recurring difference, in fact, has to do with neutrality or objectivity in the investigation of biblical texts. Some biblical scholars want to approach the texts just as historians, putting aside their own beliefs about central religious issues and their own value-laden attitudes toward the texts. They take their work to be part of the larger project of historical investigation of the ancient and Hellenistic world, which can be carried on in the same way by people of greatly varying worldviews. Some philosophers, on the other hand, are inclined to suppose that value-laden presuppositions significantly shape research on biblical texts, even research intended to be neutral or objective. They tend to think that at least with regard to biblical research no positions are properly neutral, and they want the presuppositions which inform the research brought out into the open and made part of the discussion. This is an important issue, as worth discussing in connection with a social science such as history or historically oriented biblical studies as the kindred issue is in connection with the natural sciences.

So besides constituting interdisciplinary exchange in its own right, the material published here illuminates deeper and more fundamental issues separating the two disciplines. It is our hope, then, that this volume will serve as a preliminary to future dialogue between the two disciplines, dialogue which will delve into these deeper issues to the enrichment of both disciplines.

Acknowledgments

Thanks are due to many people for their help with the conference from which this volume sprang and with the volume itself.

Because both the editors of this book are philosophers, we were concerned to enlist the help of a nationally recognized New

Testament expert to ensure that we asked the appropriate biblical scholars to participate in the conference. Therefore, we invited Adela Collins (who was at that time in the theology department at Notre Dame) to serve as a New Testament resource person for the conference, and she very generously and graciously agreed to help. The conference and this volume owe her a great debt of gratitude, which we are happy to acknowledge here. Although for the sake of getting as much local involvement as we could in our project we also asked for advice from other biblical scholars and theologians at Notre Dame, in every case the biblical scholars invited to participate in the conference were originally recommended to us by Collins.

In addition to those whose work is represented here, many other philosophers and biblical scholars took part in the conference and made valuable contributions to the discussion. We would like to offer special thanks to William Alston, Joseph Blenkinsopp, David Burrell, Adela Collins, and Alvin Plantinga, who took part in the panel discussion which concluded the conference; their discussion made a fitting conclusion for the conference, and we are glad to acknowledge their contribution here.

We also feel a debt of gratitude to the Director of the Notre Dame Press, James Langford, not only for his agreeing to the unusual feature of including comments and responses to comments in the volume but also more generally for his willingness to participate in an innovative and controversial project of this sort.

Our debt to Martha Detlefsen, secretary of the Notre Dame Center for Philosophy of Religion, is different but equally great. Without her intelligent and efficient efforts at every stage of the process, the conference and the production of this volume would have been considerably less smooth. We are grateful to her not only for her competence but for the cheerful generosity she brings to her work as well.

Finally, we owe special thanks to Alvin Plantinga, Director of the Center for Philosophy of Religion at Notre Dame, for his willingness to sponsor such a conference, different from and riskier than the Center's customary conferences. We dedicate this volume to him, in gratitude for his willingness to take that risk as well as for his many generous and courageous actions in support of Christian philosophy.

I. Faith and Philosophy: A Challenge to Contemporary Biblical Studies

The Impact of Scriptural Studies on the Content of Catholic Belief

Michael Dummett

Before Vatican II, the most lively, and perhaps the most illuminating, trend in Catholic theology was that inspired by the liturgical movement. That theology laid great stress on the communal economy of salvation and the communal character of the Christian life. In particular, the Bible figured as the book of a people, to be interpreted in accordance with their traditions as expounded by those accepted by them as having authority to do so. In the purely liturgical domain, the movement secured a total triumph at the Council and during its aftermath; but the impetus it had given to theology appeared rather abruptly to peter out. In Latin America, the vital current trend is liberation theology; but in Western Europe and North America the dominant influence on theology has been the work of present-day Catholic biblical scholars.

Unquestionably, Catholic biblical scholarship was formerly constrained by ridiculous fetters, exemplified by the Biblical Commission's reply to an inquiry whether it was necessary to teach that Moses was the author of the entire Pentateuch: the Commission answered that it could legitimately be held that some parts of the Pentateuch were of a more ancient origin. The liberation of Catholic scholars from these constraints resembled the effect of a starting-gun upon athletes straining to begin the race: they rushed to embrace all the most extreme conclusions of Protestant scholars of the nineteenth and twentieth centuries. The consequences for

theology have been dramatic. It would probably be misleading
to speak here of a theological school; rather, there is a tendency,
within which can be recognized extreme and moderate versions.
We should mistake the effect, however, if we thought it to be
confined to professional theologians, or to them together with
seminary teachers, or even to the clergy; many of the laity have
also been deeply affected by it in their understanding of their faith.
It would equally be an exaggeration to say that this trend has influenced Catholics throughout the world; doubtless many regions
and many social strata remain untouched by it. But middle-class
Catholics in Western countries have been profoundly influenced
by it, not usually through deep reading in theology or biblical
scholarship, but through that vague sense of where things are
heading that we speak of as the climate of opinion.

Although it does not strictly speaking constitute a school,
I shall, for the sake of a name, call it "exegetical theology," as
shorthand for "theology inspired by current biblical exegesis." It is
defined by two fundamental principles or axioms. The first is that
the Gospels, and the New Testament generally, do not provide
a reliable witness to what Jesus said or did. The Evangelists did
not hesitate to make up sayings and parables which they put into
his mouth but whose message was one they themselves wanted
to convey in the light of conditions prevailing at the time when
and in the area where they were writing. We can therefore arrive
at the actual words of Christ, or something approximating to
them, only by laborious critical inquiry, the conclusions of which
will be at best uncertain and speculative. It is often added that,
in writing in this manner, the Evangelists were conforming to a
literary convention well understood at the time; how it was that
their intentions came to be so soon misunderstood is usually left
unexplained. A frequent coda is that much of the apparent narrative in the Gospels was intended to be understood figuratively.
This is almost universally held to be true of the infancy narratives
but is often applied to the accounts of the Resurrection as well.
The Evangelists had no intention of being taken to say that any
women actually went to the tomb of Jesus and found it empty:
that was merely a pictorial manner of expressing their conviction
that Jesus was in some sense still alive, a sense not requiring the
absence of his body from the tomb.[1]

The second axiom is that Jesus had no powers lacked by the common run of humanity and no source of knowledge unavailable to ordinary men and women. His beliefs cannot therefore have included any which a Jewish religious reformer of his day could not be expected to have, and were accordingly as liable to error as those of any other devout Jew of the time. Some ascribe specific errors to him, such as expecting the imminent occurrence of the final Judgment, or the appearance of an apocalyptic figure, the Son of Man, distinct from himself.[2] More important, and more widespread, is the denial that he had any conception of those beliefs which we should regard as the central tenets of Christianity. He had no notion that he was God, or even that he was the Son of God in any unique sense, and therefore made no such claim. He thus had no conception of the Trinity and would have found the doctrine wholly baffling. He never prophesied his bodily resurrection in advance of the general resurrection, in which he no doubt believed. He regarded his mission as being exclusively to the Jews and had no intention of founding a church, or even a body within Judaism with its own special rites and ministers; he instituted no sacraments and created no episcopate.

Thus we cannot know with any certainty what Jesus taught, and, even if we did, we should have no special reason to believe it, since he may have been in error. We do, however, know with fair assurance that his teaching was not the source of any of the characteristic Christian doctrines. How, then, were these arrived at? The only possible answer is: by subsequent reflection. This answer seems to me preposterous. Nothing could, of itself, be evidence for the astonishing idea that a particular man was God, through whom all things were made. A man might live a very holy life, exhibit extraordinary insight or wisdom, possess a charismatic personality, work astonishing wonders: but none of that would approach being a ground for holding him to *be* God. Similarly, the doctrine of the Trinity, if purely the result of human speculation, would be no more than a bizarre theory, for the truth of which we could not have any cogent ground.

A very usual response to this epistemological quandary on the part of those influenced by exegetical theology is to thin the content of the various doctrines. To say that Jesus was God does not mean that God assumed a human nature, uniting it with his divine nature in a single person. Rather, it is not to state a *fact* at all, but to evince an attitude to the man Jesus Christ:[3] namely to see him as the unique human image of God, a unique reflection of the nature of God, to the extent that a human being can reflect it. Likewise, the Resurrection did not involve that anything unusual happened to the body of Jesus in the tomb, which must have decayed in the normal way of human bodies after death. Opinions differ about what it did involve, some holding that Jesus acquired a new, spiritual body, the materiality of which is left somewhat ambiguous, and the more radical thinking that henceforward his body consisted of the totality of the faithful, who constitute the Body of Christ.[4] The infancy narratives being merely pictorial expressions of a belief that Jesus was the holy one of God, the virginity of his mother at his conception is not to be understood in a crude biological sense; biologically, that conception took place in the usual way.[5] His birth of course occurred in Nazareth, not in Bethlehem. As for the Eucharist, there is a strong tendency to derive the presence of Christ from the unity of the participants, rather than conversely. It is in virtue of their already forming the Body of Christ that the elements of the sacred meal represent Christ for them, and in that sense become the Body and Blood of Christ: it is the "sacrament of what we are."[6]

This maneuver does not resolve the epistemological problem; whether the content of the doctrines remains robust or is thinned, we are deprived of any reason for believing them by the initial axioms. The empty tomb, for example, serves as a warrant that the Resurrection appearances (supposing them to have taken place) were authentic. Without it, they are like the various appearances of our Lady in modern times, in whose supernatural character we are not constrained to believe; and, without it, the Apostles could never have believed, or preached to Jewish hearers, that Jesus had risen from the dead. Again, how could anyone know of Jesus, on the basis adherents of exegetical theology allow, that Jesus was *uniquely* good, uniquely holy, the *perfect* image of God in the form of a man? On their own showing, we really know very little about him: so how can anyone be sure that he was a better man than any of the saints, or than any other historical figure who manifested heroic virtue? How, for that matter, can we be sure that he was a better man than any of those who lived and died during all the millennia that preceded recorded history? I see nothing for it but for the exegetical theologian to turn fideist at this point: his acknowledgment that Jesus lives and is Lord cannot be vindicated by evidence, but is prompted solely by faith.

The two axioms of exegetical theology undermine the conception of Christianity as a revealed religion. As it has been traditionally understood, it is distinguished by containing a number of astonishing and conceptually perplexing tenets at which no one would arrive by an ordinary process of rational reflection. That, indeed, is what confers plausibility on its claim to embody fundamental truth about the existence of the cosmos and the place of humanity within it. If we are to judge from what we now know about the physical universe, we should not expect the truth about any large matter to resemble what we should at first expect by looking about us and making reasonable guesses at what lay behind it: it is far more likely to be strange, puzzling, and hard to grasp. Theological truth, however, if present in Christianity, was not attained by any succession of ever more refined experiments and observations: the more amazing of Christian doctrines are inaccessible to unaided methods of discovery available to human beings, and hence, if known at all, could be known only on divine authority. On the understanding of the matter universal among Catholics up to little more than a century ago, Christ, as man, had some access to divine knowledge,[7] and hence could speak with divine authority; it was therefore possible to say of him, "Truth himself speaks truly, or there's nothing true." Exegetical theology destroys all ground for believing something because Christ said it; for, first, we cannot know that he said it, and, secondly, even if he did, he was as capable of being in error as any man.

It may be said that the epistemological problem remains. The traditional conception may provide a basis for believing in the Trinity, if the Gospels enable us to conclude that Christ said enough to convey the difficult idea that God is not one Person, but three Persons. The divinity of Christ cannot be believed on the same basis, however: some kind of bootstrap operation is needed if there is to be any reason to think that any revelation from God was made at all. It would be senseless to believe to be true whatever Christ said, on the ground that, being God, he must know and would not lie, and, on that basis, to believe that he was God because that was one of the things he said.

It remains that there would be no reason to believe him to be God unless he knew himself to be and gave us, through the Apostles, reason to think he knew himself to be. It would not be enough to suppose only that he *came to the conclusion* that he was God and subsequently gave his disciples to understand as much; for, if he had no greater source of knowledge of such matters than, say, John the Baptist, that would merely be a conclusion of whose truth there could be no assurance and which could not in fact have been reasonably, or even sanely, arrived at. Why, then, should we not simply think him deluded, a victim, as others have been, of the ultimate megalomania? That is certainly a rational option, as is the view that, contrary to what appears from the Gospels, he did not say it and we have no reason to believe it. The only irrational option is that offered by exegetical theology, that he did not say it, but that we have good reason to believe it. Should we then speak of a leap of faith at this point? I should rather speak of an act of *judgment*, involving far more than, but comparable in character to, those we perform whenever we assess the credibility of testimony or the mental balance of an individual. It is in no way irrational to judge, on the basis of what (if we reject the skeptical assessments of the biblical critics) we know from the New Testament of Christ and of the actions of his Apostles, that the astonishing doctrine of the Incarnation is more credible than the rival hypotheses.

A sufficient ground for taking something to hold good does not need to be a premise from which it follows by deductive necessity. A great many of our processes of thought require a component of judgment in the everyday sense of "estimation." We estimate probabilities in contexts where no assignment of numerical magnitudes to them is possible; and we arrive at conclusions because they appear to us to offer the best explanation of the known facts, where it is a matter of judgment what constitutes the best explanation. To some, the astounding proposition that a man who lived in first-century Galilee and Judea was God, through whom all things were made, appears so incredible that it could not be the best explanation of anything; delusion or misrepresentation should be preferred instead. Argument gives out at this point: it is a pure matter of judgment. Judgment does not dispense with the need for a rational ground: it is the discernment of such a ground. If there are facts which a given supposition satisfactorily explains, and if these facts are sufficiently bizarre that resort to an apparently bizarre explanation is not patently disproportionate, then, if no alternative supposition is truly explanatory, there is rational ground for that supposition. Judgment is required to determine what is proportionate and what is explanatory.

This raises two questions. The first is the exegetical question whether the Gospels do provide grounds for thinking that Jesus knew that he was God and expressly led his disciples to grasp that he was. I think that there is; but I will not at this point engage the exegetes on their own ground, although I will address the question briefly below. Here I will simply say instead that, if they *can* demonstrate that there is not sufficient reason to think this, then the opponents of Christianity can congratulate them for having deprived it of all rational basis, whether as traditionally understood or as understood by exegetical theology.

The second question is whether Christianity needs a rational basis. No Christian can safely deny that his belief is due to the grace of faith: the question is whether he may legitimately appeal to faith as the *ground* of his belief. It appears to me that if he does, he deprives himself of any means of convincing those who do not believe and deprives them of any motive to seek or desire faith. It may be objected that if faith is necessary for belief, no rational ground can be sufficient. This would be a confusion between a *condition* for believing something and a *ground* for its truth. Even in nontheological matters, we may rightly judge that certain beliefs could be held only by those lacking a minimal degree of human decency; by contraposition it follows that such a degree of human decency is a sufficient condition for rejecting those beliefs. It in no way follows that there is no rational ground for rejecting them: all that follows is that lack of an adequate moral sense may impede one's ability to perceive the cogency of that ground. Faith must complement, and never supplant, reason; for God is just and cannot wish or require anyone to believe that which there is no reason to believe.

Exegetical theology impugns the reliability of the Gospels and the Acts of the Apostles, questions how much of the teaching attributed to Christ was truly his, and denies that it could be trusted even if we knew what it was: what does it do for the dogmatic pronouncements of the Church? Since, according to it, there was no initial revelation, it would be natural for it to deny that any divinely appointed custodian and interpreter of that revelation was needed or could exist. The conclusion is not strictly entailed, for it would be possible to hold the Church to be the recipient of a subsequent and continuing revelation; but, although, in view of the admission of Gentiles into the Church, we must hold that revelation did not cease after the Ascension— such a claim, as extending to post-Apostolic times, would lack all warrant or credibility. It is therefore unsurprising that exegetical theology encourages its followers to sit very loosely to creeds and definitions. Formal attitudes differ considerably. Some roundly repudiate the very idea that the Church has the right to delineate the content of Christian belief. Others espouse what Father Raymond Brown calls 'centrism', in contrast to radicalism.[8] This consists, according to him, of not denying traditional doctrines but accepting them with nuance. Paul Gifford has examined five instances of this procedure;[9] I will quote just one of them.[10] "When understood with nuance," Brown wrote, "the proposition that Jesus Christ founded the one, holy, catholic and apostolic church is not necessarily foreign to modern exegetes." What does the proposition mean when so understood? That, when Jesus was no longer on earth, his disciples took the step of requiring a visible sign (baptism) for adherents to Jesus and subsequently adopted the term 'church': it does not require any explicit intention on Jesus' part during his ministry. Gifford's comment seems to me apt:

> All that 'Catholic centrist exegesis' supports is a verbal formula. Could it not be argued that . . . the understanding that Brown discounts, or says is no longer required or even tenable, is the very understanding that the formula was originally devised to convey? And . . . that the meaning Brown now gives to the formula has in the past been officially repudiated?

The centrist position resembles the celebrated attitude of Tract XC to the XXXIX Articles of the Church of England. According to Tract XC, Anglicans owe nothing to the intentions of those who framed the Articles. They merely profess their assent to those Articles as formulated; hence, in giving that assent, they are entitled to put on them whatever construction they choose, however strained, that the words will bear, no matter how little it conforms to the obvious intentions of the authors of the Articles. Some work of interpretation is indeed needed in understanding, say, the Nicene Creed. It contains some technical theological terms like the often cited 'homoousios', and some frankly metaphorical or figurative phrases like "Light from Light," "came down from heaven" and "at the right hand of the Father." It is nevertheless tendentious to represent the phrase "rose again on the third day," as either obscure or metaphorical; or to propose that the word 'virgin' admits any but a 'biological' sense, as if anyone would, in a solemn declaration apply it to a human being in any other. It is, of course, because in these two cases there is so clear a deviation from salient doctrines, understood according to the evident intentions of the credal formulas, that they are so frequently singled out; the Incarnation is well known to require delicate formulations. In fact, however, it is equally tendentious to present the interpretation of that doctrine as relating to attitudes rather than to facts as a possible reading of the weighty christological pronouncements of the Creed. In practice, the liberty of interpretation that the centrist exegetes allow themselves in construing dogmatic formulas is so wide as to impose no constraints whatever on their theological views.

The Catholic Church has always required the acceptance of certain beliefs as a condition of membership; and, until recently, the universal understanding has been that the fact of requiring them is a guarantee of their truth. The centuries-old claim of the Church has been to have a commission from Christ to safeguard the truths revealed by him and to the Apostles, and a promise to be protected from misinterpreting them. That there should be such a custodian is intrinsically plausible. For it is not credible that God should have intervened in human life in so extraordinary a manner, in part to reveal truths that we could not otherwise have known, and then allowed that revelation to suffer the garbling and distortion that is the normal fate of human theories and speculations. Obviously, not all Christians would agree that such a means of preserving the Christian revelation is likely to have been provided. My own opinion, on the contrary, is that it would be hard to accept that there had been a revelation from God if he had not also supplied such a means of keeping it intact and warding off destructive misinterpretations of it. Precisely that has been the primary point of disagreement between those who thought there was a compelling reason for membership of the Roman Church and those who saw a compelling reason for *not* belonging to it. The claim made by that Church virtually ruled out the possibility that there was no compelling reason for either.

Given that exegetical theology, whether radical or moderate, involves the falsity of clauses of the creed and other doctrinal formulas in the sense in which they were intended, the truth of that theology necessarily entails the invalidity of the Church's claim to be custodian and interpreter. For, if the claim is just, doctrines, once promulgated, are not open to revision, save insofar as they can be shown to have been subsequently misinterpreted or wrongly taken as having been proclaimed as essential to the Christian faith and consequently binding. The Church's claim is rendered void, however, not only if exegetical theology is *true*, but if it is even *tolerable*. By "tolerable" I mean "admitted, explicitly or tacitly, as consistent with membership of the Catholic Church." For it was the fact of their being required for membership that was taken to provide the guarantee of their truth. If, then, they are no longer required for membership, the claim has been renounced; and, if renounced, it can never have been warranted, for it is not the kind of claim that might be just even though withdrawn. Thus, if exegetical theology is tolerable, the Catholic Church, through most of its history, has been a fraudulent institution, making a baseless claim on the strength of which it imposed burdens it had no right to require. On the view I expressed above, that if there were no body entitled to make such a claim, it would be doubtful whether any revelation from God could ever have been given to us, this would call in question much more than the ground for membership of the Catholic Church: it would call in question the truth of Christianity altogether.

To say such a thing is, naturally, to arouse great indignation on the part of those sympathetic to exegetical theology, who will at once stigmatize it as 'divisive' (as my views were called, in print, by Nicholas Lash[11]). In a London Sunday newspaper there recently appeared a report about the draft Universal Catechism, saying:

> of particular concern is a passage which reaffirms that: 'The task of giving an authentic interpretation of the Word of God...has been entrusted to the living teaching office of the Church alone. Its authority in this matter is exercised in the name of Jesus Christ by the bishops in communion with the successor of Peter, the Roman Pontiff'.[12]

There, of course, is a statement, in traditional terms, of the claim I have been discussing. The report goes on to quote

> the Catholic theologian Jack Mahoney, Professor of Social and Moral Theology at King's College, London. He said: 'I can see enormous difficulty with this document because the Catholic Church is pluriform and the idea that such a catechism can satisfy everyone is divisive and unrealistic'.

What worries Professor Mahoney is not that teaching authority is ascribed only to those bishops who are in communion with the Roman Pontiff, but that, in a 'pluriform' Church, it is ascribed to anyone at all.

When Pope Paul V intervened in the dispute over free will between Jesuits and Dominicans to declare that both views were consistent with the Catholic faith and that neither side was to call the other heretical, his intervention healed a division. The theory has nevertheless always been that, in crucial disputes that do involve the integrity of the Christian faith, the Church has the right to intervene on one side against the other; such interventions intensify the existing division but are justified as needed to preserve the integrity of the faith. The condemnation of Monophysitism at Chalcedon resulted in one of the worst of schisms; the majority of Christians in Egypt and what we now call the Middle East fell away from Catholic unity. If avoidance of divisiveness is paramount, most of the early Councils sinned woefully against that cardinal principle. If I am to be rebuked for divisiveness, why does Lash refer to the Council of Chalcedon as having authority?[13] If the Church is to be pluriform, why are we not going to the Unitarians, the Nestorians, and the Monophysites and saying to them, "We are sorry: it was all a terrible mistake. Please think what you like; we realize now that no creed could satisfy everyone"? What is to hinder instant reunion all round? Are Mahoney and those who think like him demanding that? Or is divisiveness unobjectionable when directed at Arians and Monophysites, and offensive only when directed at Mahoney and his colleagues?

In the present instance, it is not a matter of settling a disputed question newly arisen but of responding to the raising of old questions settled long ago and, in particular, to a challenge to the Church's claim to authority to settle questions at all. The Church may reasonably say, concerning some issue, free will for example, "Diverse views are open to Christians on this question"; and it sounds modest and irenic to plead that, in a pluriform Church within which divergent opinions abound, all should be suffered to maintain their opinions undisturbed. But in this case, it is not modest: it is a demand for surrender. For the Church cannot say, "Some Catholics hold, and others deny, that the Church has the right to pronounce on what is of faith"; to say that— or, in a professedly comprehensive catechism, to say nothing on the matter—would be to renounce the claim. This is an issue that cannot remain unresolved: attempting to leave it unresolved would be a cowardly way of resolving it. And if it is resolved in favor of the pluralists, the Church will thereby be admitting to having long been a fraudulent institution, in which the pluralists will deserve no credit for continuing their membership.

I said earlier that I would not challenge the exegetes on their own ground concerning the question whether Christ manifested any consciousness of his divinity but I owe it to you to indicate why I think that an ordinary Christian or inquirer into the truth of Christianity has no need to immerse himself in this expertise in order to form a reasonable opinion on the question. Consider such a saying, attributed to Jesus, as "No one knows the Son except the Father, just as no one knows the Father except the Son and those to whom the Son chooses to reveal him" (Mt 11:27, Lk 10:22). This does not, of itself, demand interpretation in terms of full Trinitarian doctrine; but it incontestably contains a claim to be uniquely the Son of God. If neither it nor any similar saying is authentic, how are we to understand it? There are three possibilities. (1) The Evangelists knew perfectly well that Jesus had never made any such claim, but wanted their readers to believe that he did, with an eye to getting them to accept that claim. (2) When they had recuperated from the shock of Jesus's arrest and execution, the Apostles not only came to believe that he was divine, or at least not purely human, but persuaded themselves, quite falsely, that he must have said so; they therefore told others of things he had said to this effect, and these found their way eventually into the written Gospels. (3) The Evangelists did not intend their readers to suppose that Jesus made any such claim, but were confident that they would understand that, by putting those words into his mouth, they themselves were making that claim on his behalf.

Of these hypotheses, (1) quite implausibly attributes a blatantly fraudulent character to the Gospels. The hypothesis (2) that the Apostles were deluded is by far the most probable of the three, but is still unconvincing. The Apostles were all Jews. That, as a psychological defense against the horror of his death, they might have persuaded themselves that Jesus was in some special sense still alive is perfectly credible. That they should have adopted the belief, preposterous on any count, repugnant for a Jew, that he was in any sense divine, is possible only if they were quite unhinged; and if they had been unhinged, they could not have acted as they subsequently did. I call the belief preposterous because, on the present supposition, that Jesus himself made no such claim, that is what it would be: no other evidence whatever would then make it a sane idea to entertain, even if one had risen from the dead.

The popular exegetical line is hypothesis (3); but it is surely frankly incredible. How *could* the Evangelists have counted on being so interpreted? Is there the slightest indication that anyone ever did so interpret them? In a play like *Julius Caesar*, the author has converted historical characters into his dramatis personae: he does not purport to be vouching that the historical individuals acted so or spoke so. Dorothy Sayers's intentions, in *The Man Born to be King*, were plainly different: she was saying something like, "This is how I imagine that it might have happened, within the limits of how it can be represented under the constraints of a radio play." But a written text does not have to supply the details unavoidable in a play—the context, the response, and so on—and the Synoptic Gospels notoriously avail themselves of this freedom to the full. Those who were to read the Gospels would have been Christians interested in the actions and teaching of the Jesus of history. It can hardly be likely that they would take *none* of the words and deeds there attributed to Jesus as intended to be unrelated to anything he did or said; and no signals appear in the text to mark off those presented as authentic from those not so presented. Exceedingly strong evidence would be needed to convert such implausibilities into probable conjectures. It is because the theories of the exegetes rest either on the postulation of improbable literary genres without any attempt to show that the New Testament writings were ever so understood, or on a tacit ascription to their authors of an intent to mislead, that a lay person is justified in paying only minimal attention to them.

The general principle that biblical writers, like any others, must be understood as they intended to be understood, that there exists a variety of modes of writing, and that those prevalent in the ancient world do not precisely tally with those with which we are familiar is almost too obvious to need enunciation; but much, though by no means all, that is written by biblical exegetes appears to take the principle as a license to interpret the New Testament writings in defiance of all plausibility. To assign any of them to a specific genre requires clear proof that such a genre existed and that at least some of their earliest readers understood them in accordance with its supposed conventions; and such proof is frequently unconvincing and perfunctory in the extreme. I will give only one minor, though troublesome, example. There are real grounds for suspecting the Second Epistle of Peter to be inauthentic, in the sense of not having been written by St. Peter, despite its undeniable claim to have been. This difficulty is standardly treated by asserting that it was an established convention to present a literary or theological work as having some famous person as author. To make that out, it would be necessary to hold that none but the naive or uneducated were ever misled, and that the author had adequate ground for assuming that no one would be. It is plain that a convention, surely recognized as such, existed of assigning Wisdom books to Solomon; but argument seems lacking for holding that there was any more general such convention. The great host of apocryphal works with reputed Old Testament authors cannot be cited in support, unless it is shown that there was no intention to deceive. In the case of Christian literature, the claim seems quite improbable, in view of what we do know: Tertullian, for instance, records the degradation for imposture of the presbyter who composed the apocryphal Acts of Paul. Second Peter poses a problem precisely because, if in no sense written by St. Peter, it is just such another imposture, despite having been declared canonical by Trent. Resolution of the problem by casual appeal to the notion of literary genre is a species of intellectual frivolity which I strongly suspect to be involved in many other instances of the deployment of that notion.

The moderate exegete may sum up in favor of the traditional view even on such a question as the virginal conception of Christ; but he again is in epistemological difficulties. In the end, his decision can rest only on his assessment of the intentions of the New Testament writers; but this is a broken plank. However convinced we may be that Sts. Matthew and Luke meant to assert that Mary was still a virgin while she was carrying Jesus in her womb, we still require a reason to believe them. If their assertions are to be our principal ground for believing these propositions, then Hume's celebrated argument about miracles must apply: it must be more probable that the New Testament writers were mistaken, or were aiming to deceive, or had themselves been deceived by others, than that such extraordinary events in fact occurred.

The clauses of the Creed relating to the conception and birth of Jesus are, however, those from the traditional understanding of which adherents of exegetical theology most frequently deviate. This is in part because, unlike the visit to the tomb, the early chapters of Matthew and Luke do not appear as part of a continuous narrative and are written in a different style; in part also because the virginal conception of Jesus is said not to be a central doctrine.

This latter statement is a half-truth. Certainly it would be possible for someone oblivious of the doctrine and of the infancy narratives to hold all the essential other Christian beliefs. Yet whether you accept the Virgin Birth as fact or dismiss it as fable, whether you regard the infancy narratives as containing historical truth or as devoid of it, makes a deep difference to the picture you have of Jesus Christ and therefore probably to what you believe about him. If you think there is no factual truth in them, your picture will be of a carpenter's son seized, in full maturity, by the conviction of having a religious mission, his family dismayed and hostile. You *could* accept this picture and yet believe that, being God, he had sources of knowledge denied to the ordinary religious reformer, but the pressures would be against it. You would be much more likely to regard him in the manner of exegetical theology, namely to treat his being God as making absolutely no difference to what he was like as a man, and accordingly (in the words of Eamon Duffy) to "take seriously his human psychology, his frailty, his fallibility, his individuality,"[14] inquiring how he conceived his mission, exploring his self-image, and analyzing his personality. True, it might be asked how we could expect to be able to investigate the psychology of one not subject to the inherited deformation of original sin; but that is not an inquiry very likely to be made at the present day.

If, on the other hand, you accept the infancy narratives as giving a correct general conception of the birth and childhood of Jesus, the whole aspect is altered. On this picture, his parents knew, before his birth, that he was in a very particular sense from God; and he himself, while yet a boy, was yet more clearly conscious of the fact. If you accept that, it will not lead you to deny that he was truly human in all respects; but you will acknowledge that, in becoming man, he did not choose in every regard to subject himself to the conditions of our life. You will then entertain the possibility that the knowledge he possessed as man was not subject to all the limitations which the minds of fallen human beings incur.

Modern exegetes and theologians frequently assume that, to be 'scientific', biblical criticism must prescind completely from Christian faith. To treat the New Testament writings like any others demands that they be judged on the same basis as anyone would judge them, whatever religious beliefs he had or lacked.[15] That is, however, utterly irrational. Whatever has been conclusively demonstrated must be accepted: fossils were not put into the rocks by the Devil to seduce us into unbelief, or by God to test our faith. But virtually nothing proposed by New Testament scholarship has been conclusively demonstrated: it consists almost entirely of hypotheses judged to be more probable than others. Estimates of probability depend crucially on background assumptions, since probability is a relation between a proposition and a body of evidence. What is probable if there is no God, or if Christ and his disciples were misguided fanatics, becomes quite improbable if Christianity is true. Without some background beliefs, no judgment of probability can be made; there is nothing scientific about setting aside your background beliefs in order to arrive at such judgments, and then, on the basis of those judgments, either leaching most of the content out of the beliefs you started with, or explicitly rejecting them altogether.

Triumphalism has deservedly been condemned in recent years; but it has not been observed that there is a progressive triumphalism as well as a conservative one. Conservatives in the Catholic Church have been thoroughly chastened by the widespread excoriation of their former triumphalism; the new theologians have adopted a triumphalism of their own which, so far, has scarcely been noticed, or, if noticed, neither pointed out nor resisted. Their views have been propagated as endorsed by the experts, whom the uninstructed lay public may not challenge without impertinence and without showing themselves to lack respect for scientific method; opponents are ridiculed as flat-footed literalists, a species doubtless thought closely akin to the fundamentalists, and subjected to condescending explanations of the concept of a literary genre, as though they must be virtual illiterates. Theology is an intellectual discipline which, like all others, must perforce make use of technical apparatus; no plainer example of this can be found than in mediaeval theology. Yet the scholastic theologians never forgot that the laity were as capable as they of insight into the truths of faith, however imprecisely they formulated them. The new theologians have, in large measure, forgotten that. They react only with indignation to the dismay evinced by Catholics to whom it appears that the religion to which they have been loyal is apparently being whittled away from above, treating expressions of such dismay as no more than malicious attacks upon themselves. Certain of their superior knowledge, they do not ask whether this dismay might not be well founded. It is my contention that it is.

NOTES

1. See, out of many examples, Fergus Kerr, O.P., "Catholic Faith and Easter Stories," *New Blackfriars* 57 (August 1976).

2. For this and many other components of a radical version of exegetical theology, claimed to summarize 'common teaching' in Roman Catholic seminaries, Thomas Sheehan, review of Hans Küng, *Eternal Life?* in the *New York Review of Books* for 14 June 1984.

3. Eamon Duffy, "The Philosophers and the China Shop," *New Blackfriars,* 69: 449.

4. See Hubert Richards, *The First Easter: What Really Happened?* 2nd ed. (London: Mowbray 1983).

5. For one of many expressions of this view, see Uta Ranke-Heinemann, *Eunuchs for Heaven,* trans. John Brownjohn from *Eunuchen für das Himmelreich* (London: A. Deutsch 1990), 312–313; she cites Rudolf Pesch with approval as saying on p. 26 of his "On the Question of Jesus's Brothers and Sisters," in Bishop Karl Lehmann, ed., *Vor dem Geheimnis Gottes den Mensch verstehen*, "The New Testament professes and proclaims that Jesus is the son of God, but not that Jesus was conceived without an earthly father."

6. The phrase concludes one of several invitations to communion (used in place of the *Ecce, Agnus Dei*) used at Masses at Blackfriars Priory, Oxford.

7. Even this cautious phrase might have had an odor of heresy to Pope Vigilius, who in 553 issued the following condemnation, aimed at the Nestorians, at the request of Justinian: "If anyone claims that Jesus Christ was ignorant of future events and of the day of the last judgment, he who was one single Jesus Christ, at the same time true Son of God and true son of man; and if he claims that he was able only to know what was revealed to him by the deity dwelling in him as in another, let him be anathema." I am not aiming at a satisfactory formulation, but only at a rejection of the view, virtually axiomatic among exegetical theologians, that Jesus had *no* access to divine knowledge.

8. See his letter in the *Tablet* for 5 March 1988.

9. Paul J. Gifford, "The Certainty of Change," *New Blackfriars* 69 (July/August 1988): 330–339.

10. Raymond E. Brown, "Liberals, Ultraconservatives and the Misinterpretation of Catholic Biblical Exegesis," *Cross Currents* (Fall 1984): 318.

11. Nicholas Lash, "A Leaky Sort of Thing? The Divisiveness of Michael Dummett," *New Blackfriars* 68 (December 1987): 552–557.

12. The *Observer* for 27 May 1990, front page.

13. Lash, "A Leaky Sort of Thing," 556.

14. Eamon Duffy, "Mater Dolorosa, Mater Misericordiae," *New Blackfriars* 69 (May 1988): 225.

15. Joseph Fitzpatrick, "Lonergan's Method and the Dummett–Lash Dispute," *New Blackfriars* 69 (March 1988): 126–138.

The Impact of Dogmatism on Rational Discourse: Comments on the Paper of Michael Dummett

John J. Collins

The first thing that behoves a commentator on Michael Dummett's paper is to deconstruct his rhetorical strategy. Professor Dummett would have us believe that he represents the ordinary Catholic laity and that biblical scholars are a haughty elite of "experts" whom the good simple folk are forbidden to challenge. Nothing could be further from the truth. Ordinary Catholic laymen do not posture as experts on the philosophy of religion, nor do they presume to construct arguments as to the ground on which the Catholic faith stands or falls. Professor Dummett is here as an expert and he cannot so easily excuse his failure to attain even a basic literacy in the subject on which he presumes to pontificate. On the other hand, as Professor Dummett well knows, appeals to authority, whether that of "experts" or of dogmatists, carry no weight in historical biblical criticism. It is of the essence of the method that any argument must be supported by appeal to evidence and that any conclusion can in principle be challenged on the basis of new evidence or argumentation.[1] He must also be aware of the enormous efforts of biblical scholars, Catholic and Protestant, to make the material available to the laity in an accessible way. Professor Dummett does not speak for the Catholic laity but for a small group of reactionary intellectuals.

Perhaps the most surprising thing about Professor Dummett's paper is how little he knows, or has bothered to learn, about the profession he has chosen to attack. As far as I can see, his knowledge of biblical scholarship seems to be almost entirely dependent on a review by Thomas Sheehan (a philosopher) of a book by Hans Küng (a systematic theologian). He mentions only two biblical scholars, Raymond Brown (from a letter to the *Tablet* and a popular piece in *Cross Currents*) and Rudolf Pesch (from a second-hand reference). Yet he presumes to discern "two fundamental principles or axioms" of "exegetical theology." He cites no biblical scholar, or theologian, who holds these principles as axioms, and I very much doubt that any could be found. There are biblical scholars and theologians who hold such positions *as conclusions* of research, but that is a different matter, since conclusions can always be challenged if new evidence or arguments can be adduced. Professor Dummett must not be allowed to project onto biblical scholarship the dogmatism of his own mindset. For the dispute is in large part between the empiricism of historical study, which insists on appeal to evidence and is therefore quite properly called exegetical theology, and the dogmatism of Professor Dummett, which rests on assumptions about the requirements of Christian belief which remain unsubstantiated and are, I believe, unwarranted.

Rhetoric aside, what is the substance of Professor Dummett's argument? It is helpful to have some awareness of the correspondence in *New Blackfriars* to which reference has been made. Professor Dummett initiated that correspondence with an article that professed a concern for Christian unity, but concluded with an assertion that the present diversity of opinion within the Catholic Church "ought to be tolerated no longer,"[2] a fine way to promote Christian unity, no doubt. At the beginning of that article he distinguished between reasons for belonging to the Catholic Church and a rationale for it. A rationale, we are told, "for belonging to a particular church would be a proposition holding good generally and not relating to certain individuals more than to others, that, in virtue of its truth, constituted a reason, perhaps a compelling reason, for belonging to that church rather than any other."[3] Pluralism will not do. It is not enough that a particular church offer a good way of following the Gospel; it must be right, and all others wrong. Without such a proposition, according to Dummett, those who ever died for their faith were pitiably deluded.

Now this kind of "propositional Christianity" is rather obviously the construct of an analytical philosopher. The rank and file of Christians are quite content to have "reasons" to belong to their churches, and do not need such a rationale. The more dogmatically inclined, who crave certainty in matters of ultimate truth, most often appeal to faith or church dogma, oblivious to the charge of fideism. Dummett, too, would like to have us rely on the teaching of the Church rather than make our own inquiry and derides the opposing view as "scientific Protestantism."[4] But he does not want to be considered a fideist, and so he wants his appeal to Church dogma to be backed by a rationale for believing Church dogma in the first place. Herein lies the essential ambivalence of Dummett's position, which is evident again in his present article. On the one hand he flirts with a Pascalian *"credo quia absurdum"* position, claiming that the fact that no one would arrive at certain Christian tenets "by an ordinary process of rational reflection" confers plausibility on them. On the other hand he retreats from such blatant irrationalism and admits that "some kind of bootstrap operation is needed if there is to be any reason to think that any revelation from God was made at all."

Here at last there is some prospect of common ground between Dummett and biblical scholarship. On p. 9 Dummett quite correctly isolates two fundamental questions, although their logical order should be reversed. The question whether Christianity needs a rational basis must be answered in the affirmative if we are to have any hope of rational discourse. On this much we apparently agree. The crucial question, then, is the exegetical one. What do the Gospels actually say and how should they be understood? At this point Dummett's argument cries out for a treatment of the exegetical problem, but none is forthcoming. Instead he feebly declines to engage the exegetes on their own ground. But this he cannot do without conceding the argument as he himself has structured it. If the ground for Christian faith is to be sought in what Jesus said and thought, then theology must of necessity be exegetical, and the exegetical task cannot be shirked.

It must be said that Dummett's construal of the exegetical question is excessively narrow. He is not concerned with the broader questions of what the Gospels actually say, but only in the ground they give for believing in the divinity of Christ. He holds, moreover, that "there would be no reason to believe him to be God unless he knew himself to be and gave us, through the Apostles, reason to think he knew himself to be." The logic of this argument is far from apparent. We should still have to decide whether the claim was credible. Others besides Jesus claimed to be divine. Some, like Caligula, were obvious megalomaniacs. Others, like the philosopher Empedocles, were more complex. On Dummett's own account, the assessment of such a claim would involve an act of judgment, comparable in character to those we perform whenever we assess the credibility of testimony. In short it would rest on an assessment of the nature and character of the claimant, as known from other sources. The claim to be divine has no probative force in itself and does not provide any better basis for certainty than post-mortem reflection.

Most biblical critics would, I think, say that the belief in the divinity of Jesus arose from reflection on his life, death, and resurrection. There were obviously *reasons* that in fact led to this development, but no conclusive, unambiguous proof. Dummett quite rightly asks how anyone can be sure that Jesus was a better man than anyone else who ever lived. We cannot be sure. That is a problem if one craves certainty as Dummett does. It was not a problem for the early Christians, nor has it been a problem for most Christians through the ages.

One could go on to point out that even if Jesus did claim to be divine and the claim were true, this would by no means clear the way for accepting the Roman Catholic Church as the one true guardian of revelation. Dummett begs fundamental questions about the purpose of divine revelation (which he assumes must be concerned with propositional truths) and the connection between Jesus and the Church. But all of this is moot. The Achilles' heel of Dummett's position is that the Gospels do not even attribute to Jesus the kind of claim to divinity that the Church councils made on his behalf.

It is crucial here to appreciate that language must be understood in its historical context, a point which Dummett concedes in a perfunctory manner, but does not heed at all. Take the expression "son of God." Anyone who has read the Bible with a modicum of care knows that this phrase is used in a number of ways. In some cases (e.g., Gn 6) it is used of heavenly beings that we might call angels. Elsewhere it is used of Israel (Hos 11:1), the king (Ps 2, whence the later use with reference to the messiah as in 4 Ezr), or even of the righteous man (Wis 2:13, 16). The last instance is especially relevant here, as it is close in time to the Gospels. Even St. Paul says that all who are led by the Spirit are sons of God (Rom 8:14). From this range of usage it should be quite clear that the phrase "son of God," in biblical idiom, does not imply a biological relationship, or virgin birth, still less membership in a Trinity. So we may grant that Matthew 11:27/Luke 10:22 ("no one knows the Father except the Son . . . ") constitutes a claim to be son of God in some special sense, but all this can reasonably be taken to mean is a claim to a specially close relationship with God, at most a union of mind and will. The metaphysical concerns of the later Church Fathers are simply not present in the Gospels. The Gospel of John has certainly a higher Christology than the Synoptics, but even that mythical entity, the ordinary Catholic layman, can see that the idiom of John is quite different from that of the other Gospels and unlikely to preserve the words of Jesus. (In fact, even Dummett has conceded, in *New Blackfriars*, that Jesus may not have spoken "all those long speeches" in the Gospel of John.)[5] But even in John, Jesus rebuts the charge of blasphemy by citing Psalm 82, "I said, you are gods" and arguing that "he called them gods to whom the word of God came," and he makes the rather unTrinitarian statement that "the father is greater than I" (14:28). If Dummett were to take the trouble to read the Gospels carefully, even on the assumption that Jesus said everything attributed to him, he would find much that does not easily accord with dogmatic preconceptions.

Dummett's apparent ignorance of biblical usage and lack of attention to what biblical texts actually say are related to his obduracy on the question of literary genres. He makes a cursory admission "that there exists a variety of modes of writing and that those prevalent in the ancient world do not tally precisely with those with which we are familiar" but this concession is not reflected at all in his treatment of biblical texts. He complains of being treated like a virtual illiterate. Now all I know of him is what I have read in *New Blackfriars* and his present paper, but as yet I have seen no evidence that he understands any form of communication except propositional analysis and polemical diatribe. He certainly exhibits no familiarity with the literary conventions of the ancient world. Take the matter of pseudonymity, a convention that is ubiquitous in the ancient world. Dummett is at least aware of the existence of "a great host of apocryphal works with reputed Old Testament authors," but he claims that they cannot be cited in support unless it be shown that there was no intention to deceive. This is to confuse the existence of the convention with its motivation. Of the existence of the convention there can be no doubt whatever, and it is by no means restricted to works with reputed Old Testament authors. I don't suppose that Dummett wants to defend the authenticity of the Gospel of Peter or the Apocalypse of Paul. If I understand him correctly, he assumes that these noncanonical pseudepigrapha are all deceptions and worthy of moral condemnation, and that such deception is unthinkable in canonical works. Now it doesn't require much familiarity with the ancient world to see that these alternatives are too simplistic. There was a wide range of motivations for pseudepigraphy.[6] The Neo-Pythagoreans thought it most honorable and praiseworthy to publish one's philosophical treatises in the name of Pythagoras himself.[7] A priest, Salvian, who was accused of writing a letter in the name of Timothy about A.D. 440 argued that "he did not wish the obscurity of his own person to detract from the influence of his otherwise valuable book."[8] His bishop was apparently satisfied. When Tertullian condemned the author of *The Acts of Paul and Thecla*, it was because some people claimed "Thecla's example as a licence for women's preaching and baptizing."[9] The same Tertullian held that "that which disciples publish should be regarded as their masters' work,"[10] so his views on pseudonymity were evidently somewhat less stringent than Dummett's. In the case of the Old Testament pseudepigrapha, so cavalierly dismissed by Dummett, we can only guess at the self-understanding of the authors. What is amply clear, however, to anyone who takes the trouble to read these books, is that many of them contain religious and moral material that is in no way inferior to that of the canonical Scriptures. If this be deception, it is in spirit of Plato's "noble lie,"[11] and I see no reason why 2 Peter, or Colossians, should not be judged "deceptions" by the same criteria. Pseudonymity, of course, has fallen out of fashion, and Dummett finds it difficult to believe that other people may have judged truth and falsehood by standards different from his own. (I wonder, incidentally, if he would accuse George Eliot of deception.) But whether pseudonymous documents be judged deceptive or not, the existence of the convention is beyond question by anyone who is literate in the field. Equally the historiographic convention of attributing to characters things we might suppose them to have said, whether they did or not, is well attested and even explicitly defended by Thucydides. Here again we should not suppose that Dummett's all too limited historical imagination exhausts the range of logical possibilities. If there is to be meaningful dialogue between biblical scholars and philosophers about the biblical texts, the philosophers will have to learn something about the field (and Marilyn Adams's paper shows that this can be done) and not indulge in the glorification of ignorance in the guise of polemic against experts.

The fact that Dummett pays so little attention to actual biblical scholarship, or indeed to the biblical text itself, is not incidental but reflects the real structure of his thought. At the end of the *New Blackfriars* debate he complained that according to his critics "What we are supposed to do, instead of relying on the teaching of the Church, is to make our own investigations on such matters as what the New Testament writers intended."[12] Dummett clearly wants us to rely on the teaching of the Church (at least as he understands it) and ignore such matters as the researches of experts or the evidence they may adduce. In light of this dogmatic posture, his professed concern for a rational ground for faith rings hollow. As we have seen, if that ground is sought in what Jesus said or thought, it must of necessity be established by exegesis. Yet Dummett fails to engage the task of exegesis and avowedly pays minimal attention to those who do. His appeal at the end of his article to the importance of presuppositions, or "background beliefs," only underlines the circularity of his argumentation.

In the end, however, it seems to me that Dummett's quarrel with biblical criticism is not only a matter of expertise or ignorance, but reflects a basic ethical stance. What offends him is the notion of liberty, at least within the Catholic Church, the very idea that diversity of opinion should be "tolerable." He cannot abide the idea that exegetes should be free to evaluate his cherished beliefs on the basis of evidence, because then, he says, we can have no assurance of their truth, no certainty. For Dummett, the illusion of certainty is a higher value than freedom of inquiry. His insistence that "exegetical theology" is not even tolerable (p. 00) shows that he is a fideist, or dogmatist, at heart, for any pretense of rationality requires that at least the ground of his belief be established on the basis of evidence and therefore be subject to the uncertainty of criticism. I find his hostility to freedom of inquiry anomalous in a professor of philosophy, but I also find it anomalous in someone who professes to be a follower of Jesus of Nazareth. For however garbled the words of Jesus may be in transmission, we are not told that he ever said that diversity of opinion should not be tolerated. It is no small irony that Dummett should posture as a latter-day Defender of the Faith, while preaching intolerance in the name of Catholic Christianity.

NOTES

1. The classic statement of the principles of historical criticism is that of Ernst Troeltsch, "Ueber historische und dogmatische Methode in der Theologie,"*Gesammelte Schriften* (Tübingen: Mohr, 1913) 2:729–753. For a more recent formulation see Van A. Harvey, *The Historian and the Believer* (New York: Macmillan, 1966), 38–67.

2. Michael Dummett, "A Remarkable Consensus," *New Blackfriars* 68 (1987):431.

3. Ibid., 424.

4. Michael Dummett, "What Chance for Ecumenism?" *New Blackfriars* 69 (1988):531.

5. Ibid., 543.

6. See Bruce M. Metzger, "Literary Forgeries and Canonical Pseudepigrapha," *Journal of Biblical Literature* 91 (1972):3–24.

7. Iamblichus, *De Vita Pythagorica* §198.

8. Metzger, "Literary Forgeries," 8.

9. Tertullian, *De Baptismo* 17.

10. Tertullian, *Adv. Marcionem* 6.5.

11. *Republic* 382C, 414B, 459D.

12. Dummett, "What Chance for Ecumenism?" 531.

Response to Collins

Michael Dummett

Professor Collins has chosen to comment in considerable part on articles I wrote for *New Blackfriars*, as well as on my paper; since those articles may be inaccessible to readers of this volume, the editors have kindly allowed me a brief space to respond.

My original article was indeed concerned in the first instance with Christian unity: specifically, with the prospects for reunion between Catholics and Orthodox. I indicated certain obstacles that Catholics place in the way of such a reunion; and I identified as one of the gravest the widespread loss, among Catholics, of the sense that we are the custodians of truths handed down to us which it is our duty to preserve undistorted. The ensuing debate centered on this, to the complete neglect of the topic of reunion. As I saw it, the question was: is the Catholic Church a fraudulent institution? There is no doubt that that Church has, at least until very recently, claimed to be the divinely appointed guardian of a revelation and, on that basis, has made acceptance of certain doctrines a condition of membership. To those who believed the claim and accepted those doctrines on the strength of it, the answer to the question is of vital importance; to them it means: have I based my life on a lie?

The reason for asking the question is that there is now a strong current of opinion within the Church, undoubtedly stemming in the first instance from the work of New Testament exegetes, inconsistent with the historic claims. If the claims were to be expressly disavowed by the Church, that would be tantamount to a confession that, in the past, she had secured assent to what

31

were then her teachings by false pretenses. If the claims are not overtly repudiated, but those views which conflict with them are treated as compatible with membership in the Church, that is, as admissible views for a Catholic to hold, then the Church will have *implicitly* abandoned her former claims and will be presently occupying a hypocritical position. It was for that reason that I said that those views ought not to be tolerated, in the sense, which I explained clearly, that they should be unambiguously declared incompatible with membership of the Catholic Church. A 'progressive' who does not accept the historic claims of the Church may give the appearance of liberality by saying to a 'conservative' who does, "I do not deny you the right to hold your opinions; why should you deny me the right to hold mine?" But the progressive's plea is insincere: for, simply by professing the views he does, while claiming to be a full-fledged member of the Church, he *does* implicitly deny the conservative the right to his views. He does so because, if his views really are compatible with the Catholic faith as now constituted, the Church's former claims were in truth unfounded; the conservative's belief in them is therefore false, and his life has indeed been founded on a lie.

The familiar sneer at 'propositional Christianity', in which Collins indulges, is quite beside the point. No one ever suggested that adherence to the Creed was the sole, or the most important, duty of a Christian; it is undeniable that it has been treated as one indispensable such duty. The theological tendency which calls in question the Church's claims often does so implicitly, by denying central articles of the Creed, or by 'reinterpretations' that eviscerate their content. I choose, however, to concentrate on its direct attack, as being both more widespread and more fundamental. Certainly, if a revelation was made to us from God through Christ, the claim of the Catholic Church to be its guardian by no means immediately follows; but, if no such revelation was made, the claim is unquestionably spurious. A divine revelation is, *ex vi termini*, something that may be trusted absolutely; if, as is widely held, Christ had no source of knowledge other than those possessed by Jews of his time generally and was as subject to error as they, there was no revelation and we have no indefeasible reason for believing what he taught. As for the belief in his divinity, resoundingly proclaimed in the Nicene Creed, Collins has failed to take my point. Such a belief *could* not reasonably, or even sanely, arise from later reflection on anyone's life and death, or even resurrection (in a sense in which he could subsequently turn in his grave or even in one in which he could not); anyone who arrived by reflection at the conclusion *about himself* would be insane. The belief could arise only if, in addition, the one believed to be God had conveyed the fact to those who were to spread his message and if he were understood to be speaking from *knowledge*. Certainly a mere claim to divinity is not in itself self-substantiating; but to ascribe divinity to any human being who made no such claim would be at best superstition.

If New Testament exegetes can demonstrate that Christ made no such claim, or that he could not have *known* it to be true, they will have achieved what many have craved, a definitive refutation of Christianity; if they purport merely to be 'nuancing' the religion, they bring not only it but themselves into ridicule. It is the first of these conditional propositions I have been principally concerned to establish; of course I do not believe its antecedent.

II. Biblical Studies: Knowledge and Morality in Colossians

"To Walk Worthily of the Lord": Moral Formation in the Pauline School Exemplified by the Letter to Colossians

Wayne A. Meeks

"Watch out lest there be someone who is despoiling you by means of philosophy. . . ." Thus in part runs the text of Colossians 2:8.[1] The warning seems so apt for a biblical scholar thrown into a den of philosophers that I decided not merely to make it a kind of talisman for myself during the conference but to take the whole of this rather difficult letter as the subject of my paper. The fact is that biblical scholarship has not been conspicuously successful in solving the problems of the Letter to Colossians. I hope that, by suggesting an order of questions about it somewhat different from those that have become customary, I may succeed in showing that there is some booty here worth the philosopher's attention, and, far from snatching that booty away, the philosopher may be able to help clear up some of the issues that the letter raises.

In Pursuit of the Heretics

Exegetes of the Letter to Colossians have been mesmerized by the verse I quoted, which goes on to connect the φιλοσοφία viewed so ominously with "empty deceit according to human tradition, according to the elements of the cosmos and not according to

Christ." There are other warnings in similar language in the same chapter: "I say this in order that no one may delude you with beguiling speech" (2:4, RSV); "So do not let anyone judge you on food or drink or on particularities of festival or New Moon or Sabbath" (v. 16); "Let no one throw you out of the game by obsession with 'humility' and angels' rites" (v. 18); "Why do you let people lay down the law to you?" (v. 20). Linking these warnings together, interpreters have taken the main business of this letter to be a polemic against a particular "heresy" that some of the members of the Christian groups in towns of the Maeander valley must have adopted or concocted. The reconstruction of that heresy, by means of clues throughout the letter and comparisons with known or imagined religious movements from antiquity, became the interpretive key for historical exegesis of the entire letter. That is, everything else said in the letter was to be interpreted by divining its relevance to the polemic against the false teaching.

A prodigious quantity of often fine research and historical imagination has been poured into the effort to understand exactly what beliefs the Colossians were being warned against. Unfortunately the success of these efforts, if we measure success by the power to convince one's fellow scholars and thus to achieve some measure of consensus, has not been conspicuous.[2] This kind of failure, which is frequent in the history of research, does not of course prove that the question was the wrong one to ask. There are many perfectly valid and important questions, probably more than we are usually inclined to admit, that simply cannot be answered given the present state of our knowledge. That is no reason to stop asking them; something new may turn up at any moment. It would be enormously helpful and satisfying to know what were the "philosophy" and "tradition" and "dogmas" against which the author of Colossians warned. Nevertheless, while we wait for a more convincing answer to that question, this is surely an opportune time to ask whether the writer of the letter was as preoccupied with this "heresy" as we have been.

Knowledge and Behavior

The writer, following the practice of Paul, states the theme of the letter in its opening thanksgiving.[3] In 1:9–11 he or she prays that the addressees be "filled with knowledge" so as "to walk worthily of the Lord, to please him utterly, bearing fruit in every good work and growing in knowledge of God." The writer resumes this theme in 2:6: "So, as you received Christ Jesus the Lord, walk in him." If the writer is concerned with correcting the beliefs of the Colossian Christians, it is not for the sake of beliefs as such, but in order to shape the audience's moral dispositions and behavior. The contents of the rest of the letter confirm this judgment; it is predominantly a letter of moral advice, which the ancient rhetorical classifiers would call "parenetic."[4] Like a good Calvinist, the author believes that "all truth is in order to goodness."[5]

The relation between religious knowledge and moral behavior remains, I surmise, a fundamental problem in modern philosophy.[6] The author of the Letter to Colossians would not have used those terms, but the letter is a specific exercise in the relationship that we thus name. It is filled with language of "knowing," "learning," "hearing," "receiving [tradition]," "understanding," and the like, all closely tied to admonitions or statements about behavioral norms. The letter is so constructed as to bring to mind—in a particular configuration—a number of things that, the author asserts, the readers (should) already know. Looking at the statements about knowing and learning, we discover that their contents are of two sorts. On the one hand, there are statements that are, or could be put, in the form of propositions of theological belief, especially about Christ. On the other, there are a number of statements that have to do with people knowing one another or knowing things about one another, especially "Paul" and the congregations addressed. Let us look at some of each kind.

The two sorts of knowledge are tied together at the beginning of the letter. "Paul" gives thanks and prays for the Colossian saints and faithful brothers because he has "heard" of their faith and love. Their faith and love in turn are said to be warranted by an eschatological hope (διὰ τὴν ἐλπίδα τὴν ἀποκειμένην ὑμῖν ἐν τοῖς οὐρανοῖς, 1:5a), about which they "previously heard" in the gospel and "learned" from Epaphras (vv. 5b–7). Epaphras' Gospel is presumably the same as Paul's, which the author describes in 1:26–27 (in good Pauline language, cf. 1 Cor 2:6–10) as a "secret hidden from the aeons and generations but now revealed to his holy ones."[7] The Colossian Christians are included among those "holy ones" (1:2). The goal of Paul's "contest" (ἀγών) is described in 2:1–3 as the confirmation of Colossians and people like them who had not met him personally, including the neighboring Laodicaeans, in knowledge of that secret (εἰς ἐπίγνωσιν τοῦ μυστηρίου τοῦ θεοῦ, Χριστοῦ)—"in which [or, whom] all the treasures of wisdom and knowledge are hidden." Paul would not likely have demurred from this disciple's description of his mission; it is at the same time an apt description of the fictional letter's intended purpose.

The admonition in 3:9–10 certainly conveys an aura of mysterious knowledge: "Do not lie to one another, as people who have taken off the old human with the practices belonging thereto and have put on the new—the one who is being made new in [or, to attain] knowledge [εἰς ἐπίγνωσιν], according to the image of the new human's creator." This curiously elaborate warrant for a simple maxim is particularly important for answering our central question, how knowledge is connected with norms for behavior. In fact the whole series of admonitions 2:20–3:17 is a key for understanding what kind of knowledge the writer has in mind and how the addressees would have acquired it. We will turn to the latter question in a moment; suffice it here to note that this part of the letter is filled with language that alludes to the baptismal ritual and recalls interpretations and instructions that were probably associated by tradition with Christian initiation. In the "table of household duties" that follows (3:18–4:1) a lot of knowledge that was widespread in ancient urban culture is taken for granted,[8] together with some knowledge of specific Christian beliefs. "Knowing" (εἰδότες) appears explicitly as warrant for admonitions to slaves (3:24) and masters (4:1). What they know, respectively, is that in the divine judgment there is no partiality[9] and that masters themselves have a master (κύριος) in heaven. The conclusion of the letter's body sums up the admonitions with the advice, "Walk in wisdom toward those outside, exploiting your opportunity" (4:5). "Wisdom" is an all-purpose word, the content of which is not further specified; we may assume that the needed behavioral wisdom is related to the special knowledge to which the letter so often alludes, since knowing how to "walk" is its leitmotif.

Statements about interpersonal knowledge are also abundant. Friendly letters usually convey information about the writers and signal in various ways things that the writers know about the recipients. For a fictional letter, Colossians contains a surprising number of indicators of mutual knowledge. "Paul and Timothy" have "heard" about the Colossian Christians' faith and love (1:4, 9) through Epaphras, the church's founder (v. 8). In turn, it is obvious that the recipients have heard Paul (compare Eph 3:2, in another fictional letter dependent in part on Colossians, where this assumption is made explicit). The writer wants the recipients to know (θέλω γὰρ ὑμᾶς εἰδέναι, 2:1) more about Paul (after the opening "Timothy" has disappeared into the first person singular). Consequently, after introducing a poem about Christ's identity and mission (1:15–20) and a summary recollection of the recipients' conversion (1:21–22), the author inserts a note in autobiographical form (1:24–2:5). This note focuses upon Paul's service (as διάκονος) of "the Gospel" (1:23, 25–29) and of "the church" (1:25). The Gospel of which Paul is minister is of course the Gospel to and by which the Colossians have been converted and to which they are now urged to remain faithful (1:23); the brief characterization of its content as an eschatological "secret" (1:26–28) resumes the mythical picture of Christ contained in the earlier poem.

As Paul often does in the authentic letters, this writer focuses upon the sufferings entailed in his ministry (1:24) and describes it, in a favorite term of ancient philosophical moralists, as a "contest" (ἀγών, 2:1). This element, too, is closely linked both with the christological image previously invoked (by the unprecedented language of 1:24, "filling out the balance of Christ's affliction") and with the lives of the Christian groups addressed (ὑπὲρ τοῦ σώματος αὐτοῦ, ὅ ἐστιν ἡ ἐκκλησία, 1:24; ὑπὲρ ὑμῶν καὶ τῶν ἐν Λαοδικείᾳ κτλ, 2:1).

At the end of the letter "Paul" promises that Tychicus and Onesimus (who are thus the fictional and perhaps the historical bearers of the letter) will bring further information about his situation (4:7–8) and adds greetings from a number of people (vv. 10–14) and a directive for the recipients to greet others (vv. 15–17). Perhaps these friendly conventions, quite familiar in the genuine letters of Paul, are intended to add verisimilitude to the fiction. At the same time they serve an important function in the parenetic strategy of the letter by extending the circle of personal knowledge within which the recipients are to hear the apostle's admonitions.

The author of Colossians does not spell out anywhere in propositional form the precise connection between proper Christian knowledge ("in all wisdom and spiritual intelligence") and "worthy" behavior, even though we saw that connection to be the virtual theme of the letter (1:9–10). However, the passages we have looked at suggest that the two kinds of knowledge that the letter talks about—and which it is designed to enhance and to reinforce—serve the letter's hortatory aim in two encompassing ways. One function is to sketch out the symbolic realm, the other, to indicate the social realm, within which the "worthiness" of one's dispositions and behavior is to be perceived and evaluated.

A large part of the symbolic world sketched in the letter is the description of ideal figures and their actions: God, Christ, and the Apostle Paul. In much moral discourse in antiquity, including early Christian discourse, such descriptions often serve as *exempla*, models to be imitated.[10] In his undoubted letters Paul several times urges his audience to imitate him as he imitates Christ (1 Cor 4:16; 11:1; 1 Thess 1:6; see, too, 2 Thess 3:7, 9), and in later hortatory literature this pattern becomes more frequent (and often simpler). We have one straightforward instance in Colossians: "As the Lord forgave you, so also you [ought to forgive one another]" (3:13).[11]

However, the dominant strategy by which the Colossians author links myth with norm is more complex and subtle than imitation. A particularly striking instance is the way this writer uses the traditional poem or hymn quoted in 1:15–20. This is one of several similar poems that scholars have identified, with varying degrees of probability, in early Christian literature.[12] The case that has received the most attention is Philippians 2:6–11.[13] Traditionally this famous description of the Christ who, though he was in the form of God, "emptied himself" to take human form and "humbled himself" in obedience to the point of death, was taken as a straightforward model for Christian humility. In a provocative article published in 1950, Ernst Käsemann challenged that interpretation, insisting that the "hymn" was essentially a soteriological myth that could have no parenetic force whatever.[14] That is, the poem in Philippians does not describe a model life to be imitated but a foundational event to be believed in. Influential as Käsemann's essay has been, he has left many interpreters unpersuaded. Recently, for example, Ulrich Müller has argued for a position diametrically opposite to Käsemann's: not only is Paul's use of the hymn parenetic, the hymn itself was parenetic from the outset.[15] The truth probably lies somewhere between; to use Käsemann's terms, Christ is both "Urbild" and "Vorbild."[16] The case is similar in Paul's disciple's use of a poem in Colossians 1:15–20.

In Philippians the key words that link the poem with the admonitions surrounding it are "humble/humility" (ταπεινοῦν, ταπεινοφροσύνη: 2:3, 8) and "obedience/obey" (ὑπήκοος, ὑπακούειν: vv. 8, 12), but there are later resonances with the poem (especially in 3:17–21) that link the described mythic action of Christ and God not only with the behavior urged on Christians but with a mythic description of their own future, which draws the symbolic horizon within which the admonitions work. In Colossians the key words are "reconciliation" and "peacemaking." The poem says that "the Fullness" (here probably a circumlocution for God, though πλήρωμα would later become a technical term in the cosmogonic myths of some Gnostic groups) inhabited Christ in order "through him to reconcile the universe to him[self?], making peace through the blood of his cross" (Col 1:19–20). The letter-writer immediately echoes the motif of cosmic reconciliation on the personal level: "And yourselves, who then were enemy aliens by your way of thinking, in evil works, now he has reconciled in the body of his flesh through death. . . ." (vv. 21–22). Later the "peacemaking" motif is likewise transmuted from a cosmic and mythic to a personal and moral plane: "Let the peace of Christ act as umpire in your hearts, the peace into which he has called you in one body" (3:15).[17]

A similar play on keywords earlier in the letter connects moral expectations with cosmic framework in a different sense. The "word of truth, the Gospel" is described as "bearing fruit and growing—as in all the world, so also in you" (1:6). The metaphorical hendiadys, probably derived ultimately from the phrase in Genesis 1:22, 28, and elsewhere in the Torah, had apparently become a common way of speaking about the early Christian missionary endeavor. The author of Acts used a similar phrase as a refrain to punctuate the account of the Church's expansion from Jerusalem outward: "The Word of God grew and multiplied" (Acts 12:24 RSV; cf. 6:7 and Lk 8:11–15). The writer to the Colossians, however, takes up the phrase again in the letter's transition from thanksgiving to admonitions: "in every good work bearing fruit and growing in knowledge of God" (1:10). The addressees' part in the worldwide "fruitbearing and growth" of "the Word" is both their conversion and their subsequent behavior.

Significantly the poem about Christ and its application to the Colossians is followed immediately by the apostolic autobiography 1:24–2:5, and the relation of the latter to the letter's parenesis is analogous to that of the former. The central motif in the description of Paul's career is his suffering, but here nothing is said about the Colossian Christians being called to suffer. Rather the Apostle's suffering is a continuation of Christ's suffering and it is *for* the whole Church, Christ's body (1:24). Their appropriate response is to behave in accord with the teaching and admonition that the Apostle addresses to "every human person" (v. 28; note the thrice repeated πάντα ἄνθρωπον).

When employing the ideal figure of the Apostle as when using the mythic figure of Christ, the dominant logic of the ethical warrant is thus not that of a model to copy. Rather we have the description of a cosmic, divinely initiated process, into which the Colossian Christians have been incorporated and in light of which they are urged to develop their perceptions of what they ought to think and to do. The cosmic process is continuous with the Christian missionary endeavor, for which in this letter the idealized picture of the Apostle stands as prototype and warrant. The epistolary cliché, "absent in flesh, present in spirit," takes on special significance in 2:5, assuming that the letter is a pseudepigraph, for the Apostle is now permanently absent, and his presence will henceforth have to be mediated by letter and by (idealized) descriptions of his career. Christ, of course, is also physically absent, but present by word and spirit (3:16), and the faithful are destined to be "presented" to him at the Judgment (1:22; cf. 1:28; 3:4).

If the letter's reminders of the Christians' knowledge of and about Christ and Paul serve to define the symbolic universe within which Christian behavior receives intelligibility and value, the letter's allusions to other individuals and groups serve to define their social horizons. We have already noticed that the letter in several ways links the experience of the addressees with the worldwide mission of the Apostle. In several ways the connections are made concrete. Epaphras is a specific, personal link (1:7; 4:12). The six who, in addition to Epaphras, send greetings (4:10–14) and the two, besides all the brothers in Laodicaea, to be greeted (4:15–17) create the picture of a network of friends—of "brothers and sisters" in Pauline language—who are, as it were, witnesses and guarantors of the directives given to the Colossians. Most of these names duplicate the list in Paul's letter to Philemon, which this writer must have known and used. Unique to Colossians is the very close relationship that is assumed and fostered between the Christian groups addressed and those in the neighboring city of Laodicaea (2:1; 4:13, 15–16).

Elsewhere I have argued that in the process of resocialization of converts into the Christian groups of the Pauline circle, one of the central strategies is the substitution of the Christian community for the primary normative reference groups that had previously shaped the converts' perceptions and their values. There are many passages in the undoubted letters of Paul that reinforce this shift, encouraging the addressees to think of fellow Christians as the effective audience, approving or disapproving, praising or blaming, before whom their actions were performed.[18] The same strategy is clearly at work in the Letter to the Colossians. A large part of the moral wisdom that this letter seeks to induce and reinforce in the readers is the knowledge of a circle of "significant others" who care about them and about what they do. These others include the ideal figures, above all Christ and Paul, who thus become what some sociologists call "reference individuals." The others also include the whole world of Christian house-assemblies, especially those in the immediate vicinity.

The Acquisition of Christian Moral Knowledge

Early in our reading of Colossians we saw how the writer restated the theme of the letter to introduce the main, hortatory section: "So, as you received Christ Jesus the Lord, walk in him" (2:6). How *had* the addressees "received Christ," and what was it about that "receiving" that could serve as a pattern for behavior?[19] Part of the process, as we have seen, was the verbal communication of information through "the word of truth, the Gospel," presumably by preaching and instruction. We have also seen, however, that a peculiar kind of poetry or hieratic prose was known by addressees and writer, and they are likely to have learned it within a ritual context, in regular meetings of the Christian groups. We cannot be sure what specific ritual provided that context, whether Eucharist or baptism or other occasions of the Church's gathering, but there are throughout the letter many quite explicit allusions to baptism. Thus, immediately after the thematic introduction 2:6–7 and the warning against "philosophy" we noticed earlier in verse 8, the writer draws out one of the images of the poem ("in him *dwells* all the *fullness* of deity bodily, and you are *filled* in him, who is *the head* . . . , vv. 9–10; cf. 1:18, 19), and then continues with a series of relative clauses that all refer to baptism:

> in whom also you were circumcised with a circumcision made without hands, by putting off the body of flesh in the circumcision of Christ; and you were buried with him in baptism, in which you were also raised with him through faith in the working of God, who raised him from the dead. (vv. 11–12, RSV)

The primary context for "receiving Christ" that the writer has in mind is evidently baptism, or rather the whole process of resocialization into the Christian community of which baptism is the symbolic center.

The baptismal ritual that the Pauline groups received and continued was a drama of transformation. Stripping off their clothing, the converts "took off the old human" and thus "died with Christ"; descending into the water they were "buried with him." Brought up from the water, they were "raised with Christ" and reclothed, "with the new human," who was Christ himself, sometimes understood as the original Image of God after which the first human had been created. In this understanding, baptism restored the primal purity and unity of Eden before the separation of male from female and before the Fall. Receiving the Spirit of God, the baptized were "adopted" as children of God and enabled to cry out, "Abba! Father!" Sometimes there followed perhaps an enthronement, for as Christ was now enthroned in heaven his new brothers and sisters were somehow elevated to share his heavenly status.[20]

If the ritual was effective, its strong imagery and dramatic action would render an alternative reality for those who experienced it. The ritual directly challenges the stability of the everyday social world—kinship, ethnic identity, status, roles, gender—and insinuates a contrary map of fact and value. Yet we do not move easily from one symbolic world to another. The picture of the way things are that we absorbed in our primary socialization is very tough and can hardly be entirely supplanted by subsequent experience, however dramatic—our modern myths about "brainwashing" and "capture" of minds by cults notwithstanding. Furthermore, the behavioral consequences that follow from a metaphor-laden depiction of a novel world are seldom obvious; different interpreters draw different implications. "Conversion" is an extended and partial process, requiring an attentive community to reinforce the alternative reality. The Letter to Colossians is an example of such "universe maintenance."[21]

Viewed this way, ethics is a hermeneutical process. The interpretive strategy adopted by the writer of Colossians is apparent in the formal structure of the whole central section of the letter (2:6–3:17), to which the more particular directives of 3:18–4:6 are appended. The structure is implied already in the topic sentence quoted above (2:6), "So, as you received Christ Jesus the Lord, walk in him." The "so, as" (ὡς οὖν) announces the analogy to be sought between worldview and ethos, mediated, as Clifford Geertz would say, by sacred symbol—in this case the sacred symbols declared in "the Gospel" and dramatized in baptism.[22] What follows is not any particular description of appropriate behavior, but first an effort to nihilate a rival interpretation by declaring that it is "not according to Christ" (v. 8) and then a resumé of the writer's interpretation of how Christ was "received" in instruction, song, and baptism (vv. 9–15). The imperative mood of verse 8 returns in verses 16–19, tied to the preceding description of the baptismally represented reality again by the inferential particle "so" (οὖν). The imperatives here add a little detail to the picture of the rival interpretation to be avoided, which must have been a lot clearer to the original audience than it is to us.

48 / *Wayne A. Meeks*

The two conditional sentences 2:20 and 3:1–2, both in the grammatical form implying that the protasis states a factual condition, continue building the structure of analogy between ritually induced worldview and the wanted dispositions and behavior. "Since you have died with Christ [and thus been liberated] from the elements of the world, why do you let people lay down the law to you, as people living in the world?"[23] "Since you have been raised with Christ, seek the things above, where Christ is seated at the right hand of God—concentrate your moral reasoning [φρονεῖτε] on the things above, not the things on earth." In the latter admonition, and in the warrant that follows in 3:3–4, the change of symbolic worlds that the writer sees implied in conversion is almost candidly stated. The dying and rising with Christ that baptism represents means here disconnection from "the world" and "the earth" of ordinary, commonsense reality, cultivating instead a moral reasoning (a *phronesis* very different from Aristotle's) based on a reality "above." And the writer stigmatizes the "philosophy" he opposes, with its commandments and ascetic discipline, as belonging entirely to the "lower" world.

The dominant imperatives of 3:5–17 also echo the language of the baptismal ritual: "put to death" (v. 5), "take off" (v. 8), "put on" (v. 12), and so do the participles that state warrants, "having taken off" (v. 9), "having put on" (v. 10). The reference to the "peace of Christ" in verse 15 alludes, as noted above, to a line of the poem (1:20), and the "dwelling" of the word of Christ "in you" (3:16) also may possibly allude to the poem's phrase about "the Fullness" that "inhabited" Christ (1:19). For this writer a life "worthy of the Lord" is defined not by cultic or ascetic rules or by other "human commandments" but by a reasoned set of dispositions that proceed by analogy from a fundamental symbolic structure declared in preaching and instruction, elaborated in song, and enacted in ritual.

The Worthily Patterned Life

The specific contours of the appropriate "walking" are more suggested than described in this letter. Not surprisingly, peculiarly Christian features appear less in the particular directives than in the warrants and the metaphorical framework. The vices that one must "put to death" and "take off" with the "old human" (3:5–9) are oddly called "the limbs that are on earth" (v. 5), but otherwise the list might be found in the lectures of any pagan moralist. Only the added clause defining "greed" as "idolatry" bespeaks the influence of Jewish tradition. The virtues to be "put on" (vv. 12–14) include more specifically Christian or Jewish language, notably "humility" (ταπεινοφροσύνη), which in popular thinking counted not as a virtue but as a disaster that might befall one.[24] (Earlier the writer has used the same word in a pejorative sense, coupled with the neologism "will-cult," ἐθελοθρησκία, to label the "angels' cult" and its associated practices, 2:23). However, what mostly stamps these admonitions as Christian is the context referring to the experience of conversion ("as God's chosen, holy and beloved," 3:12), the prominence given to love ("above all . . . the knot tying perfection together," v. 14), the "conformity pattern" ("as the Lord forgave you," v. 13), and the fact that the virtues espoused here are those gentle traits that would ease the common life of a close and intense community.

That communal life is the locus of moral formation, as 3:16 makes clear. Mutual admonition was a practice that distinguished early Christian groups from almost all other religious associations in antiquity. Analogies could be found only in some of the philosophical schools, especially the Epicurean and Pythagorean, and in some sects of Judaism, like the Essenes and the Therapeutae. The "teaching and admonishing" that the writer of Colossians urges connects this feature of the continuing life of the local house-assemblies with the writer's summary description of Paul's mission in 1:28: "admonishing every person and teaching every person in all wisdom"; 3:16, "in all wisdom teaching and admonishing yourselves." The juxtaposition of "teaching and admonishing" with "by psalms, hymns, spiritual songs singing graciously in your hearts to God" may not be fortuitous. As Martin Hengel has argued, the tradition of "spiritual" singing in early Christianity not only created Christology, it "created community."[25] If it is true that 1:15–20 is a version of one of those "spiritual songs," then the letter's writer has given an example of the way song could be used for "teaching and admonishing."

Considering that the addressees have been told that they have "died from the elements of the world," that their life is "hidden with Christ in God," and that their moral reasoning must be set on "the things above," the worldliness of the admonitions in 3:18–4:1 is a surprise. The relationships of governance, protection, and subordination advocated here are those that were thought in antiquity to be essential to the well-ordered household.[26] The household was the microcosm and foundation of the civic life that was the fundamental context of Greco-Roman ethical reflection, even in the age of empire when the *polis* had been subjected to a new complex of power and patronage. The household's hierarchical relationships would seem, therefore, to epitomize that world that belonged to the "old *anthropos*," supplanted for the Christians by the new, "where there is not Greek and Jew, circumcision and foreskin, barbarian, Scythian, slave, free, but Christ everything and in everything" (3:11). In later centuries, as Peter Brown has shown, ascetic Christians recognized in the household the keystone of the old world, against which they must do battle or from which they must flee.[27] Yet, like other cults appearing for the first time in a city, Christianity had gained its foothold in the Greco-Roman cities within the households of friendly individuals who were in a position to offer protection and support.[28] The bishops who opposed the later extreme ascetics, according to Brown, spoke for and were dependent upon the "silent majority" for whom the household still defined their world.[29] Perhaps the battle line between the writer of the Letter to Colossians and the "philosophy" he opposed, with its ascetic rules "Touch not, taste not, handle not" (2:21), was drawn in analogous fashion.

Certainly it is clear that for the letter's writer the Christian household—Nympha's, for example, mentioned expressly in 4:15—is not part of the world to be "taken off." On the contrary, it is the very place where the Christian moral reasoning, the thinking on "things above," is to be practiced by mutual admonition, teaching, and singing; where the life that is "hidden with Christ in God" is to be rehearsed on earth; where the way of living is to be formed that will be "holy and blameless and unimpeachable" when they are "presented before him" at the coming judgment.

The ordering of the household is not materially different (with one possible exception) from what Aristotle would have approved. Only the warrants stated are novel: wives are to be subject "as fitting"—good Stoic moral concept—but "in the Lord" (3:18). No warrant is given for the husbands' rule. Children should obey "because this is well pleasing in the Lord" (v. 20). Nothing is peculiarly Christian about the reason for fathers being urged to control their anger: "lest they [sc. the children] become dispirited" (v. 21). Warrants for behavior of slaves and masters are a little more elaborate—and therein lies the one notable deviation from ordinary pagan conceptions of the household. Here (and elsewhere in early Christian adaptations of the form) slaves are directly addressed. They are persons, morally competent, able to exhibit virtue, responsible for the household's good order.[30] For slaves, "fearing the Lord" (with the previous phrase "those who are your masters according to the flesh" inserted to make plain that it is not those "lords" who are to be feared), and "work as for the Lord and not humans, knowing that from the Lord you will receive payment in the form of an inheritance"—metaphorical play on the one hope for freedom and advancement open to most slaves—"serve the Lord Christ." And a warning: "Whoever does wrong will get paid back the wrong done, for there is no partiality [i.e., as some manuscripts add, with God]" (vv. 22–25). For masters, a little less elaborate: "Knowing that you yourselves have a master in heaven" (4:1).

Perhaps the "philosophy" of the "angels' cult" wanted by cultic rules and ascetic "humility" to define the Christian existence as a continuing warfare against the fallen and transitory world. If so, the letter-writer's affirmation of the common household structures may be understood in part as a resistance to that more militant picture of reality. In any case, the metaphors that dominate the letter's imagery of the world have to do with peace and reconciliation. Even when the writer does introduce the military images of a triumphal procession, exhibiting as prisoners of war the naked "rulers and powers" (2:15), these images depict a victory already won, a peace established in the Crucifixion.

In this context, too, we can understand the special significance of two further motifs that are prominent in the letter's admonitions: the concern for the reaction of "outsiders" (οἱ ἔξω, 4:5–6) and the exceptional emphasis on thanksgiving. "Abounding in thanksgiving" describes the right way of "walking" in the thematic sentence 2:6. "Be thankful" and "Do everything. . .in the name of the Lord Jesus, thanking God the Father through him" bracket the summary admonitions in 3:15–17, and thanksgiving appears once again in the concluding admonitions of 4:2–6. By thus reiterating the key word of the customary opening thanksgiving 1:3–12, the writer has suggested a mood of gratitude, for an accomplished act of reconciliation and peace, as the defining matrix for the Christian moral reasoning here advocated.

Conclusions

I have tried simply to describe the way the Pauline Christian groups undertook to form the moral sensibilities of their members, insofar as the letter of Paul's disciple to the Colossians gives us some glimpses of that process, and as the writer undertakes to intervene in the process to shift the moral judgments of the audience in one direction rather than another. My description presupposes what George Lindbeck has called a "cultural-linguistic" theory of religion, because that family of theories seems to me to make more sense of this letter, understood as a functioning instrument of communication in a particular social and historical situation, than the "cognitivist" or "symbolic-expressive" conceptions of religion that have usually dominated modern biblical interpretation.[31]

The process by which the people to whom the Letter to Colossians was addressed became "Christian" was complex, and the letter-writer's attempt to influence their perceptions and behavior by reminding them of and reinterpreting for them parts of that process is also complicated. It is not easy to characterize either by the categories ordinarily used to define "New Testament ethics." The well-known dialectic between "indicative and imperative" defined by Rudolf Bultmann, for example, clearly names the pervasive rhetorical structure of Pauline parenesis, but his existentialist hermeneutic blunts the power of those categories to analyze the Letter to Colossians.[32] Bultmann's existentialism is perhaps the philosophy least sympathetic with those ways of construing and reinforcing that sense of the indicative to which this letter most frequently alludes and on which all its imperatives depend—ways that fall into the categories abhorred by Bultmannians, "myth" and "sacrament." Above all the subjectivism and individualism of Bultmann's existentialism is incapable of recognizing the essentially communal dimensions of the ethic this letter presupposes and seeks to foster.

The categories that modern ethicists use to sort out different styles of moral discourse, "deontological," "teleological," "consequentialist," "perfectionist," and so on, are not very helpful here either.[33] The proposal of Stanley Hauerwas and Alasdair MacIntyre to focus on the formation of character as the center of moral concern fares much better.[34] On the other hand, MacIntyre's and Hauerwas's focus on "narrative" as the primary vehicle for the formation of character is too narrow to capture the variety of ways by which the knowledge that the Letter to Colossians makes pertinent to the formation of Christian moral sensibilities was constructed and reinforced. What we have seen is rather a rich and supple set of social practices (to use MacIntyre's term) that are the foundation and context upon which the reminders and exhortations of the letter depend.

I leave untouched the question whether a description of the sort I have undertaken here is of any direct use in the shaping of normative ethics for Christian groups today. Any answer proposed to that question will have to take seriously the obvious fact that both the literary and the social context within which we hear the Letter to Colossians read is vastly different from that of its first audience. Because I believe that meaning is highly dependent upon context, any honest appropriation of a document like this one for moral discourse among Christians today is likely to be pretty complicated—but, as I have tried to show, so was the communication between the writer and his first audience.[35]

NOTES

1. Translations are my own unless otherwise noted.
2. For a sample of some of the more interesting proposals, see Fred O. Francis and Wayne A. Meeks, eds. and trans., *Conflict at Colossae: A*

Problem in the Interpretation of Early Christianity Illustrated by Selected Modern Studies, Sources for Biblical Study 4, 2nd ed. (Missoula, Mont.: Scholars Press, 1975).

3. See Paul Schubert, *Form and Function of the Pauline Thanksgiving, Beihefte der Zeitschrift für die neutestamentliche Wissenschaft* 20 (Berlin: Töpelmann, 1939). I take the letter to be the work of a disciple of Paul, probably composed shortly after Paul's death, though it could have been earlier. There can be no certainty about the authorship, and many readers resist the conclusion that a letter that admonishes its readers "Don't lie to one another" (3:9) was itself a carefully contrived fiction. Nevertheless a detailed comparison of the style of this letter with the style of Paul's undoubted letters makes this conclusion most probable: Walter Bujard, *Stilanalytische Untersuchungen zum Kolosserbrief als Beitrag zur Methodik von Sprachvergleichen*, Studien zur Umwelt des Neuen Testaments 11 (Göttingen: Vandenhoeck & Ruprecht, 1973); Mark Kiley, *Colossians as Pseudepigraphy* (Sheffield: JSOT, 1986).

4. The most useful discussion of the parenetic letter is in A. J. Malherbe's discussion of the genre of 1 Thessalonians, "1 Thessalonians as a Paraenetic Letter," a paper presented to the Society of Biblical Literature Seminar on Paul in Los Angeles in 1972 and incorporated in Malherbe's larger essay, "Hellenistic Moralists and the New Testament," to appear in the long-delayed vol. II/26 of *Aufstieg und Niedergang der römischen Welt*. See also Stanley K. Stowers, *Letter-Writing in Greco-Roman Antiquity*, Library of Early Christianity 5 (Philadelphia: Westminster, 1986), 58–70, 94–106.

5. The source of this common motto eludes me, and queries to colleagues more learned than I in the Reformed tradition have so far not produced an identification.

6. Explored, for example, by Basil Mitchell's Gifford Lectures, *Morality: Religious and Secular: The Dilemma of the Traditional Conscience* (Oxford: Clarendon, 1985). See the collection of essays edited by Gene Outka and John P. Reeder, Jr., *Religion and Morality* (Garden City, N.Y.: Anchor Books, 1973), and Jeffrey Stout, *Ethics after Babel: The Languages of Morals and Their Discontents* (Boston: Beacon Press, 1988), chap. 5.

7. Nils Dahl has shown that "once hidden/now revealed" was a pattern of early Christian preaching. It shows up several times in letters of the Pauline school, e.g. Ephesians 3:8–12, and in the editorial conclusion in most manuscripts of Romans (16:25–27). See Nils A. Dahl, "Form-Critical Observations on Early Christian Preaching," in his *Jesus*

in the Memory of the Early Church (Minneapolis: Augsburg, 1976), 30–36, esp. 32–33.

8. See David L. Balch, "Household Codes," in *Greco-Roman Literature and the New Testament: Selected Forms and Genres*, ed. David E. Aune, Society of Biblical Literature Sources for Biblical Study Series 21 (Atlanta: Scholars Press, 1988), 25–50, which includes a full, annotated bibliography.

9. See Jouette Bassler, *Divine Impartiality: Paul and a Theological Axiom*, Society of Biblical Literature Dissertation Series 59 (Chico, Calif.: Scholars Press, 1982); on Colossians 3:22–25, 178–180. Is the assertion of God's impartiality a warning to the slaves not to expect special consideration in view of the baptismal unification tradition (3:11) and positive uses of metaphors from slavery in the Pauline letters, or an assurance that in heaven, at least, their diligent service will be equitably rewarded?

10. For a detailed discussion of the general strategy, focused on a comparison of two specific traditions, see Benjamin Fiore, S.J., *The Function of Personal Example in the Socratic and Pastoral Epistles*, Analecta Biblica 105 (Rome: Biblical Institute Press, 1986).

11. This is an example of another of the "patterns of early Christian preaching" that Dahl identified, the "conformity pattern" ("Form-Critical Observations," 34).

12. For a survey of some of the results with provocative suggestions about their implications, see Martin Hengel, "Hymns and Christology," in *Between Jesus and Paul* (Philadelphia: Fortress, 1983), 78–96, notes 188–190. Among the more technical literature, the monograph by Reinhard Deichgräber, *Gotteshymnus und Christushymnus: Untersuchungen zur Form, Sprache und Stil der frühchristlichen Hymnen*, Studien zur Umwelt des Neuen Testaments 5 (Göttingen: Vandenhoeck & Ruprecht, 1967) is particularly important.

13. For an introduction to the insuperable quantity of literature on Philippians 2:6–11, see R. P. Martin, *Carmen Christi: Philippians ii.5–11 in Recent Interpretation and in the Setting of Early Christian Worship*, SNTS Monograph Series 4 (Cambridge: Cambridge University Press, 1967), 17–95 and Deichgräber, 11–21.

14. Ernst Käsemann, "Kritische Analyse von Phil. 2, 5–11," *Zeitschrift für Theologie und Kirche* 47 (1950): 313–360; reprinted in his *Exegetische Versuche und Besinnungen* 1, 2nd ed. (Göttingen: Vandenhoeck & Ruprecht, 1960), 51–95.

15. Ulrich B. Müller, "Der Christushymnus Phil 2, 6–11," *Zeitschrift für die Neutestamentliche Wissenschaft* 79 (1988): 17–44.

16. See Wayne A. Meeks, "The Man from Heaven in Paul's Letter to the Philippians," in Birger A. Pearson, ed., *The Future of Early Christianity: Essays in Honor of Helmut Koester* (Minneapolis: Augsburg-Fortress, 1991), 329–336.

17. I discussed this epistolary strategy in somewhat greater detail in "The Unity of Humankind in Colossians and Ephesians," in Wayne A. Meeks and Jacob Jervell, eds., *God's Christ and His People: Essays Presented to Nils Alstrup Dahl* (Oslo: Universitetsforlaget, 1977), 209–221. Kiley (Colossians, 76–78) has an interesting discussion of the parallel ways the author of Colossians and Paul in Philippians have used the respective poems. However, his argument that Colossians is a direct imitation of Philippians in this as in other respects is not convincing.

18. Wayne A. Meeks, "The Circle of Reference in Pauline Morality," in David L. Balch, Everett Ferguson, and Wayne A. Meeks, eds., *Greeks, Romans, and Christians: Essays in Honor of Abraham J. Malherbe* (Minneapolis: Fortress, 1990), 305–317.

19. "Walking" was obviously a long-dead metaphor; it is not easy to visualize walking while "rooted and founded...and firmed up," as Colossians 2:7 continues.

20. See Wayne A. Meeks, "The Image of the Androgyne: Some Uses of a Symbol in Earliest Christianity," *History of Religions* 13 (1974): 165–208, and *The First Urban Christians: The Social World of the Apostle Paul* (New Haven and London: Yale, 1983), 150–157.

21. The phrase, of course, is from Peter L. Berger and Thomas Luckmann, *The Social Construction of Reality: A Treatise on the Sociology of Knowledge* (Garden City, N.Y.: Anchor Books, 1967), 104–128.

22. Clifford Geertz, "Ethos, Worldview, and the Analysis of Sacred Symbols," in his *The Interpretation of Cultures* (New York: Basic Books, 1973), 126–141.

23. The identity of the "elements [στοιχεῖα] of the world" in this context (as in Galatians 4:3, 9) remains the object of much scholarly research and speculation, for which the standard commentaries may be consulted. Obviously something other than earth, air, fire, and water is meant, most likely some kind of intermediate deities commonly called by Hellenistic authors *daimones*, perhaps astral. The precise force of the "as" (ὡς ζῶντες ἐν κόσμῳ) is hard to render into English; "as if" shades too much toward unreality of the worldly existence, while my translation above does not suggest it strongly enough.

24. So in the astrological handbook by Vettius Valens 1.1 (Kroll 2.6): ταπεινότης is one of the disagreeable results of having been born under the dominance of Saturn; cf. 1.2 (Kroll 10.24) and often elsewhere.

To the point, see the important article by Albrecht Dihle, "Demut," *Realenzyklopädie für Antike und Christentum* 3 (1957): 735–778, and the monograph by Stefan Rehrl, *Das Problem der Demut in der profangriechischen Literatur im Vergleich zu Septuaginta und Neuem Testament*, Aevum Christianum 4 (Münster: Aschendorff, 1961). For a meditation on the broader implications, see Klaus Wengst, *Humility—Solidarity of the Humiliated: The Transformation of an Attitude* (Minneapolis: Fortress, 1989).

25. Martin Hengel, "Hymns and Christology," in *Between Jesus and Paul* (Philadelphia: Fortress, 1983), 96.

26. See the literature cited in n. 8 above.

27. Clearest in his discussion of Clement of Alexandria's opposition to the Encratites: Peter Brown, *The Body and Society: Men, Women and Sexual Renunciation in Early Christianity*, Lectures on the History of Religions, n.s. 13 (New York: Columbia University Press, 1988), chap. 6.

28. The seminal essays pointing out the importance of the household to the Christian mission and communal formation were Floyd V. Filson, "The Significance of the Early House Churches," *Journal of Biblical Literature* 58 (1939): 109–112, and Edwin A. Judge, *The Social Pattern of Christian Groups in the First Century* (London: Tyndale, 1960), 30–39. Their insights have been extended and elaborated by A. J. Malherbe, *Social Aspects of Early Christianity*, 2nd, enlarged ed. (Philadelphia: Fortress, 1983), 60–91; H.-J. Klauck, *Hausgemeinde und Hauskirche im frühen Christentum*, Stuttgarter Bibel Studien 103 (Stuttgart: Katholisches Bibelwerk, 1981); Wayne A. Meeks, *The First Urban Christians: The Social World of the Apostle Paul* (New Haven and London: Yale, 1983), 29–30, 75–77; Robert Banks, *Paul's Idea of Community: The Early House Churches in their Historical Setting* (Grand Rapids, Mich.: Eerdmans, 1980); and John Elliott, *A Home for the Homeless: A Sociological Exegesis of 1 Peter, Its Situation and Strategy* (Philadelphia: Fortress, 1981); among others.

29. See Brown, *Body and Society*, 54 (Paul), 78 (Tertullian), chap. 6 (Clement of Alexandria), chap. 15 (John Chrysostom), *et passim*.

30. I owe this insight to Abraham J. Malherbe.

31. George Lindbeck, *The Nature of Doctrine: Religion and Theology in a Postliberal Age* (Philadelphia: Westminster, 1984).

32. Rudolf Bultmann, "Das Problem der Ethik bei Paulus," in his *Exegetica: Aufsätze zur Erforschung des Neuen Testaments*, ed. Erich Dinkler (Tübingen: Mohr-Siebeck, 1967), 36–54 (originally published in 1924).

33. See e.g. Thomas Ogletree, *The Use of the Bible in Christian Ethics* (Philadelphia: Fortress, 1983), 15–45.

34. Alasdair MacIntyre, *After Virtue: A Study in Moral Theory*, 2nd ed. (Notre Dame and London: University of Notre Dame Press, 1984); Stanley Hauerwas, *Character and the Christian Life: A Study in Theological Ethics* (San Antonio: Trinity University Press, 1975).

35. I am grateful to members of a Yale faculty group on "Scripture and Ethics" and to Dr. Troels Engberg-Pedersen of Copenhagen University for their very helpful criticisms of an earlier version of this paper. Discussion at the Notre Dame conference stimulated many further thoughts, as did a subsequent discussion by members of Professor James M. Robinson's New Testament seminar at the Institute for Antiquity and Christianity at Claremont. Nevertheless, I have left the essay substantially unchanged.

Moral Authority and Pseudonymity: Comments on the Paper of Wayne A. Meeks

Eleonore Stump

In his clear and interesting paper Wayne Meeks undertakes a new approach to the Letter to the Colossians. According to Meeks, previous work on Colossians has focused on the heresy that the letter warns against. Interpreters have supposed that the main purpose of the letter was to inveigh against a particular heresy gaining currency among the Colossians and their neighbors, and the efforts of interpreters have been concentrated on trying to discover the exact nature of the heresy at issue. While Meeks in no way disparages this previous work, he is inclined to think it has been unsuccessful, at least in the sense that no consensus has been achieved about the nature of this heresy, and none is likely to be forthcoming. In this impasse, Meeks proposes a different approach to the letter. He suggests that perhaps the letter is not as preoccupied with heresy as previous scholars have supposed, and he directs our attention instead to the connections the letter makes between knowledge and behavior.

He takes the letter to have been written by a disciple of Paul's shortly after Paul's death. As Meeks explains, many people will be inclined to "resist the conclusion that a letter that admonishes its readers 'Don't lie to one another'...was itself a carefully contrived fiction," but he thinks that "a detailed comparison of the style of this letter with the style of Paul's undoubted letters makes this conclusion most probable."[1] According to Meeks, while the writer of the letter is concerned to correct the beliefs of the Colossian Christians and to warn them away from heresy, he is interested in their beliefs primarily for the sake of the moral dispositions and behavior that those beliefs will shape. The writer's main point, on Meeks's view, then, is not the extermination of a heresy but the moral edification and exhortation of the Colossians.

The writer achieves his aim, according to Meeks, by relying on a connection between knowledge and moral behavior. Two kinds of knowledge figure prominently in this endeavor. (In fact, one kind can be called 'knowledge' only in some extended sense of the term, since the claims constituting it are false.) The first kind is straightforwardly theological. The writer calls to the minds of his audience a number of theological claims about the nature and mission of Christ, including most notably claims about Christ's role as reconciler and peacemaker. The other kind of knowledge is apparently autobiographical and consists largely in a melange of fictional and historical claims about Paul's ministry and relations to individual Christians. Among the claims about Paul which Meeks finds useful or important for the letter-writer's project of establishing the connection between knowledge and behavior are the following. Paul has heard of the faith of the Colossian Christians and wants them to know more about him, and like Christ Paul has suffered for the sake of the Gospel in general, and for the sake of the faith of the Colossian Christians in particular. There are also various statements indicating Paul's relationships to individual people: that Paul is sending this letter to the Colossians at the hands of Tychicus and Onesimus, who will tell the Colossians more about Paul; that with Paul is a Colossian Christian, who sends greetings to his home church; that Paul is especially concerned about the ministry of one of the recipients of this letter, and so on.

The apparently autobiographical details involving Paul, Meeks says, "are intended to add verisimilitude to the fiction"[2] that the letter-writer is Paul himself. But the broader claims about both Paul and Christ are intended to stimulate the Colossians to a certain kind of moral behavior. According to Meeks, the letter-writer does not himself make explicit the nature of the connection he takes to exist between the moral behavior he is trying to promote among the Colossians and the purportedly factual claims about Paul and Christ. In some genuinely Pauline letters the claims about Paul and Christ are intended to stimulate hearers to imitation, but Meeks is inclined to find this interpretation of the connection between knowledge and moral behavior too simplistic, at least as applied to Colossians. In Colossians the "idealized picture of the Apostle" and "the mythic figure of Christ" act both as "prototype and warrant" for the behavior of the Colossian Christians. They present the Colossians with a picture of a world in which the behavior to which they are exhorted "receives intelligibility and value."[3]

How do the claims about Christ and Paul manage to make the moral behavior wanted from the Colossians both warranted and valuable? Meeks does not spell out his theory in any detail here, but the idea seems to be that these claims present the Colossians with a picture of a specifically Christian society, which includes most notably Paul and Christ. The picture, which is made more vivid by rituals, such as the ritual of baptism, conveys to the Colossians the view that the members of this society care about the Colossians, and at least some of them, those with a special claim to moral and religious authority, have labored on behalf of the Colossians and expect certain things from them.

I am unclear about Meeks's notion of a warrant for behavior, but I will assume that something warrants a person's behavior in case it warrants his belief that the behavior in question is morally acceptable or desirable. One way in which beliefs are warranted is by being accepted on the testimony of recognized authority. The scientific views most of us hold are warranted in this way, and it seems reasonable to suppose that something analogous holds for ethics. If our acceptance of certain claims about what constitutes moral behavior is based on the testimony of those we recognize as having moral authority, then our moral beliefs, obtained in this way, seem warranted. So since the Colossians believe that Paul is a person with special moral authority, they will be warranted in believing the moral claims underlying the admonitions in the letter just in virtue of accepting those claims on Paul's authority.

For this reason also the moral practices the letter urges will acquire value for the Colossians. One reasonable way to assign value to a particular sort of behavior is to emulate moral authority, to value certain actions in virtue of the fact that a person acting in his capacity as a moral authority also values those actions. So, for example, it seems reasonable for Gandhi's followers to have assigned value to the act of making salt in defiance of the legal prohibition largely because Gandhi valued that action. Furthermore, if the moral authority in question is a person to whom we owe some personal gratitude and who has some claim on our obedience, then there is additional reason to assign value to the actions to which that person exhorts us.

Of course, the order of warranting is sometimes the other way around. We might independently assign a certain positive or negative value to a behavior or believe that certain moral claims are true or false, and on those grounds accept or reject a certain person as a moral authority. We might reject Jim Bakker as a moral authority on the grounds that we assigned a negative value to certain behavior he engaged in or rejected as false certain moral claims he was concerned to promote. But this is not the order of warranting in the letter to the Colossians, according to Meeks. Rather what the letter says about Christ and Paul, made more vivid by reminders of religious ritual, leads the Colossians to see themselves as part of a community in which persons with moral or theological authority love them and want certain behavior from them. For the Colossians, then, the letter's representations of Paul and Christ give both value and warrant to the moral behavior the letter urges on the Colossians; the value and warrant of this moral behavior are founded on the claims about Paul and Christ conveyed in the letter.

These claims of Meeks's about the letter's emphasis seem to me sensible as an interpretation of the text, and his account of the connection between the letter's moral exhortations and its purportedly factual claims about Paul and Christ also seems to me plausible. What puzzles me about Meeks's paper is its putting forward these claims about the connection between knowledge and moral behavior on the hypothesis that this letter was not written by Paul. Just to ward off possible misconceptions, I want to say explicitly at the outset that in what follows I am not concerned to question the morality of writing pseudonymous letters, or to ask about the consistency of an interpretation which supposes moral admonition to be the purpose of a pseudonymous letter. What puzzles me is whether it is possible for there to be the connection between knowledge and moral behavior Meeks claims to find in the letter if we also accept the claim that the letter is pseudonymous.

Consider the possible epistemic state of the letter-writer and the Colossians, given Meeks's view of the letter. The actual author of the letter is unknown, not only to us but presumably also to the Colossians; but because it is awkward to refer to the author continually as 'the letter-writer', for the sake of convenience I will give the author a name and call her 'Pauline'. Meeks's statements about the letter imply that Pauline wrote this letter for the Colossians, intended them to receive it, and gave at least passing thought to their reaction to the letter's authorship.[4] Therefore, we must suppose either that Pauline believed the Colossians would think her letter was really written by Paul, or that she did not. And, similarly, we have two alternatives for the Colossians: either they believed Pauline's letter was really written by Paul, or they did not. There are therefore four possibilities as regards the letter.

1. Pauline believes the Colossians will think her letter was written by Paul, and the Colossians do so believe.
2. Pauline believes the Colossians will think her letter was written by Paul, but the Colossians do not in fact believe this.
3. Pauline does not believe that the Colossians will think her letter was written by Paul, but in fact the Colossians do believe it was written by Paul.
4. Pauline does not believe that the Colossians will think her letter was written by Paul, and in fact the Colossians don't believe it was written by Paul.

Some of these alternatives can be eliminated at the outset. Consider (4). The wealth of purportedly autobiographical detail about Paul in this letter is a crucial part of what is supposed to give warrant and value to the behavior the letter prescribes. But if the Colossians don't believe the letter is written by Paul, then for the Colossians the claims about Paul in the letter won't in fact succeed in giving warrant or value to this behavior. Think for a moment of a contemporary analogue. Suppose that the Director of Notre Dame's Center for Philosophy of Religion, Alvin Plantinga, received a letter which purported to be from Martin Luther King, and which recorded supposed facts about

King Plantinga hadn't previously known, including most notably claims about King's care for Plantinga's work and his suffering for the welfare of that work. And suppose that the letter went on to make a strong connection between those claims and a host of moral admonitions, such as the admonitions that Plantinga ought to start a special fellowship program for black students, to institute a mentoring program for new black students on campus, and so on. The claims about King contained in the letter might well give warrant and value to the behavior the letter urges in just the way Meeks claims occurs in Colossians: the moral authority of King would warrant the belief that such behavior was morally desirable, and the description of his care for Plantinga and his labor on Plantinga's behalf would contribute to give value to the moral behavior to which King exhorts him.

But now suppose that Plantinga knows that King is dead and so takes the letter not to be written by King at all and that Plantinga consequently believes the claims about King in the letter are largely fictional. He might still be inclined to value the behavior to which the letter exhorts him, of course; but if he did so, it would be because he valued that behavior anyway, and not because of any connection between knowledge and behavior established by the letter. If Plantinga knew that the letter-writer were not Martin Luther King but some anonymous person writing in his name, he would not accord the letter-writer the moral authority he was willing to accord King. In fact, he is not in a position to accord the letter-writer any special moral authority since he doesn't know who wrote the letter. And the apparently factual claims about King's care for him won't in themselves give value to the moral behavior to which he's being exhorted since Plantinga will believe that those claims are fictional. The letter may still occasion some reflection in him, some reflection which results in his being stimulated to just the sorts of moral behavior the letter recommended, but any value or warrant he assigns to that behavior will be based on considerations other than the claims about King. So if Plantinga does not believe that the letter is written by Martin Luther King, there will not in this case be the sort of relation between knowledge and moral behavior which Meeks attributes to the letter to the Colossians; the claims about King will not give warrant or value to the moral behavior the letter prescribes. Analogously, if we suppose that the Colossians don't believe that the letter to them was written by Paul, then the many claims about Paul in the letter can't give warrant or value to the behavior the letter recommends. Furthermore, if Pauline believes that the Colossians will have this reaction, then she will recognize that a fictional letter of this sort wouldn't succeed in giving warrant and value to the behavior she wants to promote, and so she will not write a letter she believes to be pointless. So (4) seems to me not a real possibility as regards the epistemic state of Pauline and the Colossians.

Possibilities (2) and (3) can be ruled out for similar reasons. In (2) the Colossians do not believe the letter was written by Paul. They are aware that the allegedly autobiographical details about Paul are a fiction, and so for the Colossians in that epistemic state, none of the letter's claims about Paul will support the letter's moral admonitions, in the way that Meeks says they do. As for possibility (3), if Pauline didn't believe the Colossians would think her letter had been written by Paul, then she would suppose that the many claims about Paul would be altogether unsuccessful in giving warrant and value to the behavior she intends to prescribe. For that reason she would recognize that writing in the name of Paul and providing a wealth of purportedly autobiographical detail about Paul would be pointless, since the purpose of the letter, on Meeks's account, is to stimulate the Colossians to moral behavior. And this conclusion about Pauline remains the same even if, contrary to what Pauline believes, on the receipt of such a letter the Colossians would have believed it had been written by Paul.

So to account for the fact that Pauline wrote this sort of letter to the Colossians, attempting to stimulate them to moral behavior on the basis of a variety of claims about Paul, as well as claims about Christ, we need to suppose that possibility (1) was the case.

There are some difficulties with adopting this hypothesis. For example, Pauline says that the letter will be delivered to the Colossians by Tychicus and Onesimus, who will tell the Colossians how things are going with Paul, and Meeks suggests that Tychicus and Onesimus may have been the historical deliverers of the letter. But in that case, since according to Meeks Paul was by then dead, we must suppose that Pauline instructed Tychicus and

Onesimus to deceive the Colossians with fictional stories about Paul. Otherwise, if Tychicus and Onesimus had explained that Paul had been dead for some time, or that they knew nothing about Paul and hadn't come from him, the Colossians would have learned immediately that the letter to them was fictional as regards some or all of its claims about Paul.

So since on possibility (1) Pauline believes that the Colossians will think the letter was written by Paul, we must suppose one of two alternatives to be the case: either (A) Tychicus and Onesimus were the historical bearers of the letter, and Pauline instructed Tychicus and Onesimus to continue the letter's fiction, or (B) the letter made its way to the Colossians in some way that didn't after all involve Tychicus or Onesimus, and the letter's fiction didn't extend to tales told by the bearers of the letter. The first of these alternatives has a certain moral unpalatableness, since it seems to suppose a complicated and premeditated attempt to deceive fellow Christians, and the second alternative requires us to postulate some byzantine mechanism for getting the letter to the Colossians which itself shares certain characteristics of fiction. But since these difficulties are not directly relevant to Meeks's claim that the letter's theological and allegedly historical claims give warrant and value to the moral behavior the letter urges, I'm going to suppose that these difficulties can somehow be overcome, in order that we might reflect on possibility (1).

If possibility (1) were the actual case, would we then have a situation of the sort Meeks claims we do, a situation in which the claims about Paul in the letter contribute to giving warrant and value to the moral behavior the letter prescribes? It is certainly true that in this situation the Colossians will believe that the claims about Paul warrant and give value to the recommended moral behavior. But the claim that the Colossians believe this isn't the same as the claim that for the Colossians the behavior in question has in fact been given warrant and value. What distinguishes the Colossians in this case from the Colossians in possibility (2), where the letter's claims don't give warrant to moral behavior, is just that the Colossians in (1) are mistaken in believing the claims that supposedly provide the warrant and establish the value. Can their being mistaken in this way be enough for the false claims about Paul to warrant the moral behavior in question or to give it value?

Consider an analogous case where the authority in question is scientific rather than moral. Suppose that unbeknownst to virtually all of us, the country's surgeon general dies suddenly; and the tobacco companies, seizing their opportunity, substitute one of their own people who successfully impersonates the real but deceased surgeon general. This bogus surgeon general proclaims that cigarette smoking has been discovered to be not only safe for women but even beneficial (because, say, it reduces their risk of breast cancer). She announces that she has had a terrible struggle with the male medical establishment to bring us this news but that she has endured out of her care for American women. And finally, she explains that in consequence of the new findings, she herself has taken up smoking, and she urges all other women to do so as well. Will her false statements, in virtue of our mistakenly believing them true, succeed in giving warrant and value to the behavior of smoking for women? Surely not. If they did, then women who took up smoking as a result of the bogus surgeon general's announcement would be angry at those who exposed the imposture, because in revealing the truth the exposers of the bogus surgeon general would be bringing to an end the time when smoking was warranted and valuable. But in fact the reaction of those taken in by the bogus surgeon general will not be anger at the people who exposed the imposture but rage at those who engaged in it, because, women will suppose, they have been deceived into thinking that smoking was warranted and valuable when in fact it was not. So although, as I said earlier, one way to warrant one's scientific beliefs is to take them on authority, they are in fact warranted only in case the person whose scientific testimony one accepts is in reality an authority in the relevant field of science and is speaking in his role as authority in giving that testimony.

The situation as regards moral authority seems to me analogous to this case. Consider again the case in which Plantinga receives a letter purporting to be from Martin Luther King and explaining his labor and care for Plantinga, but this time suppose that the letter was written by Marion Barry and recommends not affirmative action for blacks but rather some subtly racist practice, disguised as an instance of affirmative action. Suppose furthermore that for some reason or other Plantinga believes the letter was in fact written by Martin Luther King, whom Plantinga takes as a moral authority. (Suppose, for example, that Plantinga thinks the letter, which was never mailed, has just now turned up among King's papers.) If in consequence of his receiving this letter and holding these beliefs, he comes to believe that the racist practice is a good thing, this belief will not be warranted for him. Rather he will simply be mistaken in accepting as a moral authority someone who does not have a claim to that status (or at any rate, not nearly the same claim as King). Similarly, since the letter-writer is not only not a moral authority of the stature of King but also not someone whom Plantinga owes any debts of gratitude or is under any obligation to oblige, there is no reason for supposing that the practice the letter advocates in fact acquires any value for Plantinga. He may think that it does; but when we enlighten him about the true authorship of the letter, he will no doubt be among the first to agree that the racist practice recommended acquired no value for him in virtue of being recommended by Barry. And this will be the case even if Plantinga is quite clear that, during King's life, Barry was a follower of King's. Like virtue or wisdom, moral authority is not automatically and inevitably transferred from a moral leader to his friends and disciples. Mao's wife was regarded as a villain while Mao himself was still revered among the Chinese; Lenin was honored in the Soviet Union although his follower Trotsky was not; and Barry is currently in ill-repute with many of those who hold the highest opinion of King.

For these reasons I am inclined to think that a moral belief acquired on testimony will be warranted only in case the person on whose testimony it was acquired is in fact a recognized moral authority. Similarly, it seems to me that practices and behavior acquire value for us on being recommended by a person who has claims on our gratitude, obedience, and moral trust only in case that person actually is a recognized moral authority and really has done things for us which call for gratitude, obedience, and trust in return. In the case of the Colossians in possibility (1), since they believe that the letter was written by Paul, they will in consequence suppose that the moral beliefs Pauline wants them to adopt are warranted in virtue of being held by Paul and that the moral behavior the letter urges is valuable because it is Paul who recommends it. But since it is false that the letter is written by Paul, it is also false that their beliefs are warranted or that the recommended behavior has acquired value.

So neither in possibility (1) nor in any of the other possibilities is there the connection between knowledge and behavior Meeks ascribes to the letter to the Colossians if it is also true that the letter is pseudonymous. Possibility (1) is the best case for Meeks's interpretation of the letter, but the most we can say on possibility (1) is that the Colossians mistakenly suppose that the letter warrants certain moral beliefs and gives value to certain moral practices. So there seems to me an incompatibility between Meeks's interesting and helpful analysis of the letter and his claim that the letter was not written by Paul. Furthermore, if we accept both Meeks's interpretation of the letter and his characterization of the letter as pseudonymous, these considerations undercut the letter's worth not only for the Colossians but also for us. Some of us might be willing to accept Paul as a moral authority, but few if any of us are in a position to accord that status to the anonymous author of Colossians. We are then like the Colossians in possibilities (2) and (4): we have no reason to recognize the anonymous author of the letter as a moral authority, and so for us the letter does not succeed in establishing the connection it wants to establish between knowledge and moral behavior. So if we accept both Meeks's interpretation of the letter as having moral admonition as its main point and his claim that the letter is pseudonymous, the letter's value as a moral guide, either for the Colossians or for us, is seriously undermined.[5]

NOTES

1. All citations of Meeks refer to the paper in this volume. For this quotation, see Meeks's note 3, pp. 54.

2. P. 41.

3. P. 44.

4. Consider, for example, the following passages:

- "Tychicus and Onesimus...are...perhaps the historical bearers of the letter" (p. 41).
- "The writer wants the recipients to know...more about Paul" (p. 41).

- "The gospel of which Paul is the minister . . . is the gospel . . . to which they [the Colossians] . . . are now urged to remain faithful" (p. 41).
- "Perhaps these friendly conventions [mention of individual persons known to the Colossians] . . . are intended to add verisimilitude to the fiction" (p. 41).
- "The six who . . . send greetings . . . create the picture of a network of friends . . . who are . . . witnesses and guarantors of the directives given to the Colossians" (p. 45)
- "The process by which the people to whom the Letter to the Colossians was addressed became 'Christian' was complex, and the letter writer's attempt to influence their perceptions and behavior . . . is also complicated." (p. 52).

5. I am grateful to Adela Collins and Norman Kretzmann for helpful comments and suggestions on an earlier draft.

Response to Stump

Wayne A. Meeks

I am grateful to Professor Stump for the care with which she has read my paper and the clarity of her comments. I should be grateful also because, if I have understood her rightly, she has in effect let me off the hook by moving the discussion into an area that I did not pretend to address. That is, she has not objected to my description of the Colossian Letter's implied function, which was the sole object of my paper. She does not deny that "Pauline" seems probably to have written the letter in the way I have described with the aims I have outlined. The point is rather that Professor Stump thinks Pauline was wicked to have done so, and that the recipients would have been misguided to have paid any attention to the letter's exhortations. Despite Stump's disclaimer that she is not concerned with the question of the morality of pseudonymity, I do not see how we can understand her hypothetical examples—the pseudo-King letters, the fake Surgeon General—in any other way. Indeed that seems the only issue raised by my paper—a point I did not argue but alluded to in a single footnote—in which Stump is interested. Perhaps the original recipients of Colossians would have been better off listening to the "philosophers" against whom Pauline polemicized. In any event, Professor Stump thinks that *we* ought not to use such a fraudulent document—for that is the way she feels obliged to regard Colossians if she were to accept my stipulation about its authorship—for moral formation today.

I am puzzled why Professor Stump finds that these conclusions must follow from my description. Hence, though by rights

I should leave this kind of question to the philosophers and ethicists, as being beyond both my competence and the stated limitations of my paper, I cannot resist saying a few things in defense of "Pauline."

The key question seems to be whether beliefs may be called "knowledge" if there are grounds for others, not those who hold them, to believe them false. That is, must "knowledge" always be true? By even raising the question in this naive way I am doubtless making it even more obvious that I am not a philosopher. Still, I am forced to admit that I do find myself often in the condition of the King of Siam, for "sometimes I'm not so certain of the things I absolutely know," and I suspect this verse states, though more candidly than we usually admit, the universal human condition. Indeed, I suppose that all of our knowledge suffers from a considerable admixture of error. Perhaps I ought to have used some other word or phrase, "warranted belief" or the like. However, I am accustomed to use "knowledge" in the sense that the word has in the sociology of knowledge, believing that all our knowledge is socially constructed and highly contingent upon time, context, and circumstances. The historian is generally helped less by trying to discover whether the construction of knowledge follows appropriate rules of reason than by trying to locate the varied ways it is supported by and in turn reacts back upon the social forms and practices in which knowledge is always embedded. I've obviously said this awkwardly, and probably in a way abhorrent to many philosophers. However, I believe there are *some* philosophers who would agree with me about the socially contingent nature of knowledge.

Now the thing that puzzles me about Stump's comments is that, of all the fictions present in the Letter to Colossians, the only one that appears to disturb her is its claim to be written by the Apostle Paul. Her argument is that the moral admonitions of the letter are backed by personal authority, and if that authority is a mask of someone different, then there is no reason to heed the admonitions. What I tried to show was something quite different. The letter does not tell people to act in a certain way because its author, who has a certain recognized authority, says they should. Rather it imaginatively renders a certain kind of world in which the advocated behavior is obviously right. The "Paul" who has authority is the Paul who belongs to that world and is, so to speak, homologous with it. The Barry-forged letter imagined by Stump would not be a fair parallel to my reading of Colossians. The reason for rejecting its claims is not merely that it was written by Barry rather than King, but that it espouses values that are discordant with those of King. I take the writer of Colossians to have understood Paul rather well. I will not repeat the several ways I think the Letter to Colossians renders an imaginative world and incorporates into it a certain, partly familiar, image of Paul. I only ask why it is only the fiction about Paul—i.e., that the biographical observations are presented as if they were autobiography—and not, for example, the fictions about Christ that are problematical? Is it only that the description of Christ is not falsifiable, referring as it does for the most part to non-empirical realities?

Not to make my response longer than the comments, let me just mention two further points. One is that our judgments about the functions of a pseudonymous letter must surely take into account the historical fact that such letters were rather common in antiquity, and commonly used in teaching. Remember that every schoolchild was taught *prosopopoeia*: "Write a speech in the person of Pericles," or the like. More to the point, in the time around the writing of the New Testament, letters of Socrates, Diogenes, Crates, Hipparchia, and so on were widely circulated, and often served to inculcate the teachings of those figures, as they were understood by their later followers. I do not know whether most readers thought those letters authentic. I am not sure it would have made much difference to the purpose if they did not.

Finally, let me address the imaginary example of the pseudo-King letters to Alvin Plantinga. Ingenious as it is, this example seems to me not to fit the case. Let me pose a counterexample. Suppose instead that we were to discover that the Letter from Birmingham Jail was not in fact written by Martin Luther King, but by Bayard Rustin or Stanley Levison—both of whom knew King intimately enough by this time that they could probably have imitated his style and doubtless had a pretty clear idea of the things he would want to say in such circumstances. Clarence Jones, who according to the traditional story smuggled the papers out of the jail, and Wyatt Walker, who deciphered King's handwriting and dictated the letter to his secretary, would obviously have to have been involved in the ghost-writing—they would have been the Tychicus and Onesimus. Now would that ghost-written letter carry less moral authority—if it does in fact sum up, as I think, some of King's deepest beliefs as we know them from authentic statements elsewhere? If it does create for the reader a plausible image of King-in-prison? If it does identify central moral challenges faced by timid Christians in the face of racial injustice? That would seem to me the real analogy to Colossians.

With that in mind, let us return to one particular point that compounds the mendacity of Pauline, in Stump's view of things, namely, the conspiracy of falsehood into which Tychicus and Onesimus must have been drawn. Stump's picture of this conspiracy seems to me overdrawn. Suppose it is true that Paul had died before the letter was written—though I see no way one can be sure of that (and, contrary to Stump's impression, I did not insist on a postmortum dating; see n. 3 of my essay). Even so, all Tychicus and Onesimus have to say when they deliver the letter is this: "O holy ones of Colossae, our brother Paul has finished his race. Having been put to death at the hands of Caesar, he has departed to be with the Lord. Yet his love for you endures, and we bring you a final message to remind you of the truth he taught to all who, like yourselves, have faith in the Christ whom God raised from the dead." How serious, morally, would that deception have been?

III. Philosophy and Biblical Studies on the Empty Tomb

Was the Tomb Empty?

Stephen T. Davis

> The accounts of the empty grave, of which Paul still knows
> nothing, are legends.
>
> —Rudolf Bultmann[1]

> Today however historical criticism has made the empty tomb
> a dubious factor and the conclusions of natural science have
> rendered it suspect.
>
> —Hans Küng[2]

I

Traditional Christian belief about the resurrection of Jesus includes the claim that the tomb in which he was buried was empty on Easter morning. Despite differences in the details of their accounts of the discovery of the empty tomb, all four Gospels agree that it was empty. "He is not here; for he has risen," says the angel to Mary Magdalene and the other Mary in Matthew's Gospel (28:2). Similar notions are expressed in the other Gospels (Mk 16:6; Lk 24:5; Jn 20:2).

Despite this, the tradition of the empty tomb is frequently criticized. It is natural to expect those who doubt that Jesus was raised from the dead to deny that the tomb was empty. But what is interesting about the contemporary theological scene is that some theologians who want to affirm, in some sense or other, that Jesus was raised, either deny or struggle mightily to deemphasize the empty tomb.

Why is this? Why does the tradition of the empty tomb come in for so much criticism? The reasons are complex and fascinating. What I hope to do in this paper is take a hard look at the arguments that are given for and against the empty tomb. Let me reveal here that I am one who wants to affirm the empty tomb; accordingly, I will try to reply to the objections that are typically raised against it. All of the objections that I will discuss are interesting and thoughtful arguments; some are powerful; but in the end I will argue that they are not convincing. My conclusion will be that for both historical and theological reasons, Christians ought to continue to hold that Jesus' tomb was empty.

It is important to stress the narrowness of the scope of the paper. It is concerned only with arguments for and against the claim of the four evangelists that Jesus' tomb was found empty on Easter morning. It is clear that the empty tomb and the concept of bodily resurrection, for example, are strongly logically connected; they are usually affirmed or denied together.[3] But having discussed bodily resurrection elsewhere,[4] I will not do so here. I shall assume that the empty tomb, if it occurred, was a historical event in every relevant sense of the word and can be investigated historically. But since the empty tomb by itself does not entail the resurrection of Jesus, I will say little here (except for a few comments at the conclusion of the paper) on the complex matter of linking historical judgments to theological affirmations or to Christian faith.

II

There are five major arguments that are typically given against the empty tomb. First let me state them as fairly and strongly as I can; then I will reply to them. Some of them are closely related; the distinctions I make among them (especially the second, third, and fourth arguments) are in places somewhat artificial. Furthermore, the arguments aim in different directions—some, for example, attempt to show that the purported event of the empty tomb did not in fact occur; others attempt to show that even if it did, the empty tomb did not and should not play any important role in Christian faith or proclamation.

1. *The empty tomb tradition is unreliable because the four Gospels, which are our only sources of the tradition, give contradictory reports about it.* In order to explore this argument, let us take a thorough and rather ruthless look at the apparent discrepancies. First, the Gospels do not agree on the people who visited the tomb. Matthew mentions only Mary Magdalene and "the other Mary"; Mark mentions Mary Magdalene, Mary the mother of James, and Salome; Luke mentions Mary Magdalene (although the "we" in 20:2 can sensibly be taken to imply that others were present).[5] Second, the Gospels do not agree on the time of the visit. All agree that it occurred on the first day of the week; Matthew elaborates by saying it was after (or late on) the Sabbath toward dawn; Mark says that it was very early on the day after the Sabbath and that the sun had risen; Luke says that it was early and at first dawn; and John says that it was early and still dark.

Third, the Gospels do not agree on the purpose of the women's visit. Matthew says that it was merely to see the tomb; spices are not mentioned (perhaps given the stone and the guards, the women knew they would not be able to embalm the body); Mark says it was to anoint the body with aromatic spices bought the day after the Sabbath (16:1); Luke implies it was to anoint the body with spices and ointments the women had prepared before the Sabbath (23:55; 24:1); and John mentions no reason for the visit at all (perhaps because Nicodemus and Joseph of Arimathea are said to have anointed the body before the burial). Fourth, the Gospels do not agree on the location of the stone when the women arrived. Matthew seems to imply that it was in place when they arrived but that the angel rolled it away in their presence; while Mark, Luke, and John say that the women arrived to discover the stone already rolled away. Fifth, the Gospels do not agree on whether there was a guard at the tomb—Matthew states that there was such a guard, while the other Gospels mention no such thing.

Sixth, the Gospels do not agree on the personages the women saw, or on their location. Matthew mentions an angel of the Lord who sat on the stone outside the tomb; Mark mentions a young man in a white robe who was inside the tomb sitting on the right; Luke mentions two men in dazzling apparel who were standing inside the tomb; and John (a bit later in the story—20:12) mentions two angels who were sitting outside the tomb. Seventh, the Gospels do not agree on what the personages said to the women; the Synoptic Gospels basically agree (with a few minor, but interesting, differences) while the message delivered by the two angels in the fourth Gospel is quite different.

Finally, the Gospels do not agree in the reaction of the women. Matthew says they went away quickly with fear and great joy to tell the disciples; Mark says they fled trembling and astonished and told no one about what they had seen; Luke says the women left and told the disciples (who did not believe them); John says that Mary Magdalene ran to tell Peter and the Beloved Disciple that the body was missing.

2. *The story of the empty tomb is a late development in the pre-gospel period, and so is probably unreliable.* This claim is actually the fountainhead of most contemporary criticism of the tradition of the empty tomb. There are several reasons for regarding it as late. First, the story of the empty tomb is not so much as mentioned in Paul's writings, which are our earliest record of Christian belief about the resurrection of Jesus. (I will treat the absence of any mention of the empty tomb in Paul's epistles as a separate argument to be considered below.) Second, the empty tomb is not mentioned in the speeches Luke attributes to Peter, Stephen, and Paul in Acts. While not considered by most scholars an early document, the book of Acts, and in particular the sermons attributed by Luke to the apostles, may well give vital clues to the earliest Christian beliefs about the resurrection, and the empty tomb is not mentioned.

Third, the crucial text for the empty tomb is obviously Mark 16:1–8. (According to the vast majority of scholars, Mark was the first of the four canonical Gospels to be written, and had a major influence on both the other Synoptic Gospels, apparently including what they say about the empty tomb.) And at least some scholars, e.g., Bultmann,[6] believe that Mark 16:1–8 was formulated long after the events themselves, does not fit with what precedes it, and played a secondary and quite subordinate role in the apostolic kergyma. Furthermore, some scholars are troubled by what look like internal inconsistencies or at least improbabilities in Mark's account, e.g., the plan of the women (in hot Palestine) to anoint a body that had already been dead for three days; and their thoughtlessness in never considering, prior to their arrival at the tomb, how they could possibly enter a tomb blocked by a large stone.[7]

A slightly different version of this second argument against the empty tomb runs as follows: the empty tomb tradition was not originally meant as history, i.e., it was not meant to state facts about the tomb in which Jesus was buried. It was instead a way of elaborating, explaining, or announcing the affirmation that "Jesus is risen" that arose in the Christian community in the period prior to the writing of Mark's Gospel.[8] The empty tomb, then, is best seen not as a report of a fact but as a product of the resurrection appearances of Jesus, as a legendary elaboration of the appearances that grew up long afterward. The body of Jesus was probably just somehow lost—burned, thrown into a common grave, or the tomb in which it was buried forgotten.

3. Closely related to the above argument is this one: *The story of the empty tomb is a legendary addition to the earliest Christian proclamation of the resurrection, invented for apologetic purposes.* Several factors support this claim. First, as we have seen, the Gospels deviate sharply from each other to a surprising degree on the details of the empty tomb story, and there is evidence of the tradition developing and expanding in the later Gospels (e.g., the guards at the tomb in Matthew; Peter running to the tomb in John; Jesus' appearance to Mary Magdalene and the other Mary or to Mary Magdalene alone in Matthew and John; Joseph of Arimathea described as a follower of Jesus in Matthew and John; the disciples being increasingly involved in the story of the empty tomb). Second, the empty tomb is clearly the sort of story we might expect the early Christians to have seized upon because of its obvious apologetic value. As all scholars grant, the resurrection was crucial to early Christian proclamation, a proclamation which was subject to severe criticism by those who rejected it. Thus it is not difficult to imagine the origin of the story of the empty tomb because of its obvious apologetic value—"If Jesus was not raised from the dead, then where is his body?" Christians could have asked their enemies. Third, in Mark's Gospel (written at a time when the story of the empty tomb was perhaps not yet widely known) the empty tomb is reported as known only by a few women who keep silent about what they have seen (16:8).

But in Matthew, written perhaps a generation later when (perhaps because of the influence of Mark's Gospel) the empty tomb story was widely known, the women are reported as immediately hurrying to tell the disciples the news (28:8). This, too, is witness to the late and legendary character of the tradition.[9]

4. The second and third argument are supported by the fourth—*the case for the reliability of the empty tomb tradition is seriously weakened by the fact that Paul, the earliest and therefore most reliable of our sources about the resurrection of Jesus, does not mention it.* The closest Paul comes to mentioning the empty tomb in any of his extant writings is the brief phrase "he was buried" in 1 Corinthians 15:4 (a phrase which is meant—so critics of the empty tomb say—only to emphasize the reality of Jesus' death and not to testify to a separate event). Since this epistle is our earliest record of the resurrection (most scholars date it at ca. 54 A.D., or about twenty-four years after the events), this too supports the notion that the empty tomb is a later development, unheard of in the early days. For it seems Paul would hardly have omitted reference to something so crucial to the case for the resurrection of Jesus, a case he tries hard to make in 1 Corinthians, had he known about it. (Or, alternately, perhaps Paul knew of the empty tomb reports but rejected them because they seemed to support a crudely physicalist conception of the resurrected body of Jesus, in contrast to his own more nuanced notion of a "spiritual body.") At any rate, Paul probably believed that Jesus' "old body" remained decomposing in the tomb.

5. The final argument tries to deemphasize rather than disprove the empty tomb; its main point is that *the empty tomb played no significant role in the faith of the earliest believers and should play no significant role in ours either.* Even from the Gospels themselves it seems clear that the faith of the disciples in the resurrection of their Lord was originally based not on the empty tomb but on what they took to be his appearances to them. And the stories of the appearances contrast rather sharply with those of the empty tomb. Hans Küng points this out:

> The stories of the tomb are concerned originally only with the women and not with the disciples, the appearance statements with the latter and not the former. The stories of the tomb describe appearances of angels and not of Christ, the appearance statements

again the opposite. The stories of the tomb are narratives (artistically elaborated to some degree) about astonished listeners and were perhaps used in the readings at the eucharist; the appearance statements in their oldest versions are summaries in catechism form for learning by heart (probably in catechetical use.)[10]

Reginald Fuller argues that the disciples came to believe that Jesus was risen on the basis of appearances to them in Galilee. They then returned to Jerusalem and for the first time heard the women's story about the empty tomb. Naturally, they welcomed it as consistent with their own new belief, and presumably incorporated it into their preaching. Fuller goes on to say of the empty tomb:

> The disciples were apparently not interested in it as a historical fact and so we hear nothing of their having checked it. They were interested only in using it as a vehicle for the proclamation of the resurrection. For the disciples, faith in the resurrection did not rest upon the empty tomb, but upon their revelatory encounters with the Risen One.[11]

Furthermore, Gordon Kaufman argues that if we take the appearance stories as primary, we can easily account for the growth of the empty tomb tradition. Unsophisticated early Christians, especially those to whom Paul's concept of a "spiritual body" was incomprehensible, would accept the story of the empty tomb as something naturally entailed by their belief that Jesus had risen.[12]

III

Let me now try to respond to the above arguments.

(1) As to the first, I believe that many of the discrepancies between the Gospel accounts of the empty tomb do not present serious problems; plausible harmonizations (i.e., ones that do not involve special pleading) can be suggested without great difficulty. For example, the term "young man" in Mark and Luke was a conventional way to refer to an angel (Luke himself makes this identification in 24:23).[13] For another example, perhaps the women arose and left for the tomb while it was still dark and arrived after sunrise. However, I also believe that some of the discrepancies are difficult if not impossible sensibly to harmonize,

e.g., the location of the stone when the women arrived (here Matthew differs from the other Gospels) and the reaction of the women (where Mark, alone among the evangelists, has the women keeping silent).[14]

But the main point I wish to make is this: despite differences in details, the four evangelists agree to an amazing degree on what we might call the basic facts. All unite in proclaiming that *early on the first day of the week certain women, among them Mary Magdalene, went to the tomb; they found it empty; they met an angel or angels; and they were either told or else discovered* (Mary Magdalene in the fourth Gospel) *that Jesus was alive*. There is also striking agreement between John and at least one of the Synoptics on each of these points: *The women informed Peter and/or other disciples of their discovery; Peter went to the tomb and found it empty; the risen Jesus appeared to the women; and he gave them instructions for the disciples*. Furthermore, it may be that the discrepancies themselves lend credence to the basic facts, showing as they do that a variety of Christian interpretations of the empty tomb, obviously at many points quite independent of each other, all agree on these central points.[15]

(2) Is the empty tomb a late tradition? I find the argument unconvincing. For one thing, exactly how do critics of the empty tomb go about deciding that a given document or passage is "late"? There are doubtless provable cases of literary dependence where a convincing case can be made that one document is later than another. But when it comes to dating various strata, pericopes, or traditions in the gospels (e.g., deciding that a given text in a "late" Gospel reflects an "early" tradition, or the like), at least some of the conclusions of which critics are so confident seem tenuous.[16] Though some are based on carefully crafted linguistic arguments, others seem based on *a priori* notions about what sorts of things might have been expressed by "early" believers, and what could only have been expressed by "later" believers. Notice the circular argument in the following imagined but perhaps not unrecognizable dialogue between a critic and a defender of the empty tomb:

Defender: The empty tomb is taught in this text.

Critic: That text is a late text, and can therefore be discounted.

Defender: How do you know it is a late text?

Critic: Well, it presupposes a late theology, e.g., a physical view of the resurrection.

Defender: How do you know physical views of the resurrection weren't taught in early texts?

Critic: Well, because they just aren't. Among the New Testament texts that talk about the resurrection, only the later ones push physical views of the resurrection.

Defender: But how do you know they are the later ones?

Critic: Obviously, because they are the ones that push conceptions, like physical views of the resurrection, that only developed later.

But far more importantly, if the empty tomb is a late tradition, we are entitled to wonder why early Jewish criticism of the resurrection of Jesus never disputed it (a point I will discuss below). If the tradition had developed late, it would seem that critics of the resurrection would have disputed the claim; that they did not do so argues that the empty tomb was a fact agreed upon by all parties early in the game.

Also, it has been convincingly argued that the empty tomb stories have linguistic features indicative of early tradition.[17] Various Semitic expressions and customs are used or referred to which may suggest an early Palestinian setting for the stories—e.g., "on the first day of the week" (Mk 16:2), "angel of the Lord" (Mt 28:2), "Miriam" (as opposed to "Mary") (Mt 28:1), "[answering] said" (Mt 28:5), and "bowed their faces to the ground" (Lk 24:5). I do not wish to place great emphasis on this point; it is, after all, hard to prove that such expressions could not or would not have been used in, say, a late first-century Diaspora text. Still, the existence of Semitisms in the empty tomb stories is worth noting.

Furthermore, why is it that the empty tomb is not referred to in the speeches Luke attributes to the apostles in Acts? There is, I believe, an available explanation that is more plausible than the idea that the empty tomb was not known in the early period. To the extent that the speeches in Acts accurately reflect the earliest period of Christian proclamation, it may be that the empty tomb was not mentioned because it did not have to be mentioned, i.e., it was a widely known fact, undisputed by all parties. The question for the people of that period was not, "Is the tomb empty?" but rather, "*Why* is the tomb empty?" Furthermore, though the empty tomb is not explicitly mentioned, it seems clearly presupposed in Peter's sermon in Acts 2. See especially verses 27–29, where Jesus, who because of his resurrection "was not abandoned to Hades, nor did his flesh see corruption," is contrasted to King David, whose tomb "is with us to this day." The implication seems to be that Jesus' tomb is empty while David's is not. (See also Paul's sermon in Acts 13:29–37, where precisely the same point is made.)

Finally, what about the theory that the empty tomb stories in the Gospels are legendary products, written much later, of the earlier appearance stories? The problem with this claim is that there are many differences between the appearance stories and the empty tomb stories and the connections between them are tenuous. Accordingly, most interpreters believe that the two traditions have independent origins, i.e., that the one did not cause the other. First Corinthians 15:3–8, the earliest appearance text, contains several themes not found in Mark 16:1–8, the earliest empty tomb text (e.g., explicit citation of tradition, the appeal to the Scriptures, the death of Christ "for our sins," the title "Christ" as a proper name, and the list of six appearances). Likewise Mark 16:1–8 contains themes not mentioned in 1 Corinthians 15:1–8 (e.g., the purpose of the womens' visit to the tomb, their discovery of the empty tomb, the angel and its message, and the promised appearance to the disciples in Galilee).[18] About the only point of connection between the two texts is their common affirmation of Jesus' resurrection.

(3) Is the empty tomb an apologetic legend? Again I am doubtful. The empty tomb tradition just does not have the characteristics we would expect it to have if it were an invented apologetic device, designed to convince readers that Jesus really rose. For one thing, the empty tomb does not play an apologetic role in the New Testament (though I have little doubt that early Christians used it apologetically). Far from being pushed as an irrefutable argument for the resurrection, the empty tomb is rather depicted as an enigma, a puzzling fact that no one at first is able to account for.[19] (Notice Lk 24:22–23—"Moreover, some women

of our company amazed us. They were at the tomb early in the morning and did not find his body. . . ." Cf. also John 20:1–2, 13.) With the possible exception of the Beloved Disciple in the fourth Gospel (see Jn 20:8), *nobody* in the New Testament comes to believe in the resurrection of Jesus solely on the basis of the empty tomb—not Peter, not Mary Magdalene, not any of the other women. Only the appearances of Jesus himself moved these people to believe that he was alive. In other words, the fact that the empty tomb stories in the Gospels produce only puzzlement and ambiguity rather than proof attests to the primitive and non-apologetic character of the tradition.

The second reason for doubting that the story of the empty tomb is an apologetic legend is that it is bad apologetics. If the story is an apologetic legend invented by later Christians, why is it that the story is made to hang so crucially on the testimony of women, whose evidence was not legally admissible in Jewish proceedings? (This must have constituted something of an embarrassment to those men in Jesus' party who were later to become leaders of the church—while they were hiding, it was the women who found that Jesus was risen.) If the story is an apologetic legend invented by later Christians, why does it (in Mark's original version) lead only to fear, flight, and silence on the part of the women? If the story is an apologetic legend invented by later Christians, why is it so openly admitted that some of Jesus' followers were suspiciously in the vicinity of the tomb early on the morning of the discovery of the empty tomb? And why is there no mention made of any thorough investigation of the tomb or its environs, or of some verifying word from Joseph of Arimathea? As an apologetic argument, this one seems weak.

The third reason for denying that the story of the empty tomb is an apologetic legend is, as noted above, that the emptiness of the tomb seems to have been conceded by all parties, friend and foe alike. I frankly suspect that the tomb *was* checked; the disciples themselves would surely have rushed there to verify or falsify the women's story (again, see Lk 24:24); and later the enemies of the incipient Christian movement would doubtless have searched thoroughly in their effort to disprove the claims of the early Christians.[20] There is no record in any early anti-Christian polemic of anyone's suggesting that the tomb was not empty; what critics tried to do is argue that the disciples stole the body.[21] It should be noted that I am presupposing here my earlier argument against the claim that the empty tomb tradition is late. Naturally, the above points will not be convincing to those who believe the tradition was, for example, invented by Mark and that his Gospel was written outside Palestine during or after the Jewish war. By that time the location of the tomb could have been forgotten and verification would have been difficult. The crucial point here is that the Gospels all claim that the location of Jesus' tomb was known to the women and to the disciples (Mk 15:47; Mt 27:61; Lk 23:55; Jn 20:1). This claim should be rejected—or so I would argue—only for very cogent reasons indeed.

To put it radically, it may be that the claim that the empty tomb is an apologetic legend is *itself* an apologetic legend—a legend suggested in defense of the view that Jesus was not really raised or was raised in some non-bodily sense. It is true that Christian apologists have used the story of the empty tomb in support of the claim that Jesus was bodily raised. But that does not make the story legendary. To show that a given story does or can play an apologetic role in somebody's belief system says nothing about its historical accuracy.

In this regard, note Matthew's story of the guard at the tomb (Mt 27:62–66; 28:4). This story does seem to play an apologetic role in Matthew's Gospel, but that fact by itself does nothing to discredit it. Is the story a "legendary accretion"? I do not know. I have always thought that one point in its favor is, oddly, its own improbability; for the story would seem to have been apologetically useless to the writer of the first Gospel unless it were either widely known to be true or else completely uncheckable. But if the story is an apologetic legend, that will have to be shown on other grounds than the mere fact that the story answers certain objections (e.g., the slander that the disciples stole the body) that might be raised against the claim that the tomb was empty. Furthermore, in a similarly curious way, the story of the guard at the tomb—whether it actually occurred or is an apologetic invention of the later church—constitutes a powerful argument for the reliability of the empty tomb tradition. For the telling of the story of the guard at the tomb is quite senseless unless the tomb of Jesus really was empty. Those who denied the claim that

Jesus was raised from the dead were evidently not able to deny that the tomb was empty.[22]

(4) What about Paul's purported ignorance of the empty tomb? It is quite correct that the apostle does not mention the empty tomb per se; not even his words, "he was buried" (1 Cor 15:4), explicitly refer to it. However, it does not follow from this that Paul had never heard of the empty tomb, or that he disagreed with the empty tomb stories, or that he nowhere *implicitly* referred to the empty tomb, or even that the empty tomb was not part of early Christian proclamation. Some critics seem to come dangerously close to espousing the following obviously invalid inference:

(1) Paul, the earliest New Testament author who proclaimed the resurrection, did not mention the empty tomb;

(2) Therefore, the empty tomb was not part of the earliest Christian proclamation of the resurrection.

Why is it, then, that Paul does not explicitly refer to the empty tomb? Are there other, better, explanations available than the one which says either he had never heard of it or else he disagreed with it? Certainly. In general I imagine Paul did not discuss the empty tomb because, given his audience in Corinth, he did not find it necessary or helpful to do so. Here are several possible explanations. (1) Perhaps Paul, always at pains to prove he was a true apostle and equal with Peter, James, et al., was reluctant to mention an aspect of the resurrection story in which he had had no part (unlike the appearances of Jesus, with one of which Paul was honored—1 Cor 15:8). (2) Perhaps Paul knew the Corinthians already knew about the empty tomb and understood its importance, and so the story did not need to be repeated. (3) Perhaps Paul knew the Corinthians had never heard of the empty tomb, and he chose not to refer to it because the evidence for it, being based on the testimony of obscure women hundreds of miles away in Palestine, was unavailable to the Corinthians. (4) Perhaps Paul believed the empty tomb, by itself, could be explained (theft etc.), and that it was the appearances that were crucial. It does seem that anyone like Paul to whom the risen Jesus had personally appeared would naturally stress the appearances over the empty tomb as evidence of the resurrection. Any one of these explanations—some of which can be combined with each other—seems to me more plausible than the highly improbable claim that Paul either had never heard of the empty tomb or else disagreed with it.

But does Paul *implicitly* refer to the empty tomb in 1 Corinthians 15:4, where he mentions Jesus' burial? I believe it is quite probable that he does. Paul's own view of the nature of the resurrection, in my opinion, *requires* that the tomb be empty (which is the reverse of what is sometimes claimed). This is because his simile of the plant growing from the seed (1 Cor 15:35–43) entails material continuity between the one and the other. That is, on Paul's view Jesus' body could not still be decomposing in the tomb because it was transformed into, i.e., it *became*, Jesus' resurrection body (just as the seed becomes the plant).

Furthermore, that the tomb was empty seems clearly entailed by the claims (explicitly made by Paul) that Jesus died, was buried, and was raised from the dead. It is possible, of course, to imagine survival-of-death theories that involve death, burial, and life again with the corpse still in the grave. But such theories would not agree with most Hebraic notions of resurrection, nor with Paul's. (There were, of course, Jewish theories of survival of death that did not involve bodily resurrection, e.g., Enoch's or Elijah's translation to heaven, or the immortality of the soul doctrine of the Wisdom of Solomon. But these are not theories of resurrection, as Paul's explicitly is.) There is little evidence, for example, in favor of the claim that Paul had in mind some non-bodily notion of resurrection (like the concept of "spiritual resurrection" some contemporary Christian scholars prefer) that did not require an empty tomb. So Paul's own belief that Jesus was raised from the dead, if it is correct, *entails* that the tomb was empty.[23] Perhaps he did not mention the empty tomb because for him resurrection implies empty tomb as a matter of course.

My own view, then, is this: If it is true (1) that first-century Jews would naturally have believed that resurrection means bodily resurrection (and scholars do agree with this), and (2) that there is no convincing reason to believe that Paul had in mind some non-bodily theory, and (3) that the claim that Jesus was bodily raised entails the claim that the tomb was empty, and (4) that Paul was clever enough to recognize this entailment, then, I say, probably Paul's reference to the burial of Jesus did indeed reveal knowledge of and commitment to the tradition of the empty tomb.[24] Thus I conclude that the fact that Paul nowhere explicitly refers to or discusses the empty tomb is not a compelling argument against it.

(5) I have no quarrel with much of the fifth argument. As already noted, I happily agree that the faith of the earliest believers was based on the appearances rather than the empty tomb. But surely the first question we want to ask is not, "Should the empty tomb be emphasized as part of Christian faith today?" but rather, "Is there good reason to believe that Jesus' tomb was empty?" Once we answer the second question we can perhaps go on to the first. (I believe the empty tomb does have certain theological implications, an issue I will discuss briefly below. But to me it is curious indeed why anybody who believes that the tomb was empty should try to belittle it or suggest it has no place in contemporary Christian teaching.)

Another thing I find curious is the question which, so to speak, should take priority, the stories of the appearances or the story of the empty tomb. Kaufman[25] claims that if we regard the appearances as taking priority we can explain the growth of the empty tomb tradition, but that it is much harder to explain the appearance stories by the empty tomb tradition. Perhaps Kaufmann is correct here. But why do we have to choose between the appearances and the empty tomb? Why should one or the other be regarded as "primary" (whatever that means)? Why not accept both that the tomb was empty and that there were resurrection appearances?

Finally, Fuller's claim that the disciples were not interested in the empty tomb as a historical fact but only as a vehicle for proclamation seems almost ridiculous. The statement certainly has rather startling implications. The major one is that the disciples were slightly obtuse. Imagine, say, Peter in part basing what he took to be *the* crucial item of Christian proclamation (i.e., the resurrection of Jesus) on a historical claim (the empty tomb) whose truth value he did not care about. Even if he thought he had another, irrefutable, proof of the claim (i.e., the appearances), this would be a foolish procedure indeed. How absurd to suggest that the disciples, preaching the resurrection in an environment hostile to their message, had no interest in the truth of the claim that Jesus' tomb was empty.

IV

There are also two robust arguments in favor of the empty tomb that have not, to my mind, been refuted. Let me now briefly explain them. Both are implicit in much that I have already said.

1. The first is the fact that *the tradition of the empty tomb enjoys very broad support in the New Testament.* As we have seen, it is found in all four Gospels (note especially that both the Synoptics and John stress it), with possible indirect references in Acts and 1 Corinthians. Furthermore, the fact that it is found in both Mark, John, and in Matthew's special source (i.e., material Matthew did not gain from Mark or Q) demonstrates the broad support the empty tomb receives from independent traditions. And the discrepancies between the accounts in the Gospels (discussed above) argue against the claim that the other evangelists, or even the other synoptic evangelists, wrote about the empty tomb merely under the influence of Mark.

As noted above, I believe that those New Testament scholars who argue that the empty tomb is a late tradition have not succeeded in making their case. They have not succeeded in pinpointing a period, let alone a document, in which Christians believed in the resurrection but not the empty tomb. And if it were true that the empty tomb was a late addition to Christian proclamation, this ought to be evident in the New Testament. But all the relevant sources either affirm or presuppose the empty tomb.

A good example of what I am talking about is the association of Joseph of Arimathea with the tomb in which Jesus was buried. It is significant that this figure, who so far as we know held no position and played no role in the early Christian movement, figures so prominently in all four Gospels. No critic has been able to show that this Joseph was a late apologetic invention of the church—certainly what is said about him and his actions has the ring of truth (see Mk 15:43–46; Mt 27:57–60; Lk 23:50–53; Jn 19:33-42). As Stein argues, "the historicity of the empty tomb is supported by the fact that a specific tomb, which was known in Jerusalem as Joseph of Arimathea's tomb, was associated with the burial of Jesus."[26]

2. The second argument is even more compelling, and is often cited. It is that *early Christian proclamation of the resurrection of Jesus in Jerusalem would have been psychologically and apologetically impossible without safe evidence of an empty tomb*. The psychological point is that the earliest disciples, good Jews and believers in bodily resurrection as they undoubtedly were, would have found it psychologically impossible to preach that Jesus had been raised from the dead and was alive had they had to contend with the presence of his corpse. Or, if this *were* possible, then as Craig argues, early Christian preaching about the resurrection would have taken on an entirely different character than it in fact did.[27] The apologetic point is that the apostles would have been quite unable to convince anyone that Jesus was alive, indeed we can imagine the laughably ridiculous figure they would have cut, had the body been available.

The counter-argument that Jews had a taboo-like fear of contact with cadavers, and that this would have prevented anybody's checking the tomb,[28] is feeble. A few weeks after the crucifixion, Jerusalem was apparently seething with reports of Jesus' resurrection. The Jewish authorities, who wanted at all costs to stamp out the growing Christian movement, would have wasted no time checking the tomb, taboo or not. If worse came to worse they could have convinced Gentile allies to do the job. Perhaps they would not even have had to exhume the corpse— simply pointing to the location of the tomb would have sufficed. (The Jewish polemic against the resurrection shows they could do neither, however.)

In other words, without safe and agreed-upon evidence of an empty tomb, the apostles' claims would have been subject to massive falsification by the simple presentation of the body. As argued above, there is no convincing evidence that by the term "resurrection" the early Christians meant something akin to modern "spiritual" notions of resurrection that allow the continued presence of the corpse. We can infer, then, that the apostles' proclamation of the resurrection was successful precisely because (among other things) nobody was able to produce the corpse. The tomb was empty and the body nowhere to be found.

Of course it is possible to *imagine* scenarios which account for the inability to produce the body. Perhaps Jesus was buried in an unmarked or even mass grave by a Roman functionary and two underlings who three days later, without having told anyone how they had disposed of the body, were transferred back to Rome. Or, to turn to a scenario that has actually been suggested, here is a comment from Hans Küng:

> The disciples (returned from Galilee?), numbering no more than a hundred and twenty even according to Luke's possibly exaggerated and idealized estimate, did not start at once to proclaim the risen Christ, but only several weeks after Jesus' death (the Lucan date for Pentecost assumes fifty days). All this made verification difficult, particularly since the proclamation can scarcely have created much of a stir at the beginning or called for public control in a city of perhaps twenty-five to thirty thousand inhabitants. The story of the empty tomb therefore must not be seen as the recognition of a fact.[29]

The suggestion, then, is that contrary to the impression one receives in the early chapters of Acts, the Christian claim that Jesus had been raised did not become a matter of public controversy until perhaps years after the events immediately following the crucifixion, and that by then the tomb in which Jesus was buried had been forgotten. Thus G. W. H. Lampe says: "Even assuming that Jesus' grave was known, which is by no means certain, it seems very possible that neither party was interested in it, or regarded the truth of Easter as dependent on it, until long after the event: until the period of the controversies reflected in Matthew, which would not arise until the empty tomb had become important in Christian thought about the resurrection."[30] The argument is often combined with the theory mentioned above that the disciples fled to Galilee immediately after the crucifixion and did not return to Jerusalem till later, perhaps much later. The empty tomb story arose (so Barnabas Lindars speculates)[31] in connection with the unsuccessful attempt to locate the body of Jesus when, much later, the disciples returned to Jerusalem.

But the flight-to-Galilee aspect of this argument has been thoroughly discredited, as we saw earlier. And the story of Joseph of Arimathea's involvement in the burial of Jesus seems so strongly supported and inherently trustworthy, as we have seen, that it renders the argument we are considering implausible. And that story entails that the location of Jesus' tomb *was* known. Further, the early church's claim that Jesus' tomb was empty seems to be pointless if it was only made years after the events themselves. Such a claim would have been apologetically valueless by then; opponents could always object that the tomb was simply lost. So the Church's affirmation that Jesus' tomb was empty has the earmarks of a claim made very early indeed. As to Küng's suggestion, it too presupposes the flight to Galilee immediately after the crucifixion. But it seems clear that the location of the tomb was established *before* the return to Galilee. Furthermore, a sensible reaction to Küng's scenario is to admit that the location of an important person's tomb might be lost in fifty years—but in fifty days? And if Luke is correct (why doubt him?), the apostles' preaching *did* create a public stir, and the authorities became involved, almost immediately. (It is hard to give a precise number of days or weeks because Acts 2:43–47, which forms a bridge between the events on the day of Pentecost and the activity of Peter and John in chapter 3 that provoked the authorities, is vague on the question of how much time has passed.)

At any rate, the moral is that such scenarios, while possible, are highly improbable. There is little evidence for them. The available evidence (e.g., Joseph of Arimathea, the testimony of the women, the presupposition of the empty tomb in early anti-Christian polemic) supports the claim that the location of Jesus' tomb was known. And if it was known, then given the evident success of the apostolic preaching, it must have been empty.

V

Is it important for Christians to affirm that Jesus' tomb was empty? Fuller thinks not. What is crucial, he says, is the affirmation, "He is not here; God has raised him," not the empty tomb: "Whether the women's story was based on fact, or was the result of mistake or illusion, is in the last resort a matter of indifference."[32] I do not agree with Fuller at this point; it is time for me to make the remarks I promised earlier about the theological implications of the empty tomb.

The empty tomb tradition, in my opinion, has three important theological ramifications for Christians. The first is that it rules out all reductive theories of the resurrection, i.e., theories which explain the meaning of the Christian affirmation that "Jesus is risen" in terms that do not involve a dead man living again. The New Testament tradition of the empty tomb, in short, entails that resurrection is something that happened to Jesus rather than a convoluted way of describing things that happened to the disciples.

The second theological point is that the empty tomb makes it clear that the person who was raised was the same person as the person who died. I do not claim that such an identification logically requires the empty tomb, for I disagree with those philosophers who hold that personal identity always requires bodily continuity.[33] Still, it was the fact that Jesus was *bodily* raised, a truth underscored by the empty tomb, that made possible his recognition (usually with some difficulty) by the disciples. This was a virtual *sine qua non* of the Christian message in order to rule out misidentifications of the Risen One—that he was an angel, or some new divine being, or just a "subjective vision." The person who was raised had to be the same beloved Lord who had died.

The third theological point is that the empty tomb distinguishes the Christian view of resurrection from dualist, spiritualist theories of the immortality of the soul. To put the point emphatically, the Christian resurrection claim is an *empirical* claim— it entails the life after death of *living bodies* that can be seen and touched (although of a transformed sort).[34] The raised will be living bodies that are materially related to their old bodies (just as, in Paul's simile, the seed is materially related to the plant that it produces). Christian resurrection is not a docetic or Platonic "escape" from bodily life. The resurrection does not mean that, much to our pleasant surprise, we human beings turn out to have an indestructible aspect which survives death. It means rather that death has been defeated by a miraculous and decisive intervention by God.

An even larger point follows: on the Christian view the whole of creation is to be redeemed in Christ, not just its spiritual or "higher" aspects (cf. Rom 8:19–23). Christianity is not a form of Greek or Oriental dualism whereby the divine cannot come into relation with concrete corporeal reality.[35] All creaturely existence is to be reconciled to God—even corruptible physical bodies. Christianity says a decisive *no* to religions and philosophies that aim to liberate our true spiritual essence from its fleshly prison.

VI

The proper conclusion, then, is that Jesus' tomb was empty. The arguments against it are not convincing, and the strongest of the arguments for it have not been successfully answered. The traditional Christian belief with which we began, that the tomb of Jesus was discovered empty on Easter morning, is one which Christians ought to continue to affirm. As Karl Barth wisely put it, "Christians do not believe in the empty tomb but in the living Christ," but that does not imply "that we can believe in the living Christ without believing in the empty tomb."[36]

Does this mean that we have proved the resurrection? Is there now no room for faith? Of course not. The empty tomb, by itself, does not prove the resurrection. It is a necessary but not sufficient condition for the bodily resurrection of Jesus—if the tomb was not empty Jesus was not bodily raised; but the empty tomb itself does not prove that Jesus was bodily raised. As in the days after Pentecost, the crucial question today is: *Why* was the tomb empty? Perhaps after all the tomb was empty because of quite natural circumstances that are now unknown. That option is always available to the skeptic. My own view is that the tomb was empty because God miraculously raised its occupant from the dead.[37]

NOTES

1. Rudolf Bultmann, *Theology of the New Testament*, vol. I, trans. Kendrick Grobel (New York: Charles Scribner's Sons, 1951), 45.

2. Hans Küng, *On Being a Christian*, trans. by Edward Quinn (New York: Pocket Books, 1976), 366.

3. Some recent scholars separate them, however. Barnabas Lindars, for example, affirms bodily resurrection but denies the empty tomb. See

"Jesus Risen: Bodily Resurrection But No Empty Tomb," *Theology* 89 no. 728 (March 1986): 90–91. Luis M. Bermejo, S.J., on the other hand, affirms the empty tomb but denies bodily resurrection. See *Light Beyond Death: The Risen Christ and the Transfiguration of Man* (Anand, India: Gujarat Sahitya Prakash, 1985).

4. See Stephen T. Davis, "Was Jesus Raised Bodily?" *Christian Scholar's Review* 14, no. 2 (1985): 140–152.

5. William C. Craig, "The Historicity of the Empty Tomb of Jesus," *New Testament Studies* 31, no. 1 (January 1985): 53.

6. Rudolf Bultmann, see *The History of the Synoptic Tradition*, trans. John Marsh (New York: Harper and Brothers, 1963), 284–290.

7. Walter Kasper, for example, mentions these points and then concludes: "We must assume therefore that we are faced not with historical details but with stylistic devices intended to attract the attention and raise excitement in the minds of those listening" (*Jesus The Christ* [London: Burns and Oates, 1976], 127).

8. Hans Küng suggests this argument. See *On Being a Christian*, 364–365.

9. This conjecture is put forward by Gordon Kaufman, *Systematic Theology: A Historicist Perspective* (New York: Charles Scribner's Sons, 1968), 419n.

10. Küng, *On Being a Christian*, 364.

11. Reginald Fuller, *The Formation of the Resurrection Narratives* (Philadelphia: Fortress Press, 1970), 171. (In the light of Lk 24:24, it is hard to credit Fuller's claim that "we hear nothing of their having checked it.")

12. There are other and in my opinion less impressive arguments against the empty tomb. (1) Some claim for theological reasons that our resurrection must be like Christ's; since the tombs of Christians who have died are not empty (despite the fact that they will some day be resurrected), Jesus' resurrection must not have involved an empty tomb either. But in reply, two questions need simply be asked: first, is it an acceptable procedure to deduce a historical fact from a theological point, especially a controversial one? Second, why must Jesus' resurrection be like ours in every respect? New Testament writers do take Jesus' resurrection as a promise and model of ours, but nowhere suggest they must be alike in all respects. (2) Hans Grass suggests, following a vague reference in a speech Luke attributes to Paul (Acts 13:27–29), that Jesus' body was buried by his enemies. He accordingly dismisses as legendary the burial by Joseph of Arimathea and the empty tomb. But in reply to this argument, it need only be asked whether it is proper to base such a bold theory on such a vague reference, itself subject to a variety of

interpretations. The grounds for Grass's theory seem flimsy indeed. (See Gerald O'Collins, S.J., *The Resurrection of Jesus Christ* (Valley Forge, Penn.: Judson Press, 1973), 39, 90–91, 96, for a good discussion of these arguments.)

13. See also 2 Maccabees 3:26, 33; Josephus, *Antiquities*, V, viii, 2; Gospel of Peter 9.

14. See Eleonore Stump's article, "Visits To the Sepulcher and Biblical Exegesis," *Faith and Philosophy* 6, no. 4 (October 1989): 353–377, for a balanced and sensible critique of the approach some biblical scholars take to the discrepancies in the empty tomb accounts.

15. Even a secular historian like Michael Grant, who affirms the empty tomb as historical but not the resurrection, argues that discrepancies in secondary details do not affect the historical core of a narrative. See *Jesus: An Historian's Review of the Gospels* (New York: Charles Scribner's Sons, 1977), 176, 200.

16. See Pheme Perkins, *Resurrection* (Garden City, N.Y.: Doubleday, 1984), 169: "But frequently the judgment about which form of a story is likely to be older is difficult to make." See also p. 196.

17. See Robert H. Stein, "Was the Tomb Really Empty?" *Themelios* 5, no. 1 (September 1979): 20. Cf. also E. L. Bode, *The First Easter Morning* (Rome: Biblical Institute, 1970), 6, 58, 71.

18. Gerald O'Collins marshals the evidence effectively. See *Jesus Risen* (New York: Paulist Press, 1987), 125–127. See also Perkins, *Resurrection*, 84–94.

19. See Perkins, *Resurrection*, 123: "The restraint of the Markan story makes it evident that the empty tomb itself is ambiguous and that it is not immediately viewed as evidence for the Resurrection."

20. The theory that the disciples had fled to Galilee and so were not around to check has been shown to be utterly implausible. Hans Von Campenhausen dismisses it as "a legend of the critics." See his *Tradition and Life in the Church*, trans. A. V. Littledale (London: William Collins and Sons, 1968), 79.

21. See Raymond E. Brown, *The Virginal Conception and Bodily Resurrection of Jesus* (New York: Paulist Press, 1973), 22. See also Justin Martyr's *Dialogue with Trypho the Jew* (ca. 150 A.D.), where opponents of the resurrection still seem to grant the empty tomb.

22. I owe this point to Professor Robert Gundry, in conversation. See also William C. Craig, "The Guard at the Tomb," *New Testament Studies* 30, no. 2 (April 1984): 279, 281.

23. See the article referred to in footnote 4 for a more thorough discussion of these matters.

24. On these matters, see Brown, *Virginal Conception and Bodily Resurrection*, 70; Fuller, *Formation of the Resurrection Narratives*, 73; and Craig, "Historicity of the Empty Tomb," 40–42.

25. Kaufman, *Systematic Theology*, 419–420n.

26. Stein, "Was the Tomb Really Empty," 11. See also Grant, *Jesus: An Historian's Review*, 175. Speaking of the accounts of the work of Joseph of Arimathea, Stein says: "This story is likely to be true since the absence, which it records, of any participation by Jesus' followers was too unfortunate, indeed disgraceful, to have been voluntarily invented by the evangelists at a later date."

27. Craig, "Historicity of the Empty Tomb of Jesus," 57.

28. This is suggested by E. Hirsch. See Wolfhart Pannenberg, *Jesus-God and Man*, trans. Lewis L. Wilkins and Duane A. Priebe, 2nd ed. (Philadelphia: Westminster Press, 1968, 1977), 100–101.

29. Küng, *On Being a Christian*, 364–365.

30. See G. W. H. Lampe and D. M. MacKinnon, *The Resurrection: A Dialogue* (Philadelphia: Westminster Press 1966), 53. See also R. R. Bater, "Toward a More Biblical View of the Resurrection," *Interpretation* 23, no. 1 (January 1969): 50.

31. Lindars, "Jesus Risen," 93–94.

32. Fuller, *Formation of the Resurrection Narratives*, 179.

33. See Stephen T. Davis, "Traditional Christian Belief in the Resurrection of the Body," *New Scholasticism* 62, no. 1 (Winter 1988): 72–97.

34. This fact is grasped more clearly than anyone by Thomas Torrance. See *Space, Time, and Resurrection* (Grand Rapids, Mich.: William B. Eerdmans, 1976). See especially page 141. "It is the empty tomb that constitutes the essential empirical correlate in statements about the resurrection of Christ."

35. See ibid., 81.

36. Cited in O'Collins, *Resurrection of Jesus Christ*, 97.

37. I would like to thank Professor Adela Yarbro Collins, whose views on the empty tomb are quite different from mine, for several helpful criticisms of an earlier draft of this paper.

The Heart of the Gospel: Comments on the Paper of Stephen T. Davis

Cornelius Plantinga, Jr.

In his clear, thoughtful, and well-argued essay Professor Davis contemplates a contemporary oddity, namely, that a number of theologians who affirm Jesus' resurrection combine this affirmation with a denial of the empty tomb or with indifference toward it. Davis rightly finds this combination extraordinary. Suppose, by way of parallel, that somebody were to acknowledge that George Bush had graduated from Yale University in 1948. Suppose this same person were then to reserve judgment on the question whether Bush is still a sophomore at Yale, insisting that this question and that of his graduation were mutually independent. Such insistence would naturally put us in the interrogative mood.

Though Davis is convinced that the concept of resurrection biblically and logically includes the concept of an empty tomb, he does not direct his efforts mainly at convincing us of such inclusion. Instead, he isolates the empty tomb claim, considers five objections to it, refutes them, and then closes with three positive theological implications of the empty tomb.

Davis first considers the objection that the empty tomb tradition is unreliable because the Gospels contradict each other in presenting it. In turning back this objection Davis observes that while some details of the Gospel reports cannot easily be harmonized, the Gospels *largely* agree: they agree that early on Sunday certain women including Mary Magdalene went to the tomb, found it empty, and either discovered or were told that Jesus was alive. In other words, the narrative weave of the Gospels is tight at its center even if ragged at the edges.

According to a second objection, the empty tomb is a late and therefore unreliable accretion to the traditions of Jesus' appearances. Or, more strongly put, the empty tomb tradition is a late and oblique way of accounting for Jesus' post-resurrection appearances. Here Davis properly raises important doubts both about the lateness thesis itself and also about the suggestion that the empty tomb theory depends on and seeks to explain the appearances.

But we can go further. Suppose the lateness claim *could* be supported. Suppose someone could establish that the empty tomb reports are later than the appearances reports. Davis is right in questioning a conclusion that is then sometimes drawn, namely, that the later tradition must be an ad hoc explanation of the earlier appearance tradition.

But surely we ought to challenge as well any inevitable link between the lateness claim and the unreliability claim. While contemporary biblical scholars sometimes appear to assume that, where biblical traditions are concerned, the later they are, the falser they are, this assumption seems merely arbitrary. One could just as well imagine grounds for its opposite, namely, that the later a tradition, the truer. After all, a later version of some event has the advantage of longer, and maybe wider, perspective. Its author can hold the relevant event at arm's length. She can sift and compare seemingly rival versions of it in order to form, at the end of the day, a really balanced and mature account of this event. Take, for example, Robert François Damiens's 1757 assassination attempt on Louis XV of France. Early reports of this event assumed both that Damiens deliberately meant to kill the King and that, in this project, he had accomplices. Responsible contemporary historians doubt the former and deny the latter. Early reports and interpretations of events may or may not be more plausible than later ones.

Third, Davis takes on the assertion that the empty tomb story is a legend invented for the apologetic purpose of shoring up the claim that Jesus was raised. To this he replies that, if so, its inventors were wonderfully clumsy and ineffectual. For one thing, the empty tomb stories never do function apologetically in the New Testament. For another, even if they had, these stories would have been bad apologetics in their culture since they offer women as witnesses to their main event in a culture where women were legal non-entities. Moreover, in Luke's account the women struggle to get their amazing news through the thick skulls of male apostles—the more natural witnesses in case the empty tomb reports had been crafted as apologetic legend.

Still further, an apologetic use of the empty tomb tradition when no one disputes it appears otiose. After all, as Davis observes, the only—surely the main—issue in the neighborhood of the empty tomb is not *whether* the tomb is empty, but rather *why* it is empty.

Fourth, Davis considers a routine objection to the reliability of the empty tomb tradition, namely, that Paul never mentions it. Here Davis questions the assumption that Paul's silence implies either his ignorance of the empty tomb assertion or his rejection of it. It implies neither one. There are other perfectly possible explanations for Paul's silence and Davis suggests some plausible ones.

Fifth, Davis rightly rejects the suggestion that the empty tomb reports are largely irrelevant to Christian faith and theology. For even if the empty tomb reports are not highlighted in the New Testament as part of the core of faith, they enjoy wide support there and, in any case, seem apologetically and psychologically requisite for honest and convincing testimony to the resurrection.

In this quintuplet of refutations Davis is, in my opinion, wise, fair, and right.

But surely one question that persists is why all this is necessary. Why are scholars and others so wary of the empty tomb? Why all this speculative effort spent on the pursuit of dubious alternatives? Why are such alternatives even minimally appealing?

Possibly because the alternatives are less novel, less scandalous, less threatening to our comfortable assurance that we know pretty much where the lines of reality are drawn.

According to Matthew, on the Sabbath immediately following the crucifixion of Jesus,

> the chief priests and the pharisees gathered before Pilate and said, "Sir, we remember what that impostor said while he was still alive,

'After three days I will rise again.' Therefore command the tomb to be made secure until the third day; otherwise his disciples may go and steal him away, and tell the people, 'He has been raised from the dead,' and the last deception would be worse than the first." Pilate said to them, "You have a guard of soldiers; go, make it as secure as you can." (27:62–66)

Why is Pilate's suggestion so attractive to certain contemporary Christians, including certain contemporary scholars?

In one of his sermons Frederick Buechner comments memorably on this fatal attraction. The fear within Pilate's visitors, unspoken and maybe even unfaced, may have included

> the fear . . . that the body that now lay dead in its tomb, disfigured by the mutilations of the Cross, that this body or some new and terrible version of it would start to breathe again, stand up in its grave clothes and move toward them with unspeakable power. To the extent that deep within themselves the Jewish elders feared this as a real possibility, their being told by Pilate to make things as secure as they could was to have the very earth pulled out from under them. How does an old man keep the sun from rising? How do soldiers secure the world against miracle? ("The End is Life," in *The Magnificent Defeat* [New York: Seabury Press, 1979], 76–77)

Buechner goes on to suggest that actually quite a lot can be done to secure the world against miracle. We can domesticate and spiritualize miracles. We can turn wine into water. We can convert the miracle of the resurrection-*cum*-empty tomb into the miracle of the living spirit of Jesus which, after two thousand years, still broods over the face of human life as Lincoln's spirit broods over Gettysburg. We can center our Easter celebrations on the immortality of Jesus' teachings, or on the ageless poetry of life, death, and rebirth—especially the rebirth of hope in the despairing human soul. Any of us not addicted to crisp thought or prose can contemplate Paul Van Buren's description of the Easter miracle: the disciples "experienced a discernment situation."

But none of this preserves the heart of the Gospel and the heart of the Christian religion. For that we need a resurrection in the usual sense, namely one that, as Davis finally puts it, "*entails* that the tomb was empty."

Here Davis's three concluding theological implications of the empty tomb assume high profile. The third is especially neglected by proponents of full tomb—or possibly full tomb—theories. As Davis says, "on the Christian view the whole of creation is to be redeemed in Christ, not just its spiritual or 'higher' aspects." Creation includes bodies. That is why the classic Christian understanding of Jesus' resurrection goes beyond survival theories. The Resurrection is not merely a counterexample to the claim that death is equivalent to annihilation, not merely a piece of evidence for the immortality of the soul.

Nor, on the other hand, is it a Lazarus-like revival. Creation includes bodies; redemption includes transformation of these bodies. The particular novelty of the Resurrection of Jesus Christ is that in it he is a pioneer, he is "first fruits" of a whole new situation in history in which God's creation is both vindicated and transformed. As C. S. Lewis once put it, Jesus "forced open a door that had been locked since the death of the first man." It is not as if Jesus bails out of creation, leaving the chrysalis of his body behind him. Jesus' resurrection rather corroborates and exceeds the traditional Jewish expectations of bodily resurrection in the Day of the Lord, as the Incarnation itself corroborates and exceeds Messianic expectations. Jesus' body is both raised and transformed. It is the first fruits of a general harvest of resurrections in which our glorified bodies shall be like his (Phil 3.21).

In his essay, Stephen Davis nicely blends biblical insight, philosophical rigor, and theological sensitivity in a successful attempt to defend a non-negotiable item of Christian belief.

The Empty Tomb in the Gospel According to Mark

Adela Yarbro Collins

The narrative concerning the empty tomb in the Gospel of Mark is related to the phenomenon we call "the resurrection of Jesus." The interpretation of this phenomenon is a good topic for a volume such as this, since it is a philosophical issue. Like other questions that border on mystery, it evokes one's fundamental view of reality. A number of interpretations of the resurrection of Jesus have been articulated, each based on a different set of fundamental presuppositions.

Perspectives on the Resurrection of Jesus

Some Christians argue, "Since the resurrection of Jesus is the heart of Christian faith, if he was not raised, Christian faith is a delusion." This argument is a restatement of 1 Corinthians 15:12–19. Others assert, "What is impossible with humankind is possible with God." This is a reformulation of a widespread ancient idea that appears in the prayer of Jesus in Gethsemane according to Mark (14:36).[1] This approach to the resurrection of Jesus is based on the authority of individual passages of Scripture that function as principles. For some, such a principle solves everything as far as the Resurrection is concerned. With regard to the first example, one could dispute that the restatement accurately reflects Paul's argument. Or one could dispute that the resurrection of Jesus is the heart of Christian faith. On the latter point, one could show

107

that there are entire books of the New Testament that do not use resurrection language. The problem with the second example—that all things are possible for God—is that it does not help us much in most of the rest of life—getting a car to run, dealing with snow, solving family problems.

Another approach is what we might call the canonical perspective. The underlying argument is basically, "The New Testament says that Jesus was raised, therefore he was." At present, this perspective is growing in the number of adherents. A sophisticated version of it implies that we cannot know for certain whether Jesus was raised, or prove that he was, but the New Testament provides the language or the symbol system of Christian belief. To be Christian means to experience oneself and one's world in its terms.[2] The problem with this approach becomes apparent as soon as one recalls that the New Testament also says that slavery is to be accepted as part of Christian life. It could be objected that the resurrection of Jesus is foundational to Christianity, whereas acceptance of slavery is not. Such an objection, however, changes the rules of the game. The canonical perspective should take the entire canon into account, at least the entire New Testament. If one is to pick and choose, then criteria must be articulated for determining what is foundational and what is not.

A kind of pastoral perspective is often expressed, "People need assurance about life after death; therefore, I will tell them that the resurrection of Jesus gives them such assurance." It may well be that human beings need to believe in life beyond the grave. But most of us, except perhaps in foxholes and their equivalents, want to know that our beliefs are reliable. Some, even among the terminally ill, when presented with this argument will respond, "If that is all you can say, call the nurse."

Many of the more reflective approaches, that we may call philosophical, share as a starting point the profound idea that death is not the end. Various formulations have been proposed. One posits individual, conscious afterlife in some form. Another affirms immortality through one's children, their children, and so on. A third envisions the extension of the individual into later time by the effects of one's deeds, writings, or other accomplishments. Along these lines, process theology speaks of a kind of objective immortality through one's chemical remains and the effects of one's deeds on society.

Another type of approach reflects the apparent importance of the natural sciences for thinking about the resurrection of Jesus. One point of view says that resurrection is physically impossible. No corpse could be resuscitated. Those who take this point of view reason from an alleged general law of nature to a specific historical situation. The position taken by Rudolf Bultmann is an example of this point of view, one that has been enormously influential in New Testament studies and theology in the twentieth century.[3] This position is not based on the actual results of research in any one of the special sciences. It is rather the product of a general worldview in which the natural scientific focus on the empirical has been made absolute and functions as a secular myth.

Another perspective of this general type interprets the resurrection as the transformation of matter from one form into another. Jesus' physical body was transformed into a spiritual state as water becomes steam.[4]

Whereas Bultmann assumed that historical inquiry must work within the limits set by the natural sciences, another position is that the point of view of the historian need not be determined by the natural sciences. A historical event is always particular; all the elements of one event will never be repeated exactly. Richard R. Niebuhr, for example, asks whether it is not within the realm of historical probability that the elements of the resurrection of Jesus were present only once.[5]

Recently there has been more interest in the implications of the social sciences for understanding the resurrection of Jesus than the natural sciences. A sociological perspective begins with the function of the resurrection of Jesus for the group of his disciples. An old and negative form of this approach is the theory that the disciples consciously and deliberately fabricated the story of the resurrection to cope with the death of Jesus and continue his work. A more psychological approach has been taken by those who argue that the appearances of the risen Jesus were individual and, in some cases, collective visionary or hallucinatory experiences.

A social-psychological theory of cognitive dissonance is very persuasive for some today. Cognitive dissonance may be defined as conflict between one's view of reality or one's expectations of the future and what seems on the surface to be the case. In more technical terms, it consists of dissonant or inconsistent relations among cognitive elements.[6] Dissonance or tension among perceptions or beliefs creates pressure to resolve or reduce that tension. The means of reducing the tension include changes in behavior, changes in cognition, and the seeking out of new information. This theory was applied first to apocalyptic expectations in the United States in the mid-twentieth century.[7] Before long, it was used to explain phenomena in the ancient world, including the resurrection of Jesus.[8] This theory could provide a psychological explanation for the appearances of the risen Jesus: they were visions produced unconsciously in order to resolve the tension created by the death of Jesus. The arrest and crucifixion of Jesus seemed to be disconfirming events of his disciples' belief that he was the definitive agent of God. Most applications of the theory to biblical literature, however, have focused on changes in behavior, such as increased missionary activity, and changes in beliefs attested by hermeneutical activity.[9]

There are two final perspectives that should be mentioned: the historical and the literary. The historical approach is the attempt to determine what *probably* took place; not *possibly*. Anything conceivable is possible, for example, that Jesus rode out of the tomb on a purple toad. The historian asks the question, "What can we construct from the evidence?" The best discussion of the resurrection of Jesus from this point of view is that by Van Harvey in his book *The Historian and the Believer*.[10] The literary perspective has come into its own most recently.[11] When the debate seems to be fruitless, the participants finally ask, "What are we doing here?" The literary approach raises the question of the form and the nature of the claims being made in the sources. Are they scientific, mythological, historical, metaphorical, psychological or what?

New Testament scholarship begins with the historical and literary approaches for several reasons:

1. The resurrection of Jesus is said to have taken place in the first century. Only those who debate this claim can avoid the historical approach.

2. The evidence about the resurrection is found in literary texts.
3. Christianity has always claimed to be a historical religion. It is not founded on timeless insight or deep experience in the Jungian sense. It is founded on events among people. Therefore, the literary and historical approaches are essential.
4. All the other approaches depend on these two.

The Oldest Text: 1 Corinthians 15

In taking a historical and literary approach to the resurrection of Jesus, it is most appropriate to begin with the oldest text that refers to it in some detail, namely, Paul's first letter to the Corinthians. This letter was written in the early 50s of the first century. Very few New Testament scholars today would date the earliest Gospel before 66 C.E. In chapter 15, beginning in verse 3, Paul cites pre-gospel tradition about the resurrection of Jesus. The terms "received" and "handed over" in verses 1 and 3 are technical terms that show he is reporting tradition.[12] The use of non-Pauline words and phrases in verses 3–5 support the conclusion that we have tradition here.[13] Paul has clearly elaborated this tradition at least by adding comments about his own experience in verses 8–11. Whether he added comments to the tradition preserved in verses 3–7 is debated.[14]

First Corinthians 15 is an important historical source, not only because it is early, but also because it is written by a participant in the phenomenon under discussion. Paul's language clearly shows that he considered his experience of the risen Lord to be of the same nature as those of Peter and the rest of the Twelve: "He appeared to [or was seen by] Peter . . . he appeared also to [or was seen also by] me"(vv. 5, 8).[15] Further, in this passage Paul does not simply repeat the tradition and state his experience. He goes to considerable lengths to explain how the notion of resurrection is to be understood (vv. 35–50).

Paul's understanding of the resurrection of Jesus does not involve the revival of his corpse. The resurrected person has a "spiritual body" (v. 44) that is not a slightly modified form of the physical body. The spiritual body is as different from the physical body as the plant is from the seed (vv. 36–37). The physical body is terrestrial, whereas the spiritual body is celestial (vv. 40–41). Figurative use of language about seeds and plants was very common in the ancient world. To understand Paul's intention in using this figurative language, we must look very closely at his argument. The most important thing to notice is that Paul emphasizes the discontinuity between the seed and the plant: "what you sow is not the body which is to be. . . . But God gives it a body as he has chosen, and to each kind of seed its own body" (1 Cor 15:37–38). In other words, for Paul, the seed "dies" and God creates a plant in its place. Paul seems to have in mind here the phenomenon whereby the sprout of a new plant springs forth from that which is planted, such as a bean or a potato, and the "seed" itself shrivels and eventually decomposes. There is of course, for Paul, continuity between the dead person buried and the person who is raised. This is not, however, primarily *material* continuity in the sense of a relatively slight transformation of the body. It is rather the continuity of the personhood.

According to this interpretation, the phrase "that which you sow" in verse 36 figuratively refers to the whole (dead) person who is buried. It is the whole person who "is not made alive unless one dies." In verse 37, the referent of "that which you sow" has shifted a bit. Such a shift is not uncommon elsewhere in Paul's letters. In verse 37 "that which you sow" figuratively refers to the physical, earthly body. It is not the same as "the body that will come into being," i.e., the spiritual, resurrected body. The physical, earthly body is like a grain, bean, or potato that is used as a seed, out of which the plant comes, but that itself shrivels and decays. In verses 42–44 there is a series of verbs, all of which are in the third person singular. The implied subject of these verbs needs to be expressed in an English translation. The range of possibilities includes "he," "she," "one," and "it." The Greek is somewhat ambiguous. The antecedent of the implied subject could be the "seed" (*kokkon*) mentioned in verse 37 or "that which you sow" (*ho speireis*) mentioned in verses 36 and 37. Both of these are rather distant from the series of verbs that begins in verse 42. Since verse 42 begins with the statement "So also [is] the resurrection of the dead (plural)," the most appropriate subject to supply is "[one of] the dead." Thus, the following statements should be translated, "One is sown in corruption, one is raised in incorruption; one is sown in dishonor, one is raised in glory; one is sown in weakness, one is raised in power; one is sown as a body characterized by the principle of earthly life (*sōma psychikon*), one is raised as a body characterized by spirit (*sōma pneumatikon*). The translation "one is sown as a body" seems odd only if one is unaware that Paul sometimes used the word "body" (*sōma*) to characterize the whole human person, albeit from a specific point of view (Phil 1:20; 1 Cor 6:15 [cf. 1 Cor 12:27], 7:4, 9:27, 13:3; 2 Cor 10:10; Rom 6:12, 12:1).[16]

Paul's understanding of resurrection is like that of Daniel 12. Most English translations of verse 2 are misleading. The Revised Standard Version, for example, refers to "those who sleep in the dust of the earth." This translation is supported by the versions, but not by the Masoretic Text. The Hebrew phrase is best translated "those who sleep in a land of dust." This expression is not an allusion to bodies in graves. "The land of dust" is a description of Sheol or Hades where the shades of the dead are confined.[17] Those who "awake" are not reunited with their physical bodies, but "shine like the brightness of the firmament," "like stars" (v. 3). In other words, they are given celestial bodies, like those of the heavenly beings. That Paul's understanding of resurrection was similar to that expressed in Daniel 12 is supported by Paul's comparison of resurrection bodies to the sun, moon, and stars in 1 Corinthians 15:40–41. Both Daniel 12 and 1 Corinthians 15 express the notion of resurrection in terms of astral immortality.[18] Neither the book of Daniel nor Paul shows any interest in what happens to the physical body. Presumably it decays and has no importance for the resurrected person. This interpretation of Daniel 12 is supported by the description of personal afterlife for the righteous in the book of Jubilees, "And their bones shall rest in the earth, and their spirits shall have much joy" (Jub 23:22). It is important to note that both Daniel 12 and the book of Jubilees are of Palestinian provenance.[19]

In Paul's understanding, Jesus was transformed into a completely different kind of existence. The remark in verse 50, "flesh and blood cannot inherit the kingdom of God, nor does the perishable inherit the imperishable," implies that the resurrection "body" is not material in the same way that the earthly body is. This interpretation is confirmed by the contrast in 2 Corinthians 5 between the earthly body as a "tent" that is to be folded up or destroyed and the heavenly "body" as an eternal "building" waiting for us in the heavens.[20] Thus, for Paul, and presumably for many other early Christians, the resurrection of Jesus did not imply that his tomb was empty.

Appearances and Empty Tomb

Thus it is not surprising, although noteworthy, that the tradition cited by Paul does not mention the empty tomb. In his own elaboration and discussion of the theme, Paul also does not mention the empty tomb. The summaries of the Gospel in the book of Acts also fail to mention the empty tomb.[21] The fact that Paul, especially, does not mention it has led some scholars to argue that the tradition about the empty tomb was an apologetic invention intended to support the early Christian proclamation about the resurrection.[22] There are several problems with this theory. If such were the origin of the tradition, it is odd that it is not used apologetically in the book of Acts. Further, if the empty tomb story was invented to "prove" the resurrection of Jesus, it is odd that the only witnesses to the emptiness of the tomb, at least in Matthew and Mark, are women.[23] The status of women in the ancient world was such that a story fabricated as proof or apology would probably not be based on the testimony of women.

The empty tomb story is difficult for everyone, regardless of perspective. There is a major textual problem regarding what the original ending of Mark was. Text-critical principles and linguistic studies indicate that the original ending was verse 8.[24] The list of women varies among the Gospels; some argue that it varies even within Mark. The status of the stone varies among the Gospels. Within Mark, why do the women go without having a plan for moving the stone? Whether Jesus was anointed before burial varies among the Gospels. Within Mark, why do the women intend to anoint Jesus on the second day after his death? Assuming that Mark ended with 16:8, the women are told to tell but they do not. Why not? Was the empty tomb tradition new with Mark? Is their silence meant to explain why the tradition about the empty tomb was not known before Mark was written?

Another problem is who really buried Jesus. According to Acts 13:29, it was his enemies. According to the Synoptics, it was Joseph of Arimathea. It is quite credible that Acts 13:29 is as precise a historical report of the burial of Jesus as can be reconstructed. The Joseph story may be an apologetic legend; at least it seems to grow into one, as is evident from a comparison of the four canonical Gospels.

Some argue that the very fact that the empty tomb tradition is only loosely related to the tradition of appearances of the risen Jesus is evidence that the empty tomb tradition is equally old.[25] Most New Testament scholars at present accept the argument that the Gospel of Mark is the oldest gospel. In the opinion of this majority, Mark 16:1–8 is, therefore, the oldest attestation of the tradition that the tomb was empty.[26] One's judgment about the age of the empty tomb tradition will depend on the literary question regarding the origin of this passage.[27] The options are: (1) it is based on a pre-Markan passion narrative; (2) it is based on another source, oral or written, adapted by the author of Mark; and (3) it was composed by the author of Mark.

The Literary History of Mark 16:1–8

Those who assume that there was a pre-Markan passion narrative explain the agreements and continuities between chapters 15 and 16 as evidence for the use of the same source for the two chapters. Those who dispute the existence of such a source, or who think it ended with the burial of Jesus, explain the elements of continuity as the result of composition or editing by the author of Mark. Whether or not there was a pre-Markan passion narrative is disputed. The older form-critical view is that there was. This view was articulated by Martin Dibelius and Rudolf Bultmann.[28] The newer form-critical view is that the hypothesis of a pre-Markan connected passion narrative is untenable; the elements that connect the separate pericopes are editorial additions of the author of Mark. This view was argued in detail by Eta Linnemann.[29] For decades many scholars accepted the existence of a pre-Markan passion narrative on the basis of the authority and arguments of Dibelius and Bultmann. Although Linnemann

has not persuaded everyone, her book at least has shown that
the existence of such a document is not an assured result of
New Testament scholarship. Detailed redaction critical analyses
of Mark 14–15 have also called into question the existence of a
pre-Markan passion narrative.[30] One may not, then, begin on the
basis of such an assumption.

Several types of arguments are brought forward as evidence
that the author of Mark made use of a briefer source in composing
16:1–8. The burial scene at the end of chapter 15 and the empty
tomb story are said not to "match."[31] The names of the women
are said to differ in the two chapters.[32] The burial described in
15:46 is said not to be incomplete. Thus there is tension between
the account of the burial and the motivation for the women's
visit to the tomb. It is also claimed that, from the point of view
of the author of Mark, Jesus was already anointed for burial by
the anonymous woman in the anecdote recounted in 14:3–9. The
passage about the woman anointing Jesus was seen by the early
form critics as an insertion by the author of Mark into the pre-
Markan passion narrative.

The names of the women are given for the first time in 15:40
as Mary Magdalene, Mary the mother of James the younger and
Joses, and Salome. Here they are presented as witnesses to the
crucifixion. Two of these women are mentioned again in 15:47 as
Mary Magdalene and Mary the mother of Joses. In this context
they are presented as witnesses to the burial of Jesus by Joseph
of Arimathea. In the beginning of the empty tomb story, three
women are introduced as Mary Magdalene, Mary the mother
of James, and Salome. There is no compelling reason to think
that the three women referred to in 16:1 are not the same three
mentioned in 15:40. It is true that the references to them are not
verbally identical. But the differences may be explained perfectly
well as stylistic variations that avoid monotonous repetition. It is
the wording of the reference to the second woman that varies. In
the second two instances, the reference is shortened, first in one
way, then in another. Such shortening is understandable, given
the lengthiness of the full reference in the first instance (15:40).
Thus these differences are not evidence for the use of a source
in 16:1–8.[33]

The account of the burial of Jesus by Joseph of Arimathea in chapter 15 does not mention anointing of the body with aromatic spices. Raymond Brown has made a credible case recently that, from the point of view of the author of Mark, this burial is a dishonorable burial, the type afforded a criminal.[34] He argues that Joseph performs it, not out of reverence for Jesus, but in order to observe the commandment of Deuteronomy 21:22–23, "And if a man has committed a crime punishable by death and he is put to death, and you hang him on a tree, his body shall not remain all night upon the tree, but you shall bury him the same day, for a hanged man is accursed by God; you shall not defile your land which the Lord your God gives you for an inheritance." The relevance of this commandment, or one like it, is implied in Mark 15:42–43, "And when evening had come, since it was the day of Preparation, that is, the day before the Sabbath, Joseph of Arimathea a respected member of the Council. . .went to Pilate. . . ." The reference to sunset supplies the motivation for Joseph's request that Pilate allow him to bury the body. In the case of a dishonorable burial, anointing was not necessarily customary and should not be supplied by the modern reader. If this is an accurate reading of the burial story in its historical and literary context, this burial would have seemed incomplete to the disciples of Jesus. Thus, within the narrative of Mark, the coming of the women to the tomb to anoint the body would be motivated and would "fit" with the previous narrative.

The argument that Mark would not have composed a narrative involving women going to the tomb to anoint Jesus because he had already been anointed by the anonymous woman is not strong. The relationship between the two passages may be understood in terms of Markan compositional technique. In the first place, the intention of the women is ironic: there will be no body to anoint, since Jesus has not remained in the grave.[35] Secondly, the appearance of the motif of anointing in chapter 16 reminds the reader of the earlier passage and encourages reflection on its significance.

Another argument brought to bear is that certain verses in this passage are "overloaded" with particular kinds of markers. The point is that the source had its markers and the author of

Mark added his own. For example, 16:2 is said to "pile up" temporal indicators.[36] The first such indicator is "very early." Since a similar Greek phrase appears also in 1:35, its use here is attributed to the author of Mark.[37] The second is "on the first day of the week" or "on the first day after the Sabbath." It has been argued that this temporal expression is a Semitic phrase that Mark has retained from his source.[38] If this is a Semitic expression obscure enough to warrant the conclusion of the use of a source here, it is odd that the author of Luke preserves it without correction in the parallel to this passage (Luke 24:1) and also uses it in Acts 20:7, when, presumably, composing freely.[39] "After the sun had risen" is the third indicator. A "double step" compositional technique has been recognized elsewhere in Mark, in which a second phrase qualifies the first.[40] If one rejects the theory that the phrase "on the first day of the week" comes from a source, then the first two indicators may be seen as one: "very early on the first day of the week." Then the phrase "after the sun had risen" may be seen as a second phrase, qualifying the first in typical Markan fashion. More significantly, the temporal markers in 16:1–2 may be seen as the author's attempt to explain why the women did not attempt to anoint Jesus sooner. They had to wait until the Sabbath was over to purchase the spices (v. 1); then they went to the tomb at the earliest feasible time—as soon as it was light (v. 2).

Another kind of "overloading" has been perceived in 16:8. This verse has several references to fear. The second clause states that *tromos* (trembling) and *ekstasis* (astonishment) seized the women. The word *tromos* does not appear elsewhere in Mark. It appears four times elsewhere in the New Testament in the combination *phobos kai tromos* (fear and trembling). The word *ekstasis* is used in Mark 5:42 to express the astonishment of the onlookers when Jesus raises the daughter of Jairus from the dead. Some argue that these two words expressing fear are rare, whereas the verb used in the last clause—(and they said nothing to anyone,) for they were afraid (*ephobounto*)—and the related noun (*phobos*) occur often in Mark in connection with the disciples.[41] Against this argument it must be pointed out that *tromos* is hardly a rare word. In addition, the word *ekstasis* appears twice in Mark, in both cases in the same sense, and both times the context is related to resurrection. Linguistic arguments alone do not compel the conclusion that the "overloading" of this verse with references to fear is evidence for the use of a source.

Both cases of alleged "overloading" may be understood as features of composition rather than of editing. The several indications of time in verse 2 may be understood in various ways, for example, as an attempt at verisimilitude or at accurate reporting. The several expressions of fear in verse 8 may have been used for dramatic effect. It may well be that the last two clauses link this incident with an aspect of the theme of discipleship in the gospel. But such a link does not necessarily imply that the preceding clause comes from a source.

These linguistic arguments, weak in themselves, are meant to bolster a form critical argument against the unity of this passage.[42] Legendary elements in the passage have been pointed out, such as the motif of the large stone and the implicit quest for a helper to remove the stone.[43] Similarly, apocalyptic elements relating to narratives about the appearance of an angel, the genre "angelophany" or "angelic epiphany," have been noted. The discernment of such elements, however, does not warrant the conclusion that they could not occur together in a single, unified narrative.[44]

The command of the angel to the women to go and tell the disciples and Peter that "he goes before you to Galilee" in verse 7 is seen by some as secondary and thus as evidence of a source. Bultmann, for example, argued that the speech of the angel originally functioned simply to point out the empty tomb as evidence for the resurrection (v. 6). The command in verse 7, in his view, was added by the author of Mark to link the empty tomb tradition connected with Jerusalem to the tradition of appearances in Galilee.[45] This argument, however, is bound up with Bultmann's opinion that the Gospel of Mark could not have ended with 16:8. His reconstruction of how the gospel "must have ended" is overly speculative. Nevertheless, many scholars have agreed with him that verse 7 was added to an existing story.[46] The most obvious reason for seeing this verse as Markan composition is its connection with 14:28. In chapter 14, soon after Jesus and the disciples arrive on the Mount of Olives, Jesus tells them that after he is raised he will go before them to Galilee (v. 28). In chapter 16, the angel asks the women to remind the disciples of this promise.

Obviously, the link between 16:7 and 14:28 is insufficient evidence by itself to require the conclusion that a source was used in 16:1–8. A deeper reason for seeing 16:7 as redactional rather than as part of a unified composition by the author of Mark is the perceived tension between the command of the angel and the response of the women. Wilhelm Bousset argued long ago that the statement in verse 8, "and they said nothing to anyone" referred originally to the discovery of the empty tomb (v. 6) and not to the command that they give the disciples the message about Galilee (v. 7). The point of their silence, according to Bousset, was to explain why the story of the empty tomb had remained unknown for so long.[47] A number of scholars have argued that the reminder that Jesus goes before the disciples to Galilee implies the restoration of Peter after his denial and of all the disciples after their flight.[48] Pheme Perkins concluded that the implication of restoration may be the import of 16:7 as pre-Markan tradition, but not of the passage as a whole in the intention of the author. She seems to imply that the tension between verse 7 and the context supports the hypothesis that a source was used.[49] At the same time, however, she admits that the element of restoration may be seen as a feature of Markan redaction. Her own interpretation of the passage as a whole makes sense of the tension as a paradoxical affirmation that the disciples will be Jesus' witnesses, in spite of their incomprehension and fear, combined with an implicit warning to the readers not to repeat the pattern of both the male and the female disciples.[50] Another possibility is that the silence of the women is not to be taken literally, but is a conventional expression of the human reaction to the numinous. In any case, it should be apparent that the hypothesis of a source is unnecessary to explain or resolve the tensions in the passage.

Mark 16:1–8 as a Unified Composition

Mark 16:1–8 may be seen then as a unified and effective composition. It continues chapter 15 logically and appropriately. Joseph had buried the body of Jesus just before or just as the Sabbath was beginning. The women, however, it is implied, do not accept that burial as adequate. As soon as the Sabbath ends,

presumably at sunset or shortly thereafter, the women purchase
the aromatic spices needed to anoint Jesus (v. 1). Then they wait,
presumably for the sake of safety or propriety, until sunrise to go
to the tomb (v. 2). Their question to one another on the way to
the tomb, "Who will roll away the stone for us from the door
of the tomb," creates dramatic tension and leads the reader to
expect something extraordinary to occur (v. 3). The arrival of
the women at the tomb is narrated very strikingly. They see that
the stone has already been rolled away from the entrance to the
tomb. The extraordinary character of this situation is brought out
by the remark that the stone was very large (v. 4). Some scholars
have argued that the removal of the stone is significant for how
the reader of Mark is intended to conceive of the resurrection of
Jesus. We shall return to this point later. The next verse builds
dramatically on the previous one. The extraordinary situation of
the stone is followed by an even more uncanny incident. When
the women enter the tomb, there is a young man there dressed
in a white robe (v. 5). It is clear that this young man, in spite
of the parallel with the young man in 14:51–52, is not presented
as a human being. It was a well-known apocalyptic convention
to speak of angelic beings as "men."[51] The white robe is also a
conventional attribute of heavenly beings.[52] The reaction of the
women is described in very strong terms: *exethambēthēsan* (they
were amazed).[53]

The description of the appearance of the angel is so restrained
that it does not seem appropriate to characterize the passage
as an angelic epiphany. The role of the angel is to indicate the
significance of the empty tomb. Thus the angelic young man
plays the role of the *angelus interpres*, a narrative role common
in apocalyptic literature and other texts influenced by it.[54] His
exhortation to the women that they not be amazed (v. 6) is a
typical angelic reassurance relating to the consternation and fear
of the human recipient of revelation.[55] The rest of the speech
of the angel, including verse 7, has the narrative function of
interpreting the empty tomb. The remarks following the reassurance, from "You seek Jesus, the Nazarene, who was crucified"
to "see the place where they laid him" (v. 6), have at least the
implicit function of making the point that the women have come
to the right place. They have not confused the grave of Jesus with

another, empty grave. In the center of this first pronouncement is the key interpretation of the empty tomb, "he has been raised" (*ēgerthē*). In the narrative context of Mark 16, the announcement of the resurrection of Jesus serves to interpret the empty tomb. As I shall argue below, the author of Mark has interpreted the early Christian proclamation of the resurrection of Jesus by composing a narrative about the empty tomb.[56]

The second pronouncement of the angel, "But go, tell his disciples and Peter, 'He goes before you into Galilee; there you will see him, just as he said to you'" (v. 7), indicates the significance of the empty tomb for the disciples. It is the first stage in the fulfillment of the prophecy Jesus gave them on the Mount of Olives. At the moment in which the angel is speaking to the women within the narrative, the first part of Jesus' prophecy, "after I am raised up" (14:28), has been fulfilled. Some scholars have argued that the renewed promise, "there you will see him" (16:7), refers to the *parousia*, that is, to the return of Jesus on the clouds as Son of Man.[57] This interpretation is unlikely because language of "power" and "glory" associated with the *parousia* elsewhere in Mark (9:1, 13:26; cf. 14:62) does not occur here. The *parousia* and Galilee are not associated anywhere else in the Gospel. It is more likely that the promise alludes to the same tradition of appearances that Paul recounts in 1 Corinthians 15:5.[58]

It was standard literary practice in the ancient world to allude to well-known events that occurred after those being narrated in a text without actually narrating those later events.[59] The Iliad is perhaps the best-known example of this technique.[60] Thus the fact that the appearances are not narrated in Mark does not necessarily mean that the author believed that they did not occur or wanted to suppress them. The main problem is how to interpret the relationship between the angel's announcement and the conclusion of the narrative in verse 8.

The first part of verse 8, "And they went out and fled from the tomb, for trembling and amazement had seized them," is understandable as an example of the typical human reaction of terror in the presence of the numinous. The second part of the verse, "and they said nothing to any one, for they were afraid" is a stupifyingly abrupt ending to the Gospel. Werner Kelber has historicized this ending, claiming that it means that the Twelve and the members of Jesus' family rejected his intention that the Kingdom of God on earth, the Christian community, be established in Galilee. The Twelve never got the message. In any case, they and the family of Jesus preferred to stay in Jerusalem, closer to the center of power as they understood it and the place with which their own eschatological expectations were associated.[61] It is surprising that a scholar with so much literary sensitivity, who has argued that the Gospel of Mark is "parabolic,"[62] should insist on defining the meaning of verse 8 so absolutely. It seems more appropriate to see this ending as deliberately provocative and open-ended as numerous scholars in this century have taught us to read the parables of Jesus. It lures the reader to reflect on the events narrated and on one's own relation to those events. The disciples function in a complex way as both positive and negative examples or role models.

With regard to the eschatological events, the lack of narration of the appearances makes the impression on the reader that the chain of eschatological events is not yet completed. The narratives of the appearances of the risen Jesus in Matthew, Luke, and John, round off the story. Matthew and Luke still express eschatological expectation, but it is balanced by the sense of the presence of the risen Lord with the community. Mark lacks such a satisfying denouement. One result is that the readers are asked to complete the story, not only by imagining the fulfillment of the promise of appearances, as 14:28 and 16:7 should probably be interpreted, but also by imagining the fulfillment of the dramatic and vivid promises that the Son of Man would return (13:24–27, 14:62).

The Ancient Notion of Translation

The idea that a human being could be removed from the sphere of ordinary humanity and made immortal is a very ancient one. The oldest narrative known to me of such an event is found on a tablet excavated in Nippur that contains part of the Sumerian flood-story.[63] The hero of this story is the king Ziusudra. A deity informs him that there will be a flood and instructs him to build a huge boat. After the flood, Ziusudra offers sacrifice. Near the end of the passage that is preserved, it is said that the gods Anu and Enlil cherished Ziusudra. They give him life like a god. They give him breath eternal like [that of] a god. They cause him to dwell at the place where the sun rises. These honors are granted him apparently because he is the preserver of vegetation and the seed of humankind.

In the Akkadian Gilgamesh Epic, Gilgamesh journeys through a great mountain range and over the Waters of Death to reach the flood-hero, who in this epic is named Utnapishtim.[64] The purpose of the quest is to obtain the secret of immortality. In tablet XI of the epic, Utnapishtim recounts the story of the flood for Gilgamesh. At the end of the story he tells how the god Enlil announced, "Henceforth Utnapishtim and his wife shall be like unto us gods. Utnapishtim shall reside far away, at the mouth of the rivers."[65] Earlier in the epic it was said that Utnapishtim had joined the Assembly [of the gods].[66] In the Atrahasis Epic, that includes a Babylonian version of the flood on tablet III, a similar story is told about the flood-hero Atrahasis and his wife.

In the Hebrew Bible it is not the flood-hero Noah who was translated, but the antediluvian patriarch, Enoch. His destiny is tersely related in chapter 5 of Genesis. It is said that "Enoch walked with God" (vv. 22 and 24) and that "he was not, for God took him" (v. 24). It is not said that Moses was translated. In the book of Deuteronomy it is said that he died in the land of Moab (34:5). But it is said that God buried him and that no one knows the place of his burial (v. 6). These latter remarks suggested to later readers that Moses had in fact been translated. The translation of Elijah is described in vivid detail in the second chapter of the second book of Kings. This translation, unlike that of Enoch, is explicitly said to have been witnessed (by Elisha).

The oldest Greek texts that speak of translations of human beings are the Iliad and the Odyssey. According to book 20 of the Iliad, Tros, the lord of the Trojans, had three sons. One of these, Ganymedes, because of his unsurpassed beauty, was caught up by the gods to themselves, made immortal and made the cupbearer of Zeus (20.230–35). The mortal Tithonos is mentioned in this context as the descendant of one of Ganymedes' brothers (20.237). Earlier in the epic, his translation by the goddess Dawn is mentioned (11.1). This allusion presupposes a tradition that

Dawn had made Tithonos immortal to be her spouse and to dwell by the River Okeanos where Dawn rises (cf. Iliad 19.1–2).[67]

In book 4 of the Odyssey, Menelaos, the husband of Helen, tells Telemachos how he tricked the god Proteus into advising him how to make his way home and giving him news of his companions. Proteus' revelations include a prophecy that Menelaos will not die; rather the gods will cause him to dwell on the Elysian Plain at the end of the world, where life is as pleasant as on Mount Olympos. The reason given for this great blessing is that he is, as husband of Helen, a son of Zeus (4.560–70).[68] Menelaos is to join Rhadamanthys who apparently was transported to the Elysian Plain earlier, according to tradition. The details of his story are lost, but it is interesting to note that he was also said to be a son of Zeus (Iliad 14.321–22).

All of these traditions imply that the human beings translated became gods, i.e., immortal. They seem to assume that in these cases, the soul (*psychē*) was never separated from the body.[69] In some cases, however, the human being in question dies first and then is made immortal. The Aithiopis, a continuation of the Iliad that survives only in references to it in other authors, tells how Memnon, the Ethiopian prince, brought help to the Trojans. He is slain by Achilles, whereupon Memnon's mother, Dawn, obtains permission from Zeus to carry his body to the end of the earth in the East and there to grant immortality to her son.[70] According to the same epic poem, when Achilles was slain and placed on his funeral pyre, his mother, the divine Thetis, carried his body from the pyre to White Island. The extract does not say so, but undoubtedly she restored him to life there and made him immortal.[71]

All the traditions discussed so far involve immortal life in regions on the surface of the earth, most of which are normally not accessible to humanity. There is another type of translation-story that involves removal beneath the earth and subterranean immortality, often in a cave.[72] This type of immortality is analogous to that of the "heroes," who died, were buried, and from their graves gave proof of a higher existence and powerful influence.[73] It is noteworthy that the later belief in heroes required a grave at which the continued existence and potency of the hero was localized.[74] Erwin Rohde's reconstruction of one of the traditions associated with the hero Hyakinthos is instructive. Originally a chthonic deity, he was later transformed into a hero, who died, was buried, and then was translated to heaven.[75]

The case of Asklepios as hero is also instructive. According to this tradition, he was a mortal who was transformed into an immortal by a flash of Zeus' lightning.[76] Part of this tradition is that Asclepios was buried.[77] Thus his story is that of a hero who died, was buried, and then translated.

The focus on the tomb in Mark may have been inspired by the importance of the graves of the heroes in the Greco-Roman world. Even if the location of the tomb of Jesus was unknown to the author of Mark, and even if there were no cultic observances at the site of the tomb, it would still be important as a *literary* motif in characterizing Jesus as hero-like.[78]

An example that does not involve the death of the hero, but is instructive for the role of the angel in Mark 16, is the case of Kleomedes of Astypalaia, related by Pausanius and several other writers. Kleomedes killed his opponent in the boxing match at the seventy-first Olympic festival (486 B.C.E.) and was therefore disqualified. In his anger at this turn of events, he behaved destructively upon his return home. His behavior caused the death of some boys. He fled to the temple of Athena and hid in a chest. When the chest was forced open by his pursuers, Kleomedes was not inside. Envoys were sent to inquire of the oracle. They were told that he had become a hero and must be honored with sacrifice. The oracle is able to explain a supernatural occurrence to human inquirers because the oracle sees such events as one spirit sees another.[79] This perspective is instructive both for the role of the angel at the empty tomb and for the role of the demons or unclean spirits in Mark who know that Jesus is the son of God.

Finally, the case of Herakles should be mentioned. In agony because of the poison on his garment, he made his own funeral pyre and mounted it. Apollodorus says, "While the pyre was burning, it is said that a cloud passed under [Herakles] and with a peal of thunder wafted him up to heaven. Thereafter he obtained immortality, and being reconciled to Hera he married her daughter Hebe, by whom he had sons. . . ."[80] The traditional mythic view is obviously that immortal life is much like mortal life and that Heracles was embodied in his afterlife. Another interpretation is that the pyre burned away the mortal part of his nature, inherited from his mortal mother, so that the immortal part, inherited from his father Zeus, could ascend to the gods.[81] The Pythian priestess had promised Heracles immortality upon completion of the ten labors or tasks (Apollodorus, *Library* 2.4.12). Later writers interpreted this as an honor granted because of his great benefactions to humankind.

In the Hellenistic and early Roman periods these traditions of translation and deification were very widespread. The Hellenistic Babylonian historian Berossus, writing in Greek, retold the ancient flood-story. In his version the flood-hero is named Xisouthros. In recounting his translation, Berossus says that he "disappeared" (*aphanēs gignomai*), using a term that had become almost technical in describing such occurrences.[82] A new element in the account is Berossus' explanation of the event: he was translated because of his piety. Josephus describes Enoch's translation as "he returned to the divinity" (*Ant.* 1.85). He uses an expression similar to Berossus' in describing the translation of Elijah, "Elijah disappeared from among human beings." A little further on, he says of both Enoch and Elijah that "they became invisible and no one knows of their death" (*Ant.* 9.28). The expression "become invisible" is synonymous with "disappear" and is also typical of Hellenistic accounts of translation.[83]

The terminology used by Josephus makes clear that he was presenting Enoch, Moses, and Elijah as Jewish forefathers who had not died, but had been translated alive and made immortal, like the forefathers of the Greeks and Romans.[84] Another Jewish writer who wrote in Greek shows that the idea of resurrection could be associated with the Greco-Roman ideas of translation and deification. Phocylides was a Greek poet from Miletus who lived in the sixth century B.C.E. Around the turn of the era, a Jewish poet wrote a work under the name and in the style of Phocylides, probably in Alexandria.[85] A section of this poem is devoted to death and after-life. The author advocates moderation in grief (lines 97–98) and the duty of burying the dead (99). He then advises against opening the graves of the deceased (100–103). The rejected practice may be secondary burial[86] or the removal of bodies from their graves in order to dissect the corpses.[87] The following statement is given as the reason, "For in fact we hope that the remains of the departed will soon come to the light again out of the earth. And afterwards they become gods" (104).[88] The coming to light of the remains of the departed out of the earth is a clear expression of hope in the bodily type of resurrection, that will be discussed below. The statement that the dead become gods after being raised is an expression of the idea of resurrection in Greco-Roman terms. The word "god" in Greek is synonymous with the word "immortal." So Pseudo-Phocylides is using typical Greek language of the blessed dead to express the idea that the resurrected faithful are exalted to the angelic state. We should recall at this point that the community at Qumran referred to angelic beings as "gods" (*elim*).[89]

The Resurrection of Jesus in Mark

At the time the Gospel of Mark was written, there were two basic notions of resurrection current, one that emphasized its heavenly character and one that emphasized its bodily character. The heavenly type was expressed in Daniel 12, as was pointed out earlier.[90] The bodily or physical type is attested by the second book of Maccabees. This work contains the story of seven brothers and their mother who were tortured and killed during the persecution of Antiochus IV Epiphanes. Among the tortures were the cutting out of the tongue and the cutting off of hands and feet. Regarding the torture of the third son, the text reads, "When it was demanded, he quickly put out his tongue and courageously stretched forth his hands, and said nobly, 'I got these from Heaven, and because of his laws I disdain them, and from him I hope to get them back again' " (2 Macc 7:10–11).[91] There is no sign in the book of Daniel of a belief in bodily resurrection of the type present in 2 Maccabees. In the later period, however, the two types could be combined as the example of Pseudo-Phocylides shows.[92]

Two elements are constant, however, in Jewish literature of the time, namely, that resurrection is a collective event and that it is an event of the future.[93] The notion of resurrection was not necessarily universal.[94] The picture of Daniel 12 is collective, but not universal: "many...shall awake" (v. 2). In 2 Maccabees, the emphasis is on the restoration of individuals, because of the narrative context. Nevertheless, the implicit context of the resurrection is the apocalyptic notion of the renewal of all creation.[95] Thus, one of the innovations of the Christian movement was the claim that God had raised a single individual, Jesus. Paul explained the resurrection of Jesus as the beginning of the renewal that would be followed soon by the resurrection of those who belong to him (1 Cor 15:20–23, 51–52).

The author of Mark was heir to the shocking but simple Christian proclamation that God had raised Jesus from the dead and to the tradition that the risen Jesus had appeared at least to Peter and the Twelve. In writing an extended narrative that expressed the good news (*euaggelion*; 1:1) of God's activity through Jesus, this author was faced with the challenge of narrating the resurrection. I have argued elsewhere that the genre of Mark is history in the apocalyptic mode.[96] My working hypothesis in this paper is that Mark 16:1–8 is fiction. In composing the story of the empty tomb, the author of Mark interpreted the proclamation that Jesus had been raised.

I am aware that objections have been raised to the notion that evangelists made up episodes and speeches.[97] With regard to speeches, it is widely known that Thucydides, the ancient historian with the most rigorous standards of evidence, stated explicitly that he constructed the speeches in his history of the Peloponnesian War by giving "whatever seemed most appropriate to me for each speaker to say in the particular circumstances, keeping as closely as possible to the general sense of what was actually said" (1.22).[98] I submit that the author of Mark did something analogous. He was convinced that what actually had happened was that Jesus had been raised from the dead. In composing 16:1–8, he described that event in what seemed to him the most appropriate way. So I am not arguing that the author of Mark made up an episode out of whole cloth. He regarded the resurrection of Jesus as an event attested by those to whom the risen Jesus had appeared. Since he did not have evidence for the details regarding how Jesus was raised, he reverently supplied those details in accordance with his sense of what must have happened. Since the male disciples had fled from the scene of the arrest, presumably because their lives were in danger, and since the author apparently assumed that they were in hiding at the time of the crucifixion and burial, it seemed most appropriate to have female disciples discover the empty tomb.

The creation of the empty tomb story shows that the author of Mark had a notion of resurrection closer to that of 2 Maccabees than to that of Daniel 12. Resurrection for Mark is not the giving of a new, spiritual body to the inner person, the *psyche*, in a way that the former body does not matter. For Mark it is either a revival or transformation of the earthly body. If the text implies that Jesus pushed the stone away from the tomb and walked out, the resurrection is understood as a revival of the body.[99] But such is not a necessary implication. The stone had to be rolled aside so that the women could enter the tomb and see that Jesus was not there. The stone could just as well have been moved by the angel. At least this is how the author of Matthew rewrote the text of Mark (Mt 28:2).[100] If the text does not imply that Jesus walked out of the tomb, his resurrection, according to Mark, is best understood as a transformation of his earthly body.

If the risen Jesus is not pictured as walking out of the tomb, the alternative, in the language of the typical western Christian exegete, is that he ascended to heaven immediately.[101] It has been pointed out that the ascension of Jesus, as narrated in the book of Acts, is similar to the Greco-Roman narratives of translation.[102] I am suggesting that this tradition also influenced how Mark narrated the resurrection.[103] The Christian affirmation was that a single individual, Jesus, had been raised from the dead. Apart from the usual collective context of the Jewish notion of resurrection, this affirmation seemed quite similar to the claim made in some Jewish circles that Enoch had been taken up to heaven and to the claims made in Greco-Roman circles regarding the translation or apotheosis of heroes, rulers, and emperors.[104] I am not claiming that the empty tomb story was created with an apologetic purpose in the narrow sense. It was not meant to *prove* to outsiders that Jesus really was raised. Rather, the narrative pattern according to which Jesus died, was buried, and then translated to heaven was a natural way for an author living in the first century to narrate the resurrection of Jesus.

It could be objected that it is hard to find much influence of Greco-Roman literature in Mark. The first response that must be made to such an objection is to remind the objector that the

Gospel of Mark was composed in Greek. This simple fact speaks volumes about the cultural milieu in which the text was written. One does not learn and use a language without being influenced by the culture of which it is part. Similarly, one does not address people competent in a certain language without drawing upon the thought-world for which that language is a vehicle. Recent studies have supported older suggestions that there are significant similarities between Mark and Greco-Roman literature in form, content, and style.[105]

If, according to Mark, Jesus was translated from the grave to heaven, then there was no period of time during which the risen Jesus walked the earth and met with his disciples. The book of Acts states that he did so for forty days. The Gospels of John and Luke also imply that he did so, but, in the case of John at least, for a shorter period. Even Matthew recounts a scene in which the women meet the risen Jesus and take hold of his feet (28:9). If, as was concluded above, the author of Mark accepted the tradition that the risen Jesus had appeared to Peter and the Twelve, this appearance (or appearances) was probably of a more heavenly type, like the apocalyptic visions of heavenly beings. The appearance to the Eleven in Galilee in Matthew (28:16–20) may be understood in this way. The appearance to Paul as it is narrated in Acts is definitely of this type.

The effect of this understanding of the resurrection of Jesus is to place the accent on the absence of Jesus more than on the presence of Jesus during the time of the readers. As noted earlier, this accent is related to apocalyptic expectation. The disciples have a mission in this world (13:9–13, 8:34–37) and they will be judged on the basis of their fulfillment or non-fulfillment of that mission (8:38). The interpretation of the resurrection of Jesus as a type of translation has an effect on one's reading of the apocalyptic discourse of chapter 13. That discourse has its climax in the prediction of the coming of the Son of Man with the clouds with great power and glory. The result of his appearance is that he will send out the angels to gather the faithful "from the four winds, from the end of the earth to the end of heaven" (13:27). It is likely that this prediction refers to the same event that Paul describes in 1 Thessalonians 4:17 and 1 Corinthians 15:52. As their master was translated, so will his faithful disciples.

NOTES

1. On the widespread character of this notion in the ancient world, especially in Greco-Roman culture, see Sharyn Echols Dowd, *Prayer, Power, and the Problem of Suffering: Mark 11:22–25 in the Context of Markan Theology* (Atlanta: Scholars Press, 1988).

2. This general perspective is that of the postliberal, cultural-linguistic school of theology, that characterizes the work of George Lindbeck, Stanley Hauerwas, and others. See the discussion of this point of view (in general, not in relation to the resurrection in particular) by Frederic B. Burnham, "The Bible and Contemporary Science," *Religion and Intellectual Life* 6, *The Bible and the Intellectual Life*, (1989) 60–61.

3. Rudolf Bultmann, "Neues Testament und Mythologie: Das Problem der Entmythologisierung der neutestamentlichen Verkündigung," *Offenbarung und Heilsgeschehen*, Beiträge zur *Evangelische Theologie* 7 (1941); reprinted in *Kerygma und Mythos* vol. 1, ed. H. W. Bartsch (Hamburg-Volksdorf, 1948); English translation as "New Testament and Mythology: The Mythological Element in the Message of the New Testament and the Problem of its Reinterpretation," by Reginald Fuller in *Kerygma and Myth: A Theological Debate* (New York: Harper and Brothers, 1953).

4. C. F. D. Moule, "Introduction [to the English Edition]," *The Significance of the Message of the Resurrection for Faith in Jesus Christ*, ed. C. F. D. Moule, Studies in Biblical Theology, Second Series 8 (Naperville, Ill.: Allenson, 1968), 9–10.

5. Richard R. Niebuhr, *Resurrection and Historical Reason* (New York: Scribner, 1957).

6. Leon Festinger, *A Theory of Cognitive Dissonance* (Stanford, Calif.: Stanford University Press, 1957).

7. Leon Festinger et al., *When Prophesy Fails: A Social and Psychological Study of a Modern Group that Predicted the Destruction of the World* (Minneapolis: University of Minnesota Press, 1956).

8. Hugh Jackson, "The Resurrection Belief of the Earliest Church: A Response to the Failure of Prophecy?" *Journal of Religion* 55 (1975): 415–425.

9. John G. Gager, *Kingdom and Community: The Social World of Early Christianity* (Englewood Cliffs, N.J.: Prentice-Hall, 1975), 37–43; Robert P. Carroll, *When Prophecy Failed: Cognitive Dissonance in the Prophetic Traditions of the Old Testament* (New York: Seabury, 1979), 124–128.

10. Van A. Harvey, *The Historian and the Believer* (New York: Macmillan, 1966).

11. See, for example, Norman Perrin, *The Resurrection According to Matthew, Mark, and Luke* (Philadelphia: Fortress, 1977).

12. Compare 1 Corinthians 11:23 in which the same verbs are used in citing the words of Jesus over the bread and wine at the last supper. That these terms were technical in the Hellenistic and Roman periods is shown by Hans Conzelmann, *1 Corinthians*, Hermeneia (Philadelphia: Fortress, 1975), 195.

13. See John Kloppenborg, "An Analysis of the Pre-Pauline Formula in 1 Cor 15:3b–5 in Light of Some Recent Literature," *Catholic Biblical Quarterly* 40 (1978): 351–352 and the literature cited there.

14. See the discussion by Pheme Perkins, *Resurrection: New Testament Witness and Contemporary Reflection* (Garden City, N.Y.: Doubleday, 1984), 88–91.

15. The remark that Jesus appeared to Paul "last of all" (1 Cor 15:8) is not evidence that he distinguished the type of appearance he was granted from those of Peter and the Twelve. On the contrary, it marks his experience as the last in a series of the same type of experiences. The remark that Jesus appeared to him "as to one prematurely born" (v. 8) does not imply that the nature of the *appearance* was any different. It was Paul who was different—he was not even a disciple yet. This interpretation is supported by the remark in the following verse that he was persecuting the Church of God (i.e., even at the time that Jesus appeared to him).

16. See the classic study of the range of meaning of *sōma* in Paul's letters by Bultmann, *Theology of the New Testament*, 2 vols. (New York: Scribner's Sons, 1951, 1955), 1.192–203.

17. R. H. Charles, *A Critical and Exegetical Commentary on the Book of Daniel* (Oxford: Clarendon, 1929), 327–328; see also George W. E. Nickelsburg, Jr., *Resurrection, Immortality, and Eternal Life in Intertestamental Judaism* (Cambridge, Mass.: Harvard University Press, 1972), 17.

18. On the notion of astral immortality in the ancient world, see Franz Cumont, *Lux Perpetua* (Paris: Geuther, 1949).

19. On the variety of conceptions of resurrection and other forms of personal afterlife in Palestinian Judaism, see Friedrich Schwally, *Das Leben nach dem Tode: Nach den Vorstellungen des alten Israel und das judentums einschliesslich das Volksglaubens im Zeitalter Christi* (Giessen: J. Ricker, 1892); K. Schubert, "Die Entwicklung der Auferstehungslehre von der nachexilischen bis zur frührabbinischen Zeit,"

Biblische Zeitschrift NF 6 (1962): 177–214; H. C. C. Cavallin, *Life After Death: Paul's Argument for the Resurrection of the Dead in I Cor. 15*, Part 1, *An Enquiry into the Jewish Background* (Lund: Gleerup, 1974), 33–101.

20. Paul's language about being "further clothed" rather than "naked" does not imply material continuity from earthly body to heavenly "body" (2 Cor 5:2–4). Rather it expresses his opposition to the notion that the soul is completely immaterial.

21. Acts 2:22–24, 3:13–15, 4:10–12, 5:30–32. Whether or not one can reconstruct sources used by the author of Acts is disputed. It is generally agreed that no continuous source was used in chapters 1–5 (Ernst Haenchen, *The Acts of the Apostles: A Commentary* [Philadelphia: Westminster, 1971], 81–90). The empty tomb is presupposed in Acts 2:25–31 and 13:34–37. These passages may be dependent on older tradition, but it is not clear that such tradition is as old as the Gospel of Mark (ibid., 3–4, 409, 411).

22. Rudolf Bultmann, *The History of the Synoptic Tradition*, rev. ed. (New York: Harper & Row, 1963), 290.

23. In Matthew, of course, the guards see the angel and know that the tomb is empty. It is generally agreed, however, that the story of the guards at the tomb and the lie that they spread about the disciples stealing the body is later than the empty tomb story and is definitely apologetic. One of the problems that this story addresses indirectly is the reliability of women as witnesses.

24. At least these studies indicate that the material that follows Mark 16:8 in many manuscripts is not original. Some scholars argue that the original ending of Mark has been lost or suppressed. See, for example, Bultmann, *History*, 285, n. 2. In this paper, the assumption is made that the gospel ended with 16:8, since that is the earliest recoverable ending. Any attempt to reconstruct an earlier ending would be unduly speculative. An ending at verse 8 is also defensible.

25. So, for example, Perkins, *Resurrection*, 90.

26. P. Benoit has argued that John 20 contains an older form of the empty tomb tradition (cited by Joachim Jeremias, "Die älteste Schicht der Osterüberlieferungen," *Resurrexit: Actes du symposium international sur la résurrection de Jésus*, ed. E. Dhanis [Rome: Libreria Editrice Vaticana, 1974], 189–190; English translation in J. Jeremias, *New Testament Theology: The Proclamation of Jesus* [New York: Scribner's, 1971], 304–305); but this hypothesis is unlikely; see John Dominic Crossan, "Empty Tomb and Absent Lord (Mark 16:1–8)," *The Passion in Mark*, 138–145.

27. As Crossan puts it, there may have been a presumption that

the tomb was empty prior to the formulation of Mark 16:1–8 [or its source], but a presumption is not a tradition ("Empty Tomb," 136).

28. Martin Dibelius, *From Tradition to Gospel*, 2nd ed. (New York: Scribner's Sons, 1935), 180–181; Rudolf Bultmann, *The History of the Synoptic Tradition*, 2nd ed. (New York: Harper & Row, 1968), 262–279.

29. Eta Linnemann, *Studien zur Passionsgeschichte* (Göttingen: Vandenhoeck & Ruprecht, 1970).

30. See John R. Donahue, S.J., "Introduction: From Passion Traditions to Passion Narrative," *The Passion in Mark: Studies in Mark 14–16*, ed. Werner H. Kelber (Philadelphia: Fortress, 1976), 14.

31. See, for example, Perkins, *Resurrection*, 115.

32. Bultmann argued that Mark 16:1–8 was independent of the sections of Mark that went before. If the narrative about the empty tomb had followed upon the narratives of the crucifixion and burial, he argued, the names of the women would not have needed to be given again in 16:1 (*History*, 284–285). Given the importance of the events being narrated, however, it is understandable that the names would have been given each time. The repetition is softened by variation in the form of the name of the second woman (see above).

33. The fact that the third woman, Salome, is not mentioned as a witness to the burial does not seem to be significant for the question of sources. It does not seem to be sufficient evidence to warrant the conclusion that the pericope about the burial was once a separate anecdote.

34. Raymond E. Brown, "The Burial of Jesus (Mk 15:42–47)," *Catholic Biblical Quarterly* 50 (1988): 233–245.

35. See the discussion of irony in David Rhoads and Donald Michie, *Mark as Story: An Introduction to the Narrative of a Gospel* (Philadelphia: Fortress, 1982), 59–62.

36. Perkins: *Resurrection*, 117.

37. For example, R. Pesch, cited by Perkins, ibid. See also Crossan, "Empty Tomb," 146–147.

38. J. Kremer, cited by Perkins, ibid. Crossan argues that this phrase fits the Markan chronological framework ("Empty Tomb," 147).

39. See Ernst Haenchen, *The Acts of the Apostles* (Philadelphia: Westminster, 1971), 586.

40. Perkins, *Resurrection*, 117 and 140, n. 13, citing Rhoads and Michie, *Mark as Story*, 47–49.

41. Perkins (*Resurrection*, 121–122) and those cited in note 44, p. 143.

42. E. Bickermann attempted to define a literary form that could be called "translation-story" or "removal-story" and then to argue that

the source used by the author of Mark in 16:1–8 was such a story ("Das leere Grab," *Zeitschrift für die Neutestamentliche Wissenschaft* 23 [1924]: 281–292). Bultmann rightly disagreed and concluded that there is insufficient evidence that such a story lies behind Mark 16:1–8 (*History*, 290, n. 3). The conclusion that the literary form "translation-story" does not define Mark 16:1–8 or its alleged source does not mean that such stories or the notions they express had no influence on the passage.

43. Ibid., 118.

44. F. Neirynck has written an extensive survey of attempts to reconstruct the source used in Mark 16:1–8 (cited by Perkins, *Resurrection* 138, n. 2 and 139, nn. 9 and 10).

45. Bultmann, *History*, 285, 287. So also J. Delorme (cited by Perkins, *Resurrection*, 121, 143, n. 41). But see the reservations of Fuller and Pesch, (cited in Perkins, *op. cit.*, 143, n. 41).

46. For example, J. Kremer, J. Delorme, R. H. Fuller, and A. Lindemann (cited by Perkins) and Perkins herself (*Resurrection*, 116, 120 and 140, nn. 16 and 17).

47. Wilhelm Bousset, cited by Bultmann, *History*, 285.

48. Fuller, E. L. Bode, Rhoads and Michie (cited by Perkins, *Resurrection*, 121, 143, n. 42).

49. Ibid., 121.

50. Ibid., 121 and 122–123.

51. See, for example, Daniel 8:15–16, 9:21, 10:5. The term translated "young man" in Mark 16:5 is *neaniskos*. A related word, *neanias*, is used of angels in 2 Maccabees 3:26 and 33 and in Josephus, *Antiquities* 5.277.

52. See Daniel 7:9, 2 Maccabees 11:8–10, Acts 1:10.

53. The author of Mark is the only New Testament writer to use this word. It may express simple surprise (9:15) or the deepest kind of emotion (14:33); see Vincent Taylor, *The Gospel According to St. Mark*, 2nd ed. (Grand Rapids, Mich: Baker Book House, 1966), 396, 552, 606.

54. So Bultmann, *History*, 287, 290. The *angelus interpres* sometimes interprets a vision (Daniel 7:15–18, 8:15–26) and sometimes explains a situation (Daniel 9:21–23, 10:2–14). Note that this same device is used to comment on the significance of the ascension in Acts 1:10–11.

55. Compare, for example, Daniel 8:17–18, 10:8–12.

56. See the discussion by Perkins (*Resurrection*, 119) of the kerygmatic elements in Mark 16:6.

57. T. Weeden, *Mark: Traditions in Conflict* (Philadelphia: Fortress, 1971) 111–116; and N. Q. Hamilton, "Resurrection Tradition and the Composition of Mark," *Journal of Biblical Literature* 84 (1965):

415–421. Werner Kelber and John Dominic Crossan hold this view, but understand the *parousia* in Mark in terms of the realization of the Kingdom of God in the activity of the followers of Jesus in Galilee (Kelber, *The Kingdom in Mark* [Philadelphia: Fortress, 1974], 105, 107, 140, 146; Crossan, "The Empty Tomb," 146, 148–149).

58. Perkins, *Resurrection*, 120.

59. See J. Lee Magness, *Sense and Absence: Structure and Suspension in the Ending of Mark's Gospel* (Atlanta: Scholars Press, 1986).

60. Ibid., 30–31.

61. Werner H. Kelber, *Mark's Story of Jesus* (Philadelphia: Fortress, 1979), 83–87.

62. Werner H. Kelber, *The Oral and the Written Gospel* (Philadelphia: Fortress, 1983), 117–129.

63. An English translation of this text by S. N. Kramer is given in James B. Pritchard (ed.), *Ancient Near Eastern Texts Relating to the Old Testament* [hereafter, *ANET*] (Princeton, N.J.: Princeton University Press, 1955), 43–44.

64. An English translation by E. A. Speiser may be found in *ANET*, 73–97.

65. *ANET*, 95.

66. Ibid., 88.

67. The story of Kleitos, the mortal son of Manios, has similarities with both the stories of Ganymedes and Tithonos. Kleitos was carried off by Dawn to live among the gods because of his beauty (Od. 15.248–252).

68. Women, as well as men, were said to have been translated. There is a tradition that Helen herself was made immortal and made to dwell on the White Island or in the Islands of the Blest (Erwin Rohde, *Psyche: The Cult of Souls and Belief in Immortality among the Greeks* [New York: Harcourt Brace Jovanovich, 1925], 83, n. 21). The nereid Leukothea was once the mortal Ino (Od. 5.333–335). There was also a tradition that Iphigeneia, the daughter of Agamemnon, was not sacrificed, but was translated by Artemis and made immortal in the land of the Taurians (Rohde, *Psyche*, 64).

69. Rohde, *Psyche*, 57.

70. Ibid., 64.

71. Ibid., 64–65.

72. Ibid., 89–92.

73. Ibid., 97.

74. Ibid., 98.

75. Ibid., 99–100.

76. Ibid., 100, 582.

77. Ibid., 101.

78. On the hypothesis that there were cultic observances performed at the tomb of Jesus from an early date, see Perkins, *Resurrection*, 93–94, 119.

79. Rohde, *Psyche*, 129–130. See also the story of Aristeas, related by Herodotus and discussed by Arthur S. Pease, "Some Aspects of Invisibility," *Harvard Studies in Classical Philology* 53 (1942): 29.

80. Apollodorus, *The Library* 2.7.7, trans. James G. Frazer, Loeb Classical Library (Cambridge, Mass.: Harvard University Press, 1921), 1. 271–272.

81. So Lucian, *Hermotimus* 7, cited by Frazer, op. cit. 271.

82. For the text of Berossus, see Felix Jacoby, *Die Fragmente der griechischen Historiker, Dritter Teil: Geschichte von Staedten und Voelkern, C: Autoren ueber einzelne Laender* (Leiden: Brill, 1958) 380; for other examples of the use of this term, see G. Lohfink, *Die Himmelfahrt Jesu* (Studien zum Alten und Neuen Testament 26; Munich: Kösel, 1971), 41, n. 58.

83. On these passages, see Christopher Begg, "Josephus's Portrayal of the Disappearances of Enoch, Elijah and Moses: Some Observations," *Journal of Biblical Literature*, forthcoming. Begg's note is a response to an article by James D. Tabor, " 'Returning to Divinity:' Josephus's Portrayal of the Disappearances of Enoch, Elijah, and Moses," *Journal of Biblical Literature* 108 (1989): 225–238.

84. In spite of the statement in Deuteronomy that Moses died, Josephus did not believe that he did (see Begg, "Some Observations").

85. P. W. van der Horst, *The Sentences of Pseudo-Phocylides* (Leiden: Brill, 1978), 81–83. Van der Horst dates the work between 30 B.C.E. and 40 C.E.

86. The placement of bones in an ossuary was a common form of secondary burial in the ancient world (Jack Finegan, *The Archaeology of the New Testament* [Princeton, N.J.: Princeton University Press, 1969], 216–218).

87. Van der Horst, *Pseudo-Phocylides*, 82, 183–184.

88. Translation by van der Horst, ibid., 95; the Greek text is given on p. 94.

89. See the discussion of this clause, ibid., 186–188.

90. The heavenly notion of resurrection is also expressed in The Epistle of Enoch (chapters 91–104 of 1 Enoch). The righteous "will shine like the lights of heaven" and the gate of heaven will be opened to them. They will "have great joy like the angels of heaven" and will "be associates of the host of heaven" (1 Enoch 104:2, 4, 6; the translation cited is by M. A. Knibb in *The Apocryphal Old Testament*, ed. H. F. D. Sparks [Oxford: Clarendon Press, 1984], 312). See also the

Similitudes of Enoch, in which it is said that the resurrected righteous "will become angels in heaven" (1 Enoch 51:4; Sparks, *The Apocryphal Old Testament*, 231).

91. See also 2 Maccabees 14:37–46.

92. Pseudo-Phocylides incorporates several different understandings of afterlife with little concern for systematic coherence (see van der Horst, *Pseudo-Phocylides*, 188–189).

93. The idea that individual humans who had been translated would return to the earth at the end was widespread in Jewish literature of the second temple period, but these were men who had not died and thus did not need to be resurrected (e.g., Malachi 4:5 [3:23], 1 Enoch 90:31).

94. Many texts speak only of a resurrection of the just, e.g., Psalms of Solomon 3:10–12 [3:13–16].

95. On the apocalyptic background of the resurrection in 2 Maccabees and the reasons for its muted character, see Nickelsburg, *Resurrection, Immortality, and Eternal Life in Intertestamental Judaism*, 93–109.

96. Adela Yarbro Collins, "Narrative, History, and Gospel: A General Response," *Genre, Narrativity, and Theology*, ed. Mary Gerhart and James G. Williams, *Semeia* 43 (1988): 145–153; *Is Mark a Life of Jesus?: The Question of Genre*, the Père Marquette Lecture in Theology 1990 (Milwaukee, Wisc.: University of Marquette Press, 1990).

97. Eleonore Stump, "Visits to the Sepulcher and Biblical Exegesis," *Faith and Philosophy* 6 (1989): 367–368.

98. Cited by Oswyn Murray, "Greek Historians," *The Oxford History of the Classical World*, ed. John Boardman et al. (New York: Oxford University Press, 1986), 193–194.

99. Bultmann implies that the position of the stone when the women come to the tomb indicates that Jesus pushed it aside (*History*, 290, n. 3).

100. Compare the Gospel of Peter in which the stone rolls away by itself, presumably by divine power (Gospel of Peter 37; English translation given in David R. Cartridge and David L. Dungan, eds., *Documents for the Study of the Gospels* [Philadelphia: Fortress Press, 1980], 85).

101. Bultmann, *History*, 290, n. 3.

102. Hans Conzelmann, *Acts of the Apostles*, Hermeneia (Philadelphia: Fortress, 1987), 7, n. 26; Haenchen, *The Acts of the Apostles*, 149, n. 5.

103. Pease, citing a brief suggestion by F. Pfister, notes that there are certain likenesses between the disappearance of the body of Jesus

from the tomb and certain pagan traditions, but he does not attempt to explain them or to reconstruct the process by which they arose ("Invisibility," 29).

104. On the translation of rulers and emperors, see ibid., 16–17.

105. David E. Aune, *The New Testament in Its Literary Environment* (Philadelphia: Westminster, 1987); Vernon K. Robbins, *Jesus the Teacher: A Socio-Rhetorical Interpretation of Mark* (Philadelphia: Fortress, 1984).

Resurrection Resurrected: Comments on the Paper of Adela Yarbro Collins

Norman Kretzmann

Professor Collins's paper is illuminating and challenging. We can all be grateful to her for the illumination; as her commentator, I am especially grateful for the challenges clustered in her bold, complex hypothesis and the elaborate, learned argument she provides for it. The hypothesis and argument have to do with a written report we have received from the first century: Jesus rose from the dead.

Reflective, non-devotional considerations of this report understandably tend to focus immediately on the event it reports: Is that possible? Did it really happen? What is its theological significance? Of the nine "perspectives" on Jesus' resurrection Collins surveys early in her paper, the first seven are all focused on the reported event. The last two, the historical and the literary perspectives, are focused not on the event but instead on the report itself, asking questions such as these: In the texts that preserve it, what is that report really claiming? How are the various versions of the report related to one another? Do they agree with one another? And, as we have seen, Collins herself adopts a literary-historical approach, focusing on the report rather than the event.

It is not hard to accept her claim that such literary-historical questions are more basic than all the others we are inclined to ask about the resurrection of Jesus.[1] Still, most Christians would take those more basic questions to have been settled long ago. They would say that what is being claimed in the report that Jesus rose from the dead is that Jesus, after he died on the cross and was buried, left the tomb alive, on his own two feet. They would also say that all the various versions of this report in the New Testament are mutually compatible, differing only in their emphasis and the degree of their completeness. Collins's literary-historical results certainly challenge that standard position and call for a rejoinder from its adherents, among whom I still count myself, even after studying her paper.

Collins's main thesis is that the author of Mark's Gospel, whom I will call Mark, is the *originator* of the idea that Jesus' rising from the dead involved his leaving the tomb. She is definitely not suggesting (and indeed she denies[2]) that Mark made up the story that Jesus *rose from the dead*, just the part about his *leaving the tomb*. Before hearing her paper, we might have thought that that wouldn't be enough of a contribution to get anyone even partial authorial credit; but we now know better: "Mark 16:1–8 is fiction. In *composing* the story of the empty tomb, the author of Mark *interpreted* the proclamation that Jesus had been raised."[3] Although she refers to this claim as merely her "working hypothesis in this paper," it is actually the conclusion of an argument, which may be laid out in this form:

(1) Mark 16:1–8 contains the story of the empty tomb.
(2) Mark wrote his Gospel before the other evangelists wrote theirs.
(3) Paul wrote 1 Corinthians before Mark wrote his gospel.
(4) "Paul's understanding of the resurrection of Jesus does not involve the revival of his corpse. [F]or Paul . . . the resurrection of Jesus did not imply that his tomb was empty" (pp. 111 and 114).
(5) The summaries of the gospel in the book of Acts are embedded in speeches the apostles made before Mark wrote his gospel.
(6) "The summaries of the gospel in the book of Acts also fail to mention the empty tomb" (p. 114).
(7) Paul's letters and the summaries of the gospel in the book of Acts are the only New Testament sources

besides Mark's gospel that are relevant to these considerations.

∴ (8) Mark 16:1–8 is the earliest appearance in the New Testament of the empty tomb as part of the story of Jesus' resurrection.

(9) Mark 16:1–8 is not dependent on any earlier source.

∴(10) Mark 16:1–8 is an original composition, a fictional narrative.

Although Collins's argument is directly concerned only with some of the New Testament accounts of Jesus' resurrection rather than with the resurrection itself, her conclusions clearly bear on our understanding of the resurrection, especially because she takes the Gospels of Matthew and Luke (at least) to be dependent on Mark.[4] Her argument, therefore, deserves a careful look, even by those who, like me, are not biblical scholars.

Claim (8) does follow from (1) through (7); and, if we set divine inspiration aside for the sake of the argument, (10) follows, too. So unless we can reasonably object to one or more of her premises, we cannot reasonably reject her interpretation of Mark 16:1–8 and all that it entails.

I suppose (1) is the only utterly uncontroversial premise in the argument. From my point of view, the other premises fall into two groups. The first group are those concerned with relative dating of texts. Since I am neither equipped nor inclined to raise doubts about any premises of that sort, I accept premises (2), (3), (5), and (7). Premises (5) and (7), in any case, are merely my friendly amendments to Collins's argument. I added (7) just for completeness' sake, and (5) just because I thought it was implied by her use of (6) in the argument. After all, if she thought that the relative dating of the composition of the book of Acts rendered its summaries of the Gospel irrelevant to her argument, why would she bother to cite those summaries as if they supported her conclusion in (8)?

As for premises (4), (6), and (9), the second group of questionable premises, I have serious doubts about each of them.

The most fundamental basis for my doubts about (4) and (6) is what I take to be the natural, ordinary interpretation of 'Jesus rose from the dead', an interpretation that is also shared by most Christians, present and past: Jesus, after he died on the cross and was buried, left the tomb alive, on his own two feet. This natural interpretation artlessly weaves together the disputed revived-body thesis and empty-tomb thesis, denials of which can be found in premise (4). In fact, it really consists altogether of just those two theses. As we have seen in her paper, Collins thinks that the empty-tomb thesis can be maintained without the revived-body thesis, but she understandably shows no signs of taking seriously the possibility of maintaining that Jesus remained within the tomb even though his body had been revived. As she sees them, the revived-body thesis entails the empty-tomb thesis, but not vice versa.

In premise (6) she claims that the summaries of the Gospel in Acts do not mention the empty tomb. She must intend the emphasis to fall on 'mention', since in a footnote to the strong claim she makes in (6) she admits that "The empty tomb is *presupposed* in Acts 2:25–31 and 13:34–37."[5] In each of those passages a preaching apostle cites Psalm 16:10, "thou wilt not . . . suffer thine Holy One to see corruption," as a prophecy of Jesus' resurrection; the first preacher is Peter and the second, interestingly enough, is Paul. She might also have mentioned what strikes me as even stronger evidence for the acceptance of the disputed theses in Acts—Peter's claim in 10:40–41: "Him God raised up the third day, and showed him openly; Not to all the people, but unto . . . us, who did eat and drink with him after he rose from the dead."

Where do these considerations of passages in Acts leave premise (6)? I think it is clear that on this basis premise (6) must be considered either simply false, or, at best, true only on an irrelevant technicality—viz., that the empty-tomb thesis is only entailed, not expressly mentioned. On this basis alone, anyone who took the reports of the apostles' speeches in Acts to be historically accurate would already have evidence that the revived-body thesis and, therefore, the empty-tomb thesis were accepted before Mark wrote his Gospel. I also think that giving up the claim about the material in Acts should make a serious difference to Collins's position. But since it's clear that she herself puts more weight on her reading of the material in Paul, I will go on to consider her argument as if premises (6) and the now unnecessary (5) had simply been discarded.

Premise (4), as far as I can see, is founded on three claims about just one passage:[6] In 1 Corinthians 15 (a) Paul does not mention the empty tomb; (b) Paul takes the appearances of the risen Jesus to Peter and the others to be of the same sort as the appearance of Jesus to him on the road to Damascus; (c) Paul takes the risen Jesus to have had a spiritual body discontinuous with his physical body: "Presumably it [the physical body] decays and has no importance for the resurrected person" (p. 113).

Claim (a) is true, but this sort of argument from silence is certainly not enough to support premise (4). Neither is claim (b) strong enough for (4); and (b) itself is very doubtful. The only evidence for (b) is the fact that in verses 5–7, where Paul is talking about Jesus' appearing to Peter and the others, he uses the same language he uses in verse 8, where he is talking about Jesus' appearing to him. But, according to the story of Paul's conversion in Acts (chaps. 9, 22, and 26), Jesus' appearance to him was radically different from any of the other appearances, different in ways Paul can hardly have ignored, even though in 1 Corinthians 15 he does use just the one verb '*ophthe*', 'he was seen', for all of them.

Claim (c), then, is crucial; but (c) strikes me as the least plausible of all. It depends on Paul's discussion in verses 35–50 of the nature of resurrection. That entire discussion is concerned with the eventual resurrection of the dead, however—not with the unique resurrection of the man Paul believed to be the Son of God. And I see no reason to suppose that Paul would treat those two events as simply two instances of the same sort, especially as regards the details of the resurrection body. I conclude that Collins has not given us evidence enough to ascribe to Paul the very unnatural interpretation of 'Jesus rose from the dead' she provides for him in premise (4).[7]

All the same, even if premises (4) and the no longer needed (3) and (7) were also discarded, Collins would still have an argument for (8) based simply on the remaining premises (1) and (2). Of course, if we take the results of our investigations of the other premises to have shown that we have not been given reasons good enough to believe that the empty-tomb thesis was unknown or unaccepted before Mark wrote, then (8) will have to be construed as a claim about only *the story* of the empty tomb and not also, as originally intended, as a claim about *the very idea* that Jesus' tomb was empty after his resurrection. Furthermore, if the empty-tomb thesis may very well have been known and accepted when Mark 16:1–8 was written, premise (9) will be even harder to support.

Obviously, (9) would not have been easy to support even before questions were raised about other premises. A negative claim of that sort is by its very nature very hard to support and theoretically impossible to prove. Collins's support for (9) has two parts. She first considers the possibility that Mark drew on an earlier passion narrative, concluding merely that "the existence of such a document is not an assured result of New Testament scholarship" (p. 116). She then considers, at much greater length, the much broader possibility that Mark 16:1–8 "is based on another source, oral or written, adapted by the author of Mark" (ibid.). In doing so she very effectively criticizes the reasoning of those who have thought they saw evidence of an earlier source, concluding that "the hypothesis of a source is unnecessary to explain or resolve the tensions in the passage" (p. 120).

But neither of these considerations rules out or even diminishes the likelihood that Mark relied on oral or written testimony about the empty tomb. So premise (9) remains unsupported. And, for everyone inclined toward the natural interpretation of 'Jesus rose from the dead', (9)'s implausibility has not been lessened.

So I am irresistibly led to believe that on the basis of the argument we have been reviewing we cannot be expected to accept or even to feel a tendency to accept its conclusion—viz., that Mark 16:1–8 is an original composition, a fictional narrative.

The argument, however, is not all there is to consider in assessing that hypothesis. Collins's narrative development of her interpretation of Mark 16:1–8 contains many details that do not emerge in the argument, and so it also deserves to be taken seriously. In order to examine it in a way that is suited to these circumstances, I will present it again, largely in her own words, interjecting my comments as we go through it.

As I see it, then, Collins's account of Mark's achievement in 16:1–8 may be spelled out in this way. "In writing an extended narrative that expressed the good news...of God's activity through Jesus, this author was faced with the challenge of narrating the resurrection" (p. 129). Mark had to include the resurrection in his narrative because he "was convinced that what actually had happened was that Jesus had been raised from the dead" (p. 129); and he was convinced of it because he "regarded the resurrection of Jesus as an event attested by those to whom the risen Jesus had appeared" (p. 129). But narrating the resurrection was a challenge for him because "he did not have evidence for the details regarding how Jesus was raised" (ibid.).

Collins does not tell us how she knows Mark had no such evidence; and his story does, after all, say that there were witnesses to the empty tomb and the angel's explanation of it. Presumably she is partly relying on the line of reasoning in her main argument, which, I have already claimed, is unconvincing. But when we review in more detail what she takes Mark's Easter story to be, we may be able to come up with further reasons for thinking that Mark could not have had evidence for its details.

Faced with the challenge just described, Mark "reverently supplied those details in accordance with his sense of what must have happened" (p. 129); "he described that event in what seemed to him the most appropriate way" (p. 129). "The creation of the empty tomb story shows that . . . [r]esurrection for Mark is not the giving of a new, spiritual body to the inner person, the *psyche*, in a way that the former body does not matter" (p. 130). That is, the account of Jesus' resurrection that Collins attributes to *Paul* is clearly ruled out immediately by the fact that in Mark's story the tomb is empty. Friends of the natural interpretation of 'Jesus rose from the dead' might have thought they knew what must be coming next, but in that case Collins's development of Mark's story would have surprised and disappointed them.

Her very next move is cautious, introducing a set of three alternatives. "For Mark it [Jesus' resurrection] is either a revival or transformation of the earthly body" (p. 130). Revival, of course, just is the natural interpretation (or the essence of it); transformation, it turns out, is ascension or bodily translation to heaven.

Collins proposes a literary test on the basis of which to decide between these alternatives: "If the text implies that Jesus pushed the stone away from the tomb and walked out, the resurrection is understood as a revival of the body. . . . If the text does not imply that Jesus walked out of the tomb, his resurrection, according to Mark, is best understood as a transformation of the earthly body" (p. 130).

The first thing to notice about the transformation alternative is that it would radically alter the Apostles' Creed to read 'the third day he rose again from the dead, *that is*, he ascended into heaven'.

Notice, second, that if, "according to Mark, Jesus was translated from the grave to heaven, then there was no period of time during which the risen Jesus walked the earth and met with his disciples" (p. 131). In that case those appearances the testimony of which is supposed to have convinced Mark of the resurrection must have been not of a Jesus who ate and drank with Peter and the others but "probably of a more heavenly type, like the apocalyptic visions of heavenly beings" (p. 131).

In the third place, notice that if the transformation alternative had been the one Mark intended, Matthew and Luke, who are supposed to have used Mark's Gospel in composing their own, would have failed utterly to understand their source; for Matthew and Luke agree with John in telling the Easter story along the lines of the natural interpretation of 'Jesus rose from the dead'.

Notice, finally, how weak a criterion is proposed for so strong and unusual an interpretation: *not* 'If the text *implies* that Jesus did *not* walk out of the tomb' but merely 'If the text does *not* imply that Jesus walked out of the tomb'. But surely the text is not the only source of relevant implications in a case like this. Common sense and natural expectations have an important part to play as well, providing a default explanation. If the *text* says *nothing* that implies *either* that Jesus walked out of the tomb *or* that he did not walk out of the tomb, the natural conclusion is that he walked out of the tomb.

And yet, as we know, it is Collins's view that Mark intended the transformation alternative. What is more, she thinks it is only natural that he should have done so: "the narrative pattern according to which Jesus died, was buried, and then translated to heaven was a natural way for an author living in the first century to narrate the resurrection of Jesus" (p. 130). I think I speak for most people when I say that I can't believe it could ever have been natural for anyone to "narrate the resurrection" in such a way that the resurrection simply disappeared altogether into the ascension. More particularly, I find it very hard to believe that this would have been natural for Mark, in whose Gospel the notion of resurrection generally seems clearly physical. In Mark 5:22–43 the daughter of Jairus walks after being raised from the dead, and in Mark 6:14–16 Herod is reported as believing that Jesus, going about doing miracles, might be John the Baptist risen from the dead. Since Mark 16:1–8 says nothing to suggest that Jesus' resurrection involves no physical presence of the sort that characterizes resurrection or the concept of resurrection elsewhere in Mark's Gospel, it is only natural to infer that Mark is presenting the resurrection of Jesus as also being of this sort. Why does Collins infer otherwise?

Here is where her six-page survey of more than a dozen stories involving "the ancient notion of translation" comes into play. As she says, "It has been pointed out that the ascension of Jesus, as narrated in the book of Acts, is similar to the Greco-Roman narratives of translation. I am suggesting that this tradition also influenced how Mark narrated the resurrection" (p. 130). It is this familiar pagan literary background that makes the adoption of the transformation alternative in her view "a natural way for an author living in the first century to narrate the resurrection of Jesus" (p. 130). And Collins tries to underline the culturally relative naturalness of this unnatural interpretation of 'Jesus rose from the dead' with observations that tie Mark's Gospel into Greco-Roman literature (ibid.). Still, as she observes, what characterizes all the pagan translation narratives on which Mark is supposed to have drawn is the "idea that a human being could be removed from the sphere of ordinary humanity and made immortal" (p. 123). And that idea alone, I think, would have ruled out these narratives as literary models for the author who described his book as "the Gospel of Jesus Christ, the Son of God."

I conclude, then, that neither in her argumentation nor in her narrative explanation of her hypothesis has Collins given us reasons good enough to think that the empty tomb is Mark's invention.

NOTES

1. "All the other approaches depend on these two" (p. 111).

2. Mark "regarded the resurrection of Jesus as an event attested by those to whom the risen Jesus appeared" (p. 129).

3. P. 129; emphasis added.

4. See, e.g., pp. 118 and 130.

5. Note 21, emphasis added.

6. Near the end of her section on Paul she cites 2 Corinthians 5 as confirming her interpretation of Paul's theory of "the resurrection 'body'" (pp. 113–114), but that is the only other Pauline passage she alludes to in developing (4). The parenthetical list of passages on p. 113 supports only an incidental point about Paul's use of '*soma*'.

7. As some evidence that he accepted the natural interpretation one might cite, besides his speech in Acts 13:34–37, 1 Corinthians 6:13–15, where Paul speaks of the resurrection of Jesus in the context of talk about *bodies*, and Romans 10:7: "Or, Who shall descend into the deep? (that is, bring Christ again from the dead.)"

Response to Kretzmann

Adela Yarbro Collins

I would like to thank Professor Kretzmann for his gracious comments on my paper, even though he remains unpersuaded.

The first part of my response relates to his outline of my argument, specifically to point (5). It reads: "The summaries of the Gospel in the book of Acts are embedded in speeches the apostles made before Mark wrote his Gospel." He admits that this statement is not in fact part of my argument, but states that he added it because he thought it was implied by (6), namely, my observation that "The summaries of the Gospel in the book of Acts also fail to mention the empty tomb" (p. 114). In fact, (5) is in no way implied by (6). The consensus among New Testament scholars today is that the author of Acts, who was also the author of the Gospel according to Luke, composed the speeches in Acts and that these speeches reflect the point of view and milieu of that author, who wrote after Mark. The only reason for mentioning the summaries of the Gospel in these speeches is that scholars of the last generation argued that *these summaries*, not the whole speeches, represented earlier Christian preaching. That argument seems dubious to many today in any case.

In his critical comments on premise (6), Kretzmann failed to notice the distinction made in the note that he cited between the *summaries of the Gospel* and the rest of the speeches. The passages that presuppose the empty tomb do not come from the summaries, but from their elaboration by the author of Acts. Since the author of Acts had narrated a form of the empty tomb story in the first volume of his work, it is not surprising that the empty tomb would be presupposed in the speeches of Acts. It would be naive, however, to assume that these speeches represent in accurate detail what was actually said on some specific occasion.

Kretzmann's "fundamental basis" for doubting my interpretation of Paul's understanding of resurrection shows an unfortunate lack of historical imagination and of appreciation for cultural differences. It should be remembered that the notion of resurrection does not represent an "ordinary" or "natural" event. Further, it is a notion that developed in two specific cultures, Jewish and Persian, probably with some influence of one upon the other. The presence of the notion in any system of beliefs can be traced back to one or the other of these cultural traditions. The idea of resurrection appears not to have been part of these cultures from the beginning, but to have evolved over time. Since the notion deals with matters beyond ordinary human experience, it is shortsighted to claim that it has always had one simple meaning.

In my paper I argued that Paul considered the appearance of the risen Christ to him to be of the same type as the appearances to Peter and the Twelve. Kretzmann points to the "radical" differences between the appearances to the apostles and the appearance to Paul in the book of Acts and claims that Paul could hardly have overlooked these differences! But this argument overlooks the fact that the book of Acts was written later than Paul's letters! Although Paul never speaks of his experience as occurring "on the road to Damascus," the account of Paul's experience in Acts does fit with the impression given by 1 Corinthians 15, Galatians 1, and 2 Corinthians 12 that the appearance of the risen Jesus to him was of a visionary or apocalyptic type.[1] Thus, Paul's description of his experience in the same terms used for those of the Twelve suggests that their experiences were also of this type. The distinction in kind between the appearances of Jesus to the Twelve and the appearance to Paul has long been seen as part of the agenda of the author of Luke-Acts. The experiences of the apostles were reinterpreted and recast, whereas the basic character of Paul's experience was preserved.

Kretzmann rejects my conclusion that Paul considered the spiritual body of the resurrected Jesus to be discontinuous with the earthly, physical body of Jesus. He apparently accepts my interpretation of 1 Corinthians 15:35–50, but objects that here

Paul is speaking only of the eventual resurrection of Christians. He denies that the resurrection of Jesus and the later collective resurrection are two instances of the same sort of event. But that is exactly the point of Paul's argument. Some in Corinth deny the eventual resurrection of Christians ("some among you say that there is no resurrection of the dead"; 1 Cor 15:12). Paul's argument in verses 12–19 depends on two premises: (1) that Christ was raised from the dead, and (2) that the resurrection of Christians is the same type of event as the resurrection of Jesus: "If the dead are not raised, Christ has not been raised" (v. 16). This interpretation is supported by the image Paul uses for the resurrection of Jesus in verse 20: he is the first fruits of those who have fallen asleep. This image implies that the resurrection of Christians will be the completion of the harvest begun when God raised Jesus: i.e., the events are of the same order; in fact, they are two phases of the same event.

On page 146 of Kretzmann's written response is an argument that I find very strange. He remarks that I criticized very effectively the reasoning of those who have thought that they saw evidence for the use of an oral or written source in Mark 16:1–8. But then he goes on to say that this refutation does not rule out or even diminish the possibility that Mark relied on oral or written testimony about the empty tomb! If there is no evidence that the author relied on a source, how can one conclude that he did? This willingness to hold a conclusion without evidence relates to a comment I made in the opening part of my paper regarding historical method. Historians deal in probabilities not possibilities. It is of course possible that Christians before Mark thought that the tomb of Jesus was empty. The point I have tried to make, however, is that there is no *evidence* that anyone so thought or taught before the Gospel of Mark was written. If there is no such evidence, then it is reasonable to conclude that the story of the empty tomb was invented by Mark to narrate the resurrection of Jesus.

I argued in my paper that the best way to interpret the resurrection of Jesus in Mark 16 is as the transformation of his earthly body. It is not obvious that this interpretation requires a radical alteration of the Apostles' Creed, as Professor Kretzmann claims. The Creed of Nicea reads, "He suffered and the third day he rose, and ascended into the heavens."[2] The Apostles'

Creed, a statement of faith used only in the Western Church, at an early stage in its development contained also a reference to Jesus' descent into hell. This article is omitted in the form of the Creed that is now recited in the liturgies of many churches. In *Worship II*, used in many Catholic parishes, the relevant part of the creed reads, "On the third day he rose again in fulfillment of the Scriptures; he ascended into heaven. . . ." In both of these creeds, the "rising" and "ascending" may be seen as two phases of the same event. I cannot resist pointing out that neither Creed says that Jesus walked out of the tomb on his own two feet.

The interpretation of the resurrection in Mark 16 as transformation does not entail the conclusion that the authors of Matthew and Luke misunderstood their source. Matthew presents two types of appearance of the risen Jesus. The appearance to the women implies that Jesus' body was revived. The appearance to the Eleven makes the impression of the more spiritual or heavenly type of appearance. I do not suggest that Matthew was illogical. Rather, he was aware of two distinct understandings of resurrection and reverently included both. The authors of the Gospels of Luke and John had their own reasons for emphasizing the point of view that Jesus' resurrection entailed the revival of his earthly body.

The issue of historical imagination and appreciation for cultural differences comes up again in Kretzmann's reluctance to consider my interpretation of Mark 16 seriously. What is a matter of common sense and natural expectations for a twentieth-century reader of Mark 16 is not necessarily so for the author and first readers. If the text does not necessarily imply that Jesus walked out of the tomb and if it does not describe appearances that entail a revival of his body, it is reasonable to conclude that the understanding of resurrection embodied in this text is the transformation and translation of the body. As I pointed out in my paper, such ideas were extremely widespread in the culture in which Mark was written.

The narratives about the raising of Jairus' daughter and about Herod thinking that Jesus was John the Baptist raised from the dead are indications only that there were various types of notions about "resurrection" current in the culture. They do not imply that the author considered the resurrection of Jesus to be identical with either of these types.

Kretzmann's final argument is that the author of Mark could not have adapted a tradition according to which "a human being could be removed from the sphere of ordinary humanity and made immortal" because he described his book as "the gospel of Jesus Christ, the Son of God." Let me point out first of all, lest there be misunderstanding, that "the sphere of ordinary humanity" means the realm or realms in which most persons were believed to pass their existence between birth and death and after death, i.e., the earthly, physical world and Hades or Sheol. The interpretation offered in my paper of Mark 16 is by no means incompatible with the opening of the gospel. As was pointed out in the discussion, "son of God" in Mark 1 is equivalent to "messiah." Neither term implies divinity in the Nicene sense. In fact, Kretzmann unwittingly has pointed out a further similarity between Mark and the texts I cited. In many cases, it is precisely because a person was perceived as both human and divine that he or she was said to have been translated. Menelaos and Herakles were each translated because he was a "son of God."

NOTES

1. Even if the account in 2 Corinthians 12 is not an allusion to the same experience mentioned in Galatians 1, it is evidence that Paul had ecstatic, visionary experiences of an apocalyptic type.
2. English translation from John H. Leith, *Creeds of the Churches*, 3rd ed. (Atlanta: John Knox, 1982), 31.

IV. Faith and Philosophy: A Reaction to Contemporary Biblical Studies

Critical Studies of the New Testament and the User of the New Testament

Peter van Inwagen

By *users* of the New Testament, I mean, first, ordinary church-goers who read the New Testament and hear it read in church and hear it preached on, and, secondly, the pastors who minister to the ordinary churchgoers, and, thirdly, theologians who regard the New Testament as an authoritative divine revelation.

By *critical studies of the New Testament* (hereinafter, "Critical Studies"), I mean those historical studies that either deny the authority of the New Testament, or else maintain a methodological neutrality on the question of its authority, and which attempt, by methods that presuppose either a denial of or neutrality about its authority, to investigate such matters as the authorship dates, histories of composition, historical reliability, and mutual dependency of the various books of the New Testament.[1] Source criticism, form criticism, and redaction criticism provide many central examples of Critical Studies as I mean to use the term, but I do not mean to restrict its application to Gospel studies. An author who argues that Paul did not write the letter to the Ephesians or that 2 Peter was composed well into the second century is engaged in what I am calling Critical Studies. For that matter, so are authors who argue that Paul *did* write Ephesians, or who (like the late J. A. T. Robinson) argue that 2 Peter was probably composed about A.D. 61, provided that they do not argue for those conclusions from premises concerning the authority or inspiration of the New Testament.

159

I exclude from "Critical Studies" all purely textual studies, studies that attempt to determine the original wording of the New Testament books by the comparative study of ancient manuscripts. Thus, the well-known arguments purporting to show that the last chapter of John was not a part of the original composition (arguments based mainly on a supposed discontinuity of sense in the text) belong to Critical Studies, while the well-known arguments purporting to show that the last twelve verses of Mark were not a part of the original composition (arguments based mainly on the fact that important early manuscripts do not contain those verses) do not belong to Critical Studies.

Again, a close study of a New Testament book or group of books or idea may not be an instance of what I am calling Critical Studies, for it may be that it does not raise questions of dates, authorship, historical reliability, and so on, but, so to speak, takes the texts at face value. An example of such a study would be Oscar Cullmann's famous Ingersol Lecture, "Immortality of the Soul or Resurrection of the Dead?"[2] But it is unusual for a book or article or lecture about the New Testament to be a "pure" example of the *genre* Critical Studies, and it is even more unusual for a book or article or lecture on the New Testament to contain no material that belongs to that *genre*. Most recent works on the New Testament (to judge from the very small sample of them that I have read) are mixtures of Critical Studies with many other things. My term 'Critical Studies' should therefore be regarded as a name for an aspect of New Testament scholarship, rather than for something that is a subject or discipline in its own right.

It is taken for granted in many circles that pastors and theologians must know a great deal about Critical Studies if they are to be responsible members of their professions, and it has been said that even ordinary churchgoers should know a lot more about Critical Studies than they usually do. My purpose in this paper is to present an argument against this evaluation of the importance of Critical Studies to users of the New Testament. I present this argument first in the form of a schematic outline, and proceed to fill in the detail of the argument by commentary on and defense of the premises.

Premise 1. If a user of the New Testament has grounds for believing that the New Testament is historically and theologically reliable, grounds that are independent of Critical Studies, and if he has good reason to believe that Critical Studies do not undermine these grounds, then he need not attend further to Critical Studies. (That is, once he has satisfied himself that Critical Studies do not undermine his reasons for believing in the historical and theological reliability of the New Testament, he need not attend further to Critical Studies.)

Comment on Premise 1

The famous Rylands Papyrus, a fragment of the Fourth Gospel, has been dated to around A.D. 130 on paleographic grounds. Clearly the methods by which this date was arrived at are *independent of* radiocarbon dating. But if radiocarbon dating of the fragment assigned it to the fourth century, this result would *undermine*—if it were incontrovertible, it would refute—the paleographic arguments for the second-century date. (The radiocarbon dating, would not, of course, show where the paleographic arguments went wrong, but, if it were correct, it would show that they went wrong somewhere.)

Premise 2. The liturgical, homiletic, and pastoral use the Church has made of the New Testament, and the Church's attitude towards the proper use of the New Testament by theologians, presuppose that the New Testament is historically and theologically reliable.

Premise 3. These presuppositions of reliability do not depend on accidents of history, in the sense that if history had been different, the Church might have held different presuppositions and yet have been recognizably the same institution. If the Church's use of the New Testament had not presupposed the historical and theological reliability of the New Testament, the Church would have been a radically different sort of institution—or perhaps *it* would not have existed at all; perhaps what was called 'the Christian Church' or 'the Catholic Church' would have been a numerically distinct institution.

First Comment on Premise 3

If the Constitutional Convention of 1787 had established a political entity called 'the United States of America' by uniting the thirteen former colonies under a hereditary monarchy and an established church, the United States would have been a radically different sort of political entity; perhaps, indeed, the nation that was called 'the United States' would not have been the nation that is called that in fact.

If the New Testament books had never been collected into a canon and portions of this canon read at Mass and as part of the Divine Office, if preachers had not been assigned the task of preaching on New Testament texts, if Christians had not generally believed that the New Testament narratives presented a reasonably accurate account of Jesus' ministry, death, and Resurrection, and of the beginnings of the Church, if they had not believed that God speaks to us in the pages of the New Testament on particular occasions (as in the story of Augustine's conversion), if theologians had not generally believed that their speculations must be grounded in the spirit of, and subject to correction by the letter of, the New Testament—then the Church would have been a radically different institution. We might in fact wonder whether an institution that regarded what we call the New Testament as nothing more than twenty-seven venerable but non-authoritative books would really be the institution that is referred to in the Nicene Creed as the one, holy, Catholic, and Apostolic Church. I think that we should have to say that if it *was* the same institution, it was that institution in a radically different form.

Second comment on Premise 3

One might wonder why I am conducting my argument in terms of what the Church has presupposed about the New Testament, rather than in terms of what the Church has *taught* about the New Testament. The answer is that it is much clearer what the practice of the Church presupposes about the New Testament than it is what the Church has taught about the New Testament, the main reason for this being that the Church's practice as regards the New Testament has been much more uniform than its teaching. I grant that there can be disputes about just what it is that a given practice presupposes, but I prefer dealing with disputes of that sort to dealing with the disputes that would attend any very specific attempt to define the Church's teaching about the New Testament.

> *Premise 4.* There are grounds, grounds independent of Critical Studies, for believing that whatever the Church has presupposed is true—provided that presupposition is understood in the strong or "essential" sense described above.

Comment on Premises 3 and 4

There are things the Church has pretty uniformly presupposed in certain periods that are false. I would say, for example, that Paul, and probably all first-century Christians, presupposed that Christians would never be able to do much to change the large-scale features of what they called the World and people today call 'society'. This was doubtless partly because they expected that the World was not going to last long enough to be changed by *anything*, but they seem also to have thought of Christians as necessarily held in contempt (if not actively persecuted) by those on whom the World has conferred power and prestige. Today we know that, for good or ill, it is possible for there to be a formally Christian society, and that even in a society that is not formally Christian, or is formally anti-Christian, it is possible for Christians to exert significant influence on society as a whole.

No doubt there are false presuppositions that the Church has held uniformly from the day of Pentecost to the present, though it is not for me, who do not claim to be a prophet, to say what they might be. The combined force of premises 3 and 4 is this: Any such universally held but false presupposition of the Church is not essential to the Church's being what it is. And (the two premises imply) any presupposition of the Church that is essential to the Church's being what it is is true—or, more exactly, there are grounds for believing that it is true.

> *Premise 5.* Critical Studies do not undermine these grounds, and there are good reasons for believing that they do not,

reasons whose discovery requires no immersion in the minu-
tiae of Critical Studies, but which can be grasped by anyone
who attends to the most obvious features of Critical Studies.

These five premises entail the following conclusion:

Once users of the Nest Testament have satisfied themselves
that Critical Studies do not undermine their independent
grounds for believing in the historical and theological reliability of the New Testament, they need not attend further
to Critical Studies.

First Comment on the Argument

I have already said that by Critical Studies I do not mean just
any historical studies of or related to the New Testament. I have
explicitly excluded from the category of Critical Studies purely
textual studies and studies of aspects of the New Testament that,
as I said, take the texts at face value. Many other historical studies
related to the New Testament are obviously essential to pastors
and theologians, and advisable for ordinary churchgoers who have
the education and leisure to be able to profit from them.

Pastors and theologians should obviously know something
about the history and geography of the ancient Mediterranean
world. They should know something about who the Pharisees,
Sadducees, and Zealots were, what the legal status of the Sanhedrin was, what the powers and responsibilities of a procurator
were, what it meant to be a Roman citizen, and how an appeal
to the Emperor worked. They should know something about the
Jewish religion and the other religions of the Roman world. They
should know something about second-century Gnosticism, and
something about its probable first-century roots. They should
know something about the social, agricultural, and legal facts and
customs, knowledge of which is presupposed in the parables of
Jesus. (I have found facts about fig trees to be enlightening.) All
of this is obvious, and a lot more that could be said in the same
vein is obvious. I mention it only to show that I do not mean
to deny the obvious.

It is worth mentioning that there are historical studies that
users of the New Testament need know little if anything about,
but on which things that they must know something about are

based. (The painstaking comparisons of manuscripts by which our present New Testament texts have been established would be an example, but far from the only example, of what I mean.) It is my position not only that users of the New Testament need know little about Critical Studies, but that nothing that they need to know much about is so much as based upon Critical Studies.[3]

Second Comment on the Argument

The conclusion of the argument applies to users of the New Testament *qua* users of the New Testament. Consider, for example, theologians. The conclusion is consistent with the thesis that *some* theologians, in virtue of the particular theological vineyard in which they labor, may need to be well versed in Critical Studies. For example, a theologian trying to reconstruct Luke's theology from clues provided by the way Luke used his sources would obviously need to have an expert's knowledge of Critical Studies. This qualification is strictly parallel with the following statement: A physicist *qua* physicist need have scant knowledge of biology, but a *bio*physicist has to know a great deal about biology.

Third Comment on the Argument

The conclusion of the argument is not that users of the New Testament must not or should not have an extensive acquaintance with Critical Studies, but that they need not. Biophysicists need to know a lot of biology, but it is not generally supposed that physicists working in the more abstract and general areas of physics need know much about biology. Erwin Schrödinger, however, set out to educate himself in biology because he thought that the observed stability of the gene was inexplicable in terms of known physics, and that the study of living systems therefore held important clues for the theoretical physicist. Well, he was wrong about the gene, but he was no fool, and the matter was certainly worth looking into. I want to say that something like that should be the case in respect of theology and Critical Studies: that Critical Studies are not, in general, particularly relevant to the theologian's task (except in the case in which the task is to reconstruct the theology of the writer of a New Testament book, or something of that sort); but a theologian may conclude at a certain point in his or her investigations that those investigations require a deep knowledge of Critical Studies. But this is no more than a special case of what I would suppose to be a wholly un-controversial thesis: A theologian may conclude at a certain point in his or her investigations that those investigations require a deep knowledge of just about anything—physics, say, or formal logic, or evolutionary biology. I am arguing that Critical Studies cannot be said *a priori* to be of any greater relevance to the concerns of the theologian (or the pastor or the ordinary churchgoer) than physics or formal logic or evolutionary biology.

Fourth Comment on the Argument

Users of any very recent edition or translation of the Bible are going to be exposed to the judgments of those engaged in Critical Studies and the corresponding historical studies of the Old Testament. I mention the Old Testament because my favorite example of the way in which one can be exposed to such a judgment is Genesis 1:2. If one's translation says, "and a mighty wind swept over the face of the waters," instead of, "and the Spirit of God moved over the face of the waters," one may want to know what the arguments in favor of the former reading are. Or if in one's Bible the twenty-first chapter of John has some such heading as "An Ancient Appendix," one may want to know what the arguments are upon which this editorial comment rests. No such example as these is individually of any very great importance, but a large number of such translations and editorial comments may combine to produce an impression of the nature of the biblical texts, an impression that may be correct, but which certainly reflects views of editors and translators that are at least partly conditioned by Critical Studies. If one wants to make up one's own mind about the views that have shaped modern editions and translations of Scripture, one may have to devote more time to Critical Studies than the conclusion of my argument suggests— in self-defense, as it were. An analogy: in ideal circumstances, a student of Plato would not need to know much about nineteenth-century British Idealism; but if the only available edition of Plato were Jowett, such knowledge would be prudent.

Fifth Comment on the Argument

The argument refers to Critical Studies as they actually are. For example, the thesis of Premise 5, that Critical Studies do not undermine the user's grounds for believing in the historical and theological reliability of the New Testament (the grounds alleged to exist in Premise 4), does not imply that Critical Studies could not possibly undermine these grounds, but only that they have not in fact done so.

Even when the qualifications contained in these five comments have been taken into account, the argument is unlikely to win immediate and unanimous approval. The place of Critical Studies in theological education is more eloquent testimony to the strength of the convictions opposing the conclusion of the argument than any chorus of dissent could be. In the seminaries maintained by my own denomination, for example, seminarians spend more time reading works that fall in the area I am calling Critical Studies, or works which are deeply influenced by the supposed results of Critical Studies, than they do reading the Fathers of the Church. I doubt whether things are much different in typical Roman Catholic and "mainline" Protestant seminaries. And, no doubt, any suggestion that Critical Studies should have at most a marginal role in doctoral programs in theology would be greeted with the same sort of incredulity that would attend a suggestion of a marginal role for the study of anatomy in the training of physicians. As to the laity (as opposed both to the ordained clergy and the theologically learned), probably no small number of diocesan vicars of education, and their Protestant counterparts, would agree with the proposal of Ellen Fleeseman-van Leer that the Bible be taught to the laity, " . . . in such a way that the question of its authority is for the time being left to one side and that modern biblical scholarship is taken into account at every step."[4]

The remainder of this paper will be devoted to further clarification of some of the ideas contained in the argument, and to a defense of its premises. Unfortunately, I haven't the space to perform either of these tasks adequately. I must either touch on all of the points that deserve consideration in a very sketchy way, or else be selective. I choose the latter course.

The ideas that figure in the argument that are most in need of clarification are the ideas of "historical reliability" and "theological reliability." The premises most in need of defense are the fourth and the fifth.

Despite the fact that the idea of theological reliability is badly in need of clarification, I am not going to attempt to clarify it, because that would be too large a task. I could not even begin to explain what I mean by the words 'The New Testament is theologically reliable' in the one or two pages I could devote to the topic here. I shall, therefore, attempt to clarify only the idea of *historical* reliability. It is certainly true that the idea of historical reliability is more directly related to the topic of Critical Studies than is the idea of theological reliability. There are plenty of people who believe that Critical Studies have shown that the New Testament cannot be, in any sense that could reasonably be given to these words, theologically reliable. But the primary argument for this thesis would, surely, have to be that Critical Studies have shown that the New Testament is not theologically reliable *by* showing that it is not historically reliable. (After all, if we cannot believe the New Testament when it tells us of earthly things, how can we believe it when it tells us of heavenly things?)

But what thesis do I mean to express by the words 'The New Testament is historically reliable?' What is meant by historical reliability?

The concept of historical reliability, although it is much simpler than the concept of theological reliability, is sufficiently complex that I am going to have to impose two restrictions on my discussion of it. I hope that what I say within the scope of these restrictions will indicate to the reader what I would say about other aspects of the topic of historical reliability.

First, I am going to restrict my attention to the narrative passages of the New Testament: Passages written in the past tenses or the historical present, in which the author represents himself as narrating the course of past events (one typical sign of this being the frequent use of connecting and introductory phrases like 'in those days' and 'about that time'), passages in which what is presented is not represented as a dream or a vision, and in which the references to persons and places are in the main concrete and specific. Secondly, I am going to restrict my attention to descriptions of the words and actions of Jesus. I do this because there are certain stylistic and expository advantages to my focusing my discussion on a strictly delimited class of events, and this class of events has attracted more attention from those engaged in Critical Studies than any other strictly delimited class. I will attempt to explain what I mean by saying that the descriptions of the words and actions of Jesus in the narrative passages of the New Testament are historically reliable. It should be kept in mind that in what immediately follows, I am explaining what I mean by this thesis and not defending it. I give three explanations of historical reliability, which I believe are consistent and, in fact, mutually illuminating.

I begin with a formal explanation—roughly, an explanation in terms of how much of what is said in the texts is historically accurate—for obviously the notion of historical reliability must be closely related to the notion of historical accuracy. I mean by saying that the New Testament narratives are historically reliable (as regards the words and acts of Jesus) that (i) Jesus said and did at least most of the things ascribed to him in those narratives, and (ii) any false statements about what Jesus said and did that the narratives may contain will do no harm to those users of the New Testament who accept them as true because they occur in the New Testament. But clause (ii) of this explanation is itself in need of an explanation.

I will explain the idea of "doing no harm" by analogy. Suppose that a general who is fighting a campaign in, say, Italy, is separated by some misadventure of battle from all of his military maps and reference materials. Suppose he finds a pre-war guidebook to Italy with which he makes do. Suppose that this guidebook is in some respects very accurate: its maps, tables of distances between towns, statements about the width of roads, and so on, are all without error. On the other hand, it has wrong dates for lots of churches, contains much purely legendary material about Italian saints, and it has Garibaldi's mother's maiden name wrong. If the general, so to speak, treats the guidebook as gospel, and as a consequence, believes all of the legends and wrong dates and mistakenly concludes that he is related to Garibaldi, it will probably do him no harm. At any rate, it will do him no military harm, and that is the kind of harm that is relevant in the present context. And if he later comes to believe that God providentially put the guidebook into his hands in his moment of greatest need, it is unlikely that he will be argued out of this belief by a skeptic who shows him that it contains a lot of misinformation about churches and saints and Italian patriots.

The false statements in our imaginary guidebook were militarily irrelevant. So it may be that there are false statements about the words and acts of Jesus in the New Testament that are irrelevant to the spiritual warfare. Let us examine this possibility.

Suppose that Jesus never said, "Blessed are the peacemakers, for they shall be called sons of God."[5] Suppose, however, that this is something he might very well have said. Suppose that it in no way misrepresents his teaching, and is in fact an excellent expression of something he believed. If these things are so, it is hard to see how anyone would be worse off for believing that he said these words. We may contrast this case with the following one: If the early Church had twisted the story of the widow's mite into an injunction to the poor to give to the Church, even to the point of starvation, the changed version of the story would have done grave harm to those who believed it.

My explanation of the notion of historical reliability, therefore, is consistent with the supposition that Jesus did not say all of the things ascribed to him in the Gospel narratives. But this statement naturally raises the question, How much? Is it possible that these narratives ascribe to him *lots* of things he never said or did, all of them being nevertheless things he might well have said or done? I think that there is no contradiction in the idea that the narratives are perfect guides to what Jesus might well have said and done, even though they are most imperfect guides to what, in point of historical fact, he did say and do. I do not, however, regard their having this feature as a real possibility. I believe that if very *many* of the ascriptions of words and acts to Jesus in the New Testament narratives are historically false, then it is very unlikely that any significant *proportion* of those ascriptions attribute to him things he might well have said or done. I shall presently touch on my reasons for believing this.

We can see a second kind of "harmless" historical inaccuracy if we consider the order in which events are narrated. Suppose that, as most scholars apparently believe, the things Jesus is represented as saying in Matthew 5, 6, and 7 (the Sermon on the Mount), are things that—assuming that Jesus said all of them—he did not say on any single occasion. But it has certainly never done anyone any harm to believe that he did; not, at least, if he did say all of them, and said them in contexts that give them the same significance that the "Sermon on the Mount" narrative framework gives them. It is not an altogether implausible thesis that the order in which many of the sayings and acts of Jesus are recorded is of no great importance to anyone but New Testament scholars trying to work out the relations among the Synoptic Gospels. If Mark, as Eusebius said Papias said, " . . . wrote down accurately all that [Peter] mentioned, whether sayings or doings of Christ; not however in order,"[6] and if a simple reader of Mark believes that X happened before Y because that is what it says in Mark, when in fact Y happened before X, it is hard to see how this could have done the simple reader any harm.[7]

This completes my formal explanation of what I mean by historical reliability. I now give a *functional* explanation of this notion.

As I have said, the Church has made very extensive liturgical, homiletic, and pastoral use of the New Testament, including the narrative portions thereof. These texts have been read to congregations and preached on for getting on towards a hundred thousand Sundays. My functional explanation of what is meant by the historical reliability of the New Testament narratives is this: the narratives are historically reliable if they are historically accurate to a degree consonant with the use the Church has made of them. Again, the explanation needs to be explained. Let us consider a rather extreme suggestion. Suppose that most of the New Testament stories about the sayings and actions of Jesus were made up in various communities of the early Church in response to certain contemporary and local needs. (We suppose that when the Evangelists eventually came to hear these stories, they took them for historical fact and incorporated them into their Gospels, adding, perhaps, various fictions of their own composition.) This suggestion is, I believe, *not* consonant with the use the Church has made of the New Testament historical narratives. The Church has caused these stories, these past-tense narratives bursting with concrete and specific historical reference, to be read, without any hint that they should not be taken at face value, to fifty generations of people the Church knew full well *would* take them at face value. If these narratives were indeed largely a product of the imaginations of various people in the early Church, then the Church has, albeit unwittingly, been guilty of perpetrating a fraud. (We might compare the position of the Church—if this suggestion is right—with the position of the paleoanthropological community in the thirties and forties in respect of Piltdown Man. The comparison is not an idle one: it would be hard to find a better case of a fraud that was accepted because it met the needs created by the *Sitz im Leben* of a community.)

What, then, is the degree of historical accuracy that is required of the New Testament narratives (as regards the words and actions of Jesus) if they are to satisfy the present functional characterization of historical reliability? Not surprisingly, I would identify it with the degree of accuracy that figured in our formal explanation of historical reliability. Last Sunday,[8] for example, many churchgoers heard a reading from the gospel according to John that began, "There was a man of the Pharisees named Nicodemus, . . . this man came to Jesus by night. . . ." The degree of historical accuracy exhibited by this passage is consonant with the use the Church has made of it only if (i) there was a Pharisee named Nicodemus who came to Jesus by night and had a certain conversation with him about being born again, or (ii) the passage falls short of historical accuracy in ways that will do no harm to those who hear it read and accept it as an historically accurate narrative. As to the latter possibility—well, perhaps it isn't very important whether Jesus said those things to *Nicodemus*. Perhaps (despite Jesus' characteristic depreciation of the knowledge of "the teachers of Israel") the passage has its historical roots in a conversation Jesus had with some wholly unimportant person, although he might well have said the same things to a distinguished Pharisee if the occasion had arisen. Perhaps the passage is woven together from things Jesus said on several different occasions, or perhaps it records a set speech that he delivered many times with only minor variations. Perhaps the "voice" Jesus is represented as using is to some degree a literary device of the Fourth Evangelist, or displays a way of speaking that Jesus sometimes used in the presence of a few people like the Apostle John, but rarely if ever used in conversations with strangers. All of this, and a great deal more in the same line, would be consonant with the Church's use of John 3: 1–17. If historical inaccuracies of all these kinds were present in that passage, and if someone heard or read the story and took it as unadorned historical fact, it would be a hard critic of the Church indeed who accused her of deceiving that person.[9] If, on the other hand, Jesus never talked about being "born again" at all, the charge of ecclesiastical deception would have considerable merit.

The third explanation I shall give of the notion of historical reliability is *ontological*, an explanation that proceeds by describing the basis in reality of the fact (supposing it to be a fact) that the New Testament narratives possess the degree of historical accuracy that I have characterized formally and functionally. In giving this explanation, I adapt to the New Testament narratives what I have said elsewhere about a very different part of the Bible, the creation narrative in Genesis.[10] What I said there had to do with the work of the Holy Spirit in the transformation of myth. What I say here pertains to the work of the Holy Spirit in the preservation of tradition.

It was natural for primitive Christian communities to tell stories about what Jesus had said and done. (I continue to restrict my discussion to this class of events. But what I shall say is applicable with no important modification to those parts of the Gospel narratives that are about people other than Jesus, and to the Acts of the Apostles.) Every reporter, lawyer, and historian knows that the stories people tell about past events are not always entirely consistent with one another—and therefore not entirely true. Intelligent, observant, and wholly disinterested witnesses to a traffic accident will shortly afterwards give wildly different descriptions of the accident. The four ancient writers who provide our primary documentation of the life of Tiberius Caesar give accounts of his reign that are at least as hard to "harmonize" as the four gospels.[11]

Now let us assume that God was interested in Christians' having an account of the things Jesus said and did during the years of his public ministry, an account that conforms to the standard of "historical reliability" described above; let us in fact assume that he was sufficiently interested in there being such an account that he was willing to take some positive action to ensure its existence.

(But let us put to one side the question why God would have this interest.) Given the facts about the unreliability of witnesses briefly touched on in the last paragraph, and the many mischances that a piece of information is subject to in the course of its oral transmission, what might God do to ensure the existence of such an accurate account?

I suppose that no one seriously thinks that God might have chosen to achieve this end by dictating narratives of Jesus' ministry, Greek word by Greek word, to some terrified or ecstatic scribe. (People are often accused of believing that God did this, but I have never seen a case of anyone who admits to it.) Though I firmly believe in miracles, I do not believe—I expect no one believes—that God's governance of the world is entirely, or even largely, a matter of signs, wonders, and powers. God created the natural processes whose activity constitutes the world. They are all expressions of his being, and he is continuously present in them. The natural process of story formation and transmission among human beings is as much an expression of God's being as is any other natural process, and there is no reason to suppose that he would choose, or need, to circumvent this process to ensure the historical reliability of the New Testament narratives. Nevertheless, I believe that his presence in the formation of the New Testament—and, more generally, Scriptural—narratives was different from his presence in the formation of all other narratives, just as his presence in the formation of Israel and the Church was different from his presence in the formation of all other nations and institutions.

I suppose that the New Testament writers and their communities were chosen by God and were rather special people. I suppose that if, say, St. Luke was told one of the bizarre stories about Jesus' boyhood that survive in the apocryphal infancy gospels, the Holy Spirit took care that his critical faculties, and, indeed, his sense of humor, were not asleep at the time. I suppose that if an elder of the Christian community at Ephesus in A.D. 64 was tempted by want of funds to twist the story of the widow's mite into an injunction to the poor to buy their way into the Kingdom of God, the Holy Spirit saw to it that his conscience was pricked, or that no one believed his version of the story, or that the changed story never got out of Ephesus and soon died out.

I suppose that the Holy Spirit was engaged in work like this on many occasions in many places during the formation of the New Testament books. I suppose that the Holy Spirit was at work in the Church in similar modes during the process of canonization and during the formation of the opinion that the canonical books were the inspired word of God. I suppose that (although no good book is written apart from the work of the Holy Spirit) the Holy Spirit is present in just *this* way only in the formation of Holy Scripture, and that this mode of presence is part of what we mean by inspiration. (I say 'part of' because we are touching here only on the narrative aspect of Scripture.)

If I am right, God has guided the formation of the New Testament historical narratives by acting on the memories and consciences and critical faculties of those involved in their formation. His employment of this "method" is certainly consistent with there being historically false statements in the New Testament. A false saying of Jesus might have arisen and gained currency without dishonesty or conscious fabrication on anyone's part. (No doubt many did.) And if it were in his "voice," and if its content were consistent with his teaching, then it would not be of a sort to be "filtered out" by the critical faculties of those who transmitted and recorded it, however perfect the operation of those faculties might be. The inclusion in the New Testament of such a false saying would, as I have said, do no one any harm, for it would by definition be consistent with his teaching. (There are many other, if less important, ways in which historically false but harmless ascriptions of words to Jesus might arise: the attribution to him of an apposite quotation of a well-known proverb in a situation in which he said something less memorable; the substitution of one arbitrary place-name for another in a parable. . . .) But if this method is consistent with there being some inauthentic sayings of Jesus in the New Testament (the same point, of course, applies to actions), it does not seem to allow any real possibility of a very high proportion of inauthentic sayings. One's critical faculties need something to work on: one cannot judge that an alleged saying of Jesus is not the sort of thing he would have said unless one has at one's disposal a large body of sayings characteristic of Jesus. And the only real possibility of having at one's disposal a large body of sayings characteristic of Jesus is this: having at one's disposal a large body of actual sayings of Jesus.

If the Holy Spirit has indeed been at work in the formation of the New Testament narratives in the way I have described, what would the results be? I think we could expect two results. First, we could expect the narratives to be historically reliable in the formal sense. Secondly, I think that we could expect them to look pretty much the way they do—or at least we can say that the way they look is consistent with their formation having been guided by the Holy Spirit in the way I have described. In one sense, the New Testament narratives are far from coherent. That is, while "harmonization" of the narratives is no doubt logically possible, any attempt at harmonization is going to look rather contrived. (The same could be said of the Tiberius sources.) But these incoherencies are of little consequence to the people I have called users of the New Testament, however important they may be to those engaged in Critical Studies. Let us grant for the sake of argument—I am in fact very doubtful about this—that it is impossible to reconcile Jesus' representation of himself in John with his representation of himself in, say, Mark. How Jesus represented himself to his audiences and to the authorities and to his disciples at various points in his ministry is no doubt of great interest to certain scholars, but what has it got to do with the Christian life, or with Christian ministry, or even with Christian theology? Or does this incoherency (supposing always that it exists) show that the Holy Spirit cannot have guided the formation of the New Testament narratives in the way I have supposed? How, exactly, would an argument for this conclusion go?

This completes my tripartite explanation of the meaning of 'historically reliable'. I now turn to my promised defense of premises 4 and 5. This was premise 4:

> There are grounds, grounds independent of Critical Studies, for believing that whatever the Church has presupposed is true.

I am a convert. For the first forty years of my life I was outside the Church. For much of my life, what I believed about the Church was a mixture of fact and hostile invention, some of it asinine and some of it quite clever. Eventually, I entered the

Church, an act that involved assenting to certain propositions. I believe that I had, and still have, good reasons for assenting to those propositions, although I am not sure what those reasons are. Does that sound odd? It should not. I mean this. I am inclined to think that my reasons for assenting to those propositions could be written down in a few pages—that I could actually do this. But I know that if I did, there would be many non-Christians, people just as intelligent as I am, who would be willing to accept without reservation everything I had written down, and who would yet remain what they had been: untroubled agnostics, aggressive atheists, pious Muslims, or whatever. And there are many who would say that this shows that what I had written down could not really constitute good reasons for assenting to those propositions. If it did (so the objection would run), reading what I had written on those pages would convert intelligent agnostics, atheists, and Muslims to Christianity—or would at least force them into a state of doublethink or intellectual crisis or cognitive dissonance. Perhaps that's right. If it is, then among my reasons there must be some that can't be communicated—or *I* lack the skill to communicate them—like my reasons for believing that Jane is angry: something about the corners of her mouth and the pitch of her voice, which I can't put into words.

Philosophers are coming to realize that the fact that one cannot articulate a set of reasons that support one's assent to a certain proposition, reasons that are felt as having great power to compel assent to that proposition by everyone who grasps them, does not mean that one does not have good reasons for assenting to that proposition. And they are coming to realize that being in this sort of epistemic situation is not the peculiar affliction of the religious believer. Let me give an example of this that is rather less abstract than the examples that philosophers usually give, a political example. When I was a graduate student, in the Vietnam era, it was widely believed among my friends and acquaintances that there was something called "the socialist world" that was at the forefront of history and which was soon (within ten or fifteen years) to extend over the entire surface of the globe through the agency of something called "the Revolution." Now I believed at the time that all of this was sheer illusion. In fact, I didn't just believe it was sheer illusion, I *knew* it was sheer illusion.

Nevertheless, although I knew this, if you had asked me why I thought it was true, I could not have cited anything that was not well known to, and which would not have been cheerfully conceded by, any reasonably alert campus Maoist: that such-and-such a story had appeared in the *New York Times*, that George Orwell had once said this, or that Leopold Tyman was currently saying that.

A second illustration of this philosophical point is provided by philosophy itself. A philosopher I deeply respect once told me that he could not accept any religion because there were many religions and they disagreed about important matters. I pointed out to him that he himself accepted many philosophical positions that other, equally able philosophers rejected, philosophers who knew all the arguments *he* knew. (He resisted the parallel, but on grounds that are still opaque to me.) And his situation is not unique. Every philosopher, or so it seems to me, accepts at least some philosophical theses that are rejected by some equally able and equally well-informed philosopher. But I am not willing to say that no philosopher knows anything philosophical.

Such examples can be multiplied indefinitely. What do you think of psychoanalysis, the theory of evolution by natural selection, or the Documentary Hypothesis? Someone as intelligent and as knowledgeable as you rejects your position. Are you willing to say that this shows that you lack reasons that support your opinions on these matters? If so, why do you continue to hold them? (Why, in fact, did you hold them in the first place, since you were perfectly well aware of the disagreements I have alluded to?) If not, then it would seem to follow that you should agree that it is possible for one to have reasons that support a belief, even if one is unable to give an account of those reasons that has the power to compel belief in others.

In my view, I have such reasons with respect to the propositions assent to which is essential to membership in the Church—although, as is typical in such cases, many will dispute this claim. One of these propositions is the proposition that Jesus Christ (who, in addition to being the Way and the Life, is the Truth) is the head and cornerstone of the Church. I cannot reconcile assent to this proposition with assent to the proposition that falsehoods are presupposed in the essential operations of the Church. I have argued that the historical reliability of the New Testament is presupposed in the essential operations of the Church. I therefore claim to have good reasons for believing that the New Testament is historically reliable—they are just my reasons for accepting the whole set of propositions essential to membership in the Church. And those reasons are independent of the findings of Critical Studies.

Or so I say. But are they really, *can* they really be, independent of the findings of Critical Studies? Some would perhaps argue as follows. Among the propositions essential to Christianity are certain historical propositions; for example, that Jesus was at one time dead and was later alive. Therefore (the argument proceeds), if the believer has reasons for accepting the propositions essential to Christianity, reasons that actually warrant assent to those propositions, they must be partly historical reasons, reasons of the kind that historians recognize as supporting a thesis about the past. (And it is in Critical Studies that we see the methods of objective historical inquiry applied to the task of sifting historical fact from myth, legend, and fancy in the New Testament narratives.) I have said "some would perhaps argue . . ."; I concede, however, that the only people I can remember actually arguing this way are avowed enemies of Christianity like Antony Flew. And they of course believe that it is impossible to demonstrate, on historical grounds, certain of the historical propositions essential to Christianity. While I would agree with them that it is impossible to demonstrate on historical grounds that, for example, Jesus was at one time dead and was later alive, I see no merit in the thesis that the only grounds that could warrant assent to that proposition are grounds of the kinds that historians recognize. If I have, as I believe I have, good grounds for accepting what the Church teaches, and if the Church teaches certain things about the past, and if some of those things cannot be established by the methods recognized by historians, why should I cut myself off from those truths about the past by believing only those statements about the past that are endorsed by the methods recognized by historians?

I think it is worth noting that, whether the thesis that propositions about the past should be accepted only if they can be established by the methods recognized by historians is true or false, it is certainly incompatible with Christianity. A more careful statement of the thesis would be this: a proposition about the past should be accepted *by a given person* only if *that person knows* (or at least *has good reason to believe*) *that* it can be established by the methods employed by historians. Now it is obvious that many of the historical propositions essential to Christianity are rejected by large numbers of historians. I do not know whether it is possible for there to be a historical proposition that is (i) rejected by large numbers of historians, and (ii) such that some people know, or have good reason to believe, that its truth can be established by the methods recognized by historians. But if this is possible, it can hardly be doubted that only a very well-educated person could know, with respect to a proposition that is rejected by large numbers of historians, that its truth could be established by the methods recognized by historians. It follows that some of the propositions essential to Christianity have the following feature: only a very well-educated person–if anyone—should accept them. This conclusion is, of course, radically inconsistent with the Gospel. It is, in fact, very close to Gnosticism, for it entails that a form of knowledge accessible only to an élite is necessary for salvation.

I conclude that I do have grounds for accepting the historical reliability of the New Testament that are independent of Critical Studies. As we have seen, however, it is still possible that my grounds may be *undermined* by Critical Studies. Let us therefore see what can be said in defense of Premise 5:

> Critical Studies do not undermine these grounds, and there are good reasons for believing that they do not, reasons whose discovery requires no immersion in the minutiae of Critical Studies, but which can be grasped by anyone who attends to the most obvious features of Critical Studies.

That discoveries by those engaged in Critical Studies have undermined whatever grounds anyone may ever have had for accepting the historical reliability of the New Testament is not an unknown opinion. The late Norman Perrin, for example, says:

> In revealing the extent to which the theological viewpoint of the evangelist or transmitter of the tradition has played a part in the formation of the Gospel material, [redaction criticism] is forcing us to recognize that a Gospel does not portray the history of the

ministry of Jesus from A.D. 27–30, or whatever the dates may actually have been, but the history of Christian experience in any and every age. At the same time this history of Christian experience is cast in the form of a chronicle of the ministry of Jesus, and some parts of it—whether large or small is irrelevant at this point—are actually based on reminiscence of that ministry. The Gospel of Mark is the prototype which the others follow and it is a mixture of historical reminiscence, interpreted tradition, and the free creativity of prophets and the evangelist. It is, in other words, a strange mixture of history, legend, and myth. It is this fact which redaction criticism makes unmistakably clear. . . . [12]

It is obviously a consequence of the point of view expressed in this quotation that whatever grounds I may have for believing in the historical reliability of the New Testament have been undermined by Critical Studies—just as F. C. Baur's grounds for believing that the Fourth Gospel was a product of the late second century (whatever they may have been) have been undermined by the discovery of the Rylands Papyrus.

How shall I, who possess none of the tools of the New Testament critic, decide whether this evaluation (or other less extreme but still highly skeptical evaluations) of the historical reliability of the New Testament is to be believed? Someone might well ask why reasoning parallel to my earlier reasoning does not show that I need not raise this question. Why not argue that if one needed to decide that the findings of Critical Studies did not undermine one's grounds for believing in the historical reliability of the New Testament before accepting the historical reliability of the New Testament, this would entail the false conclusion that only highly educated people—if anyone—could accept the historical reliability of the New Testament? The answer is that there are good reasons for thinking that Critical Studies do not cast any doubt on the historical reliability of the New Testament, and that one does not have to be a highly educated person to understand these reasons.[13]

This is not surprising. In general, it is much harder to find reasonable grounds for deciding whether a certain proposition is true than it is to find reasonable grounds for deciding whether so-and-so's arguments for the truth (or for the falsity) of that proposition are cogent. If the proposition under consideration is one whose subject-matter is the "property" of some special field of study (like 'The continents are in motion' and unlike 'Mario Cuomo is the governor of New York'), and if the "reasonable grounds" are those that can properly be appealed to by specialists in that field of study, then it is almost certain that only those specialists can find reasonable grounds for deciding whether it is true. (I suppose it is reasonable for me to decide that the continents are in motion on the basis of the fact that it says so in all the geology textbooks. But this is not the sort of fact that *geologists* can properly appeal to when they are asked to explain why they believe that the continents are in motion.) But if the "reasonable grounds" are ones that it is appropriate for the laity to appeal to, then it is almost always possible for the laity to find reasonable grounds for deciding whether the arguments employed by some group of specialists are cogent.

Suppose, for example, that the director of the Six Mile Island Nuclear Facility delivers to Governor Cuomo a long, highly technical case for the conclusion that the Facility's reactor could never possibly present a radiation hazard. The Governor, of course, doesn't understand a word of it. So he selects ten professors of nuclear engineering at what he recognizes as leading universities to evaluate the case he has been presented with. Eight say the reasoning on which the case is based is pretty shaky, one says it's abominable, and one—who turns out to be married to the director of Six Mile Island—says it's irrefutable. It seems to me that the Governor has found reasonable grounds on which to decide whether the director's arguments in support of the proposition *Six Mile Island is safe* are cogent. And this is true despite the fact that he is absolutely unable to judge the case "on its merits"—that is, unable to judge it using the criteria employed by nuclear engineers.

It is not impossible, therefore, that it turn out to be a comparatively easy matter for me to decide whether the findings of Critical Studies undermine my grounds for believing in the historical reliability of the New Testament. I say this in full knowledge of the fact that the field of New Testament scholarship is as opaque to me as nuclear engineering is (I suppose) to Governor Cuomo. I am aware that an academic field is an enormously complex thing, and that it takes years of formal study and independent research to be in a position to find one's way about in one of them. (Independent research in a field is absolutely essential for understanding it. This fact leads me to take with a grain of salt what some of my fellow philosophers who have had some seminary or university training in New Testament studies tell me about the field. I think of new Ph.D.s in philosophy from Berkeley or Harvard or Pittsburgh, whose mental maps of academic philosophy are like the famous Steinberg *New Yorker* cover— the world as two-thirds midtown Manhattan—the philosophical world as two-thirds Berkeley or two-thirds Harvard or two-thirds Pittsburgh.)

Nevertheless, some facts about New Testament studies are accessible even to me. One of them is that many specialists in the field think—in fact, hold it to have been demonstrated—that the New Testament narratives are, in large part, narratives of events that never happened. I have quoted Perrin to this effect. On the other hand, one can easily find respectable workers in the field who take precisely the opposite view. In this camp I would place F. F. Bruce, John Drane, and (to my astonishment, given *Honest to God*) John A. T. Robinson. Could it be that these people are *not* respectable? Well, their paper or "*Who's Who*" qualifications are excellent, and how else shall *I* judge them? That, after all, was how I judged Perrin: if he had not had impressive paper qualifications, I should have picked someone else to quote.

How can one expert in a field say what I have quoted Perrin as saying, when two other experts—as nearly simultaneously as makes no matter—write books called *The New Testament Documents: Are They Reliable?*[14] and *Can We Trust the New Testament?*[15] and answer their title questions Yes? (Drane's *Introducing the New Testament*[16] is if anything more trusting of the New Testament than the writings of Bruce and Robinson are.) A philosopher, at any rate, will not be at a loss for a possible answer to this question. A philosopher will suspect that such radical disagreement means that New Testament scholarship is a lot like philosophy: Either there is little *knowledge* available in the field, or, if there is, a significant proportion of the experts in the field perversely resist acquiring it.[17]

Is New Testament scholarship a source of knowledge? Or, more exactly, is what I have been calling Critical Studies a source of knowledge? Well, of course, the *data* of Critical Studies constitute knowledge: we know, thanks to the labors of those engaged in Critical Studies, that about ninety percent of Mark appears in closely parallel form in Matthew, and that the phrase *en tois epouraniois* appears several times in Ephesians but in none of the other letters that purport to be by Paul, and many things of a like nature. But such facts are only as interesting as the conclusions that can be drawn from them. Do any of the conclusions that have been reached on the basis of these data constitute knowledge? Or, if you don't like the word *knowledge*, can any of these conclusions be described, in Perrin's words, as a "fact" that Critical Studies "make unmistakably clear"? (We know, thanks to the geologists, that the continents are in motion. This is a fact, which their investigations make unmistakably clear. Is there any thesis that we know in this sense that we can credit to the practitioners of Critical Studies?) I suppose that if any of the conclusions of Critical Studies is known to be true, or even known to be highly probable, it is this: Mark's Gospel was composed before Luke's or Matthew's, and both Luke and Matthew used Mark as a source. But this thesis, while it is almost universally accepted (at least everyone I have read says it is) has periodically been controverted by competent scholars, most recently by C. S. Mann in his Anchor commentary on Mark.[18] One might well wonder whether this thesis is indeed known to be true. If it is, how can it be that Mann, who is perfectly familiar with all the arguments, denies it? If it is unmistakably clear, why isn't it unmistakably clear to *him*? And if the *priority* of Mark has not been made unmistakably clear, can it really be plausible to suppose that the much more controversial thesis that Mark is "a strange mixture of history, legend, and myth" has been made unmistakably clear?

My suspicion that Critical Studies have made nothing of any great importance unmistakably clear, or even very clear at all, is reinforced when I examine the methods of some of the acknowledged experts in that field. Here I will mention only the methods of Perrin and his fellow redaction critics, for it is they and their predecessors, the form critics, who are the source of the most widely accepted arguments for the conclusion that the New Testament is historically unreliable; if someone supposes that Critical Studies undermine my supposed grounds for believing in the historical reliability of the New Testament, he will most likely refer me to the redaction critics for my refutation. (No doubt there are highly skeptical New Testament critics who reject the methods of redaction criticism. I can only say that I am very ignorant and don't know about them. I suppose them to exist only because it has been my experience that in the world of scholarship every possible position is occupied. I shall have to cross their bridge when I come to it.)

I have few of the skills and little of the knowledge that New Testament criticism requires. I know only enough Greek to be able painfully to work my way through a few sentences that interest me, using an interlinear crib, a dictionary, and the tables at the back of the grammar book. I have more than once wasted time looking for a famous passage of Paul's in the wrong letter. But I do know something about reasoning, and I have been simply amazed by some of the arguments employed by redaction critics. My first reaction to these arguments, written up a bit, could be put in these words: "I'm missing something here. These *appear* to be glaringly invalid arguments, employing methods transparently engineered to produce negative judgments of authenticity. But no one, however badly he might want to produce a given set of conclusions, would 'cook' his methods to produce the desired results quite so transparently. These arguments must depend on tacit premises, premises that redaction critics regard as so obvious that they don't bother to mention them." But this now seems to me to have been the wrong reaction, for when I turn to commentaries on the methods of the redaction critics by New Testament scholars, I often find more or less my own criticisms of them—although, naturally enough, unmixed with my naive incredulity.

I could cite more than one such commentary. The one I like best is an article by Morna Hooker, now Lady Margaret Professor of Divinity in Cambridge University. The article is called "On Using the Wrong Tool,"[19] and it articulates perfectly the criticisms I would have made of the methods of redaction criticism if I had been as knowledgeable as she and had not been hamstrung by my outsider's fear that there had to be something I was missing. If Professor Hooker, as she is now, is right, I have certainly not missed anything: All of the premises of the redaction critics are right out in the open. If she is wrong—well, how can *I*, an outsider, be expected to pay any attention to redaction criticism? If its methods are so unclear that the future Lady Margaret Professor couldn't find out what they were, what hope is there for me? I might add that Professor Hooker's witness is especially impressive to an outsider like me because she does not criticize the methods of the redaction critics in order to advance the case of a rival method of her own; rather, their methods are the very methods she herself accepts. She differs from a committed and confident redaction critic like Perrin mainly in her belief that these methods can't establish very much—perhaps that certain *logia* are a bit more likely on historical grounds to be authentic than certain others—and she adheres to these methods only because (in her view) these methods are the only methods there are. (But if she accepts Perrin's methods, she would appear to dissent from one of his premises: that, owing to the pervasive influence in the formation of the Gospels of the theological viewpoints of the transmitters and evangelists, the Gospel narratives are intrinsically so unreliable as historical sources that, in the absence of a very strong argument for the authenticity of a given saying, one should conclude that that saying is not authentic. If I understand Hooker, however, she would say in such a case that nothing can be said about its authenticity; she would conclude that a saying was inauthentic only if there were good arguments—arguments relating to the content and Gospel setting of the particular saying—for its inauthenticity.)

I conclude that there is no reason for me to think that Critical Studies have established that the New Testament narratives are historically unreliable. In fact, there is no reason for me to think that they have established *any* important thesis about the New Testament. I might, of course, change my mind if I knew more. But how much time shall I devote to coming to know more? My own theological writings, insofar as they draw on contemporary knowledge, draw on formal logic, cosmology, and evolutionary biology. I need to know a great deal more about these subjects than I do. How much time shall I take away from my study of them to devote to New Testament studies (as opposed to the study of the New Testament)? The answer seems to me to be: very little. I would suggest that various seminaries and divinity schools might consider devoting a portion of their curricula to these subjects (not to mention the systematic study of the Fathers!), even if this had to be done at the expense of some of the time currently devoted to Critical Studies.

Let me close by considering a *tu quoque*. Is not philosophy open to many of the charges I have brought against Critical Studies? Is not philosophy argument without end? Is not what philosophers agree about just precisely nothing? Are not the methods and arguments of many philosophers (especially those who reach extreme conclusions) so bad that an outsider encountering them for the first time might well charitably conclude that he must be missing something? Must one not devote years of systematic study to philosophy before one is competent to think philosophically about whether we have free will or whether there is an objective morality or whether knowledge is possible?—and yet, is one not entitled to believe in free will and knowledge and morality even if one has never read a single page of philosophy?

Ego quoque. If you are not a philosopher, you would be crazy to go to the philosophers to find anything out—other than what it is that the philosophers say. If a philosopher tells you that you must, on methodological grounds, since he is the expert, take his word for something—that there is free will, say, or that morality is only convention—you should tell him that philosophy has not earned the right to make such demands. Philosophy is, I think, valuable. It is a good thing for the study of philosophy to be pursued, both by experts and by amateurs. But from the premise that it is a good thing for a certain field of study to be pursued by experts, the conclusion does not follow that that field of study comprises experts who can tell you things you need to attend to before you can practice a religion or join a political party or become a conscientious objector. And from the premise that it is a good thing for a certain field of study to be pursued by amateurs, the conclusion does not follow that anyone is under an obligation to *become* an amateur in that field.

This is very close to some of the depreciatory statements I have made about the authority of Critical Studies. Since I regard philosophy as a Good Thing, it should be clear that I do not suppose that my arguments lend any support to the conclusion that the critical study of the New Testament is not a Good Thing. Whether it is, I have no idea. I don't know enough about it to know whether it is. I have argued only that the very little I do know about Critical Studies is sufficient to establish that users of the New Testament need not—but I have said nothing against their doing so—attend very carefully to it.[20]

NOTES

1. This is a purely stipulatory definition. My conclusions about "Critical Studies" apply only to those studies that meet the strict terms of this definition.

2. Oscar Cullmann, *Immortality of the Soul or Resurrection of the Dead?* (London: The Epworth Press, 1958).

3. Many studies of the New Testament presuppose the results, or the alleged results, of Critical Studies. The conclusion of our argument applies to such studies to the extent that these presuppositions are essential to them. Consider, for example, the following quotation from Professor Adams's paper in the present volume (p. 258): ". . . Luke's Gospel was written in the 80s C.E. and arguably reflects the conflict between Christian and non-Christian Jews over who is to blame for the destruction of Jerusalem. . . ." The thesis that Luke's Gospel was written in the eighties is an alleged result of Critical Studies. To the extent, therefore, that this thesis is essential to her paper (I do not claim that this extent is very great; it seems to me that most of what Professor Adams says in her paper could be true even if Luke's Gospel was, as I myself believe it to have been, written in the early sixties), the conclusion of our argument applies to her paper. Any study of Luke that is *wholly* dependent on the thesis that Luke was written well after the destruction of Jerusalem is, if our argument is sound, a study that users of the New Testament may, if they wish, ignore with a clear intellectual conscience.

4. The quotation is taken from a sort of open letter written by Dr. Fleeseman–van Leer to the New Testament scholar Christopher Evans, and included, under the title "Dear Christopher," in a *Festschrift* for the latter. See Morna Hooker and Colin Hickling, eds., *What about the New Testament? Essays in Honour of Christopher Evans* (London: SCM Press, 1975), 240.

5. I learn from reports in the press that the seventh Beatitude has been established as inauthentic by the majority vote of a group of biblical scholars, and will be so marked in the group's forthcoming edition of the New Testament, in which the words the evangelists ascribe to Jesus

are to be printed in four colors, signifying "certainly said," "probably said," "probably didn't say," and "certainly didn't say."

6. *Ecclesiastical History*, iii, 39.

7. In correspondence, Harold W. Attridge has suggested that the various New Testament texts that have been used to justify persecution of the Jews pose a difficult problem for my thesis about historical reliability. In connection with this question, it is important to realize—I don't mean to imply that Professor Attridge is confused on this point—that my thesis does not entail that these texts, or any texts, have done no harm; it entails only that, if any of these texts is not historical, no one has come to any harm by believing that it was historical. Nevertheless, I am willing to defend the strong thesis that Matthew 27:25, John 8:44, 1 Thessalonians 2:14, and Revelation 2:9 have done no harm. These texts have indeed been used as proof-texts by persecutors of the Jews, but it seems wholly obvious to me that only people who were already dead to both reason and the Gospel could use them for such a purpose. As to the masses who may have been swayed by such texts—well, they must have been pretty easy to sway. ("There are in England this day a hundred thousand men ready to die in battle against Popery, without knowing whether Popery be a man or a horse.") I doubt whether the Devil needs to quote Scripture to get people to murder Jews or any other harmless and inoffensive people. At any rate, I'd need a strong argument to believe that any New Testament text has been anything more than a sort of theological ornament tacked on the racks and gas chambers, like a cross on a Crusader's shield. The only harm involving these texts I'm willing to concede is this: to attempt to use scripture to justify murder and oppression is blasphemy, and those who have done this may have been damned for six reasons rather than five.

8. That is, the Sunday preceding the conference at the University of Notre Dame the proceedings of which are printed in this book: the second Sunday in Lent, 1990.

9. I am myself inclined to take this passage as at least very close to unadorned historical fact. (This is, of course, merely one of my opinions—like my opinion that Anglican orders are valid—and not a part of my Christian faith.) If, on another shore, in a greater light, it should transpire that this opinion of mine had been incorrect, I should not regard the Church as having deceived me.

10. Peter van Inwagen, "Genesis and Evolution," the Kraemer Lecture, the University of Arkansas, 1989. To be published in Eleonore Stump, ed., *Reasoned Faith*, forthcoming from Cornell University Press.

11. See A. N. Sherwin-White, *Roman Society and Roman Law in the New Testament* (Oxford: Clarendon Press, 1963), 187–189.

12. Norman Perrin, *What is Redaction Criticism?* (Philadelphia: Fortress Press, 1969), 75.

13. At any rate, one does not have to have the tools of a trained New Testament scholar at one's disposal. It is certainly true that the reasons I shall give for believing that Critical Studies do not cast any doubt on the historical reliability of the New Testament could be understood only by someone who had enjoyed educational opportunities that have not been available to everyone to whom the Gospel has been preached. I would say, however, that these reasons could be understood by anyone who could understand the passage that I have quoted from Perrin's book.

14. F. F. Bruce, *The New Testament Documents: Are They Reliable?*, 6th rev. ed., (London: Inter-Varsity Press, 1981). Bruce was Rylands Professor of Biblical Criticism and Exegesis in the University of Manchester.

15. John A. T. Robinson, *Can We Trust the New Testament?* (Oxford: A. R. Mowbray & Co., 1977). Robinson was the Bishop of Woolwich and the Dean of Trinity College, Cambridge.

16. John Drane, *Introducing the New Testament* (New York: Harper & Row, 1986). Drane is Lecturer in Religious Studies at Stirling University.

17. In the case of philosophy, my own view is that, while certain people know certain philosophical propositions to be true, it would be very misleading to say that the field of academic philosophy has any knowledge to offer. I consider cases of philosophical knowledge—a particular person's knowledge that human beings have free will, say—to be something on the order of individual attainments. A philosopher who knows that human beings have free will is not able to pass the grounds of his or her knowledge on to other persons in the reliable way in which a geologist who knows that the continents are in motion is able to pass the grounds of his or her knowledge on to other persons.

18. C. S. Mann, *Mark* (Garden City, N.J.: Doubleday, 1986).

19. Morna Hooker, "On Using the Wrong Tool," *Theology* 75 (1972): 570–581.

20. I am grateful to Ronald Feenstra for his generous and careful comments on this paper, which are included in the present volume. I am also grateful to Harold W. Attridge who sent me a long and thoughtful letter about various of the points raised in the paper. I have tried to address one of his concerns in note 7. I should also like to express my indebtedness to the writings of Professor E. L. Mascall, particularly his *Theology and the Gospel of Christ: An Essay in Reorientation* (London: SPCK, 1977), which directed me to many of the authors I have cited.

Critical Studies of the New Testament: Comments on the Paper of Peter van Inwagen

Ronald J. Feenstra

Professor van Inwagen's essay, "Critical Studies of the New Testament and the User of the New Testament"[1] offers a probing, thoughtful challenge to the place of "Critical Studies" of the New Testament within the discipline of theology and in the life of the Christian Church. In this brief comment, I first summarize the position advocated by the essay and then offer an evaluation of the essay's thesis. In the end I accept Professor van Inwagen's claim that the believer's grounds for accepting the claims of Scripture lie outside of Critical Studies and that Critical Studies do not undermine these grounds. However, I also challenge Professor van Inwagen's rejection of the value of Critical Studies for users of the New Testament and propose that Critical Studies, properly understood, should operate, not out of an artificial methodological neutrality, but on the basis of central Christian presuppositions about the nature and purpose of the New Testament.

I. Summary of the Position

In his paper, van Inwagen defines two central terms: "users of the New Testament" and "Critical Studies of the New Testament." *Users* are ordinary churchgoers, pastors, and "theologians who regard the New Testament as an authoritative divine revelation"

191

(p. 159). *Critical Studies* are historical studies that either deny or are neutral regarding the authority of the New Testament and attempt "to investigate such matters as the authorship, dates, histories of composition, historical reliability, and mutual dependency of the various books of the New Testament" (p. 159). Professor van Inwagen observes that, although there are few pure examples of Critical Studies, most recent works on the New Testament contain an element of such scholarship. He therefore considers Critical Studies to be "an *aspect* of New Testament scholarship," not "a subject or discipline in its own right" (p. 160).

Given these definitions, van Inwagen argues to the conclusion that, "Once users of the New Testament have satisfied themselves that Critical Studies do not undermine their independent grounds for believing in the historical and theological reliability of the New Testament, they need not attend further to Critical Studies" (p. 164). In commenting on his argument, he adds that "nothing that [users of the New Testament] need to know much about is so much as based upon Critical Studies" (p. 165). He also points out that he is not arguing that users of the New Testament *must not* or *should not* know Critical Studies, but only that they *need not* (p. 165). Finally, he admits that, although Critical Studies as they actually are do not undermine "the user's grounds for believing in the historical and theological reliability of the New Testament," this does not imply that they *could not* undermine these grounds (p. 167). Therefore, although they may, users of the New Testament need not attend very carefully to Critical Studies (p. 188).

II. Evaluation of the Argument

I find van Inwagen's overall argument to be clear and powerful. Central to his argument, it seems to me, is his claim that the believer's reasons (or grounds) for accepting those propositions central to church membership are her grounds for accepting the essential propositions of the Church, including the presupposition that the New Testament is historically reliable (in his specified sense of historical reliability). I share van Inwagen's belief that Critical Studies (as he has defined them) have not undermined the believer's grounds for accepting the New Testament's historical reliability.

Yet I am not fully satisfied with van Inwagen's treatment of Critical Studies in his essay. My criticisms will appear in ascending order of importance. First, van Inwagen begins his essay by stating that the term "Critical Studies" refers to an *aspect* of New Testament studies, not to a subject or discipline in its own right. But he concludes the essay by comparing Critical Studies to the discipline of philosophy, pointing out that both involve interminable disagreements about nearly everything. A better comparison might have found some aspect of philosophy similar to Critical Studies that produces as little knowledge as do Critical Studies. As it is, it seems hard to believe that van Inwagen, as a professional philosopher, holds as little regard for the value of philosophy as a means of access to truth as he does for Critical Studies; or alternatively, that he thinks as highly of the value of Critical Studies—even for the amateur—as he does of philosophy, which he presumably teaches to amateurs as a discipline well worth learning and one likely to hone one's intellectual skills. Or are we to conclude that the whole *discipline* of philosophy offers as little sure and certain knowledge as does just this one small *aspect* of New Testament studies?

Secondly, it seems odd to me that van Inwagen groups ordinary churchgoers, pastors, and theologians together as *users* of the New Testament without making any further distinctions among them and then argues that none of them needs to have much knowledge of Critical Studies (except, perhaps, in self-defense against biblical translations that use Critical Studies). It seems to me that some of the matters treated by Critical Studies—matters such as the authorship and mutual dependency of various books of the New Testament—could contribute to our understanding of the New Testament and might properly be of more interest to theologians than to ordinary churchgoers.

A study of the mutual dependency of the Gospels, for example, that maintains a "methodological neutrality" regarding the authority of the Gospels would, on van Inwagen's definition, count as an example of Critical Studies. Yet it seems that such a study could provide significant insights into the distinctive message of each Gospel, thereby aiding the theologian or pastor in the task of studying and preaching on these documents. The point here is that Critical Studies of a certain sort might contribute to a New Testament user's understanding of, say, the gospels and therefore should be studied by at least some users of the New Testament.

Of course, such studies may prove to be quite technical and may require a significant background in the original languages, literary theory, or some other specialized field. In such cases, at least, it seems plausible to make distinctions among users of the New Testament, holding that theologians and, perhaps, pastors should be equipped for and introduced to such studies, while ordinary churchgoers might safely avoid such specialized studies.

In sum, it seems possible that some forms of Critical Studies might be of some value to New Testament scholarship and that some users of the New Testament—perhaps only theologians and pastors—should be introduced to these studies for whatever light they might shed on the meaning of the New Testament writings.

Thirdly, it seems incorrect for van Inwagen to say that nothing users of the New Testament "need to know much about is so much as based upon Critical Studies" (p. 165). The formation of the New Testament canon itself seems to have been based upon a type of Critical Studies.

During the process of canon formation, the early Church used a variety of tests and arguments in order to determine which writings should have canonical status. The Church appealed to apostolic authorship, orthodoxy of teaching, the antiquity of the document, divine inspiration of the text, and the Church's use of the document as various tests or criteria for inclusion in the canon.[2] J. N. D. Kelly argues that the first of these criteria was most important:

> The criterion which ultimately came to prevail was apostolicity. Unless a book could be shown to come from the pen of an apostle, or at least to have the authority of an apostle behind it, it was peremptorily rejected, however edifying or popular with the faithful it might be.[3]

The Church used arguments that were not based upon the authority or inspiration of the books in question and that attempted— whether correctly or incorrectly—to show that Paul, John,

Thomas, or one of the other apostles either did or did not write or lend his apostolic authority to a certain Gospel or Epistle. The investigations upon which such arguments were based would appear to meet the definition of Critical Studies: historical studies that are neutral regarding the question of authority and attempt to investigate the authorship and dates of a document. If, as seems likely, these investigations were an early form of Critical Studies, then van Inwagen is in error in contending that nothing users of the New Testament need to know about is based on Critical Studies. However, if these investigations were *not* Critical Studies, then we need a clearer definition of Critical Studies so that we can see the difference between the latter and the work involved in the formation of the canon.

Finally, I want to challenge and extend van Inwagen's remarks by focusing on his definition of Critical Studies. According to him, Critical Studies are historical studies of the New Testament that either deny or are methodologically neutral regarding its authority. But is such methodological neutrality even *possible*? Moreover, would not a Christian theologian be permitted—or even obligated—to approach the New Testament documents as authoritative statements inspired by the Holy Spirit? If a Christian theologian has the sort of grounds that van Inwagen mentions for accepting the historical reliability of the New Testament, then why should she accept a version of Critical Studies that would prohibit her from using those truths that she has good grounds to accept?

To begin, then, is methodological neutrality really possible in biblical studies? In his essay, van Inwagen discusses an important article by Morna Hooker in which she argues that the "tools" used by New Testament scholars are inadequate to the task of uncovering the "authentic" teaching of Jesus.[4] She concludes the article by observing the importance of presuppositions in affecting the outcome of a New Testament scholar's work:

> For in the end, the answers which the New Testament scholar gives are not the result of applying objective tests and using precision tools; they are very largely the result of his own presuppositions and prejudices. If he approaches the material with the belief that it is largely the creation of the early Christian communities, then he will interpret it in that way. If he assumes that the words of the Lord were faithfully remembered and passed on, then he will be

able to find criteria which support him. Each claims to be using the proper critical method. Each produces a picture of Jesus—and of the early Church—in accordance with his presuppositions. And each claims to be right. . . . They cannot all be right—though they may well all be wrong.[5]

In this passage Hooker points out that a scholar's presuppositions and prejudices will deeply affect the conclusions that are drawn. If Hooker is correct on this point—and I think she is—then Critical Studies that operate from complete methodological neutrality on the question of the authority of the New Testament are not really possible.

I suggest, then, that we should declare the impossibility of pursuing Critical Studies that are neutral on important questions such as the nature and authority of the New Testament and should argue instead that Christian biblical scholars ought to work out of basic Christian presuppositions regarding the nature and purpose of Scripture. Christian biblical scholars ought not, therefore, to pretend to hold a methodological neutrality about the nature, authority, and purpose of the biblical texts, but ought instead to acknowledge the authority of those biblical texts whose "authorship, dates, histories of composition, historical reliability, and mutual dependency" (the topics mentioned by van Inwagen) are being investigated by whatever scholarly tools are available.[6] If, as Hooker argues, biblical scholars cannot escape the effect of presuppositions on their work, and if Christian biblical scholars accept (as they should) the truth of basic Christian presuppositions about the nature and authority of Scripture, then why should they deny themselves access to truths they already accept as they press onward in the pursuit of truth? Affecting a methodological neutrality toward Scripture should be recognized, then, as neither possible nor desirable.

To conclude my discussion of this point, I observe that the above suggestion is not foreign to highly regarded professional biblical scholars. In his paper for this conference, John Donahue mentions an important recent article by Joseph Fitzmyer.[7] In that article Fitzmyer argues that the historical-critical method has fallen under suspicion within the Church because it has been linked with rationalist, anti-supernatural, demythologizing, or existentialist presuppositions that affected the outcomes the method produced. The historical-critical method itself, says Fitzmyer, is neutral; and therefore in use it can be—and has been—combined with a variety of presuppositions.[8] Fitzmyer suggests that a modern Christian biblical scholar should combine historical-critical tools with Christian presuppositions about the authority, inspiration, and purpose of canonical documents. By means of such faith presuppositions, he says, the historical-critical method becomes a *"properly-oriented* method of biblical interpretation."[9]

I think we should endorse Fitzmyer's suggestion. Properly oriented Critical Studies of the New Testament would not be methodologically neutral, but would work out of basic Christian presuppositions about the nature and purpose of the New Testament. Critical Studies of this sort would investigate matters of authorship, dates, histories of composition, historical reliability, and mutual dependencies of various New Testament books. The results of such investigations, I submit, would advance the theological task and deeply enrich the life of the Church.

NOTES

1. In this volume, future references to this essay will be made parenthetically in the body of the text.

2. Lee Martin McDonald, *The Formation of the Christian Biblical Canon* (Nashville: Abingdon Press, 1988), 146–163.

3. J. N. D. Kelly, *Early Christian Doctrines*, 5th ed. (San Francisco: Harper & Row, 1978), 60.

4. M. D. Hooker, "On Using the Wrong Tool," *Theology* 75 (1972): 570–581.

5. Ibid., 581.

6. Alvin Plantinga makes a similar suggestion with respect to the task of Christian philosophers ("Advice to Christian Philosophers," *Faith and Philosophy* 1 [July 1984]: 253–271, esp. 260–261).

7. Joseph A. Fitzmyer, S.J., "Historical Criticism: Its Role in Biblical Interpretation and Church Life," *Theological Studies* 50 (June 1989): 244–259.

8. Ibid., 252–254.

9. Ibid., 254–255.

V. Biblical Studies and Philosophy on Christology

Calling Jesus Christ

Harold W. Attridge

What I would like to do in this essay is to explore some issues of method in biblical studies. I intend to illustrate what it is we do, or at least what it is I think some of us do, in the contemporary study of Scripture and then invite critical reflection on that enterprise from our colleagues in philosophical theology. This exploration of methods will not be divorced from content and I shall be making two substantive claims (a) that there is undeniable diversity within the New Testament on issues central to it and (b) that early Christian documents are obviously and profoundly conditioned by their environment. For those of us who have an interest in biblical texts as somehow disclosive or revelatory of the divine, these facts present obvious, but not insurmountable challenges, and along the way I shall offer some suggestions about appropriate theological appropriations of critical biblical scholarship.

Let me begin with some preliminary, rather general and, I suspect, rather obvious methodological considerations and then proceed to a more concrete illustration involving the Christology of the New Testament.

1. Preliminaries: Contemporary Biblical Scholarship

It may be useful to begin by reminding ourselves of the institutional arrangements that form the context of contemporary biblical studies. Biblical texts are investigated today in two major environments and with a variety of tools and heuristic strategies. They are, that is, the subject of inquiry within various secular humane disciplines: the study of religion, ancient history, semitic or classical languages, or comparative literature. In such contexts the texts are investigated without any commitment to their normative status for communities of faith. Within the world of theology, however, that normative status is recognized and perhaps taken for granted, although the function of the biblical text *qua* norm is construed quite differently by different religious and confessional traditions. Furthermore, even within religious or confessional traditions, there are significant differences of opinion over Scripture's normative function(s). That Scripture plays a role in the mix that constitutes revelation is acknowledged, but how it is to be balanced with other sources of revelatory insight such as reason and tradition remains a matter of debate.[1]

It is also worth reminding ourselves of the contemporary diversity in approaches to exploring Scripture. Methods of study and heuristic strategies cut across institutional and disciplinary lines. Virtually all approaches to scriptural texts rely on the on-going work traditionally labeled "lower criticism" (the study of textual traditions, grammar, etc.). I presume that these aspects of scriptural study raise few philosophically interesting issues. Biblical texts, moreover, are studied as sources for ancient history and for the history of ancient religious beliefs and practices. These types of inquiry, in principle at least, subject scriptural texts to the same sort of scrutiny exercised on other ancient witnesses to social, institutional, or conceptual phenomena. With increasing frequency, biblical texts are also studied as literature in ways that often abstract them from their ancient environment.[2] In such studies, analysis of form, narrative style, rhetorical strategy, and underlying structures of various sorts tends to dominate discussion. Philosophical theologians surely have questions of these approaches to Scripture, but these questions are properly addressed to the contributory disciplines of historical and literary inquiry. One might ask about, e.g., the epistemological status of historical reconstructions, the nature of the warrants adduced in making historical arguments, the value and uses of aesthetic judgments, the limits of historical or literary inference, etc.

What distinguishes the theological study of Scripture from other approaches is not the appropriation or refusal to appropriate one or another of these heuristic strategies, but rather the context and goal of the investigation and the intended audience to whom the results of that investigation are directed. As a constituent of theological reflection, scriptural study shares in the overall aim of that enterprise, which is to explore the meaning and truth of the claims of a faith tradition. Scriptural study makes its contribution to that overall enterprise in several ways. It does so, first of all, by exegesis narrowly defined, i.e., the explication of the plain (although perhaps not always obvious) meaning or literal sense of the biblical text. That sense is a primary datum for theological reflection (and not the end result of such reflection) because of Scripture's authoritative status in a community of faith. Discussion of the literal sense of a biblical text is, of course, no simple operation and cannot be easily separated from the results of applying to scriptural texts the various heuristic strategies that have already been mentioned. In fact, the questions of interest to this conference have no doubt arisen because some of the heuristic tools involve presuppositions or lead to results that pose theological or philosophical problems. Scriptural study also contributes to the theological enterprise when it engages in hermeneutical reflection on the contemporary significance of the biblical text. As scriptural study moves in this direction, it overlaps with more systematic theological and philosophical concerns. It is a characteristic of most contemporary reflection of this sort by scriptural scholars that it takes seriously the results of investigation of the literal sense of Scripture produced by the various heuristic methods generally used in contemporary humanistic study of ancient texts. I hope that my probes into contemporary types of biblical study will suggest some of the ways that theologically relevant concerns emerge from such study.

2. A Test Case: Christology

Let me now move to specifics. Certain central questions for Christian theological reflection generally, and, perhaps, for philosophical theology, revolve around the claims made by Christians about Jesus of Nazareth. Christians call Jesus "Christ," usually as a focus for a large number of other epithets, and they call on Jesus Christ in prayer. (Yes, the title of this essay is systematically ambiguous.) Christian theologians of any stripe will no doubt want to explain what Christians are doing when they engage in such activities.

One element of a response to that question involves exploration of Christian foundational documents, including the New Testament, and biblical interpreters have been trying at least to provide data for an answer for quite some time. I would like to take four probes into problems of New Testament scholarship, to sketch briefly four areas in which New Testament scholars have contributed to the discussion of Christology. Each of these areas involves a slightly different combination of methodological approaches or heuristic strategies; two are primarily historical and two more literary.

3. Calling Jesus Christ in early Christian Communities

A seemingly trivial problem surfaces in planning any introductory course on the New Testament. If the introduction observes any chronological scheme, the instructor must choose whether to follow an absolute chronology and begin with Jesus and his environment or to adopt a literary chronology, begin with our earliest written records and eventually reason back to the historical events that some of them describe. An analogous problem confronts us here. We could begin by considering what we know of the claims that Jesus made for himself or we could begin with the early communities that arose after his death and resurrection and with the evidence that they have left in what is now the New Testament. I prefer the latter starting point, simply because it offers fewer initial problems.

We begin, then, with the evidence of the New Testament, which provides at least a sample of the assessments of Jesus in the early Christian movement. Our investigation is primarily a historical one, asking what followers of Jesus made of him in the first half century or so after his death.[3] Unless we approach the question with dogmatic blinders, our initial perception is that there was considerable diversity, both formal and contentual, in what early Christians meant by calling Jesus "Christ."

3.1 *Two models*: It is not too much of an oversimplification of this diversity to distinguish two major overarching models.

In one, Jesus is identified as the anointed instrument by which God will effect a final righteous judgment. In the other, he is the embodied agent of God who has entered human history to do something for humankind. In terms of later dogmatic categories, the first model tends more toward an "adoptionist" understanding of the special status of Jesus, the latter tends more toward an "incarnational" understanding, although both categories require considerable clarification. In terms of religio-historical terms, the first model reflects Jewish ways of thinking about the exaltation of the righteous, as well as hopes for final redemption. The latter tends to reflect other Jewish models, which derive primarily from the sapiential tradition, although the dichotomy is not airtight.

3.2 *The majority model*: If we had to take a vote of New Testament authors, what I have labeled as the first model for describing what they meant when calling Jesus "Christ" would win a clear plurality, if not an outright majority. There are several particularly striking examples of the pattern. The most memorable is perhaps the opening of Romans, written by Paul around 56 A.D.:

> Paul a slave of Christ Jesus, called an apostle set apart for God's good news, which he foretold through his prophets in holy scriptures, the good news about his son, who came from David's seed according to the flesh, but who was designated son of God through a mighty act, by the spirit of holiness, by resurrection from the dead, his son, namely, Jesus Christ our Lord. . . .

For Paul, at least in this passage, to call Jesus "Christ" means to recognize him to be the "anointed one," designated as such by the resurrection event. What he is designated for is explained in the following verse and discussed throughout much of Romans. I do not at this point want to pursue the soteriological implications of Paul's Christian confession.

Two other clear examples of the same christological perspective are attributed to Peter in the pages of Acts, written in the last decades of the first century or early in the second. The first comment is in Peter's speech at Pentecost which concludes:

> God raised up this Jesus, of whom all of us are witnesses. He was exalted to the right hand of God, receiving the promise of the holy spirit from the father. This he has poured out, which is what you see and hear. For David did not go up to heaven, but he says,

"The Lord said to my lord, 'Be seated at my right hand until I make your enemies a stool for your feet.'" Let all the house of Israel know, then, with assurance, that God *has made this Jesus* whom you crucified *to be both lord and Christ*. (Acts 2:32–36)

In the next chapter, in his address to the people in Solomon's stoa, Peter calls for repentance:

Repent therefore and turn so that your sins might be wiped away, so that the times of refreshment might come from the Lord and he might send Jesus, the one who has been predesignated for you as the Christ, whom heaven must receive until the times of restoration of which God spoke through the mouth of his holy prophets from of old. (Acts 3:19–21)

There may be some archaizing in Luke's presentation of the earliest apostolic community and its chief spokesman. The Christology of the Petrine speeches is not, however, repudiated or explicitly corrected anywhere in the third Gospel or the book of Acts. In fact, the "prophetic" model that Peter (Acts 3:22–23) goes on to apply to Jesus is probably at the heart of Luke's reflections on the significance of Jesus. It may be that the eschatological Christology of the Petrine speeches is implicitly nuanced by virtue of the overall program of the two-volume work of Luke-Acts. At the very least we must acknowledge that to cite the formulas of the Petrine speeches is not to exhaust Luke's reflections on the significance of Jesus. Neither, for that matter, does Romans 1:3 exhaust all that Paul has to say about the significance of Jesus. To the issue of situating christological formulations in their literary contexts we shall return.

At this point we can, however, conclude that one thing that some early Christians meant in calling Jesus "Christ" was that he was the designated agent of God's expected intervention into human history to fulfill his promises to Israel.

3.2.1 *Calling on Jesus Christ*: Let me add one reminder relevant to the ambiguity of the title of this essay. Early Christians called upon Jesus Christ in prayer. One early form of such Christ prayer is preserved in Aramaic in 1 Corinthians 16:22, written around 55, and in Greek in Revelation 22:20, written nearer the end of the century. In the former the prayer is *Marana tha*, "Come Lord"; in the latter, ἔρχου κύριε Ἰησοῦ, "Come, Lord Jesus."

Interestingly, the title "Christ" does not appear in either prayer, but I take "Lord" (Marana, Kyrios) to be the functional equivalent of the title "Christ," an equivalence suggested by the juxtaposition of the two terms in Acts 2:36. However we construe the formula *lex orandi, lex credendi*, it is clear that there is a correlation between the way in which some early Christians conceived of the significance of calling Jesus "Christ" and their liturgical acts of calling upon him.

3.3 *The Minority Model*: The second mode of calling Jesus Christ that we need to consider may be more familiar from its development in the dogmatic tradition, but it is certainly the less well attested of the two. This is the incarnational model, best known from the poetry of the Fourth Gospel, written in its final form in the last decade of the first century or the opening years of the second, which first describes the primordial existence of God's agent:

> In the beginning was the Word
> and the Word was with God
> and the Word was God.
> This one was in the beginning with God
> and all things were made through him
> and apart from him nothing came into being.

According to the prologue, this Word eventually became flesh (1:14). This came about so that he who was in the bosom of the Father might instruct human beings about that Father (1:18). The rest of the Gospel explains what that instruction or revelation contains.

At least one other passage presupposes the same schema. In its rhetorically sophisticated prologue, the Epistle to the Hebrews, a homily probably composed in the last decades of the century, evokes the Son through whom God has spoken at the end of days, a Son

> who, being the radiance of his glory
> and the imprint of his very being
> bearing all things by his powerful word
> having effected a cleansing of sins
> has taken a seat at the right hand
> of the Majesty on high (Heb 1:3).

The third text that probably gives expression to this christological pattern appears, interestingly enough, in an epistle of Paul written in the 50s. I say "probably" because the interpretation of the poetic imagery of Philippians 2:6–11 has been hotly debated in recent years. Nonetheless, I would maintain that the text is of a piece with the prologues of John and Hebrews.[4] In its familiar cadences it celebrates Christ Jesus:

> who, though being in God's form
> did not consider it a prize to be equal to God,
> but emptied himself,
> taking the form of a slave.
> Having become like human beings
> and being found in human form,
> he humbled himself,
> becoming obedient even to death,
> yes, the death of the cross.

The hymn, of course, continues beyond the incarnational moment and incorporates a description of the exalted one. At this point I simply want to highlight the incarnational model and its claim that what Jesus is and what he does is somehow connected with what he has been "in the beginning," or at least prior to his "becoming like human beings."

3.4 *Other Models*: I don't want to go into great detail describing other New Testament models for thinking about the person of Jesus and his relationship to God. There are many points along the spectrum between the exaltationist and the incarnational poles. Most can be seen as extensions or modifications of elements in one or the other.

3.4.1 *The New Adam*: One example of a variant would be the image, prominent in Paul (e.g., 1 Cor 15:20–28; Rom 5:12–21), of Jesus Christ as the New Adam. This image, I suggest, is best understood as an extension of the exaltationist model of thinking about Jesus. The primary motivation for the extension, as for the generation of most christological models, is soteriological, that is, it arises from a consideration of the effect of what God has done in Jesus. The image suggests that God's eschatological intervention in human history is nothing less than a new creation. Paul, of course, qualifies that exuberant claim when he insists on the unfinished dimensions of this new creation (Rom 8:18–30).[5]

3.5 *The Theological Significance of Diverse Christological Models*: The presence of such diverse ways of describing who Jesus is as the Christ creates a set of interesting problems, more for the theological appropriation of the texts than for a strict historical assessment, although even a hard-nosed historian might be led to quasi-theological speculation. The historian, that is, might be content to say that various early followers of Jesus blithely proceeded to use various images, models, and patterns of thinking to describe the significance of Jesus. Those images, models, and the like are not reducible to any simple essence. Conceptual diversity is simply a fact of life in this period (as in most others) of Christian history.

Yet even the theologically neutral historian might be led to wonder whether the people who gathered these disparate materials into a single collection of literature saw some unity within the diversity. She may answer that they did, that they read simpler or more "primitive" patterns as implicative of the more complex or developed. Or she may hold that the incorporation of diverse models was an attempt to create an institutional synthesis of various ecclesial factions.

Given enough time and energy we might try to sort through these and other options for explaining the diversity within the canon of the New Testament.[6] If we could agree on one solution to the historical problem, it might be of assistance in dealing with the contemporary problem of what the community of faith is to make of its scriptural heritage. In fact, both of the historical positions that I have sketched have been used in constructive theologies. A more traditional approach to the phenomenon of the development of doctrine would opt for the first historical assessment. For those who hold some variety of this position, the diversity within the New Testament is testimony to the growth in insight and awareness of the truths of the Christian message. There is a progression from the inchoate affirmations of the significance of Jesus in the Synoptic Gospels upward to the Prologue of John and on to Nicaea and Chalcedon. A more revisionist approach might attempt to validate the multiplicity of perspectives as itself normative for contemporary theologizing, or insist that the less-developed models with their attention to the humanity of Jesus have greater validity.

Yet a third approach represented in various forms across the theological spectrum would try to find some coherence behind or beneath the diversity of early Christian confessional affirmations. For instance, the existentialist demythologizer might argue that all types of affirmations of Jesus as the Christ are to be seen as ways of challenging the human subject to understand and accept "authentic existence." Such an approach involves explicit or implicit judgments about the nature and function of the confessional affirmations of Jesus as Christ and on this point, I suspect the interests of philosophical theologians and philosophers of religion might be mildly aroused. The approaches I have in mind suggest, in effect, that Christian confessional affirmations are not descriptions of states of affairs whose truth value can be tested. They are, rather, images or metaphors that evoke commitments, express values, or inspire action. The unity, more or less tight, underlying the various biblical Christologies is found in the actions, commitments, and values that they inspire.

Let me leave this all too brief sketch of various options for dealing with the diversity and historicity of explicit christological affirmations and move to a second probe.

4. The Jesus of History and the Christ of Faith

Thus far we have been exploring one element of contemporary biblical, or more specifically, New Testament scholarship. We have noted the way in which that scholarship has been concerned with the historical phenomenon of diversity in early Christian affirmations of the significance of Jesus. Yet another historical issue has long intrigued students of the New Testament, whether or not they include a theological dimension in their work. This is the relationship between the Christ proclaimed by the early post-Easter communities and the Jesus who lived and died in the land of Israel in the first century.[7]

4.1 *Jesus' Christology as Criterion*: Intense interest in the historical Jesus arose in large part for theological reasons. One way to adjudicate the validity of competing christological models, ancient or modern, is to appeal to the teaching of Jesus about himself. Whatever we might think about the validity of the appeal, it simply does not resolve the problem. What the inquirer encounters when searching for the teaching of Jesus in the pages of the New Testament, particularly in the Gospels, is not immediately Jesus' own voice, but testimonies to him on the part of his followers written some forty to seventy years after his death. The appeal to Jesus as a touchstone of christological adequacy has led to the increasingly refined historical enterprise of sorting through the evidence for his beliefs and teachings in order to establish a reliable core. This task in various ways has engaged New Testament scholars for over two hundred years, but its results are controverted.

4.2 *The State of the Quest for Jesus and His Christology*: There remains enormous diversity among those who attempt to describe what Jesus really did, taught, and thought about himself. For some contemporary scholars he was a Hellenistic magician; for others, a Galilean charismatic or rabbi; for yet others, a prophetic reformer; for others, a sly teller of wry and engaging tales;[8] for some, he had grandiose ideas; for others, he eschewed them. In general, the inquirer finds the Jesus that her historical method allows her to see. It is as true today as it was at the end of the liberal quest for the historical Jesus catalogued by Albert Schweitzer[9] that we moderns tend to make Jesus in our own image and likeness.

Despite the enormous diversity that obtains in contemporary research on Jesus, I think that it is fair to say that most critics interested in the historical question agree that Jesus made few, if any, *explicit* claims about his own status as "the" or "an" "anointed one." He made few, if any, claims that he was in some extraordinary sense, a "son of God." Passages in the Gospels where he makes such claims[10] consist most likely of post-Easter confessional expressions of his followers and are not grounded in explicit teachings of Jesus about himself.

4.2.1 *The "Historical Truth"*: What then did Jesus claim or stand for? Although I share the skepticism that a cursory examination of the history of research tends to inculcate, I do think that we can answer that question. I would argue that some things can be affirmed with a high degree of probability about Jesus' actions, his teachings and, with a lesser degree of probability, his self-conception. He was, first and last, a Jew, who believed in the validity of Yahweh's promises to and demands on his people. He hoped that those promises would be realized and he tried to live as if they would soon be. In other words, he had a vision of a world where an equally balanced justice and compassion prevailed, a world where God ruled. While he prayed to that God for deliverance, he denounced the shortcomings of his environment, where that divine rule was not the case. He gathered a group of followers or disciples whom he taught, by provocative words and actions, to catch the vision and let it govern their lives. He ended his life a victim of the world as it was, and, even in the days of perestroika, still remains, a world where justice is not always done, compassion not always shown, and the two more seldom still held in any semblance of equilibrium. He had spoken powerfully about his vision of things and probably understood himself to be authorized to do so by the one who had made promises to Israel. Bold proclamation and provocative action led to his death. Jesus died as a political criminal, executed for sedition by the Roman authorities governing Palestine.

So much, for now, for the historical Jesus, a selective, distorted and tendentious reading of the evidence, but such is the nature of telling historical tales.

4.3 *Theological Problems*: Historical examination of the New Testament record about Jesus, motivated either by "pure" historical considerations, or more often, by the theological concern to find an adequate historical ground for faith and theology, has uncovered a major point of discontinuity in the development of the Christian movement. It is not immediately clear how to construe the identity between the somewhat visionary wit and activist of Galilee and the exalted Christ of Peter's speeches in Acts or the eternal Word of God in the Fourth Gospel.

4.4 *Solutions*: The range of solutions to the problem parallels the attempts to deal with the diversity of confessional affirmations in the earliest Christian communities. For some theological interpreters of the biblical text, there is continuous development from the one who proclaims the inbreaking reign of God and those who proclaim him as God's agent. This position will usually involve a claim that there is at least an implicit Christology in the teaching or action of Jesus. Although he may not have styled himself the "anointed one", the authoritative way he spoke, prayed (calling

God "Abba"), and acted indicates a claim to a special role in God's plans, at least in God's plans for Israel.[11] For other scholars, the surface diversity between the two historical phases is held together by an identity of function between the two forms of proclamation. Such scholars would be less interested in establishing what might have been the claims or assumptions of Jesus about himself. They would argue that the summons to recognize God's present and future rule is a call to adopt certain values, commitments, and programs of action. They would argue that the call to recognize Jesus as the Christ, with whatever explicit content that predicate involves, is an analogous summons.[12]

4.5 *Calling Christ Jesus*: Both those who opt for development between the Jesus of history and the Christ of faith and those who opt for identity or similarity of function between proclamation of the kingdom of God and of the messianic status of Jesus can make a useful case for bridging the gap between the Jesus of history and the Christ of the believing community. We could build a case one way or another, but for the moment I want to reflect on the way in which the collection of writings known as the New Testament engages the issue. (In doing so I suppose that I am exemplifying a bit of "canonical criticism.") For, however skeptical we may be of the precise historical reliability of various accounts about Jesus and however limited we may find the basis for christological affirmations in the explicit teachings of Jesus himself, we cannot fail to recognize the overall thrust of the spectrum of canonical witnesses. The New Testament says rather little about the significance of the predicate "Christ." It says a great deal in story form about the activities and teachings of Jesus. We might, in fact, say that the investigation of New Testament Christology is mistaken if it focuses too heavily on the models that inform the term "Christ." In the New Testament's claim that Jesus is the Christ, Jesus is as much the logical predicate as the subject. "Christ" is but a cypher that derives whatever meaning it has for the Christian community of faith because of the Jesus to whom it is applied, Jesus as remembered and revered in that community of faith.

Our exploration of the second historical line of inquiry into the New Testament, the quest for the historical Jesus, has led to an interesting result. The phrase "to call Jesus Christ" could be construed as having yet another meaning, to summon up the image of Jesus in order to give meaning to the confession that he is the Christ. In simpler words, to engage in theological reflection on the significance of early Christian claims about Jesus is, as I have done a few moments ago, to tell his story, tendentiously no doubt, but consciously so.

The very fact that the New Testament spends so much energy telling the story of Jesus has of late been taken as an important datum for christological reflection. That leads us to my next exploratory probe.

5. Calling Jesus Christ: A Narrative Model

Thus far we have been reflecting on two sets of issues that have engaged New Testament scholars. The issues are posed by literary data, but are primarily historical. What is one to make of the diverse models deployed by the early Christian community for describing the significance of Jesus and what is one to make of the obvious differences between what Jesus was about in his public activity and what his followers claimed about him?

As I indicated in my introductory comments, New Testament scholars these days tend to be as much interested in strictly literary as in historical questions. Some take their literary methods to a formalist extreme to which I do not subscribe, but all have become aware of questions and issues that were long ignored or slighted by exegetes. As a third example of a contemporary biblical scholar's exploration of the New Testament's claims about Jesus as the Christ, let us take a particular Christology that happens to be developed through narrative.[13]

5.1 *The Christology of the Fourth Gospel*: The voice of the narrator and implied author[14] of the Fourth Gospel as we now have it, a composition of the late first or early second century, explicitly claims that the text was written in order to enable the reader to know that Jesus is the Christ (20:31). This sounds like a missionary claim and, largely on the basis of this verse, many interpreters have argued that the text is a proselytizing document, designed to convert Jews or perhaps Gentiles. Others have noted problems with this construal. The hostility to Jews (8:44) and the opacity to gentiles of the imagery in John militate against the hypothesis of simple propaganda. Two interpretations of the verse result. For more traditional, diachronically oriented critics, it is a remnant of a source document that was a simple proselytizing text.[15] For others, who may not deny the source hypothesis, the verse is of a piece with the irony that forms so much a part of the narrative.[16] The author toys with the reader here as elsewhere. For the implied reader is one who already knows that Jesus is the Christ. She is included in the "we" who have seen the glory of the incarnate one (1:14) and who have received amazing grace from him (1:16). She should know already that Jesus is the Christ, but perhaps does not understand that claim in the way that the author of the text would prefer. Perhaps, that is, the reader is like so many of the interlocutors of Jesus within the story, grasping a truth at some inadequate, partial, or inchoate level. The sensitive reader of the Gospel might be led to ask what is the deeper level of understanding at which the text aims.

We could pursue various strategies for examining this question. The simplest way would perhaps be to trace the explicit Messianic motif. Within the narrative of the Fourth Gospel, Jesus never simply calls himself the Christ. He is identified as such early on, by Simon (1:41, "the Messiah, which is interpreted, the Christ") on the basis of the testimony of John the baptizer (1:30, 36) and Jesus' summons (1:39). The Samaritan woman questioningly believes him to be the Christ (4:29, 41). Jerusalem crowds suspect it (7:26), but have reasons to doubt (7:27, 41; 10:24; 12:34). In connection with the case of the man born blind, the narrator informs us that "the Jews" had agreed to excommunicate any who confessed Jesus to be the Christ. Martha firmly believes it and calls Jesus "Christ" in no uncertain terms: "I have come to believe that you are the Christ, the son of God, who has come into the world" (11:27).

Jesus does use the title Christ of himself at least once, in the context of the Johannine version of the Lord's prayer. In the midst of the petition that the Father glorify the Son through his action of bringing life to the world, Jesus affirms at 17:3, "This is eternal life, that they may know you, the one true God, and the one whom you have sent, Jesus Christ." There is a point of similarity between this self-affirmation of the Johannine Jesus and the solemn declaration of 11:27. The term "Christ" is really a subsidiary element in the confession. Another phrase "the one who has come into the world" or "the one whom you have sent" achieves more prominence, and in a diachronic view might be regarded as a Johannine redactional addition to a more primitive confessional formula. Be that as it may, the affirmations that Jesus is the Christ point beyond themselves to some other aspect of the figure being identified with the title.

A similar point could be made on the basis of the narrative structure of episodes where Jesus is identified as the Christ. A clear example is the case of Peter's confession, which takes place not late in Jesus' ministry, but at the very beginning (1:41). Peter's recognition of Jesus as the Messiah is one of several recognitions and confessions that the first disciples make. Jesus climactically responds to all of them in 1:50–51 with the affirmation: "You will see greater things than these. . . .Amen, amen, I say to you, you will see heaven opened and the angels ascending and descending on the Son of Man."[17] The hint of irony in the programmatic statement of 20:41 is confirmed in the structure of this pericope. To call Jesus "Christ," as Peter had done, on the basis of Jesus' preternatural knowledge, is not the most that can and should be said about him. It is more important for the Fourth Gospel to see him as the Son of Man who has come from and returned to heaven.

The importance for the Fourth Gospel of imagery associated with the Son of Man or the Man from Heaven, has long been recognized. There may well be social functions for the Johannine community that this imagery serves, functions explored in a well-known article by Professor Meeks, one of our colleagues at this conference.[18] Those functions do not interest me at the moment. There are also interesting ways that the Son of Man imagery relates to the epithet deployed of and by Jesus in the Synoptic Gospels. John probably knows those usages and is involved in subtle reinterpretations of them. Time precludes consideration of the mechanics of those interpretations. I rather want to explore the internal associations forged by the narrative in its spiral play on identifications of Jesus.

Recognition of Jesus as the Son of Man involves for the Fourth Gospel an insistence on the various elements of the image of Jacob's ladder utilized in 1:51. Through the Son of Man a way to God is opened: there is movement from God and to God. The movement from God was hinted at in the two explicit christological confessions at 11:27 and 17:3 that we have already noted. The claim that Jesus is from God is the basic warrant for accepting whatever other claims he makes in the Fourth Gospel. In the first half of the text he constantly reiterates that claim in one way or another. Warrants for that basic claim are explored, particularly in chapter 5, but the works that Jesus does (5:36) and the testimony of the prophets (5:39), the sorts of things that the Synoptic Gospels emphasized, don't seem to convince anyone. The claim to have come from the Father is finally grounded in the "glory" that Jesus receives from the Father (5:41). Although the Gospel hints that glory is visible in the life of Jesus (2:11), it insists that his true glorification takes place in the hour of his passion (12:23; 13:31) when he returns to the Father.

The structure of the Gospel's Christology is encapsulated in the Son of Man saying at 3:14–15: "As Moses lifted up the serpent in the desert, so it is necessary for the Son of Man to be lifted up, so that everyone who believes in him might have eternal life." The return of the Son of Man to the "glory" that he had before the world was (17:5) is the second part of the movement hinted at in the image of Jacob's ladder at 1:51. In what this "glorification" consists and how it is perceived (1:14) is at the heart of the Fourth Gospel's christological claim.

The Fourth Gospel revels in irony and does so because of the outrageous claim that so many early followers of Jesus made, that the Christ had died on a cross. Like Paul before him in the hymn from Philippians and elsewhere (e.g., 1 Cor 1:23; 2:2), but even more forcefully, the fourth evangelist insists on the centrality of the cross. Christ's lifting up in shame, degradation, and pain is the moment of his greatest glory, his return to the eternal glory of the Father, by which he draws all to himself.

Irony and paradox offer antinomies that call for reconciliation. The Fourth Gospel offers some relief to the bedazzled reader, but it is the relief of evocative poetry, not philosophy. The last supper discourses of John 13–17 are in effect the evangelist's comment on the significance of the moment of glorification of Jesus. Their comment on the paradox of glory in shame and suffering is made through yet another paradox, that of presence in absence. In these discourses Jesus tells his disciples of his imminent departure and promises that he will abide with them (14:3). It is in fact only by his departure that he can abide with them (16:7). The opposition between absence and presence is mediated on one level by the mysterious figure of the "paraclete." On a somewhat less mysterious level it is mediated by Jesus' command to love. Abiding, like branches in a vine, takes place through love (15:9–10) and through obedience to the example of Jesus in giving himself for his friends (15:13).

Insofar as John resolves his paradoxes it is by interpreting the death of Jesus as an act of love, embodying the principle of love that has been with God from the beginning, the principle, that is, in the words of the Johannine epistolographer (I Jn 4:8), Godsself. For John to call Jesus "Christ" is finally to respond appropriately to this revelation of the glory of God, and to live a life devoted to love as defined by the life of Jesus.

6. Calling Jesus Christ: A Rhetorical Model

Another literary approach to New Testament texts that has found some favor of late is to give attention to their rhetorical dimensions. Since I have spilled considerable ink elsewhere over one of the more sophisticated rhetorical products of the New Testament, i.e., the Epistle to the Hebrews,[19] I shall keep my final exploratory probe quite brief. Nonetheless, Hebrews will serve as a useful focus to conclude our reflections.

6.1 *The Christological Models of Hebrews*: One reason for exploring Hebrews, however briefly, is the fact that it deploys in its first chapter two of the alternative christological models that we spoke of in the first section of this paper. We have already noted the preexistence Christology of the exordium. The following verses, like the conclusion to the hymn to Christ in Philippians 2, focus instead on Christ's exaltation. Although the first chapter might leave the impression that the preexistence Christology of the exordium dominates the author's thought, most of the remainder of the text concentrates on the moment of exaltation as decisive. Hence, a traditional crux for interpreters has been to determine when, if ever, the "Son" is first named, at or before the moment of creation (1:3) or at the exaltation (5:5).

The author probably had some way of reconciling the alternative perspectives of his tradition. I have argued that he maintained an incarnational Christology, and understood the exaltation to be the installation of the incarnate one to a new function, that of heavenly high priest. Yet what is surely remarkable for those of us with neatly categorizing minds is how ambiguous the author's handling of christological predicates is. Whatever the text is about, it is not in the business of explicitly reconciling the tensions between christological schemes.

Instead, the author uses the image of Jesus as priestly messiah (2:17; 5:5–6; 9:11) in the "heavenly sanctuary" (8:3–6; 9:11–14) to undergird his pastoral program of renewing and deepening the commitment of his congregation. The practical goal is abundantly clear from the exhortations of the last several chapters (10:19–13:25). What requires some further explanation is the way in which the christological portrait plays its role. The author operates within the genre of Hellenistic Jewish homiletics and argues exegetically, exploring scriptural texts and images in strikingly playful ways, which all have a serious point. Two passages at the heart of the complex central exposition illustrate his procedures. One (9:15–17) involves an untranslatable play on the term *diatheke*, which can mean either testament or covenant. Christ's death has significance for his followers because it is the necessary precondition for leaving his testament to them. This testament is no ordinary one, however. It is, in fact, the covenant which was promised by Jeremiah in the text that forms the basis for this portion of the homily (Jer 31:31–34, cited in Heb 8:8–12). Covenants, as the author suggests on rather artificial grounds, require sprinkling of blood (9:19–23). Christ's death is the sacrifice of the priestly messiah that provides the shedding of blood for the new covenant.

The connections established here between Jesus and the text of Jeremiah constitute, to say the least, an exegetical *tour de force*. What follows is equally dazzling. The author pushes to its logical extreme the image of Jesus as heavenly priest. He brings his blood into the supernal sanctuary to effect atonement and "cleanse heavenly realities" as does the earthly high priest on Yom Kippur

(9:23–25). If some in the audience had been tempted to take all this imagery literally when the author began the exposition, even they might be hard pressed to follow him at this point. The audience, however, was probably familiar with the metaphorical pyrotechnics of authors like Philo and might suspect that the homilist has something in mind other than a ghostly supernal altar. In fact, the Platonic language that he uses to describe the heavenly sanctuary (9:24) prepares the way for the final exegetical moves of chapter 10, where it becomes clear that the sacrifice of Christ which has lasting effects and leaves behind a new covenant is indeed his death, the one time offering of his body (10:10), an offering which was indeed "spiritual" and "within the heavenly veil" because it was a fully human act of conformity to God's will (10:5–9).

For Hebrews to call Jesus the Christ is to identify him as the priestly messiah foreshadowed by the figure of Melchizedek and the Aaronid high priests. To give him that title with that meaning is to acknowledge him as the paradigm of fidelity to God, the inaugurator and perfecter of faith (12:2). To make that acknowledgment is to commit oneself to follow in the way (10:19) that he has inaugurated. That way to what is true and real is the covenant of faith, hope, and love (10:22–25). Within that covenant, by the way, one calls upon Jesus as the Christ, the same yesterday, today, and forever (13:8).

6.2 *Christology and Rhetoric*: Our last probe into New Testament Christology has been an attempt to illustrate one form of New Testament criticism relevant to our overall theme. Attention to a text's rhetoric, in this case the exegetical rhetoric of an elaborate early Christian homily, shows what some early followers of Jesus were doing as they called him Christ in the various senses of that term. It also provides, I would suggest, a useful model of a constructive Christology. Hebrews is content to use traditional images, but it recognizes them for the metaphors they are. It plays with them and teases them out, always with a view to their application in the ongoing life of the faithful. This is not philosophical or even systematic theology as they might be practiced today, but what Hebrews does is theology in a significant sense. Such theology, the reinterpretation and application of traditional categories, is, moreover, the stuff with which we New Testament critics, whether we be historians, literary critics, theologians, or some combination of the above, have to deal. If we are theologically committed New Testament critics, it is also the kind of theology that we normally do.

7. Conclusion

What I have tried to do in this essay is to explore with you four issues of New Testament criticism, illustrating different methods that have been and continue to be deployed by New Testament critics. I have attempted to illustrate some of the range of problems with which New Testament critics have to deal in encountering the diverse body of literature that the Church chose to recognize as authoritative and to indicate some of the strategies that they find useful. This survey has no pretensions to be exhaustive, either of method or of content. I hope that it provides useful grist for the mills of this conference.

NOTES

I want to express my delight in having this opportunity to explore, across disciplinary boundaries, issues of common interest to biblical scholars and philosophical theologians (or philosophers of religion). Let me also offer a particular word of thanks to my old friend Eleonore Stump, one of the prime movers of this conference, for offering me this opportunity to meet so many members of the Notre Dame philosophy department. Perhaps one thing that I shall be able to clarify for myself is the nature of the differences between philosophical theology and the philosophy of religion on the one hand and philosophical theology and systematic theology on the other.

1. For some examples of the diverse approaches to Scripture as a norm, see David H. Kelsey, *The Uses of Scripture in Recent Theology* (Philadelphia: Fortress, 1975.)

2. For some recent examples of literary critical methods currently applied to New Testament texts, see Daniel Patte, *Paul's Faith and the Power of the Gospel: A Structural Introduction to the Pauline Letters* (Philadelphia: Fortress, 1983); idem, *Structural Exegesis for New Testament Critics*, Guides to Biblical Scholarship (Philadelphia: Fortress, 1989). Less formalist are Vernon K. Robbins, *Jesus the Teacher: A*

Socio-Rhetorical Interpretation of Mark (Philadelphia: Fortress, 1984); Norman R. Peterson, Rediscovering Paul: Philemon and the Sociology of Paul's Narrative World (Philadelphia: Fortress, 1985); idem, Literary Criticism for New Testament Critics, Guides to Biblical Scholarship (Philadelphia: Fortress, 1978): Robert Jewett, The Thessalonian Correspondence: Pauline Rhetoric and Millenarian Piety, Foundations and Facets (Philadelphia: Fortress, 1986); Burton Mack, Rhetoric and the New Testament, Guides to Biblical Scholarship (Philadelphia: Fortress, 1989). Literary theory has been particularly prominent in parable research. See most recently Bernard B. Scott, Hear Then the Parable: A Commentary on the Parables of Jesus (Philadelphia: Fortress, 1989), with extensive bibliographies, and John R. Donahue, The Gospel in Parable: Metaphor, Narrative and Theology in the Synoptic Gospels (Philadelphia: Fortress, 1988).

3. Studies abound of the development of New Testament Christology, with the focus on historical-critical exegesis. Two fairly recent works provide useful overviews and extensive bibliographies: James D. G. Dunn, Christology in the Making: A New Testament Inquiry into the Origins of the Doctrine of the Incarnation (Philadelphia: Westminster, 1980), and Marinus de Jonge, Christology in Context: The Earliest Christian Response to Jesus (Philadelphia: Westminster, 1988).

4. For a detailed treatment of the hymn, see Ralph P. Martin, Philippians 2:5–11 in Recent Interpretation and in the Setting of Early Christian Worship, Society of New Testament Studies Monograph Service 4 (Cambridge: Cambridge University Press, 1967), rev. ed. (Grand Rapids: Eerdmans, 1983).

5. For a treatment of the theme and further literature, see Dunn, Christology, 98–125.

6. For various attempts to wrestle with the theological problem of early Christian diversity, see James D. G. Dunn, Unity and Diversity in the New Testament: An Inquiry into the Character of Earliest Christianity (Philadelphia: Westminster, 1977); Helmut Koester, "The Theological Aspects of Primitive Christian Heresy," in The Future of Our Religious Past: Essays in Honor of Rudolf Bultmann, ed. James M. Robinson (London: SCM, 1971), 65–83; Reginald H. Fuller and Pheme Perkins, Who Is the Christ? (Philadelphia: Fortress, 1983); and Raymond E. Brown, "Christology" in The New Jerome Bible Commentary (Englewood Cliffs, N.J.: Prentice Hall, 1990), 1354–1359.

7. The opposition is enshrined in several famous titles: David Friedrich Strauss, The Christ of Faith and the Jesus of History: A Critique of Schleiermacher's the Life of Jesus, trans. and ed. Leander E. Keck (Philadelphia: Fortress, 1977); Martin Kähler, The So-called Historical

Jesus and the Historical Biblical Christ, trans. and ed. Carl E. Braaten (Philadelphia: Fortress, 1964).

8. For the magician, see Morton Smith, *Jesus the Magician* (San Francisco: Harper & Row, 1978); the charismatic, Geza Vermes, *Jesus the Jew* (London: Macmillan, 1973; New York: Macmillan, 1974; Philadelphia: Fortress, 1981); the rabbi, Bruce Chilton, *The Kingdom of God in the Teaching of Jesus* (London: SPCK; Philadelphia: Fortress, 1984) and idem, *A Galilean Rabbi and His Bible: Jesus' Use of the Interpreted Scripture of His Time*, Good News Studies 8 (Wilmington, Del. and London: Glazier and SPCK, 1984); the reformer, Ricard A. Horsley, *Jesus and the Spiral of Violence: Popular Jewish Resistance in Roman Palestine* (San Francisco: Harper & Row, 1987); the Cynic wit, Burton Mack, *A Myth of Innocence: Mark and Christian Origins* (Philadephia: Fortress, 1988).

9. Albert Schweitzer, *The Quest of the Historical Jesus: A Critical Study of Its Progress from Reimarus to Wrede*, the English translation of *Von Reimarus zu Wrede* (1906) (New York: Macmillan, 1968).

10. Cf., e.g., Matthew 11:27; Luke 10:22.

11. For emphasis on the importance of the prayer life of Jesus, see Joachim Jeremias, *New Testament Theology*, vol. 1: *The Proclamation of Jesus*, the English translation of *Neutestamentliche Theologie*, vol. 1: *Die Verkündigung Jesu* (New York: Scribner's, 1971). This emphasis is developed in E. Schilebeeckx, *Jesus: An Experiment in Christology* (New York: Collins, 1979).

12. This approach is exemplified in one form in the classic liberal Protestant work of Rudolf Bultmann, *Theology of the New Testament*, 2 vols., trans. Kendrick Grobel (New York: Scribner's, 1951–55).

13. For a constructive attempt to build a narrative Christology, see Robert A. Krieg, C.S.C., *Story-Shaped Christology: The Role of Narratives in Identifying Jesus Christ* (New York: Paulist, 1988).

14. For the literary-critical categories used here, see R. Alan Culpepper, *The Anatomy of the Fourth Gospel* (Philadelphia: Fortress, 1983), or more recently, Jeffrey Lloyd Staley, *The Print's First Kiss: A Rhetorical Investigation of the Implied Reader in the Fourth Gospel*, Society of Biblical Literature Dissertation Service 82 (Atlanta: Scholars, 1988). A more structuralist critical strategy is adopted by Hendrikus Boers, *Neither on This Mountain Nor in Jerusalem: A Study of John 4*, Society of Biblical Literature Monograph Series 35 (Atlanta: Scholars, 1988).

15. Source criticism of the text is still an important pursuit, see Robert T. Fortna, *The Fourth Gospel and Its Predecessor: From Narrative Source to Present Gospel* (Philadelphia: Fortress, 1988).

16. Several recent works have explored the function of the Gospel's ironic mode. See, e.g., Paul D. Duke, *Irony in the Fourth Gospel* (Atlanta: John Knox, 1985), and Gail R. O'Day, *Revelation in the Fourth Gospel: Narrative Mode and Theological Claim* (Philadephia: Fortress, 1986).

17. The complex Son of Man question, i.e., whether and how Jesus used the term, may be left aside for this discussion. John knows of something like the Synoptic tradition and reinterprets it for his own ends. On this point see Francis J. Moloney, *The Johannine Son of Man* (Rome: Ateneo Salesiano, 1976).

18. Wayne Meeks, "The Man from Heaven in Johannine Sectarianism," *Journal of Biblical Literature* 91 (1972): 44–72.

19. Harold W. Attridge, *The Epistle to the Hebrews*, Hermeneia Commentaries (Philadelphia: Fortress, 1989).

Interpreting the New Testament: Comments on the Paper of Harold W. Attridge

Richard Swinburne

In the course of asking "what the followers of Jesus made of him in the first half-century or so after his death" (p. 204), Harold Attridge has described four different Christologies which we find in the New Testament. Two of them are moderately well developed and peculiar to their own books—St. John's Gospel and the Epistle to the Hebrews—and two of them vaguer but more pervasive. They illustrate two substantive claims which he made at the beginning of the paper: "That there is an undeniable diversity within the New Testament on issues central to it, and . . . that early Christian documents are obviously and profoundly conditioned by their environment" (p. 201). I do not wish to deny these claims so long as "diversity" is not read as "incompatible diversity"; much of the diverse things said and presupposed about Jesus are quite compatible with each other. Whether or not there remains a number of incompatible things depends on the sense in which you read the texts; and I'll come to that issue in due course. Diversity of approach to a historical phenomenon by different writers who respond to it and conditioning by environment are however all part of our semi-rational human condition. While not wishing to disagree with very much of what Attridge has explicitly said, I do find implicit in the paper a feeling that the New Testament is too uncertain a source of reliable information to form the basis of a religion. Whether or not I am right in attributing it to Attridge—I believe that feeling to be mistaken, and to derive from three fundamental mistakes which many biblical scholars, conservative as well as liberal, have tended to make over the last two hundred years.

The first mistake is to suppose that it is a mark of rationality to approach biblical texts without any assumptions about whether or not there is a God and whether or not he is likely to intervene in human history. On the contrary, it is a mark of rationality to approach evidence about some particular historical event armed by what else you know about the world. If a scientific theory, well established on other grounds, leads you to expect that stars will sometimes explode, then some debris in the sky of a kind which could have been caused by an exploding star but which (though improbably) just might have some other cause, may nevertheless be reasonably interpreted as debris left by an exploding star. But if a theory well established on other grounds says that stars can't explode, you'll need very strong evidence indeed that the debris could not have had another cause before interpreting them as debris of an exploding star. Similarly we must approach texts which claim that God intervened in human history having considered whether wider evidence (from the fact and nature of the world as a whole) makes it likely that there is a God and whether it is likely that the kind of God whose existence that evidence best supports is at all likely to intervene in human history. I have argued elsewhere[1] that that wider evidence does make it quite likely that there is a God, who is among other things perfectly good. I suggest also that a perfectly good God, surveying the human race, would see that we badly need two things—atonement and revelation.

For reasons of space I cannot argue for either of these latter claims here—I have argued for our need of atonement at some length elsewhere[2]—but my present point does not depend on them. That point is that there are arguments for my view and for rival views about whether there is a God and what he may be expected to do. We need to form an opinion about how likely the different views are and come to biblical books armed with that opinion. If we know that a certain sort of event which they describe is quite likely to happen, we will ask for a lot less in the way of detailed historical evidence in favor of the claim that it did happen than we would otherwise ask. If from our reflection on the nature of God we see that it is quite likely that he would reveal things to humans and show that he had done so by violating the laws of nature in such a way as symbolically to bless and make flourish that teaching, then we will need fewer and less obviously trustworthy witnesses of such a purported violation, e.g., the Resurrection of Christ, if we are rationally to believe that it has occurred. And the reverse, of course, if our wider reflection suggests to us that there is no God or no God at all likely to do that sort of thing.

The second mistake of biblical scholars is to fail to distinguish two quite separate roles for biblical books—their role in providing historical evidence that a revelation from God has occurred through Christ and their role as part of the content of that revelation. The first role of the biblical books is, in the light of our overall worldview justified by wider considerations, to provide historical evidence about what was done and said in Palestine in the first century A.D. I share Dr. Attridge's view that, so treated, they provide a pretty blurred picture, but I believe that he has failed to draw our attention to all the features of that picture.

"Acts speak louder than words." The words of Jesus were not recorded by a stenographer, let alone on tape, and historians dependent on the memories of others about what he said at least forty years before are likely, with the best will in the world, to read back into history some of their views about what he ought to have said. But deeds are better remembered, and even if the historian is biased, his bias is more likely to give rise to biased commentary on what was done rather than a total misreporting of it.

I comment very briefly on the significance of three groups of acts of Jesus which, as I see them, seem to me to have enormous importance. The first group centers on the appointment by Jesus of twelve apostles. That there were twelve chief followers is known to many New Testament writings, though those which have lists differ slightly on who the twelve were. The old Israel deriving from Abraham had (in the common belief of first-century Jews) twelve tribes deriving from twelve tribe-founding individuals. A Jewish prophet who founded a community based on twelve leaders could only be read as claiming to found a new Israel, a church. Further, the Gospels report or acknowledge the institution by Jesus of a ceremony in which he and the original twelve were the first participants, the Eucharist. Early Christian communities were all characterized by the celebration of the Eucharist. These two acts make clearer than words could an intention to found a church deriving from the twelve and characterized by a special ceremony.

The second group of acts are those centered on the 'passion', the story of Jesus' betrayal, arrest, trial, and crucifixion which all the Gospels record in considerable and very similar detail. Jesus allowed himself to be put to death for proclaiming a true message as the victim of an unjust judicial process, rather than use force to prevent this. Hence a life of great goodness. Central to the eucharistic ceremony which Jesus instituted at that time was the interpretation of the bread as his 'body', the wine as his 'blood', implying that the Eucharist was constituted to commemorate a sacrificial death, which of course occurred only after that institution; and our reception of the elements to be the reception of the benefits of that sacrifice.

And thirdly, of course, the Resurrection. The witness of the apostles to the empty tomb and the resurrection appearances, as recorded in the Gospels, is clearly a claim to have seen and touched certain things—an empty tomb and a risen Lord. And, to my mind, equally clearly the body had disappeared—for the reasons given by Stephen Davis in his paper in this volume.

If the events of the first Easter occurred in anything like the form recorded in the Gospels,[3] there is a clear case of a violation of a natural law. As a violation of natural law, it would, since God alone can violate the laws which he keeps operative, be plausibly explained by the action of God intervening in human history. The community for whom this event occurred must, given their own conventions of understanding—and all acts and words must be interpreted in the light of the conventions for understanding them current in the community in which they are performed— put at least this interpretation upon it: bringing to life a prophet crucified for saying certain things is par excellence vindicating that message, declaring it to be true.

The historical evidence (if we ignore the crucial route of argument, to which I am about to draw attention) may be a bit shaky as to what Jesus said when, and what the early community said; but it is a great deal less shaky on what he did. And, I suggest, interpreted in the light of reasonable prior beliefs, it indicates that he taught a message, died on the cross for it (and by that death intended to make available for us an atoning sacrifice) and was brought to life again by God. God thereby signified that the message was true. If God through Christ proclaimed an important message, so important that he gave that unique signature of the Resurrection to its truth, he must have made provision for its continued proclamation—and since he founded a church to carry on his work, it must be the authorized proclaimer of that message. Messages can get misremembered or misunderstood or blown away in the wind unless they are entrusted to a body who can in the end be relied on to proclaim them aright. If Christ founded a church, he taught what it said he taught. I say that without judging between the many different views ranging from a conservative Roman Catholicism to a conservative Protestantism about just how and when the Church has given us authorized teaching about Christ's message; but one thing that all Christians for a millennium and a half have agreed is that the Church has taught that the New Testament is a faithful guide to what Christ said; and that the Old Testament is true—if taken in the way and with the limits that Christ or his Church as his expositor declare. The first role of the New Testament as historical evidence leads it via the Church to authorize its second role as the content of revelation. We trust it because, by normal historical criteria, a part of it shows that a community is reliable and that community says that the rest of it is reliable (at any rate, when interpreted in the way the Church says it is to be taken).

Biblical critics have wrongly supposed that only exact detailed historical work on the texts would reveal Jesus' message. We do indeed need historical work—for Christianity is a historical religion—but only to legitimize a broad framework. If historical work, in the light of an overall worldview justified by wider considerations, cannot do that, then there is no authority to the scriptural text. But if it can do that, the text gains its own authority without the need for detailed proof with respect to each passage.

And the third mistake of the modern biblical critic is to suppose that there is one "plain meaning or literal sense of the biblical text" (to quote Attridge's giveaway phrases, see p. 203). But what a sentence means depends on the paragraph in which it is set. And what a paragraph means depends on the book in which it is set. And what the book means depends on the volume in which it is set. And what the volume means depends on who issues it with what explanations, when, for whom, with what conventions of genre for interpreting it. For that context determines what is the reference of the referring expressions and also which sentences, paragraphs, and books are to be taken literally and which metaphorically, and among ambiguous sentences which meaning is to be preferred, since it is that one which is consonant with other parts of the volume or other known beliefs of its author.

What the sentence "Larry is an elephant" means depends on the kind of literary work in which it occurs. If it occurs in a guidebook to "London Zoo," it is clearly to be taken literally as a statement describing the zoological genus of one of the inhabitants of the zoo. Which zoo this concerns will depend on who published the book and which town was understood in that context by "London"—London, England or London, Ontario. If that sentence occurs in a children's story, although to be taken literally it is not to be taken as having a truth-value on its own with respect to how things are in the actual world. The story of which it is part may nevertheless be making an important moral or other claim with a truth-value about the nature of the actual world—consider Orwell's *Animal Farm,* which made by means of such sentences powerful claims about the history and nature of the Soviet Union. Or if the sentence occurs in the course of a poem or article about someone called "Larry," known by all the readers to be human, it can only be read metaphorically, e.g., as saying that he is clumsy, and so read, it will be true or false. The obvious falsity or inappropriateness to conversation or narrative of some sentence understood literally forces upon it a metaphorical interpretation; which metaphorical interpretation will depend on which of the things commonly believed about the properties attributed to the subjects of conversation would be most appropriate to say in that context. If elephants are believed to be long-lived with long memories, strong, kind, and bulky, and Larry has (it is believed) some of these properties or behaved in some of these ways, then what is being said is that he has some of these properties or behaved in just those ways.

Now the Bible is a patchwork. It was formed of small units (each written or uttered in one original context), put together into larger units (at later times in different contexts) and finally put together (at yet later times in different contexts) into a Bible. So what a given sentence will mean depends on whether we consider it as part of its original unit, its biblical book, or the Bible as a whole. In each case it has a different author—the original utterer for the unit, the compiler for the biblical book—and the latter issues it in a different context, often in a work of a quite different genre from the original unit. Thus Psalm 21 was probably used as a hymn in a New Year festival for the enthronement of the king in the first Temple; by "the king" it will therefore refer to whichever king is currently being enthroned. But the book of Psalms was put together for synagogue use when there were no longer kings of Judah. So neither the compiler of the book nor those who used Psalm 21 in the synagogue will have understood "the king" in that way (although some of them may well have known what was the original context); and it is their use which determines its new meaning. And presumably, in view of their expectations of a new king, a Messiah, "the King" when part of a psalm belonging to the Book of Psalms is to be taken as referring to him. So too a sentence of some story in the New Testament may have had one meaning in its original context but another when forming part of St. Luke's Gospel.

But the biblical books were finally put together into a Bible, and it was that which the Church proclaimed as the content of revelation, true and inspired by God. Now maybe the Bible is not inspired by God. Whether it is reasonable to believe that it is partly a matter of my two earlier considerations (my two earlier positive points against the mistakes of many biblical critics)—the probability on other grounds of a revelation, and the historical evidence of a miracle apparently vindicating one—and also a matter of whether the Bible, interpreted as such a revelation, is at all likely in those areas where we have any independent check on it to be true. But in order to consider the latter, we must consider the Bible in the terms in which the Church proclaimed it. We must consider its sentences as having the meaning they would have if issued by God (with his beliefs, i.e., knowledge, of how things are) for the Church of many centuries, a meaning consonant with all the other sentences in the Bible, and above all consonant with the Church's central doctrines, proclaimed in creeds, which were recognized as containing the content of revelation in a much clearer and more precise form. (By my previous argument these doctrines must be true if God raised Jesus from the dead.) A sentence with its earlier meaning may provide valuable historical evidence, but it is the sentence with its whole-bible-context meaning which the Church claims to be part of the content of revelation, and so is authoritative for Christians. So, since it is an invariable rule for interpreting a text that, if at all possible, you interpret it so that various passages within it are consistent with each other and with the beliefs of its author, any doubts about what is the meaning of a passage of the whole Bible are to be settled by looking at God's beliefs (i.e., knowledge) insofar as we can discover them. Since God has true beliefs on all matters, any knowledge of the world—e.g., of science and history—is relevant in helping us sort out the meaning of scriptural texts. If you know that Genesis 1 is not literally true, then God does too; and so if he inspired it, as a message for the Church of many centuries, some of whom have also come to know this, God did not intend it to be taken as literally true. Both Origen and Augustine (among others of the Fathers and Scholastics) believed that they had good scientific reason for supposing that Genesis 1 was not literally true, and so they interpreted it metaphorically. Also the Church's central message about Jesus and his teaching constrains the way in which particular biblical passages are to be interpreted—e.g., it forces us to interpret certain vengeful passages of the Old Testament metaphorically—in view of the centrality in the Church's exposition of the teaching of Jesus of his Sermon on the Mount.

So, returning to Attridge's four Christologies, I don't see them basically as inconsistent, just different. Yet there are biblical passages which, if interpreted as passages on their own written by some unknown or even known first-century writer, would on the most natural reading be inconsistent with other passages. But the meaning which is authoritative for Christians is not that meaning (even if it was that writer's original intended meaning), but the meaning in the context of an authorized Christian document. And so, while saying "designated Son of God through a mighty act" *might* be most naturally interpreted as asserting that Jesus was made Son of God by the Resurrection, that is certainly not the most natural meaning to ascribe to the passage as a passage of a book recognized as expounding its doctrine by the Church which finally gave it canonical status in the fourth century A.D. The passage in that context must mean that Jesus was publicly proclaimed as Son of God by the Resurrection, proclaimed as being what he had been from all eternity.

None of the points I have made are altogether new. The first was well emphasized by Paley,[4] the second by Newman,[5] and the last one was hammered out by many of the Christian Fathers who were strongly conscious, *at least* as strongly conscious as we are, both of the diversity of interpretations which can be given to many biblical passages and the obvious falsity of some passages if taken on their own and read literally. Irenaeus, for example, stressed the importance of the Church's doctrinal tradition as a constraint on interpretation: "Every word [of Scripture] shall seem consistent [to someone] if he for his part diligently read the Scriptures in company with those who are presbyters in the church, among whom is the apostolic doctrine."[6] Augustine wrote: "We must show the way to find out whether a phrase is literal or figurative. And the way is certainly as follows: whatever there is in the word of God that cannot, when taken literally, be referred either to purity of life or soundness of doctrine, you must set down as figurative." And so many other writers said similar kinds of thing in the course of the centuries from the first to the sixteenth, or even eighteenth.[7] But the detailed historical work of the last two centuries on the original meaning of the small units which came eventually to be put together into the Bible, combined with the view of later (not classical) Protestantism that the Bible was to be interpreted solely on its own terms—i.e., independently of Christian creeds or scientific and historical knowledge—led many in the Anglo-American world of the nineteenth and twentieth centuries to think that the meaning of the Bible was the meaning of its original units, which could somehow themselves be interpreted independently even of the context of their original utterance. But no text can be interpreted naked, without a context; and if you interpret the Christian Bible in the way in which the Christian Church proclaimed it, it comes out with the kind of meaning which I have analyzed. In their careful work on the New Testament, for which we all remain very grateful—especially for its relevance to supporting (or overthrowing) the broad Christian framework—

biblical critics must not forget the important lessons about evidence and meaning which have been learnt in the many centuries between the first and the twentieth.[8]

NOTES

1. Richard Swinburne, *The Existence of God* (Oxford: Clarendon Press, 1979.)

2. Richard Swinburne, *Responsibility and Atonement* (Oxford: Clarendon Press, 1989).

3. Of course the Gospel writers, like the subsequent Church, regarded the Resurrection as something vastly more mysterious and of vastly greater significance than "the resuscitation of corpse"—to use a phrase coined by those who seek to reject the normal view of the Resurrection, to characterize that view—but it has also normally regarded that Resurrection as involving "resuscitation" as a minimal mundane historical element. And by speaking of the Resurrection occurring "as reported" it is to the mundane elements of the Empty Tomb and the bodily appearances of the Risen Christ that I am referring.

4. William Paley, *A View of the Evidences of Christianity* (first published London: Faulder, 1794), Prefatory Considerations.

5. J. H. Newman, *An Essay on the Development of Christian Doctrine* (first published London: Toovey, 1845). I refer approvingly to Newman without committing myself to his view about exactly how the authority of the Church is manifested.

6. *Adversus Haereses* 4.32.1.

7. See, for example, Origen, *De Principiis* 4.3; and for the medieval period the influential *Didascalion* of Hugh of St. Victor, Books 5 and 6. The Augustine quotation is from *De doctrina Christiana* 3:10.14.

8. The points made in this paper, although set in the context of a reply to another paper at a conference, are developed by me at book-length in a book entitled *Revelation* (Oxford: Clarendon Press, 1992).

The Role of Miracles in
the Structure of Luke-Acts

Marilyn McCord Adams

1. Introduction

The topic of miracles is standard in courses on analytic philosophy of religion. Not surprisingly, we puzzle over *how the concept 'miracle' is to be analyzed*: whether as a violation of natural law (obstruction of a natural potency), or in terms of a humanly/religiously significant coincidence of events each of which has an ordinary explanation? In terms of an interference in nature by something beyond nature? or as a surprising but humanly/religiously significant event caused by God?[1] Such definitional questions take us into issues of *natural philosophy* about the nature of causality, whether causal laws can admit of exceptions (causal potencies, of obstruction), whether a causal nexus at the sub-lunary/phenomenal level must or can be underwritten by a first cause behind the scenes?[2] Likewise, we are vexed by *epistemological* questions, such as whether it could ever be reasonable to believe that a miracle had occurred? Whether the occurrence of miracle is epistemologically prior or posterior to the existence of God?[3]

For New Testament authors, the issues are different. On the whole, they take for granted that personal explanations are basic, and hence that psycho- or spiritual-physical causation is both possible and actual. They assume that the occurrence of humanly/religiously significant events, not only can in principle, but has in fact been recognized as the product of supernatural powers. Their epistemological questions concern rather the

235

nature, character, and policies of such supernatural agency (e.g., Lk 11:14–26). Because miracle-working is part of the ministry of Jesus, and hence "the work of Christ," answers to the latter questions disclose the writer's *Christology*. Because Jesus and his disciples are presented as instruments of divine redemption, the function of miracles in the plot is an issue in *soteriology* as well.

My purpose in this paper is to urge that we Christian philosophers widen the scope of our attention to miracles. To be sure, there has been method in our madness: the metaphysical and epistemological possibility of miracles are presuppositions, without which questions about the christological and soteriological implications of miracles cannot arise. Nevertheless, I would contend, the former issues are already well charted, our homework there more or less done. Those of us (which I suspect includes most of us) who are firmly committed to the miraculous resurrection of Jesus Christ and/or to belief in miracle-working activities on the part of Jesus and his disciples ought to spill as much ink saying why they are important as to how they are possible: i.e., to the questions of how miracles figure in the way God defeats the powers of darkness; of when, where, and what sort of rescue we can expect God to provide.[4]

To practice what I preach, I begin by going "back to the Bible," to explore what answers various New Testament writers gave regarding the place of miracles in Christology and soteriology. Luke-Acts seems a good place to start, not only because of its scope—the two-volumes cover both the ministry of Jesus and the earliest decades of the Church—but also because scholars argue that, of all New Testament books, it makes the most of miracles. For example, not only do nine of the fourteen New Testament couplings of 'signs' with 'wonders' occur in Acts;[5] Luke even inserts 'signs' into his quotation of Joel 2:28 ff. to create a proof text for this emphasis.[6] But the extent to which Luke-Acts reflects a heightened interest in miracles is a subject to which I shall return in section 5 below.

2. Achtemeier's Theses Extended

In his valuable article "The Lukan Perspective on the Miracles of Jesus: A Preliminary Sketch," Paul J. Achtemeier lifts out the following three theses as distinctive of Luke's treatment of miracles in the Gospel:[7]

(T1) As contrasted with the other synoptics, Luke "in several instances attempts to balance Jesus' miraculous activity and his teaching in such a way as to give them equal weight."[8]

For example, in Jesus' keynote sermon, Luke 4:18-22 refers to his activity as a proclaimer; 4:23-27, to his role as a miracle worker. The account of his first miracle represents both teaching (Lk 4:32) and miracle-working (Lk 4:36) among his authoritative acts. Again, people come to Jesus both to hear and to be healed of their diseases (Lk 5:17). And editorially, Luke rearranges blocks of material in order to bracket the Sermon on the Plain with accounts of miracles (Lk 6:17b-19; 7:1-17).[9]

(T2) According to Luke, miracles have the capacity to validate Jesus and his ministry.[10]

For example, when John the Baptist asks whether Jesus is the one (Lk 7:18-23), the immediate Lukan context is two miracle stories (Lk 7:1-17); and by way of answer, Jesus performs a variety of miracles *in that very hour*.[11] Likewise, a typically Lukan response to Jesus' miracles is for people to glorify *God*, the presumed source of such activity (Lk 5:19; 8:39), thereby implying that Jesus is *his* agent.

(T3) For Luke, the miracles of Jesus are intended as an effective device for turning people to faith.

Thus, their witnesses praise God (Lk 5:25; 7:16; 9:43; 13:13; 17:18; 18:43) and respond with numinous fear (Lk 5:26; 7:16; 8:35, 37; 24:5) which detects the presence of God in Jesus' action.[12] Again, in Luke, Jesus' ability to perform miracles is amply demonstrated (Lk 4:31-41) and reported (Lk 4:23) before any disciples are called. The first disciples follow because of the wondrous power (Lk 5:1-11), and the calling of Levi, the second disciple, immediately follows a miracle story (Lk 5:26-29). Finally, only Luke mentions that the women who follow Jesus have been cured by him (Lk 8:2-3). In sum, "for Luke, knowledge of Jesus' miracles is a legitimate cause for faith in him."[13]

Turning to Luke's second volume (see Chart I for a complete list of miracles in Acts[14]), we can distinguish two broad categories of the miraculous: signs and wonders done through human agency, on the one hand, and theophanies, angelophanies, inSpirations, and visions, on the other. Achtemeier has focused on the former, and his three theses apply to them. In addition to validating their recipients in the eyes of the readers or (sometimes) onlookers, the latter category serves an additional function which we may express as follows:

(T4) For Luke, theophanies, angelophanies, inSpirations, and visions often signify the appointment of their recipient(s) to a special task by God or provide guidance (individual or collective) about what God wants to happen.[15]

I think it is fairly plausible to argue that (T4) as well as analogues of (TI)–(T3) hold for Luke's treatment of miracles in Acts as well.

Jesus' parting commission to his disciples promises that they "shall receive power when the Holy Spirit has come upon" them and that they shall be his "witnesses" (Acts 1:8). A survey of Chart II suggests that Luke has them practice their ministry in Acts in terms of the twin modalities of preaching-teaching and miracle-working, just as much as the Lukan Jesus does his. To be sure, not all of the miracles are paired with preaching sessions; as we shall see below, some are included for different reasons. And there is a stretch of Paul's missionary work in Greece that includes no miracle reports. Nevertheless, it seems to me that the balance of evidence sustains the analogue of (TI) for Acts.

Similarly, it seems to me, Chart III shows how Luke uses miracle reports to validate the preacher-teacher and/or his message, so that the analogue of (T2) is true. Chart IV shows how Luke has used theophanies, angelophanies, visions, etc. to describe the vocation of a particular missionary or the commissioning of disciples to special tasks or to indicate divine guidance to the community. Finally, I believe, Chart V suggests that in Acts the missionary-miracles, as much as the preaching, are *intended* to elicit the response of faith.

Hence, I conclude that, so far as they go, Achtemeier's hypotheses about the function of miracles in Luke's Gospel can be extended to cover the book of Acts as well.

3. Christo-morphic Structure

Even in the Bible, however, intention and fact are not the same. Chart V outlines how the miracles in the book of Acts (like the preaching) in fact get a mixed response. Some people rejoice, glorify God, and are converted, while others are jealous and become increasingly dangerous enemies of the cause. Twice miracles in the book of Acts are met with an unwittingly blasphemous response, when their human agents are mistaken by pagan onlookers for gods in human form (14:8–18; 28:3–6). Although I will not take time to document it here, the same is true for Jesus' miracles (and preaching) in the gospels. Thus, if we probe the structure of Acts (and the Gospel) more deeply, we will see that Achtemeier's essentially correct conclusions can be integrated into a more comprehensive scenario summarized on Chart VI.

As Luke tells the story, human beings are appointed to be agents in the divine plan of salvation by some sort of miraculous happening—a theophany, angelophany, vision, or annointing with the Holy Spirit. The more visible figures then embark on a two-pronged ministry that includes both preaching and miracle-working. Both activities elicit a divided response: some accept the Good News, some are non-committal, and some are hostile. The latter reaction intensifies to the point of persecution. In Acts, the disciples bear witness to Jesus, not only in their preaching and miracle-working, but in their persistent testimony in the face of persecution and death (Lk 9:22–27, 21:12–17). But just as Jesus is vindicated by the God who resurrects him, so the disciples are vindicated by miraculous rescues in the short run and special places in the kingdom in the life to come (Lk 18:29–30; 22:28–30). Given these structural parallels, we see that Luke not only uses individual miracles of both kinds to vindicate and validate a given missionary leader; he distributes them through the person's life in a pattern that imitates the paradigm of Jesus' life and ministry. What is true for individuals, holds also for the collectivity: the Christian community is shown to be God's people, because her early history, both in segments and in the overall pattern of the book recapitulates the experience of her crucified and risen Lord.

4. Sampling the Finer-Grained Structure

Luke-Acts also makes miracles the currency of divine guidance, especially regarding controversial issues, such as the role of Paul in and the admission of Gentiles into the Church. Paul was doubly anomalous: he had been a zealous persecutor of the Church (8:1; 9:1–2, 13–14; 22:4–5; 26:9–11), and we know from his letters (e.g. Gal. 2; 6:11–16; 1 Cor. 8:1–13) that he took a radical view regarding Gentile observance of Jewish customs. His legitimacy as a missionary to the Gentiles is secured with the help of the double-vision formula, involving an appearance of none other than the Lord Jesus himself (9:5; 22:8; 26:15), and the second visionary being Ananias, an apparently unexceptionable man, whether from a Christian (9:13–14) or a Jewish (22:12) point of view. Further, Luke fixes a parallel between Paul and Peter by selecting Pauline miracles that are similar to Peter's: the healings of the lame are even form-critically similar[16] but others are similar in type—Peter's shadow (5:15) and Paul's handkerchiefs and aprons (19:12) are believed by crowds to be efficacious by touch; Peter raises Dorcas (9:36ff.), Paul Eutychus (20:9) from the dead; both are involved in punitive miracles (5:1–11; 13:6–12). In short, their miracle-working activities are roughly comparable in kind and quantity.

The first Gentile conversion is handled with equal delicacy. Notwithstanding that Paul has just been elected by Jesus as missionary to the Gentiles in chapter 9, Peter, who has emerged into the projected role as number-one apostle (Lk 22:31–32; as preacher of the first two sermons, instrument of the first healing, etc.), is God's chosen evangelist for Cornelius. Not enough that Peter has preached the Pentecost and Temple Sermons, acquired a great reputation as a healer, and been miraculously released from prison; Luke prepares the way for this new mission with a Petrine healing of the paralytic Aeneas (9:32–35) and the raising of Dorcas from the dead (9:36–43), both of which have parallels in the healing ministry of Christ (Lk 5:19–26 and Lk 8:40–42, 49–56).

These are but instances of what Howard Clark Kee claims is the general rule: "that *God demonstrates his approbation* of each new stage in the cosmic process of redemption by divine manifestation."[17] Thus, the birth of John the Baptist and Jesus are each attended with angelophanies and anointing with Holy Spirit (Lk 1–2); the launching of Jesus' public ministry, with the descent of the Spirit-dove and the heavenly voice (Lk 3:21–22). Miracles extend the ministry beyond Jewish national and ritual boundaries (Lk 7:1–17, 8:26–39, 17:11–19), the resurrection of Jesus (Lk 24) and the commissioning of the disciples (Lk 5:1–11; 10:9, 17–20; 24:48–49; Acts 1:6–11, 2:1–13), the inclusion of great numbers of Gentiles in the Christian community (see previous paragraph), the geographical spread of the community (Acts 8:4–8, 26–40; 13:2–4; 14:3, 8–10; 15:8–9; 16:6–10; 18:9–10; 19:6–7, 11–12, 21; 27:23–26).

5. The Meaning of Miracles, Christological and Soteriological

Granted that miracles punctuate the careers of Jesus, the disciples, and missionary leaders, and the Church as a whole, according to a definite pattern (viz., that of Chart VI), more needs to be said to articulate their precise christological and/or soteriological meaning.

Numerous commentators begin christologically, arguing that Luke-Acts makes apologetic use of miracle stories to depict Jesus and Christian heroes as conforming to certain Hellenistic paradigms.

(5.1) *Jesus and Primitive Church Figures as Magicians?* In his book *Hellenistic Magic and the Synoptic Tradition*,[18] John Hull sees Luke-Acts as out to advertise the Christian movement to a Hellenistic audience by presenting Jesus and primitive church leaders as magicians. Semantic issues greet us at once: what are we to understand by the word 'magic'?

(5.1.1) *Hull's Causal Criteria:* Hull begins on target when he surmises that "the most central characteristic of magic" is "the desire to compel the gods to do our will."[19] When he comes to offer criteria, however, he seems to define the magical in terms of a cause-effect connection of a sort not explicable in terms of natural laws of the sort studied by scientists. He maintains that miracle-working counts as magic, where (i) the event has no cause but the will of the miracle-worker, (ii) if cause and effect are indicated, their connection is based upon a theory of sympathetic bonds or mana, etc., and/or (iii) the cause of the event is said to be the performance of certain rituals which are efficacious in themselves.[20] Since (i) is inconsistent with each of (ii) and (iii), Hull presumably regards these conditions not as individually necessary but disjunctively sufficient. He suggests that by (i), God's activity in creation is represented as magical when his willing something makes it so. Two ideas are included in (ii): on the one hand, the notion that spirits are somehow bound to elements here below in such a way that knowledgeable mixing of chemicals could compel spirits to do one thing rather than another,[21] or perhaps that rubbing Alladin's lamp makes the genie come out and give one three wishes; on the other, the idea that persons or objects may be "charged" with power which produces effects by contact. Criterion (iii) is exemplified by the idea that merely pronouncing the right word or formula (often a foreign word, or nonsense sequences of vowels, or special names[22] is sufficient to produce an effect for which the phonemes are not naturally sufficient causes (e.g., as when the door opens at the utterance of "Open Sesame!").

Hull contends that many New Testament miracles count as magic by these criteria. For (a) the exorcisms and healings of Jesus and his disciples are form-critically similar to exorcism and healing rituals described in magical treatises; in early Acts, miracles are performed "in the name of Jesus," parallel to the practice among non-Christian wonder-workers of invoking help from the spirits of humans who died a violent death. Again, (b) in some passages, Jesus (Lk 9:42–48) and his disciples Peter (Acts 5:15) and Paul (Acts 19:11–12) are assumed to have mana-like power that is transmitted by mere contact. In Paul's case, it is sufficient to detoxify a snake bite (Acts 28:3–6).

Against this, Achtemeier notes that (b) the objective power is attributed to Jesus in all four Gospels and so is not a special feature of Luke.[23] He also points out respects in which Luke is less "magical" by Hull's criterion than his sources: (1) In the raising of Jairus's daughter (Lk 8:40–42a, 49–55), Luke leaves out the foreign phrase (Mk 5:41) which is part of the magicians repertoire;[24] (2) Luke emphasizes the relevance of Jairus's faith for the miracle (Lk 8:50); (3) unlike magicians, Luke's Jesus usually performs his acts openly—e.g., the raising of the son of the widow of Nain (Lk 7:11–17); and (4) Luke omits from the story about the epileptic boy (Lk 9:37–43) all details about how to deal with especially difficult demons (Mk 9:29).[25]

My quarrel is with Hall's criteria, which in effect assume that any belief in

(T5) the performance of a prescribed ritual is reliably followed by phenomena not *naturally* producible thereby

or

(T6) natural objects may have supernatural properties that produce supernatural effects,

is magical. But this is not true. Whether (T5) and (T6) carry a commitment to magic or to the miraculous depends upon the wider framework of meaning into which they are imbedded: e.g., upon such factors as which spirit is supposed to account for the sequence in (T5) or to endow the properties in (T6), as well as on the presumed relation of human beings to that spirit.

(5.1.2) *Magic as Supernatural Engineering*: Recognizing that some of the feats performed by Jesus and Christian heroes bear an outward resemblance to those of magicians and sorcerers, other commentators have attempted to distinguish the former from the latter by reference to the last-mentioned factor, i.e., in terms of *attitude* and *motivation*.[26] Thus, they represent the magician as an engineer of the supernatural. When human beings try to get control over their environment, they employ generalizations about natural phenomena wherever possible. But when features of the world (such as the weather) elude human control by scientific means, the magicians may claim, by means of esoteric knowledge referred to in (T5) and (T6), to harness supernatural forces to produce the desired end. The magician approaches the spirit with a kind of service-contract mentality: the magician is not interested in relating to the spirit for its own sake, but merely for its ability to "get results" and for the power of position of such trafficking with a successful spirit can bring to the magician himself. Likewise, effectiveness, not understanding, is the focus of the magician's "customer."

If Jesus and his disciples and Luke shared with contemporary magicians a commitment to (T5) and (T6), Luke-Acts says much to repudiate the idea that by doing signs and wonders Jesus and his disciples are manipulating God to produce humanly desired ends and to aggrandize themselves in the process. Where the disciples are concerned, it is God who does the signs and wonders through them as instruments, and God who endows them with super- natural power (1:8). So far from controlling God, they assume their roles as miracle-workers because he has commissioned them (Lk 9:1–2, 10:1, 17–19; Acts 1:8), and not for ends of their own. Jesus himself successfully resists the temptation to aggrandize or save himself by miracle-working (Lk 4:9–12) and he warns the disciples not to "rejoice in this, that the spirits are subject to you; but rejoice that your names are written in heaven" (Lk 10:20). Later on, in Acts, Peter and John insist that the lame man was not cured "by" their "own power or piety" but by the God of Abra- ham, Isaac, and Jacob, the One who raised Jesus from the dead (Acts 4:12–15), while Paul and Barnabas rend their garments and vehemently protest the crowd's attempt to deify them at Lystra in response to a similar healing (Acts 14:8–18) through their hands (Acts 14:3). Conversely, those who accept for themselves the glory due to God alone—viz., Simon Magus (Acts 8:12–24) and Herod (Acts 13:20–23)—merit a curse.[27] Rather, for Luke, healings and exorcisms are part of Christian proclamation,[28] which invites their recipients into a relationship with the God who created them and raised and exalted Jesus, the God who invites them to enter into the promises of his kingdom of which healing and exorcism are only down-payments.

(5.1.3) *'Magic' as a Sociological Category*: The above two approaches assume that the concept of 'magic' is "absolute," in the sense of not varying significantly from culture to culture. They advance a pre-established definition that purports to capture the essence of magic, and then use it to measure the contents of New Testament accounts.[29] Significant disagreement in the secondary literature, together with the difficulty in pinning the category down, have led others to suggest that the criteria for what counts as magical may vary with the cultural context. If it does, however, then—so far as our interest in Lukan Christology is concerned— how Lukan wonder-working stories fit with modern definitions of 'magic' is of secondary importance. What is relevant in the first instance is *Luke's own understanding of and attitude towards magic* in relation to the Christian movement.

Again, many commentators stress the importance of distinguishing *external* (anthropological observer) from *internal* (community member) points of view on wonder-working activities.[30] They question whether there is evidence that wonder-workers ever saw their own activities as "supernatural engineering," or whether the latter does not merely express the assessment of hostile outsiders.[31] These reflections suggest that 'magic' is fundamentally a *polemical* category, a pejorative label used to discredit the wonder-working activities (wonder-workers) of the rival/enemy group.[32] Such a category would involve at least two components: (i) criteria for what sorts of activities are eligible for this label (e.g., broadly and vaguely, "wonders"; or, more determinately, those of the sort mentioned in Hellenistic magical papyri); and (ii) some explanation of what distinguishes acts of type (i) that count as magic from those superficially similar to them—a "theory" that accounts for the pejorative force of the label. So understood, the concept of magic would be social-context-relative twice-over: first, in that it would represent the evaluation of a rival social group; second, in that specifications of (i) and (ii) might differ from culture to culture, group to group.[33]

(5.1.4) *Magic as a Polemical Category In Luke-Acts*: Even superficially, it seems likely that Luke deploys 'magic' as a polemical category. For it occurs explicitly only in Acts, where Luke decisively rejects the practice of magic (as he conceives of it) for Christians. Simon Magus is severely reprimanded by Peter for thinking to augment his powers by an alliance with the Holy Spirit (Acts 8:18–24). Paul's punitive miracle puts an end to Elymas's attempt to draw on his credibility as a magician to block the progress of the Gospel (Acts 13:8–11). Likewise, Paul exorcizes the spirit of divination from a slave girl, thereby foiling her owners' perverse profit-taking from it (Acts 16:16–19). The sons of Sceva get attacked by the demons they are trying to exorcise, when they try to "steal the disciples' formula" and cast out demons in the name of Jesus (Acts 19:13–17). As a result, believers confess and eschew further practice of the magical arts and burn valuable handbooks of magic (Acts 19:18–19).

Susan R. Garrett backs up this impression convincingly in her book *The Demise of the Devil: Magic and the Demonic in Luke's Writings*, where she finds Luke's explanation of the difference between magic and Christian miracles in the apocalyptic myth of cosmic warfare between God and the devil,[34] which she summarizes in the following quote from P. Samain:

> Without embracing Iranian dualism, the world is understood as the arena of struggle between God who incarnates Good and an Adversary who incarnates Evil; two empires are in opposition, one governed by God and his Angels, the other by Satan and the demons. The battle has been fought ever since these demons, fallen angels, undertook to bring evil to the human race. Each party is represented visibly on earth by a series of human-lieutenants. Prophets are countered by false prophets, apostles by false apostles, Christ by the Antichrist. And as God gives his 'saints' the power to accomplish miracles giving credence to their mission, Satan and his satellites give to their agents the power to accomplish wondrous feats which are, or at least appear to be, equivalent. These "sons of the devil" who perform wonders are the magicians.[35]

This understanding is reflected in Luke's version of the Beelzebul controversy, in which Jesus reverses *ad hominem* (in Lk 11:19) the charge of his rivals (Lk 11:15) that he casts out demons via an alliance with the prince of demons, while Jesus' implication that his own exorcisms are wrought "by the finger of God" (Lk 11:20) recalls Moses' defeat of Pharoah's magicians (Exodus 8:19). The apostles' cursing of magicians (Acts 8:20–23; 13:10) presupposes the same view. Regarding Simon Magus, Garrett adduces biblical and extra-canonical literary parallels to show that

> every one of Simon's characteristics–his use of magic, his self-deification, his attraction of the people, his secretly sinful heart, his attempt to procure divine authority, and even his submission when condemned—is a stereotyped feature of contemporaneous portrayals of Satan or those who belong to Satan's lot, especially false prophets. . . .[36]

Likewise, Luke pits Bar Jesus (alias Elymas) (Acts 13:6, 8), a Jewish "magician" and "false prophet" (Acts 13:6) against Saul (alias Paul) (Acts 13:9) the missionary herald of the Gospel, as "son of the devil" (Acts 13:10) against one "filled with the Holy Spirit" (Acts 13:9). By contrast with John the Baptist, Bar Jesus makes "crooked the straight paths of the Lord" (Acts 13:10; cf. Lk 3:4). If both Bar Jesus and Saul were made blind for a time for their opposition to the Gospel (Acts 9:8–9; 22:11; 13:11; cf. Dt 28:29), the mist and darkness that fall on the former unrepentant magician and false prophet (Acts 13:11; cf. Acts 26:18; Lk 22:53) consign him to the authority of his master Satan, while Saul/Paul converts (Acts 9:17–19) and receives a commission to evangelize the Gentiles: "to open their eyes" and cause them "to turn from darkness to light, and from the authority of Satan to God" (Acts 28:18).[37]

Obviously, the correctness of Garrett's analysis entails that Luke was not attempting to win converts in the Hellenistic world by presenting Jesus and primitive church leaders as magicians! On the contrary, he is insisting that rival wonder-workers are magicians and hence servants of Satan, while Christian miracle-workers are empowered by God's gift of Holy Spirit.

(5.2) Theios aner *Christology?* Other scholars insist that Luke-Acts commends Christianity to a Hellenistic audience by turning Jesus and Christian heroes into Hellenistic *theioi andres*. Once again, this question is semantically vexed, because *'theios aner'* is a fluid concept, in both ancient propaganda and contemporary secondary literature.

In his book *Theios Aner in Hellenistic Judaism*, Carl Holladay formulates the "*Theios Aner* Hypothesis" in four theses:

(T7) Within the Hellenistic world, the *theios aner* was a widespread and popularly known figure who possessed the following set of traits: (a) divinity, (b) itinerancy, (c) miracle-working, and (optionally) (d) prophesying, oracular and ecstatic utterances, (e) wisdom, and (f) rhetorical ability.[38]

(T8) Within Jewish life and thought, especially the Old Testament, the notion of a *theios aner* was a contradiction in terms and was not applied to priests, prophets, judges, kings, etc.

(T9) Hellenistic Jews reinterpret ancient biblical heroes to conform to the model of a *theios aner* and so present their heroes to non-Jews by the first century A.D.[39]

(T10) This tendency of hero-depiction developed simultaneously within Christianity in the first century A.D. and influenced early Christian conceptions of Jesus and early church leaders.[40]

If we take the list in (T7)—(a)–(c), optional (d)–(f)—as criterial, it is easy to see how (T10) suggests itself for the heroes of Luke-Acts. Jesus, Peter, and Paul are all travelling, miracle-working preachers; they exhibit wisdom and rhetorical ability; Jesus and Paul are represented as having prophetic foreknowledge (Acts 27:10, 24), and Peter may be presumed to speak in tongues (Acts 2:4ff.; 10:46–47). Again, we see some of these features in Stephen's catalogue of Old Testament heroes who possess wisdom (Acts 7:10, 22; cf. 7:47), do signs and wonders (Acts 7:36), and migrate from place to place (Acts 7:2–4, 9, 12–15, 29, 36, 45).

Nevertheless, it is unlikely that Luke really intends to represent primitive church heroes as (a) divine, because human acceptance of credit for miracles or appropriation of the title 'god' is staunchly repudiated in Acts. The early chapters lay great stress on the fact that it is not the apostles themselves who do the miracles (Acts 3:12); rather it is the name of Jesus, and faith in that name, that heals (Acts 3:16) or God himself who heals through that name (Acts 4:30). Again, *God* did mighty acts *through* Jesus (Acts 2:22) and continues to do signs and wonders "through" or "by the hands of" the apostles (Acts 2:43, 5:12) as instruments. Moreover, despite the fact that Old Testament enthronement terminology occasionally refers to the king as "a god" (Is 9:6; Ps 45:7), Luke does not apply it to Jesus, the one whom God has made Lord and Christ (Acts 2:36). By contrast with Paul, deutero-Pauline epistles, John, and Hebrews, Luke never attributes to Jesus preexistence, a role in creation, or dominion over the universe.[41] Herod is smitten by the Lord with a plague of worms, because he acquiesced in the title and "did not give God the glory" (Acts 12:22–23). When crowds at Lystra infer from the healing of the lame man that "The gods have come down to us in the likeness of men!" Paul and Barnabas rend their garments and protest, "Men, why are you doing this? We also are men, of like nature with you" (Acts 14:15ff). The fact that a like inference at Malta is not explicitly repudiated does not signal any theological change of mind. For the focus of Acts 28:1–10 is elsewhere—viz., on working a parallel between Paul and Jesus (cf. Chart I): both are arrested due to false charges raised by the Jews (Acts 22–24); both remain in charge after their arrest—their true prophecies fulfilled by the course of events (Acts 27:9, 21–26; 13–20, 27–44); each continues the ministry of bringing healing/salvation to strangers (Acts 28:8–9); what happens first presents each to onlookers as guilty of a capital crime (Acts 28:4); in each case the impression is reversed, and righteousness is recognized by Gentiles (Acts 28:6).

In his careful study *The Charismatic Figure as Miracle Worker*, David Tiede challenges both (T7) and (T9) by separating two distinct hero-paradigms in Hellenistic and Hellenistic-Jewish literature. He finds that the ideal of the perfectly rational, philosophically wise, and pragmatically virtuous man was in ascendency in such circles during the first century, while miracle-working, prophecy, and ecstatic utterances were disparaged as superstitious.[42] Luke himself apparently recognized that the decoration of heroes with "special effects" would not serve the ends of effective advertising among the sophisticated; for he records a drop in Athenian interest, even mockery, as soon as Paul mentions Jesus' resurrection from the dead (Acts 17:31–32). Interestingly, the *term 'theios aner'* is rarely used in Hellenistic Judaism, and never occurs in the New Testament.[43]

Some scholars meet such diversity in hero-depiction, by suggesting that *'theios aner'* is a malleable, "umbrella" concept.[44] Holladay notes how Josephus, in his apologia for Judaism, converts the Stoic ideal of virtue and piety, by understanding the virtuous man as one who lives in accordance with the law of the universe, and the pious as one who lives attuned to divine providence. But divine providence has revealed the law of Moses![45] If the notion of *theios aner* is adapted by Josephus along these lines, a Lukan variation would also be available. The *theios aner* of Acts is one who, as attuned to divine providence, believes what God has done in Jesus, receives the Holy Spirit, and obeys its promptings. Once again, Luke-Acts, insofar as it contains miracle-pericopes, can be seen as offering its own distinctive shaping and contextualization of them (according to Chart VI). But now the epistemological priorities run in the wrong direction: *'theios aner'* is no longer a preidentified concept which can be used to illuminate the textual data; rather analysis of Luke-Acts itself is required to supply the distinctive, christological content of that term.

In some cases, the very analytical techniques deployed by scholars guarantee that they will find the miracle-working style of *theios aner* in the texts of the Gospels. Taking over the hypothesis that the canonical Gospels draw on several preexisting sources—a sayings-, a parable-, and a signs-source, as well as passion narratives—Hans Dieter Betz[46] and Helmut H. Koester[47] conjecture that each was controlled by its own distinctive theological principles and assumptions, those of the former three markedly different from "the pattern of the classic passion/resurrection creed and the 'Gospel' produced by it."[48] Betz (apparently following the lead of Martin Dibellius) dissolves the text, not only into source-critical but into form-critical units, and appears willing to speak of the Christology of a single pericope.[49] But this approach teeters between circularity and vacuity. Once we have identified a unit as a miracle-pericope, it is hardly surprising if Jesus is presented as a miracle-worker therein. Even if we use independent criteria to identify the form-critical units, it seems ridiculous (except perhaps in the more developed "narrative tales") to see the features of Jesus in a single pericope as more than evidence for a Christology (just as a single action of a person is rarely sufficient to reveal the depth of his/her character or meaning and purpose in life).

Koester seems to envision collections of similar materials. Positing a signs-source containing only miracle stories, he not surprising classifies them under the literary genre of aretalogies, which he identifies as collections of miracle stories designed to recommend their human channel as a *theios aner*, where he understands a *theios aner* to be (i) a person through whom divine power is present and available, (ii) who does/can make the benefits of miraculous acts available to others, and (iii) whose followers may expect to imitate their leader in being a channel of such wonder-working power.[50] Yet, Koester's method runs the same twin risks as Betz's, except where we have independent evidence that pericopes of a given kind (miracle stories, parables, or sayings) travelled together *and* in isolation from collections of other kinds and/or from the passion narratives. For even if there were sayings-, parables-, and signs-sources distinct from one another and from the passion-narratives (the way the Episcopal prayer book and hymnal are books distinct from one another and from the Bible), if they were all used in conjunction with one another, so that the contents of each were allowed to interact with those of the others in worship, preaching, and the believers' minds, it would be misleading to speak of the separate sources as representing distinct theologies.

Once again, to discover a distinctively Lukan understanding of the role of miracles requires us to look not merely at the source- and form-critical trees, but also to the forest in which they are planted. Betz, Koester, and Weeden admit this in principle, but ignore what Chart VI makes obvious, in their application of it to Luke-Acts. At the ground level, examination of the texts shows the earthly careers of Lukan heroes to be decidedly mixed, punctuated by significant if not individually fatal set-backs. In advancing the ideal of imitative discipleship, Luke emphasizes (he adds 'daily') crossbearing (Lk 9:22–26; 21:12–15). The theme of Jesus as "the suffering prophet" or "suffering righteous one" runs right through his two-volume work.[51] Mentions of the wisdom (Acts 7:10) and wonder-working (Acts 7:36) in Israel's heroes is subordinated in the speech of Stephen to an indictment of Israel for its habitual rejection and abuse of God's chosen "righteous" agents—of Joseph (Acts 7:9), of Moses (Acts 7:17–19, 25–28, 35), of "the prophets" "who announced beforehand the coming of the Righteous One" (Acts 7:52), most recently in Jesus "whom you have now betrayed and murdered" (Acts 7:52), and momentarily in Stephen himself (Acts 7:8, 15, 54–60)! There follows a generalized and "great" persecution of the Church in Jerusalem (Acts 8:1); Herod starts a second, killing James the brother of John by the sword (Acts 12:1–2) and arresting Peter with the intention of killing him "after the Passover" (Acts 12:4; cf. Lk 22:1–2). Likewise, if the death of Paul is not recorded, his wonder-working is inextricably bound up with a series of "close calls." For example, Paul and Barnabas flee from persecution by hostile Jews and Gentiles at Iconium, to Lystra, where the healing of the cripple (Acts 14:8–10) first prompts the idolatrous response that they must be gods (Acts 14:11–18), only for Jews to come and persuade the people to stone Paul and drag him out of the city, (mistakenly) supposing him to be dead, whereupon Paul rises and moves on to Derbe (Acts 14:19–20)—according to the pattern of Chart VI. Similarly, at Philippi, Paul's preaching wins the conversion of leading citizens (Acts 16:12–15), but the exorcism of the slave girl with the spirit of divination (Acts 16:16–18) wins Paul and Silas judicial beating and imprisonment (Acts 16:19–24), followed by a midnight hymn-sing and miraculous earthquake (Acts 16:26) which precipitates the conversion of the jailer and his household (Acts 16:29–34), and an official apology and release (Acts 16:35–40)—likewise according to the pattern of Chart VI.

My conclusion is that, so far as illuminating Lukan Christology is concerned, the concept *'theios aner'* is at worst highly misleading and at best a red herring.

(5.3) *Theologia gloriae*? Commentators who find a *theios aner* Christology in Luke-Acts, also defend a parallel thesis that Lukan emphasis on signs and wonders leads to triumphalism in soteriology. Thus, Koester concludes that where the theology of Mark is controlled by the passion narrative, "the theme of aretalogy" so dominates the theology of Luke that the passion narrative is no longer "the focal point of revelation" but has become "no more than the last chapter of the 'Aretalogy' of Jesus."[52] Moreover, Koester finds, "this same theology" "even more blatantly present" "in the Lukan Acts of the Apostles": the missionaries are "successors" of Jesus who imitate him, being endowed with the same power and guided by the same Spirit, performing the same sort of mighty acts.[53] Betz agrees, remarking that

> the pre-Synoptic Divine Man Christology decided that Jesus' suffering and death were not essential to the Christian message and were to be regarded as a failure that God has made good by raising Jesus from the dead. . . .[54]

He reckons that by contrast with Mark, "Luke . . . does not regard Jesus' death as salvation event, and, in this regard, maintains the theological position of his sources."[55] Theodore J. Weeden, Sr., also echoes Koester, noting how in Luke's Gospel (by contrast with Mark's and Matthew's) "the strong interest in the legendary details of Jesus' life" and "emphasis on the wonder-working ability of Jesus" lead to "his replacing of Mark's *theologia crucis* with a *theologia gloriae*, and his presentation of the crucifixion as the unfortunate death of a *theios aner*. . . ."[56]

Closer examination of these quotations shows that the common charge of triumphalism splits into claims of varying strengths:

(T11) For Luke-Acts, the passion narrative is no longer *the* focal point of revelation. (Koester)

(T12) For Luke-Acts, Jesus' death is not *a* salvation event. (Betz)

(T13) For Luke-Acts, Jesus' death is merely a failure that God has made good. (Betz)

(T14) For Luke-Acts, Jesus' death is no more than the last chapter of an aretalogy. (Koester)

(T15) For Luke-Acts, the crucifixion is merely the *unfortunate* death of a *theios aner*. (Weeden)

—which fare very differently when measured against the complexities of the text of Luke-Acts. (T14) is obviously false, since Luke concludes in chapter 24 with resurrection appearances, and Acts continues the story. On the other hand, insofar as Chart VI captures the Lukan soteriological pattern, it makes *revelation* a process with numerous focal moments, thereby lending credence to (T11). More troubling are the claims that Luke-Acts (T12) robs the death of Jesus of any soteriological significance by treating it as (T15) merely unfortunate, as (T13) a failure that God reverses.

If Betz and Weeden infer these conclusions from Luke's positive deployment of signs-materials, additional apparent support comes from what he does *not* say about the meaning of the death of Jesus itself. (a) First, with the possible exception of the eucharistic formula at Lk 22:19–20, Luke-Acts does not contain the expression found elsewhere in the New Testament that Christ has died for us[57] or for our sins.[58] (b) Moreover, other New Testament writers describe the death of Jesus in *sacrificial* terms,[59] comparing it with covenant sacrifice,[60] or passover sacrifice,[61] with expiation generally,[62] or with the expiating death of the Servant of YHWH.[63] (c) As for the eucharistic formulae—'This is my body which is *given for you*. . . . This cup which is *poured out for you* is the new covenant in my blood' (Lk 22:19–20)— (i) their authenticity is controverted because they are missing in some Western manuscripts; (ii) if authentic, they would be more reflective of older liturgical language than of Lukan theology in particular; and (iii) in any event the language suggests covenant sacrifice (the beginning of a new regime) rather than expiation.[64] (d) While Luke-Acts contains numerous allusions to the Servant-

Songs of Isaiah, by contrast with the other Synoptics, it uses them to speak of Jesus' subordination to God (Acts 3:13, 26; 4:27, 30) and humiliation (Lk 22:37; Acts 3:13, 8:7–35), and avoids the verses having to do with ransom (cf. Mk 14:24/Mt 26:38) and vicarious suffering.[65] (e) Even Acts 20:28, which speaks of "the church of God which he obtained with the blood of His own Son," does not explain what the blood has to do with the foundation of the Church, and leaves it open that nothing more than a covenant sacrifice is meant. These data support the conclusion that whatever meaning Luke-Acts assigns to the death of Jesus, it is not that of vicarious or expiating sacrifice.

(5.4) *The Soteriology of Luke-Acts: Hopeful Realism*: In my judgment, it is theologically narrow-minded to equate the death of Jesus' "being a salvation event" (cf. (T12)) with its functioning as a vicarious or expiating sacrifice. My contrary contention is that so far from crude triumphalism, Lukan soteriology combines confidence in God's victory with sober realism (which is what Chart VI straightforwardly suggests).

First, examination of the text shows that, so far from (T15) merely unfortunate, Luke-Acts represents the death of Jesus as occurring according to the definite plan and foreknowledge of God (Acts 2:23). (a) First, by contrast with Mark and Matthew, Luke's use of *dei* in connection with Jesus' life and ministry becomes thematic. Jesus must be about his Father's business (Lk 2:49), must preach the Kingdom (Lk 4:43), must be on his way for three days (Lk 13:33), must first suffer many things (Lk 17:25, 24:7, 24:26), must stay at Zacchaeus's house (Lk 19:5); likewise, it was necessary for the Scriptures written about him to be fulfilled (Lk 22:37, 24:44).[66] (b) Moreover, God's will (*thelema*) is behind it (Lk 22:42); it is his design (*boule*) (Acts 2:23; 4:28), which he foreordained (*horizo*) (Lk 22:22; Acts 2:23; 10:42; cf. 17:31).[67] (c) Again, Luke-Acts emphasizes how Christ's passion conforms to God's will as revealed in Scripture.[68] (d) Again, the journey motif, which makes Jerusalem and the cross the *telos* of Jesus' ministry, threads through the text. From early on, Jesus is a traveller (Lk 4:42; 7:6, 11). Only the Lukan transfiguration narrative makes reference to his exodus (Lk 9:31). Once the final journey begins (Lk 9:51), the reader is repeatedly reminded that Jesus is on his way (9:52, 53, 56; 10:38; 17:11).[69] All of these show that the death of Jesus is no (T13) mere failure or (T15) misfortune; it was foreknown, planned for, and intended by God.[70] Chart VI shows how God weaves it, along with signs and wonders, into a tapestry; the meaning of the death of Jesus is to be found in the context of that pattern.[71]

Yet, if the map in Chart VI undermines ascriptions of simple-minded triumphalism, it is still abstract. The question remains, why, according to Luke-Acts, events fall into this pattern, and what positive meaning can be assigned to the death of Jesus and the persecution of his followers? The sketch of a response can be found in four, characteristically Lukan themes.

(1) *The Theme of Martyrdom:* One attractive answer, sponsored by Martin Dibelius among others,[72] interprets the Lukan pattern with the theme of martyrdom. Jesus is the herald of God's kingdom; his disciples are called to bear witness to him (Lk 22:31–34; 24; Acts 1:8). These vocations are exercized, not only through the twin ministries of preaching and miracle-working, but also through willing loyalty in the face of persecution, if necessary, to the death. The martyr's death has meaning both as an act of testimony, and as a necessary precondition of divine vindication. Jesus was the pioneer martyr, whose life-death-resurrection sets the pattern for those who follow. Death is not *the* salvation event, but (contrary to (T12)) it may be *a* salvation event, in that it is a *means* to the end of Divine rescue and exaltation.[73] Alternatively, one might say that the death of Jesus is an *efficient* partial cause of Jesus' own vindication, while the whole pattern of his life is an *exemplar* cause of the salvation of his followers.[74] Correspondingly, tracing Christ's pattern through persecution and death acquires further positive meaning for the disciple as an act of loyal identification with his/her Lord.

(2) *Apocalyptic Cosmic Warfare:* A complementary framework for interpreting Chart VI is provided by Lukan appropriation of apocalyptic themes.[75] As noted above (in section 5.1.4), Luke accepts the apocalyptic picture of the earth as the battleground of cosmic warfare. During the old age the powers of darkness have been allowed to overrun God's territory; at the turn of the age (Lk 16:16), God has sent John the Baptist as forerunner, and Jesus as Son to reclaim what is rightfully his. The temptation narrative is a trial by ordeal which pits the newly anointed Son

of God against the devil. The latter finds himself bested and withdraws from direct confrontation "until a more opportune time" (Lk 4:13). That "strong man" bound, Jesus proceeds to take away his armor and divide the spoils (Lk 11:21–22) with a series of exorcisms and healings. Likewise, in a passage unique to Luke, the seventy (arguably post-resurrection missionaries to the Gentiles) recognize the cosmic dimensions of the vocation, as they exclaim "Lord, even the demons are subject to us in your name!" and Jesus replies, "I saw Satan fall like lightning from heaven!" (Lk 10:17–19). The Lukan Jesus' claim to cast out demons by "the finger of God" (Lk 11:20) echoes the language of Exodus 8:19, thereby comparing his activity to God's deliverance of Israel from bondage in Egypt. The journey narrative moves Jesus towards Jerusalem for his final, decisive confrontation with Satan, the commander-in-chief of demons, who seizes his better opportunity by entering Judas (Lk 22:3) and his hour in which to do his worst (Lk 22:53). Yet, even while bound to the cross, Jesus wins the battle: his faithfulness to the divine plan through death shows the final impotence of the devil's weapons; his resurrection-ascension to God's right hand results in Satan's falling like lightening from heaven (Lk 10:18). Satan continues to prowl the earth; rejection and persecution are permitted by God's battle strategy, which allows the powers of darkness to spend themselves, in order to maximize the humiliation of their defeat. Acts tells the story of further skirmishes, in which Christians empowered by Holy Spirit have "authority to tread on serpents and scorpions, and over all the power of the enemy" in Jesus' name (Lk 10:17–19).[76]

(3) *The Theme of Judgment*: Shifting from military to legal imagery, the ministry of Jesus, God's special agent, was to bring judgment (Lk 3:16–17) and to proclaim salvation through repentance and the forgiveness of sins (Lk 5:31–32; 1:76–78). Already Simeon prophesies,

> "Behold this child is set for the fall and rising of many in Israel, and for a sign that is spoken against . . . that the thoughts out of many hearts may be revealed." (Lk 2:35)

God judges, not outward appearances, but the heart. And the contents of the heart are inevitably expressed in its fruit (Lk 6:43–45; cf. 3:8–9). Some—notably the Pharisees in Luke—try to obstruct this appearance through ritually controlled behavior (Lk 11:37–42), but in the longer run this strategy will not work (Lk 12:1–3). For Luke-Acts, John the Baptist, Jesus, and Christian disciples are lightning rods which draw out of human individuals (Lk 7:31–35) and collectivities (Lk 10:9–16) the secrets of their hearts. People and cities judge themselves by their divided reactions to God's anointed agents (Lk 1:41–45; 3:21–22; 4:1; Acts 2). For the latter, experiences of resistance and persecution have the positive meaning, because in them they cooperate in God's program to judge the earth.

The Lukan crucifixion scene is one of judgment and division. Jesus' opening intercession (Lk 23:34) makes clear that it is a trial which holds open the possibility of repentance and forgiveness for his persecutors (as proclaimed in Peter's sermons, Acts 2:24–42; 3:12–26). Divided reaction to Jesus is most sharply focused in the criminal scene (Lk 23:39–42). We may assume that Luke intends both criminals to be Jewish—the first because of his use of the title 'Christ' rather than 'King of the Jews' (Lk 23:39), the second because in Lukan context his speech betrays familiarity with Jewish apocalyptic literature (Lk 23:40–43). Thus, Simeon's prophecy has its paradigmatic fulfilment in the antithesis between the justly condemned sinner who blasphemes in his dying hour, and the repentant sinner who recognizes Jesus as Savior and asks him for mercy. But Jesus, in his dying, has also judged its other witnesses, with their graduated reactions. In arranging it, the rulers of the people have allowed themselves to become tools of the powers of darkness; they have perverted the people into collaborating, and they scoff at the foot of the cross. Their failure to confess Jesus as Christ and contrivance of his death is a blasphemy well epitomized by the first criminal. The people show themselves to be fickle; precipitously persuaded to demand Jesus' crucifixion, they then follow him to the place of the Skull to watch, and then are moved to grief, which in some will bear the fruit of Pentecost conversion. There is likewise a division among Gentile soldiers, some of whom slide from indifference to mockery (Lk 23:34–36), while their commander recognizes in the death of Jesus a mighty work of God (Lk 23:47). Finally, Jesus' disciples and companions withdraw to a distance, but their watching from afar makes them eligible to be witnesses after the resurrection (Lk 22:31–34; ch. 24). Luke's treatment of Gentile reactions anticipates not only the vindication of Jesus with the spread of the Gospel to the Gentiles (second half of Acts), but also the divided response it will meet with there (its many successes balanced, e.g. by Gentile division at Athens [Acts 17:23–34] and hostility at Ephesus [Acts 19:23–41]). Thus, Luke's treatment of the witnesses goes beyond any historical reporting, as he develops in them a spectrum of typical reactions to Jesus, among the Jews first, but then among the Gentiles.

Having prepared himself with prayer in the garden (Lk 22: 40–42), Jesus remains confident and dignified throughout Luke's crucifixion narrative. He practices what he preaches by interceding for his persecutors (Lk 23:34). He continues to bring judgment and to offer salvation by repentance and the forgiveness of sins, even in the hour of the power of darkness. By remaining faithful to the divine plan to the end, he is satisfying his mocker's taunt to save himself (Lk 23:35–37, 39). Confident of his Father's vindication, he reaches into the future and exercises his authority to open the gates of Paradise to the repentant criminal (Lk 23:43), whose estimate of Jesus' apocalyptic role is further vindicated by cosmic irregularity in the failure of the sun's light (Lk 23:44). Once again, Jesus reigning even from the throne of the cross, is a model for the disciples who will also sit on thrones judging the twelve tribes of Israel (Lk 22:30); their dignified confidence in the face of persecution (cf. the saga of Paul in Acts) allows their suffering the further positive meaning as an identification with him.

(4) *The Prophetic Interpretation of Salvation–History*: History itself resists the charge of crude triumphalism. For Luke's Gospel was written in the 80s C.E., and arguably reflects the conflict between Christian and non-Christian Jews over who is to blame for the destruction of Jerusalem: the latter argue that disaster is due to the Christians who blasphemed by worshipping a false prophet; Luke insists, on the contrary, that the fault belongs to those who resisted conversion, for not recognizing the hour of their visitation (Lk 19:41-44).[77] Acts tells a story of Christians on mission, facing conflict on multiple fronts: hostility from the Jews marches right through to the book's end, but Gentiles put up violent resistance as well. What words of encouragement can

the evangelist address to those who confront the bitter realities of persecution, perhaps even daily (cf. Lk 9:23–25)?

Luke-Acts reminds them that they are partners in the new covenant (Lk 22:20); that they have already received the Holy Spirit as a down-payment on covenant blessings (Acts 2; 3:25–26); that the testimony of their predecessors was well attested with signs and wonders (e.g. Acts 2:22); and that a miraculous vindication awaits them in the final consummation. I suggest that, so far from blinding, signs and wonders permit Luke-Acts to be grimly realistic about resistance and individually fatal opposition, and at the same time to proclaim a message of confidence and hope.

CHART I

LIST OF MIRACLES IN ACTS taken from F. Neirynck, "The Miracle Stories in the Acts of the Apostles," *Les Acts des Apotres: Traditions, redaction, theologie*, ed. J. Kremer (Leuven University Press, 1977), 170–171.

H = healings
R = raisings from the dead
E = exorcisms
N = nature miracle

P = punishments
L = liberations from prison
S = summary reports

Marginal numbers = Peter-Paul parallels.

1. S	Many signs and wonders performed by the apostles (2:43)	See 15
2. H	Peter heals the lame man at the Temple gate (3:1–10)	See 16
3. P	The death of Ananias and Sapphira (5:1–11)	See 14
4. S	Many signs and wonders by the apostles (5:12)	
5. S	Peter's shadow (5:15)	See 19
6. S	Healing of the multitudes (5:16)	See 17, 24
7. L	Apostles delivered from prison (5:17–21)	See 18
8. S	Signs and wonders by Stephen (6:8)	
9. S	Signs and wonders by Philip (8:6–7:13)	
10.	Peter and Simon Magus (8:18–24)	See 14, 17, 20

11. H Peter heals Aeneas (9:32–35)   See 23
12. R Peter raises Tabitha (9:36–42)   See 21
13. L Peter delivered from prison (12:3–17)   See 18
14. P Paul blinds Elymas the Magician (13:9–12) See 3, 10
15. S Signs and wonders by Paul and Barnabas
        (14:3)   See 1
16. H Paul heals the lame man at Lystra
        (14:8–10)   See 2
17. E Paul exorcises the Pythoness (16:16–18) See 6, 10
18. L Paul and Silas delivered from prison
        (16:25–34)   See 7, 13
19. S Paul's handkerchiefs and aprons
        (19:11–12)   See 5
20. E The sons of Sceva (19:13–l9)   See 10
21. R Paul raises Eutychus (20:7–12)   See 12
22. N Paul shakes off viper from his arm
        (28:3–6)
23. H Paul heals Publius's father of dysentery
        (28:7–8)   See 11
24. S Paul heals the sick on Malta (28:9)   See 6

JESUS-PETER PARALLELS (Neirynck, 188)

Luke	Acts
A lame man is healed by the authority of Jesus (5:17–26)	A lame man is healed by the name of Jesus (3:1–10; cf. 9:32–35)
Conflicts (5:29–6:11)	Conflicts (4:1–8, 13–22)
A centurion (7:1–10)	A centurion (10)
A story involving a widow and a resurrection (7:11–17)	A story involving a widow and a resurrection (9:36–43)
A Pharisee criticizes Jesus (7:36–50)	The Pharisaic party criticizes Peter (11:1–18)
Intention to kill Jesus after the feast (22:1)	Intention to kill Peter after Passover (12:4)

JESUS-PAUL PARALLELS

Luke	Acts
A lame man healed by Jesus (5:17–26, 7:22)	A lame man healed by Paul (14:8–10)
Jesus raises the dead (7:11–17)	Paul raises the dead (20:7–12)
Jewish plots to kill Jesus (4:29, 6:11, 20:19–20, 22:5–6)	Jewish plots to kill Paul (9:23–24, 23:12–21)
Touching Jesus' garment heals (8:44)	Touching Paul's garment heals (19:12)
Jerusalem-associated passion predictions (9:22, 30, 44, 51; 18:31–33)	Jerusalem-associated passion predictions (19:21, 20:22–23, 21:11)
Jesus as King besides Caesar (23:2–3)	Paul accused of recognizing a king besides Caesar (17:7)

CHART II

*Texts Which Pair Teaching/Preaching
with Miracle–Working Through Humans*

2:14–42: Pentecost sermon, subsequent teaching
2:43: many signs and wonders through the apostles

3:1–11: Peter's healing the lame man
3:12–26: Temple Sermon

6:8: Stephen's great signs and wonders
6:10: Stephen's wise disputations in the synagogue

8:4: Philip's preaching
8:6–8: Philip's healings and exorcisms

13:5: Paul and Barnabas's preaching at Salamis
13:6–12: Punitive blinding of Elymas

14:1, 3: Paul and Barnabas's preaching at Iconium
      Their signs and wonders there

14:6–7: Paul & Barnabas preach at Lystra
14:8–10: Paul's healing of the lame man

16:13–15: Paul and Silas preach at Philippi
16:16–18: Paul's exorcism of the girl with the spirit of divination

19:1–10: Paul's preaching at Ephesus
19:11–12: Paul's extraordinary miracles at Ephesus
(19:13–16: Sons of Sceva incident)

20:7–8: Paul's preaching at Troas
20:10–12: Paul's raising of Eutychus

Blocks of Miracles Not Paired with Teaching/Preaching

5:1–11: Punitive miraculous deaths of Ananias and Sapphira

5:12–16: Signs and wonders by the apostles, especially Peter

9:32–43: Two healings by Peter

23:1–10: Paul on Malta: snake-bite recovery; healings.

Blocks of Miracle-Free Preaching/Teaching

13:13–41: Synagogue Sermon by Paul

17:1–3: Preaching at Thessalonica

17:11-12: Preaching at Beroea

17: 16–34: Preaching at Athens

18:5-6: Initial preaching at Corinth

CHART III

Passages Where Miracles Validate the Preacher or His Message

2:42: Pentecost sermon is followed by many signs and wonders done through the apostles.

4:31: Miraculous earthquake reassures disciples that prayer for boldness will be answered.

5:19–21: Miraculous prison release of Peter and John validates their preaching and healing ministry.

7:55: Vision of Jesus at the right hand of God vindicates Stephen's innocence.

12:6–19: Peter's miraculous release from prison validates his leadership and the Church's activity.

16:25–28: Earthquake and prison-release of Paul and Silas vindicates them and their preaching and exorcism.

19:15: The repudiation of the sons of Sceva validates Paul's preaching and healing ministry by contrast.

18:9–11: Paul's vision at Corinth gives him encouragement.

23:11: Paul's vision at Jerusalem gives him encouragement.

27:10, 24: Paul's foreknowledge of the weather and angelic vision validate his claim to be God's chosen servant.

28:3–10: Miraculous snake-bite recovery and healings validate Paul as innocent and God's servant.

CHART IV

Theophanies or Angelophanies or InSpirations
as Vehicles of Divine Vocation and/or Guidance

2:1–13: Descent of the Holy Spirit on Pentecost

5:19–20: Angelic release from prison with direction to teach in the Temple

8:26: Angelic direction to Philip to take a trip from Jerusalem to Gaza

8:29: Spirit's direction to Philip to join the Ethiopian in the chariot

9:1–22; 22:6–21; 26:9–18: Double vision effects the call of Saul

10:1–48; 11:1–18: Double vision arranges for the first gentile conversion

13:2–4: Holy Spirit directs that Barnabas and Saul be set apart

16:6-10: Holy Spirit forbids Paul and Silas to preach in Asia; Spirit of Jesus disallows trip to Bithynia; vision bids them to Macedonia.

18:9–11: Vision encourages Paul to stay in Corinth and speak out.

19:21: Paul's resolve in the spirit to go to Jerusalem and Rome

20:22; cf. 21:4; 20:23; 21:11: Paul bound in the Spirit to go to Jerusalem; Holy Spirit testifies to future afflictions

23:11: Vision tells Paul that he will get to Rome.

CHART V

Miracles as Testimony Precipitating Division in the Audience

(a) *Miracles met with Faith:*

2:1–42: Descent of the Holy Spirit at Pentecost with the disciples speaking in other languages

3:1–4:4: Peter's healing of the lame man

5:12–14: General miracle-working activity

9:35: The healing of the paralytic Aeneas

9:36–42: The raising of Dorcas by Peter

13:9–12: The punitive blinding of Elymas

16:25–34: The earthquake-release of Paul and Silas

19:17: The punishment of the sons of Sceva

(20:7–12: Raising of Eutychus comforts the Christians)

(b) *Miracles met with Opposition:*

4:1–3: Healing of the lame man brings imprisonment for Peter and John.

5:17–18: The apostles' (especially Peter's) reputation for healing brings imprisonment at hands of jealous Jews

5:33ff: Sadducees have the "urge to kill" after the miraculous prison release of Peter and John

6:8ff: Hellenistic Jews debate with and try to frame Stephen after his signs and wonders

7:57–58: The stoning of Stephen

16:16–24: Exorcism of the girl with the spirit of divination brings beatings and imprisonment

(c) *Miracles met with Idolatry:*

14:8–18: Paul's healing of the lame man at Lystra

29:3–6: Paul's miraculously being unaffected by the snake bite

CHART VI

STRUCTURAL PARALLELS

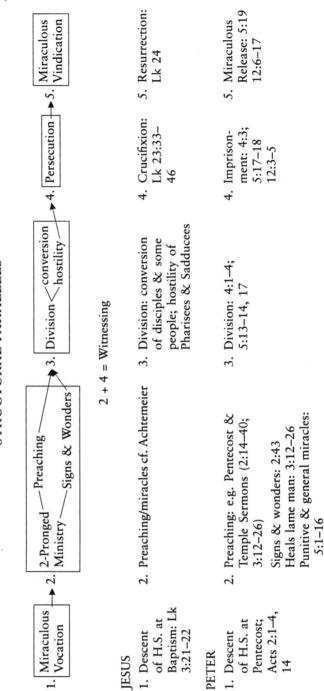

1. Miraculous Vocation → 2. 2-Pronged Ministry ⟨ Preaching / Signs & Wonders → 3. Division ⟨ conversion / hostility → 4. Persecution → 5. Miraculous Vindication

2 + 4 = Witnessing

JESUS

1. Descent of H.S. at Baptism: Lk 3:21–22

2. Preaching/miracles cf. Achtemeier

3. Division: conversion of disciples & some people; hostility of Pharisees & Sadducees

4. Crucifixion: Lk 23:33–46

5. Resurrection: Lk 24

PETER

1. Descent of H.S. at Pentecost; Acts 2:1–4, 14

2. Preaching: e.g. Pentecost & Temple Sermons (2:14–40; 3:12–26)
Signs & wonders: 2:43
Heals lame man: 3:12–26
Punitive & general miracles: 5:1–16

3. Division: 4:1–4; 5:13–14, 17

4. Imprisonment: 4:3; 5:17–18 12:3–5

5. Miraculous Release: 5:19 12:6–17

PAUL

1. Damascus Rd. Vocation: 9:1–22; 22:6–21; 26:9–18

2. Preaching; e.g. Philippi 16:13 Exorcism at Philippi: 16:16–18

3. Division: 16:14–15; 16:19–21

4. Beating & Imprisonment: 16:22–24

5. Miraculous Release: 16:25–34

STEPHEN

1. Ordained deacon: 6:5–6

2. Debates with wisdom: 6:9–10 Signs & wonders: 6:8

3. Division: (favorable implicit; 6:11–15; 7:1, 54)

4. Stoning: 7:57–58

5. Vision of Jesus at God's right hand; Will join Jesus: (7:55, 59)

THE CHURCH: repeated pattern of 1–4, leads to church growth:

2:47: And the Lord added to their number day by day those who were being saved.

6:1: Now in these days when the disciples were increasing in number....

9:31: So the church throughout all Judea and Galilee and Samaria had peace and was built up; and walking in the fear of the Lord and in the comfort of the Holy Spirit it was multiplied.

12:24: But the word of God grew and multiplied.

19:20: So the word of the Lord grew and prevailed mightily.

28:30–31: And he lived there (Rome) two whole years at his own expense, and welcomed all who came to him, preaching the kingdom of God and teaching about the Lord Jesus Christ quite openly and unhindered.

NOTES

I am indebted to A. Orley Swartzentruber for originally suggesting this topic to me and to David Adams, Harold Attridge, David Balch, Wayne Meeks, and Thomas H. Tobin for comments on earlier ancestors of this paper.

1. Richard Swinburne, *The Concept of Miracle* (London: Macmillan, St Martin's Press, 1970), chap. 1; R. F. Holland, "The Miraculous," *American Philosophical Quarterly* 2 (1965), reprinted in *Readings in the Philosophy of Religion*, ed. Baruch Brody (Englewood Cliffs, N.J.: Prentice-Hall, 1974), 450–463; Augustine, *The City of God*, Book 21, sec. 5–8; Book 22, secs. 8–10; Thomas Aquinas, *Summa Theologica*, I, q. 105, a. 7; I–II, q. 113, a. 10.

2. Spinoza, *Theological-Political Treatises*, Preface, chaps. 4, 6: Leibniz, *Discourse on Metaphysics*, sec. 1–16; Kant, *Religion within the Bounds of Reason Alone* (New York: Harper & Row, 1960), 79–84; Schleiermacher, *On Religion* (New York: Harper & Row, 1958), Second Speech, 88–90; idem, *The Christian Faith* (Philadelphia: Fortress Press, 1976), 12–18, 62–76, 137–140, 170–184; Thomas Aquinas, *Summa Theologica* I, q. 105, a. 7; I–II, q. 113, a. 10; C. S. Lewis, *Miracles: A Preliminary Study* (New York: Macmillan, 1960), chaps. 3–5, pp. 12–38.

3. These epistemological worries were forcefully pressed by David Hume, *Enquiry Concerning Human Understanding*, section X, and taken up by that latter-day Humean, Antony Flew, "Miracles," *Encyclopedia of Philosophy* 5 (New York: Macmillan and Free Press, 1967), 346–353; *Hume's Philosophy of Belief* (London: Routledge & Kegan Paul, 1961), chap. 8; and *God and Philosophy* (London: Hutchinson, 1966), chap. 7. Replies have been mounted by many, including the following: R. F. Holland, "The Miraculous," *American Philosophical Quarterly* 2 (1965), reprinted in *Readings in Philosophy of Religion*, ed. Baruch Brody, 450–463; Ninian Smart, "Miracles and David Hume," *Philosophers and Religious Truth* (London: SCM Press, 1964), chap. 2, pp. 25–49; and Swinburne, *Concept of Miracles*, chaps. 3–6.

4. Ironically, many biblical scholars (notably Bultmann and company) have the mirror-image problem: they have let inarticulate philosophical assumptions about the impossibility of miracles drive their hermeneutics and thereby dramatically affect their christological and soteriological results. My advice to them would be to acquaint themselves with the variety of defensible philosophical positions regarding the metaphysical and epistemological possibility of miracles. This could open minds and liberate hermeneutics, to let the texts say what they say!

5. Viz., at 2:19, 22, 24; 4:30; 5:12; 6:8; 7:36; 14:3; 15:12. Cf. Theodore J. Weeden, Sr., *Mark: Traditions in Conflict* (Philadelphia: Fortress Press, 1971), 74.

6. Weeden, *Mark: Traditions in Conflict*, 75.

7. Paul J. Achtemeier, "The Lukan Perspective on the Miracles of Jesus: A Preliminary Sketch," in *Perspectives on Luke-Acts*, ed. Charles H. Talbert (Danville, Vir.: Association of Baptist Professors of Religion, 1978), 153–167, esp. 165.

8. Ibid., 156. Cf. Howard Clark Kee, *Miracle in the Early Christian World* (New Haven, Conn.: Yale University Press, 1983), chap. 6, p. 202.

9. Achtemeier, "Lukan Perspective on the Miracles of Jesus," 156–157.

10. Ibid., 158.

11. Ibid.

12. Ibid., 159.

13. Ibid., 161.

14. Which I borrow from F. Neirynk, "The Miracle Stories in the Acts of the Apostles," *Les Actes des Apotres: Traditions, redaction, theologie*, ed. J. Kremer (Leuven: Leuven University Press, 1978), 169–213, esp. 170–171.

15. See Kee, *Miracle in the Early Christian World*, chap. 6, pp. 208–211, where he classifies these as portents.

16. Neirynk, "Miracle Stories in the Acts of the Apostles," 176.

17. Kee, *Miracle in the Early Christian World*, chap. 6, p. 210.

18. John Hull, *Jesus and Primitive Church Figures as Magicians?* (London: SCM Press, 1974), chap. 6, "Luke: Tradition Penetrated by Magic."

19. Ibid., 27.

20. Ibid., 54.

21. Ibid., 30, 35, 37.

22. Ibid., 35, 38.

23. Achtemeier, "Lukan Perspective on the Miracles of Jesus," 162.

24. Ibid., 162-163.

25. Ibid., 163.

26. See Kee, *Miracle in the Early Christian World*, chap. 1, pp. 23–24; chap. 2, pp. 62–64; chap. 6, pp. 211–219. Cf. Susan R. Garrett, *The Demise of the Devil: Magic and the Demonic in Luke's Writings* (Minneapolis: Fortress; 1989), chap. 1, pp. 29–31.

27. Cf. Garrett, *Demise of the Devil*, chap. 3, pp. 63, 65.

28. As Garrett notes, the miracles of Jesus and the Christian miracles are not random stunts, rather "effect what" the preachers' words "figure," bringing release to the captives in some concrete way (*Demise of the Devil*, chap. 3, pp. 63, 65).

29. Ibid., Introduction, p. 4; chap. 1, pp. 22, 26, 30.

30. Ibid., 27, 30.

31. Ibid., 31.

32. This perspective was originally brought to my attention by Professor Thomas H. Tobin, S.J., in his comments on my paper at the conference. Garrett explicitly endorses this view in several places (*Demise of the Devil*, Introduction, pp. 4–5; chap. 1, p. 16).

33. This two-component analysis seems to be what Garrett has in mind, but she doesn't make herself fully explicit.

34. Garrett, *Demise of the Devil*, especially chap. 2 and *passim*.

35. P. Samain, "L'Accusation de magie contre le Christ dans les Evangiles," *Ephermerides theologicae lovanienses* 15 (1938): 449–490, esp. 454–455, trans. and quoted by Garrett, *Demise of the Devil*, chap. 1, p. 21.

36. Garrett, *Demise of the Devil*, chap. 3, pp. 65–75; quotes from 74–75.

37. Ibid., chap. 4, pp. 79–87.

38. Carl H. Holladay, *Theois Aner in Hellenistic Judaism* (Atlanta: Scholars Press, 1977), 15.

39. Ibid., 16–17.

40. Ibid., 17.

41. Cf. Hans Dieter Betz, "Jesus as Divine Man," *Jesus and the Historian: Written in Honor of Ernest Cadman Colwell*, ed. F. Thomas Trotter (Philadelphia: Westminster, 1968), chap. 6, pp. 114–133, esp. 126.

42. David Lenz Tiede, *The Charismatic Figure as Miracle Worker* (Missoula, Mon.: SBL, 1972), *passim*. Cf. Holladay, *Theios Aner in Hellenistic Judaism*, 99–100.

43. Tiede, *Charismatic Figure as Miracle Worker*, chap. 3, p. 254. Cf. Betz, "Jesus as Divine Man," 117.

44. Cf. Tiede's review of this secondary literature in *Charismatic Figure as Miracle Worker*, chap. 3, p. 254.

45. Holladay, *Theios Aner in Hellenisic Judaism*, 99–100.

46. Betz, "Jesus as Divine Man," 114–133.

47. Helmut H. Koester, "One Jesus and Four Primitive Gospels," *Harvard Theological Review* 61 (1968): 203–247.

48. Ibid., esp. 207–211.

49. Betz, "Jesus as Divine Man," 117, where he speaks of "form-critical units" and p. 124, where he envisions that traditions "circulated . . . as singular units."

50. Koester, "One Jesus and Four Primitive Gospels," 232, 235. Tiede argues that the genre of aretalogy is wide; participating in the same ambiguity as *theios aner* (between divine man as philosophical sage and

paragon of virtue or as miracle worker) (*Charismatic Figure as Miracle Worker*, chap. 1, pp. 1–13).

51. Cf. David L. Tiede, *Prophecy and History in Luke-Acts* (Philadelphia: Fortress Press, 1980). Also, Robert J. Karris, *Luke: Artist and Theologian: Luke's Passion Account as Literature* (New York: Paulist Press, 1985), esp. chap. 3, pp. 23–46.

52. Koester, "One Jesus and Four Primitive Gospels," 234–235; emphasis added.

53. Ibid., 235.

54. Betz, "Jesus as Divine Man," 129.

55. Ibid.

56. Weeden, *Mark: Traditions in Conflict*, 75.

57. Mk 14:24. Jn 6:51; 10:11, 15; 11:50–52; 15:13; 17:19. Rom 5:6, 8; 8:32; 14:15. 1 Cor 1:13; 8:11; 11:24. 2 Cor 5:15. Gal 1:4; 2:20; 3:13. Eph 5:2, 25. 1 Thes 5:10. 1 Tim 2:6. Tit 2:14. 1 Pet 2:21. 1 Jn 3:16. Cf. Richard Zehnle, "The Salvific Character of Jesus' Death in Lucan Soteriology," *Theological Studies* 30 (1969): 438; and Augustin George, S.M., "Le Sens de la Mort de Jesus pour Luc," *Revue Biblique* 80 (1973): 186.

58. Rom 4:25. 1 Cor 15:3. Gal 1:4. Heb 9:26, 28; 10:12. 1 Pet 2:24; 3:18. 1 Jn 1:7; 2:2; 4:10. Rev 1:5. Cf. George, "Le Sens de la Mort," 186.

59. Rom 5:9. 1 Cor 10:16–21. Eph 1:7; 2:13; 5:2. Col 1:20. Cf George, "Le Sens de la Mort," 186.

60. Mk 14:24. Mt 26:28. 1 Cor 11:24. Heb 8:6–13; 9:15; 10:18. This idea appears in Luke 22:20 in the eucharistic formula considered below. Cf. George, "Le Sens de la Mort," 186.

61. Jn 1:26; 19:36. 1 Cor 5:7. 1 Pet.1:19. Rev 5:6–12; 13:8. Cf. George, "Le Sens de la Mort," 186.

62. Rom 3:24–25. Heb 7:27; 9:1–14. Cf. George "Le Sens de la Mort," 186.

63. Mk 10:45; 14:24. Mt 20:28; 26:28. Rom 4:25. 1 Cor 15:3. Heb 9:28. 1 Pet 2:22–25. Cf George, "Le Sens de la Mort," 186; and Zehnle, "Salvific Character of Jesus' Death." 438–439.

64. Cf. George, "Le Sens de la Mort," 193–194; and Zehnle, "Salvific Character of Jesus' Death," 439–440.

65. George "Le Sens de la Mort," 195–198; and Zehnle, "Salvific Character of Jesus' Death," 442–443.

66. Zehnle, "The Salvific Character of Jesus' Death," 420–444, esp. 426–427; George, "Le Sens de la Mort," 186–217, esp. 205.

67. Cf. George, "Le Sens de la Mort," 205; Zehnle, "Salvific Character of Jesus' Death," 427.

68. First, there are general references to Scripture: in the passion prediction (Lk 18:31), to Moses and the prophets (Lk 24–27), to the psalms (Lk 24–45), and to the prophets (Lk 24:25, 44; Acts 3:8; 13:27, 29). Explicit citations include Luke 22:37 (to Is 53:12), Acts 2:25–28 (to Ps 16:6–11), 4:25–28 (to Ps 2:2–1) and 8:32–33 (to Is 53:7–8). Implicit citations include Acts 3:13 ("sheep to the slaughter"), 4:11 (to Ps 118:22), 5:30, 10:30, 13:29, (to Dt 21:22). Cf George, "Le Sens de la Mort," 205–206.

69. Zehnle, "Salvific Character of Jesus' Death," 427–428; cf. Anton Buchele, *Der Tod Jesu im Lukasevangelium: Eine redaktionsgeschichtliche Untersuchung zu Lk 23* (Frankfurt am Main: Verlag Josef Knecht, 1978), 114–145.

70. As Buchele (*Der Tod Jesu im Lukasevangelium*, 94) and George ("Le Sens de la Mort," 216) both insist.

71. Richard Zehnle insists on this, although he grasps only the last part of the pattern: "Essential to the understanding of the role of Jesus in Lk/Acts is the recognition that the complex, life-death-resurrection-ascension/glorification, constitutes a whole whose individual parts find their full meaning precisely in relation to the whole" ("Salvific Character of Jesus' Death," 425). Anton Buchele (*Der Tod Jesu in Lukasevangelium*, 193–194), H. Flender (in Buchele, *op. cit.*, 16–17) and Augustine George ("Le Sens de la Mort," 215–217) also concur in a general way.

72. Cf. George, who comments: "On a souvent remarque depuis M. Dibelius que Luc donne a son recit de la Passion le caratere d'un recit de martyre. Cette observation est fort juste: du Mont des Oliviers au sanhedrin, du pretoire au Calvaire, Jesus apparait comme le juste souffrant, le modele de l'obeissance a Dieu et du courage, le temoin fidele. Et quand Luc raconte la mort d'Etienne, il prend soin de fair ressortir comment la mort du martyr reproduit celle de Jesus" ("Le Sens de la Mort," 208).

73. Anton Buchele quotes W. Pilgrim as using such means-end language, as follows: "Luke does not attribute any atoning significance to the death of Christ. The focus of his soteriology is upon the resurrected and exalted Lord. Nevertheless, the suffering and death cannot be removed from salvation history. His death is the necessary means to his glorification as Messiah and the fulfilment of his Messianic destiny. The cross and resurrection thus provide the pattern of the believer's own life . . ." (Buchele, *Der Tod Jesu im Lukasevangelium*, 20).

74. Zehnle concludes that "the relation between the death of Jesus and the salvation of the individual Christian" is to be explained "along the lines of formal (exemplary) causality rather than efficient causality" ("Salvific Character of Jesus' Death," 444).

75. Cf. my article "Separation and Reversal in Luke-Acts" (in *Philosophy and the Christian Faith*, ed. Thomas Morris [Notre Dame, Ind: University of Notre Dame Press, 1988], 92–117, esp. 111) where I argue that the soteriology of Luke-Acts represents an interaction between apocalyptic and prophetic plot-lines.

76. This is the part of Luke's plot-line that Garrett focuses on (cf. *Demise of the Devil*, chap. 2, pp. 37–60).

77. Cf. Tiede, *Prophecy and History in Luke-Acts*.

Miracles, Magic and Modernity: Comments on the Paper of Marilyn McCord Adams

Thomas H. Tobin, S.J.

I want to begin by thanking Professor Adams for her very stimulating and insightful paper. She has shed a great deal of light on both the miracle stories in Luke-Acts and on the appropriate context in which they should be interpreted. In my response I shall first comment on several aspects of Professor Adams's paper and then make some more general remarks on the vexing question of magic and miracle.

To begin with, Professor Adams is correct to emphasize that miracles play parallel roles in both the Gospel of Luke and the Acts of the Apostles. In both, miracles were meant to validate the ministry of Jesus and his disciples; they were also meant to turn people to faith; finally they serve to signify the appointment of their recipient(s) to a special task by God or provide guidance about what God wants to happen. In addition, the parallel roles of miracles in Luke and Acts serve Luke's larger concern with continuity. As a third-generation Gentile Christian, Luke was concerned about the continuity between Gentile Christian communities and their roots in a different culture and religion (Judaism) and especially in the central figures of Jesus and his disciples with whom no one in his community probably had had any contact.[1] The intricate parallelisms between Jesus, Peter and the apostles, and Paul (whom Luke saw as the link to his own community) were crucial in establishing that continuity. Miracles played an integral part in this intricate parallelism.

Adams is also correct, I think, in rejecting several christological interpretations of the Lukan Jesus which are based at least partially on views about the role of miracles in Luke-Acts. First, the Jesus who emerges from the pages of the Gospel of Luke should not be characterized as a magician, although I shall have a bit more to say about this later in my response. Second, I also agree with Adams that the use of the concept of *theios aner* in describing Luke's portrait of Jesus creates more confusion than clarity. We would do better to realize that the complexity of views about holiness in the Graeco-Roman world is not well served by the use of a term such as *theios aner* to cover so many different phenomena.[2] Finally Adams is also correct to reject the notion that Luke's theology is a *theologia gloriae*. In addition to the points Professor Adams made, one can add the testimony of the speeches in Acts. Since these speeches are almost certainly Lukan compositions, they tend to reflect Luke's own interpretation of Jesus. Jesus' death plays a significant role in several of these speeches (Acts 2:23; 3:18; 4:27–28; 7:52; 13:27–29). Jesus' death is part of a plan (βουλή) by which God determined (ὁρίζω, προορίζω) what was to take place (2:23; 4:27–28). Jesus' death was also the fulfillment (πληρόω) of what had been foretold (προκαταγγέλλω) by the prophets, (3:18; 7:52; 13:27).[3] While it may not be the *theologia crucis* of either Paul or Mark, Luke quite obviously has a *theologia crucis*.[4]

Adams also quite rightly sets Lukan soteriology in the context of such larger themes as martyrdom, judgment, and the prophetic interpretation of salvation history. She also describes Luke's soteriology within the context of what she calls an "apocalyptic cosmic warfare." While it is true that Luke shares a number of apocalyptic viewpoints and motifs with many other early Christians, it is also important to realize that Luke shifted his emphasis from an imminent end of the world to an interpretation of the present situation of Christians.[5] His viewpoint is less apocalyptic and more historically oriented than was Mark's.

I should now like to discuss in a bit more detail the concepts of magic and miracle and their use in the interpretation of early Christian texts, especially the New Testament. Discussion of these concepts is often quite confusing. If it is any consolation to us, they were also confusing to the ancient world. Nevertheless, some sorting may be of value. I shall briefly treat only three of a number of problem areas, building on some of Professor Adams's remarks.

The first problem area concerns description. In the Graeco-Roman world (and in our own world for that matter) magic was often someone else's miracle. It involved an inherently pejorative evaluation of someone else's apparently extraordinary religious events.[6] The other person was really a charlatan, a fake. As in the case of Apuleius of Madaura, it could serve as the basis of a criminal indictment. Magic was often a term used to describe not only a certain kind of activity but also the motivation behind that activity, that is, greed and fraud. The classic example of this is Lucian's Alexander of Abonoteichus, an example used by David Hume in Section X on miracles in *An Inquiry Concerning Human Understanding*.

One does not have to be a cynic to admit the validity of that description for many magicians. But I want to suggest that this was probably not always the case and that it is not the only way to describe magic. Rather magic can profitably be described not only on the basis of motivation but also on the basis of the type of activity involved and the worldview it implied. In that case magic would be "a technique grounded in a belief in powers located in the human soul and in the universe outside ourselves, a technique that aims at imposing the human will on nature or on human beings by using supersensual powers."[7] This description leaves aside the question of motivation.

It may be helpful to expand on this description a bit. First, magic is a technique, a τέχνη, an art or craft which can and often must be learned. This craft may be more or less complex, but, as Georg Luck suggests, the various concepts, formulas, and rituals seem to have been systematized during the Hellenistic period and so reached a certain stability by the first century C.E.[8] Second, the purpose of these formulas and rituals was to impose the human will on nature or on other human beings. There was a significant element of compulsion; if the formulas and rituals were performed correctly, then the results should follow. Finally, magic was rooted in a particular worldview. In this view, the world was filled with various sorts of supersensual powers whose energies could be controlled and channeled through magical knowledge and technique.[9]

On this description of magic, Adams is quite right in maintaining that the miracle stories in Luke-Acts (as well as in other New Testament texts) are for the most part not examples of magic. There is practically no knowledge or use of standard magical techniques, formulas, or rituals, that is, of the τέχνη of magic. Nor is there a sense that either Jesus or the disciples, through their knowledge of the supersensual powers of the universe, are imposing their wills on either nature or other human beings. Rather they are portrayed as empowered by God or as instruments through which God's power works in extraordinary ways. If one were to imagine stories of healings or exorcisms based on texts from the Greek magical papyri, they would sound very different than do most of the miracle stories of the New Testament.[10]

One also has to realize, however, and this is my second problem area, that early Christians had a variety of attitudes toward the miraculous and its significance. The miracles in the Gospel of John are significant primarily, although not exclusively, because of their symbolic significance.[11] For example, the cure of the blind man in John 9 is told in a very condensed fashion (John 9:1, 6–7). The real significance of the story is at the symbolic level, brought out in the rest of the story (John 9:2–5, 8–41), which is devoted to describing the process of coming to see spiritually or becoming spiritually blind. The miracle of physical healing, while important, is secondary. This differs significantly from the story of the cure of the blind man in Mark 8:22–26 where Jesus spit on the man's eyes, then laid his hands on him and asked him if he saw anything. The man replied that he saw men, but they looked like trees walking. Then Jesus laid hands on him again and the man's sight was fully restored. The use of spittle as well as the effort required to make the technique work correctly seem much closer to what I have described above as magic. Interestingly enough, both Luke and Matthew omitted this story, perhaps because they found it too close to magic. A similar use of "technique" is described in Acts 19:11–12, where handkerchiefs and aprons which had touched Paul's body were carried away to the sick who were then cured. Even more revealing is the story of the strange exorcist (Mark 9:38–41; Luke 9:49–50). John reports to Jesus that an exorcist who is not a disciple of Jesus is casting out demons in his name. Jesus replies, "Do not forbid him; for no one who does a mighty work in my name will be able soon after to speak evil of me.

For he that is not against us is for us" (Mark 9:39–40). What Jesus tolerates here is someone neither called nor commissioned in effect using Jesus' name as a kind of magical formula. Similar to this, but with a different outcome is the cautionary, sorcerer's-apprentice story of the seven sons of a Jewish high priest Sceva (Acts 19:14–16). They try to cast out a demon in Jesus' name. The demon, however, refuses to recognize them and beats them up. They are forced to flee the house naked. Apuleius' Lucius would have sympathized with their indecorous exit. Immediately prior to this, however, Luke mentions other itinerant Jewish exorcists who cast out demons in Jesus' name, apparently without the unhappy results experienced by the seven sons of Sceva. The point of these examples is not to deny that most of the miracle stories in the New Testament are not magical. It is simply to suggest that a variety of attitudes toward the extraordinary coexisted in early Christianity and some of them bordered on what can fairly be described as magical.

The final problem area that I want to discuss briefly is the plausibility of the miracle stories. This is, perhaps, the most difficult area to deal with, not only because of the difficulties inherent in the question of the plausibility of miracles generally but also because in biblical exegesis opinions about the plausibility of the miracle stories are often implicit and are neither argued nor even articulated. This means that the historical character of the miracle stories in early Christianity and in the New Testament is often either affirmed or denied on grounds that remain at best implicit. Another quite different approach is to treat the miracle stories on a purely literary level, leaving aside altogether the question of their historical character. It is probably fair to say that all three of these approaches (affirmation, denial, or abstention) are rooted in general notions of plausibility as much as they are in the actual interpretations of texts.

Perhaps, however, there is a fourth possibility which admittedly does not ultimately answer the question about the plausibility of miracles as such but does offer a helpful and appropriate way to look at the miracle stories of the New Testament. Historians, in critically examining evidence of past events, use the broad analogy of contemporary events and motivations to help them critically sort through evidence and come up with the most plausible explanation of past events. The use of these analogies is both necessary and inevitable. Without such broad analogies of antecedent plausibility it becomes impossible to make critical judgments about the evidence of past events. One must certainly keep an open mind, but that is not the same as an empty head.

My suggestion is that such a broad analogy also ought to include accounts of contemporary events often described as extraordinary or miraculous. I think that it would be fair to say that such contemporary descriptions by intelligent, critical observers of unquestioned good will, while considerably less numerous than the credulous would hope for, nevertheless do exist. Even Hume had to admit as much in describing the miracles connected with the Abbé Paris.[12] Admitting this does not mean that one is inevitably forced to admit that these apparently extraordinary events are miracles in the narrow Humean sense of the term, that is, violations of a law of nature by a god. It only means that such apparently extraordinary events are attested to by intelligent, critical people of good will. If that is the case, then the occurrence of such extraordinary events should be part of the broad analogy of contemporary events that an exegete takes to an interpretation of the miracle stories of the New Testament and the assessment of their historical character.

I suspect that the result of such an assessment would be that at least some of miracles in the Gospels and elsewhere in the New Testament were a significant factor in early Christianity from the outset. At least some of the miracle stories were also an important part of the Jesus tradition and were part of the historical core of that tradition, even though heavily embellished in the process of transmission.[13]

I am not sure to what extent these comments clarify or confuse the points made in Professor Adams's fine paper. At least they are intended to carry the discussion begun in her fine paper several small steps further.

NOTES

1. For the identity of the author of Luke-Acts, see Joseph A. Fitzmyer, *The Gospel According to Luke*, Anchor Bible, vol. 28 (Garden

City, N.Y.: Doubleday, 1981), 35–53; *Luke the Theologian* (New York: Paulist, 1989), 1–26.

2. Ironically, Ludwig Bieler who wrote the single most significant study of the *theios aner* was more aware of the constructive nature of his results than are some later scholars (*ΘΕΙΟΣ ΑΝΗΡ: Das Bild des "Göttlichen Menschen" in Spätantike und Frühchristentum*, 2 vols. [Vienna, 1935–36; reprinted, Darmstadt: Wissenschaftliche Buchgesellschaft, 1967] 1967] 1.1–9).

3. For a study of the speeches in Acts, see Ulrich Wilkens, *Die Missionsreden der Apostelgeschichte* (Neukirchen-Vluyn: Neukirchener Verlag, 1961).

4. This point is also made by Fitzmyer, *Gospel*, 22–23, 219–221.

5. Luke does this in a number of ways: (1) Luke has at times either omitted sayings from his sources that express an imminent eschaton or modified them so as to dull, at least, their eschatological edge (Lk 4:15; 4:18–21; 9:27; 17:20–21; 19:11); (2) there are a number of statements in Luke that imply a delay or postponement of the end-time (Lk 12:38, 45; 13:8); and (3) some of the apocalyptic stage props in the eschatological discourse of Mark 13 have been either eliminated or reduced in the Lukan parallel (Lk 21) which describes the destruction of Jerusalem as an historical rather than as an immediately eschatological event. See Fitzmyer, *Gospel*, 231–235.

6. See Susan R. Garrett, *The Demise of the Devil: Magic and the Demonic in Luke's Writings* (Minneapolis: Fortress, 1989).

7. Georg Luck, *Arcana Mundi: Magic and the Occult in the Greek and Roman Worlds* (Baltimore: Johns Hopkins University Press, 1985), 3.

8. Ibid., 14, 20.

9. Ibid., 3; Howard Clark Kee, *Miracle in the Early Christian World* (New Haven: Yale University Press, 1983), 1–77; idem, *Medicine, Miracle, and Magic in New Testament Times* (Cambridge: Cambridge University Press, 1986), 123–124.

10. These papyri are collected in *Papyri Graecae Magicae: Die Griechischen Zauberpapyri*, ed. and trans. Karl Preisendanz and Albert Henrichs, 2nd ed., 2 vols. (Stuttgart: Teubner, 1973–74). An English translation is found in *The Greek Magical Papyri in Translation*, ed. Hans Dieter Betz (Chicago: University of Chicago Press, 1986).

11. Kee, *Miracle in the Early Christian World*, 88–90.

12. Hume, *An Inquiry Concerning Human Understanding*, Section X.

13. This is essentially the same as the conclusion of Kee, *Miracle in the Early Christian World*, 124–125.

VI. Overview
of Biblical Studies

Between Jerusalem and Athens: The Changing Shape of Catholic Biblical Scholarship

John R. Donahue, S.J.

Any dialogue between the philosophy of religion and biblical exegesis must face the challenges arising from the acceptance of the historical-critical method by the official teaching office of the Church (the Magisterium) and from its use by the majority of biblical scholars. With its roots in Renaissance humanism and its flowering in the Enlightenment, the relation of the historical-critical method to questions of belief is a variation of Tertullian's question: "What indeed does Athens have to do with Jerusalem? What is there in common between the Academy and the Church?"[1] Its more theological formulation deals with the roles of faith and reason, and of revelation and of history, in the quest for human understanding and knowledge of God.

The pilgrimage of biblical studies within Roman Catholicism from a marginal role with a defensive posture toward emerging historical-critical methods to its flowering after Vatican II, when it joined the mainstream of biblical studies, did not begin with Vatican II.[2] Historians often date it from the work of the French Oratorian Richard Simon (1638–1712), who published a series of works applying critical methods to the Bible.[3] Simon's aim was apologetic, to show that the Protestant *sola scriptura*, "when carried to its logical extreme, makes confidence in the Bible impossible."[4] His fate, however, was to be expelled from the Oratorians (1682) and to have his writings put on the Index of Forbidden Books.

Historical criticism within Catholicism, as within Protestantism, is a child of the Enlightenment and of the attempts to grapple with rising historical consciousness by members of the Catholic Tübingen school in nineteenth century. It gained momentum with the cautious opening toward critical methods in the encyclical of Pope Leo XIII, *Providentissimus Deus,* issued on November 18, 1893. The years immediately following his encyclical witnessed the beginning of modern Catholic biblical scholarship at the recently founded École Biblique in Jerusalem (1890) and at the Pontifical Biblical Institute in Rome (1909).

The first seedlings of emerging biblical scholarship, however, soon fell on the rocky ground of the anti-modernist reaction, amid attempts of Roman integrists to tar biblical scholars with the brush of Modernism. The early decrees issued by the Biblical Commission (1905–15) mandated for Catholic scholars the most traditional position on virtually every issue raised by critical scholarship.[5] Anti-modernist reaction was especially destructive of Catholic biblical scholarship in the United States, still in its infancy in the first decades of the twentieth century. In his recent history of American Catholic biblical scholarship Gerald Fogarty describes its long-term effects as follows:

> The state of Catholic biblical scholarship in the United States at the end of the 1930s was bleak. Whatever scholarship there had been at the beginning of the century had either been destroyed or gone underground.... The type of Neo-Thomism, formulated in the nineteenth century to combat rationalism, had become so pervasive that Catholic writers confused rationalism with doctrine. Jesuit professors like Peirce and Gruenthaner took as their starting point, not the criticism of texts, but the declarations of the popes or the Biblical Commission.... In effect, integrism had become a habit of mind, even after Benedict XV had condemned it. The American church gave little indication that it was ready to undertake any type of scholarly endeavor.[6]

Though our pilgrim seemed to be in long hibernation, her journey was surprisingly renewed at the end of the 1930s by the founding of the Catholic Biblical Association (1937), which grew out of the need to provide a new translation of the Scriptures to supplant the older Douay-Rheims version. More significantly, amid the darkest days of World War II, the dedication and patience of biblical scholars such as Marie-Joseph Lagrange and Augustin Bea bore fruit in the encyclical *Divino Afflante Spiritu*, issued by Pope Pius XII, September 30, 1943, to commemorate the fiftieth anniversary of Leo XIII's encyclical.[7] Here Pius rejects those Catholic conservatives who " . . . pretend that nothing remains to be added by the Catholic exegete of our time to what Christianity has brought to light."[8] The letter also approved critical methods urging that exegetes "endeavor to determine the peculiar character and circumstances of the sacred writer, the age in which he lived, the sources written or oral to which he had recourse and the forms of expression he employed."[9] Exegesis of the text was to be determined by the literal (or literary sense) defined as "the literal meaning of the words, intended and expressed by the sacred writer" and while exegetes were also exhorted "to disclose and expound the spiritual significance intended and ordained by God, they should scrupulously refrain from proposing as the genuine meaning of Scripture other figurative senses."[10]

Divino Afflante Spiritu contributed to the acceleration of biblical studies in the United States, especially in the 1950s, which witnessed a changing of the guard as younger scholars were trained as before not only at Catholic institutions such as Catholic University and the Pontifical Biblical Institute, but also at secular institutions such as Johns Hopkins, under the direction of William Foxwell Albright.[11] Still, the progress of biblical studies was far from smooth. Biblical scholars continued to be attacked by conservatives in the United States, encouraged and supported by the heirs of integrism in Rome. For example, Edward F. Siegmann who, as editor from 1951–58, transformed the *Catholic Biblical Quarterly* into a solid scholarly journal, was constantly attacked by integrists, leading to his dismissal from Catholic University in 1961 on purported grounds of ill health. At the beginning of the pontificate of Pope John XXIII (1958) important biblical scholars were attacked, culminating in the removal of Stanislas Lyonnet and Maximilian Zerwick from their teaching positions on the eve of the Second Vatican Council.[12] When John XXIII shocked the world on January 25, 1959 by announcing that he intended to call an ecumenical council, the theological atmosphere did not bode well for the future of biblical studies. Yet it was to be the dogmatic constitution on revelation, *Dei Verbum*, in the context of the general renewal of church life and theology accomplished in Vatican II, which spawned a full flowering of Catholic biblical studies.

The new directions in Catholic biblical scholarship stimulated by *Divino Afflante Spiritu* and the Second Vatican Council provide the larger framework for the contemporary discussion of the relation of philosophical theology to biblical exegesis. To describe better this framework and its impact on contemporary theology, I will first describe briefly the journey of the Decree on Revelation from its preconciliar status to its final approval, with attention to the hermeneutical principles within the document, and then sketch certain movements and tensions as Catholic biblical scholarship joined the mainstream of biblical scholarship in the decades following the Council, with special attention to the present situation. I will conclude with a tentative proposal on one direction biblical scholarship might take to meet the challenges of the present situation.

I. The Journey of a Document

On June 18, 1959, under the direction of Cardinal Tardini, the Secretary of State, invitations were issued worldwide to bishops, other church officials, and theological faculties to make recommendations on the Council.[13] By May 1960 over 2,000 responses were gathered. On June 5, 1960, two years before the Council was to begin, Pope John XXIII set up a central preparatory commission, ten subcommissions, and two Secretariats.[14] The president of the important theological commission was Cardinal Alfredo Ottaviani, the prefect of the Holy Office, known for his rigorous conservatism.[15] A month later on July 5, 1960, Pope John charged this commission to deal with "Sacred Scripture and Sacred Tradition."[16]

During the summer of 1960 a summary was prepared of thirteen points which was sent to the members of the commission on October 27, 1960. A subcommission was then formed to develop these original thirteen points into a draft or schema which was eventually discussed by the central preparatory commission on November 10, 1961.[17] Though substantial objections were voiced against this schema by Cardinals Frings, Koenig, Döpfner, and Bea, these were seen as merely advisory by Cardinal Ottaviani.[18] With small changes this was the document sent to the Council participants in the summer of 1962 and presented at the first session of the Vatican Council under the title, "A Dogmatic Schema on the Sources of Revelation."[19]

This schema crystallized the reactionary tendencies of post-Tridentine and anti-modernist theology. It also rarely refers to *Divino Afflante Spiritu* and never cites those passages where Pius XII explicitly authorized use of modern methods of criticism. Going beyond what was stated at Trent this schema says explicitly that there are two sources of revelation.[20] The schema also states "it is completely forbidden to admit that the sacred author could have erred, since divine inspiration of its very nature precludes and rejects all error in every thing, both religious and profane."[21]

In contrast to the later view of Pope John XXIII in his opening address to the Council, that "she [the church] meets the needs of the present day by demonstrating the validity of her teaching, rather than by condemnations," this schema "condemns those errors" by which it is asserted that the evangelists or "what is far worse, the primitive communities" attributed statements to the historical Jesus which he did not utter.[22] Behind this condemnation is a rejection of form and redaction criticism, which were emerging as the dominant methods of New Testament studies.

When this draft was presented during the first session of the Council on November 14, 1962, a procession of speakers stood to urge rejection of this schema, led off by Cardinal Achille Lienhart's ringing "Hoc schema mihi non placet."[23] As Joseph Ratzinger comments: "the inevitable storm broke which had been building up in a private counterdraft, circularized by the presidents of the bishops' conferences of Belgium, Germany, France, Holland and Austria."[24] Bishop Emile DeSmedt of Bruges, Belgium, offered a crucial intervention, noting that the Theological Commission had not consulted the Secretariat for Promoting Christian Unity as the pope had advised, with the result that: "The schema is a step backwards, a hindrance, it does damage. The publication of the theological schema in the form of the drafts we had before us would destroy all the hope that the Council could lead to the drawing together again of the separated brethren."[25]

It was during this debate that the bishops of the world asserted that the Council was to represent the Church universal and not the anti-modernist theology of the Roman Curia. Giuseppe Alberigo, one of the leading interpreters of Vatican II, notes: "Had the conciliar fathers done nothing else, that action alone would have been credited to Vatican II—and John XXIII—as a meritorious deed of the first importance: a refusal to succumb to an oligarchy, and the restoration of full freedom in the Church."[26] Nonetheless, despite strong voices against this draft, partly because of parliamentary confusion, the vote to reject the schema did not receive the required two-thirds majority necessary to send it back to the drafting committee. The drama of this first session was further heightened when on the morning of November 21 Cardinal Felici, the General Secretary of the Council, announced that the pope had removed discussion of this schema from the agenda and handed it over to a mixed commission of which Cardinals Ottaviani and Bea, representing the Secretariat for Promoting Christian Unity, were to be co-chairs.

The decree on revelation would not again be discussed until the third session of the Council (September 30 to October 6, 1964) and would then go through three major revisions before its final adoption on November 18, 1965. Though it was not a decree on scripture but on revelation, its new understanding of revelation would shape both exegesis and theology. In place of a neo-Scholastic emphasis on revelation as revealed truth which transcends human reason, revelation is historical, dialogic, and personal. While both Vatican I and Vatican II say that God reveals himself, Vatican II stresses that God is revealed not only in word ("the decrees of his will") but in deeds, which are recorded in the Bible.[27] Revelation as personal communication in word *and deed* is thus wider than the record of it in the Bible. If revelation is primarily the self-disclosure of God in Israel's history and in the Christ event, then tradition cannot simply be the handing on of a series of doctrines or practices contained in the unwritten traditions of the Church. Tradition is the ongoing witness to the Christ-event expressed in language and other aspects of church life.

On important issues of biblical interpretation *Dei Verbum* remains dialectical, reflecting its origin as a document combining traditional perspectives with cautious openings to more progressive thought. The text states simultaneously that the "Magisterium," the teaching office, is not above the word of God, but serves it, and continues, "the task of authentically interpreting the Word of God, whether written or handed on, has been entrusted exclusively to the living teaching office (Magisterium) of the church" (art. 10). Thus the teaching office is simultaneously the servant of the Word and its authentic interpreter; the whole Church determines the development of tradition, but is subordinate to the teaching authority.[28]

Chapter Three of this decree, "The Divine Inspiration and Interpretation of Sacred Scripture," was of most interest to biblical scholars. After describing inerrancy in article 11, in one of the most debated sentences of the Council, as extending to "that truth which God wanted put into the sacred writings for the sake of our salvation," article 12 turns to biblical interpretation. The principal norm of interpretation is that "the interpreter of sacred Scripture in order to see clearly what God wanted to communicate to us, should carefully investigate what meaning the sacred writer really intended and what God wanted to manifest by means of their words" (art. 12). Selective methodological principles are then given to attain the original sense of the text: (1) attention must be paid to the literary forms; (2) the interpreter must consider the historical circumstances of the time of writing, and (3) attention must be paid to "the customary and characteristic patterns which people in that period employed in dealing with each other." In principal no method of scholarly inquiry is precluded in seeking the meaning of texts.

The Council then turns to theological exegesis, introduced by a citation from St. Jerome that "the holy Scripture must be read and interpreted according to the same Spirit by whom it was written" (*Dei Verbum* 12).[29] This "pneumatic" or spiritual exegesis means consequently that "serious attention must be given to the content and unity of the whole of Scripture"; interpretation must take into account "the living tradition of the whole church along with the analogy of faith (*analogia fidei*)." This final recommendation recalls the earlier statement from paragraph 8 of

Dei Verbum that "the tradition which comes from the Apostles develops in the Church with the help of the Holy Spirit," in a number of ways: by growth in understanding (*perceptio*) of the realities and words handed down; through contemplation and study of believers (*contemplatione et studio*); through the intimate understanding of the spiritual realities they experience (*intima spiritualium . . . experientia*); and through the preaching (*praeconio*, also translated as proclamation) of those who through episcopal succession have received the sure charism of truth. Historical exegesis, the work of scholars, the experience of believers, the prayer of the Church as well as preaching by church leaders all contribute to understanding divine revelation.

From a perspective of over twenty-five years, while we can appreciate the achievements of the Decree on Revelation, both its own conditioning by history and its unresolved theological tensions begin to emerge. These tensions have provided recently a "conflict of interpretations" about the Council.

While I cannot treat adequately the difficult issue of conciliar "reception" or how council documents are rightly interpreted, I will offer a few suggestions. *First*, Vatican II is not simply a collection of documents. It is a process begun in the preparatory stages of the Council, worked out dramatically in the Council sessions, and continued in the ongoing history of the Church.[30] In this arena history is hermeneutics. To see either the scriptural hermeneutics fostered or employed by the Council as the last word would be unfaithful to the Council's own recognition of the pilgrim nature of the Church and the need for development of doctrine. *Second*, the Council intentionally left certain disputed issues open, among which were the nature of inspiration and the relation of historical criticism to theological interpretation.[31] *Third*, since the Council was a historical event its documents should be interpreted by the same rules the Council chose to apply to Scripture. Specifically the historical circumstances and mode of thinking of the participants should be evaluated. Concretely this means that in order to interpret the intention of the Council documents, and not simply their statements, interpreters must engage in a careful reading of the *Acta* of the Council, retracing the various redactions of the documents. The conciliar documents manifest a blend of continuity with church tradition and openness to new perspectives. Interpretation of specific documents must be based on their internal dialectic of adapting tradition to new historical circumstances and warranting methods of exegesis and theology which allow this process to continue, rather than selection by "conservatives" or "liberals" of specific passages congenial to their respective positions.[32]

The history of Catholic biblical scholarship since Vatican II, though not consciously planned as such, presents a sequential grappling with the Council's promotion of historical criticism and its simultaneous caution that this is not totally adequate for Christian faith but must be joined to theological interpretation. Until the mid-seventies issues of historical criticism dominated, followed by issues of theological hermeneutics which are most alive today. I now turn to an admittedly inadequate survey of the post-conciliar development.

II. Sketches of the Post-Conciliar Development

The immediate history of post-Vatican Catholic biblical scholarship, in concert with other theological disciplines, presents a dazzling kaleidoscope. One immediate effect was the commitment to biblical and theological studies by a great number of people. More and more talented lay people, especially women scholars, entered the field. Roman Catholic scholars quickly became leaders in the scientific study of the Bible. The biblical renewal became the soul of bilateral ecumenical dialogues, as groups turned to the scriptural roots of disputed issues only to find that a historical critical reading of the Scriptures challenged positions once thought to be set in concrete.[33] Theologians such as Küng, Schillebeeckx, and Kasper all wrote significant studies of Jesus solidly informed by biblical scholarship. Redaction criticism helped to recognize the theological creativity and literary achievement of the evangelists and disclosed a multi-colored pluralism in the New Testament itself. Fresh translations such as the *Bible of Jerusalem* and the *New American Bible* were produced and Catholics participated in the production of commentaries, no longer divided along confessional lines. Creative theological movements such as feminist and liberation theology wrestled critically with the biblical texts as a source of their insights. Literally thousands of religious and lay people flocked to summer institutes and workshops, sustained by joyful discovery of the manner in which the Bible touched their lives.

As meticulously surveyed by Terrence Curtin in a recently completed dissertation from the Gregorian University (1987), *Historical Criticism and Theological Interpretation of Scripture*, two major movements characterize the post-conciliar period.[34] They are: first, the acceptance and use of biblical-historical criticism in both official church documents and by the vast majority of biblical scholars, and second, continuing attempts to relate historical criticism to theological interpretation. In this section I would like first to offer some clarifications about the nature and use of historical criticism, and then to indicate how historical criticism itself was gradually supplemented by other methods of inquiry.

Along with acceptance of the historical-critical method, its conclusions and its leading practitioners, such as Raymond Brown and Joseph Fitzmyer, have been subjected to constant attacks from "neo-integrist" writers.[35] Joseph Fitzmyer has recently written:

"Though widely used by Catholic, Jewish and Protestant interpreters of the Bible, the historical-critical method of interpretation has come under fire in recent years. Criticism of it has been voiced in various quarters. For instance, (1) integrists in the Catholic Church label it Modernist or Neo-Modernist, because they see it as emphasizing the human elements in the Bible, and not paying sufficient attention to the Bible as "the Word of God."[36]

Historical criticism in a general sense is "the disciplined interrogation of sources to secure a maximal amount of verified information."[37] In studies of the biblical text its primary aim is to discover the "literal," or better, "literary" sense, defined by Raymond Brown as "the sense which the human author directly intended and which the written words conveyed."[38] To achieve this historical criticism uses a wide variety of methods, for example, textual criticism, source criticism, studies of the background and influence on a given writer, examination of literary genres and literary styles of a given document, study of related literature of antiquity. The historical-critical method *as method* should not be determined by theological commitments or philosophical perspectives, even while the practitioners of the method may reflect widely different religious attitudes and world-views. Objectivity is a *sine qua non* when attempting to hear the voice of an ancient writer or to see the pattern of life in an ancient culture.

While it is accurate to say that official Catholic teaching accepted historical criticism in study of the Bible, it is equally true that it never claimed that historical criticism is adequate to determine the meaning of the biblical texts in the ongoing life of the Church.

While historical criticism is indispensable for arriving at the literal sense of an ancient text, of itself it is incapable of judging the trans-historical referent or claim to truth made by the texts. Paul, for example, on the basis of an early church tradition handed down to him (1 Cor 15:1–11) and on the basis of his own experience (1 Cor 9:1; Gal 1:11ff.) can claim that the risen Lord has been revealed to him. Historical criticism can analyze this claim, but cannot verify or describe in historical terms just what constituted this experience for Paul. An appearance of the risen Lord or even "resurrection from the dead" is not an event subject to the normal canons of historiography. The statement that these claims are true and of ultimate significance for people living twenty centuries after Paul requires different methods and different criteria of authority.

For this reason most Roman Catholics who employ historical criticism reject historical positivism, anti-dogmatism, and rationalism. Biblical scholars are partners in a theological enterprise where exegesis is but one stage in assessing both the meaning and significance of biblical texts. Joseph Fitzmyer, for example, has written that "modern Catholic interpreters" of the Bible employ the philological tools and techniques of the historical-critical method with a theological perspective, "a plus or presupposition" that it is "the Word of God couched in ancient human language."[39] This "plus" consists of elements of faith: that the book being critically interpreted contains God's Word set forth in human words of long ago; that it has been composed under the guidance of the Spirit and has authority for the people of the Jewish-Christian heritage; that it is part of a collection of sacred, authoritative writings; that it has been given by God to his people for their edification and salvation; and that it is properly expounded only in relation to the tradition that has grown out of it within the communal faith-life of that people.[40] In Fitzmyer's view historical criticism exists in service of and in dialogue with belief and church life.

While Fitzmyer's view represents the voiced or unvoiced perspective of a generation of Catholic exegetes, it leaves unanswered a host of problems, principally how objective historical criticism is related to theological interpretation, itself a variation on the relation of faith and reason.

This concern evolved differently in various countries.[41] As noted earlier, scholars in the United States were concerned primarily with defense of the historical-critical method and with exposition of its contributions to faith and church life. Issues of theological hermeneutics are a rather late arrival on the scene. By contrast, the French "are already questioning the overall effect of this emphasis [the historical-critical method] in biblical interpretation."[42] Whereas the Americans constantly turn to papal and conciliar teaching as a warrant for their approach, "the French review the teaching and find it tinged with the assumptions of historical positivism."[43] Given the longest tradition of historical criticism among Catholic scholars it is not surprising that the Germans stressed an ideal of exegesis that is both historical and theological.[44] While the French are concerned for the actualization of Scripture in the life of the Church the Germans call for greater reflection on the hermeneutical implications of the use of historical-critical exegesis.[45] Method, rather than content, becomes the preoccupation of theology.

Since limitations of space do not allow us to retrace this history, I would like to direct my attention principally to the situation in the United States.

By the late 1970s the intellectual atmosphere had shifted dramatically. At least five new factors emerged. *First*, no longer was dissatisfaction with historical criticism characteristic only of conservative Catholics. Theologians and ethicists were at times justifiably bewildered by the excessive technical nature of biblical scholarship, by the avalanche of seemingly arbitrary interpretations, and by the absence of a reflective method for the theological interpretation and pastoral application of Scripture.

Second, this period also witnessed the emergence of two new specialities within New Testament studies: social scientific criticism and literary criticism, understood (and used from now on) not as "source criticism" but as it is used in the field of literature in general.[46] "Social scientific methods" is an umbrella phrase for a host of emergent subdisciplines: study of social *realia*, uncovering the social world *behind* the text; social history involving both descriptive and methodological issues (e.g., Marxist and feminist interpretation of social history), social organization and reconstruction of the social, symbolic world of early Christianity.[47] In recent years the methods have been broadened and enriched to include considerations from cultural anthropology as well as from social theory and the sociology of literature. Literary criticism is equally comprehensive, covering approaches such as "close reading," reader response criticism, rhetorical criticism, semiotic exegesis, narrative analysis, and deconstruction. While the social scientific methods disclose primarily "the world behind the text," these methods address "the world of the text."

The panorama of critical options facing the biblical scholar is well described by Christopher Ricks in a review of Giles Gunn's *The Culture of Criticism and the Criticism of Culture* (New York: Oxford University Press, 1987):

> The sights stretch as far as the eye can see—to the immense zoo of Kenneth Burke, the bracing gymnasium of Lionel Trilling, the chaffering marketplace of Clifford Geertz, the broadcasting house of Mikhail Bakhtin with its phone-in programs on the logic of the dialogic; all this and then low on the horizon the bog of deconstruction, swallowing everything in readiness for the final exquisite pleasure of swallowing itself. Milton's vast Serbonian bog where whole armies have sunk.[48]

A *third* factor consequent on this and on the entry of Catholic biblical scholarship into the mainstream is that the divisions within biblical scholarship are often no longer primarily confessional, but often methodological.

A *fourth* factor is the conscious attempt by Catholic scholars in dialogue with non-Catholic biblical scholars, philosophers, and theologians to evolve a theory of hermeneutics bridging the gap between historical criticism and theological interpretation. Again, Curtin notes, much of the ferment for this takes place in France in important articles by François Dreyfus and François Refloulé,[49] but especially in the United States in the work of Sandra Schneiders and Elisabeth Schüssler Fiorenza.[50]

A *fifth* factor is the "linguistic turn" in biblical studies, itself part of a larger revolution in both theology and the humanities, which Werner Kelber describes as "a shift from a referential to a formalist model, from theological categories to narratological apparatus, from extra-textual standards of correctness to fictional purpose and from meaning-as-reference to meaning-as-narrative."[51] A negative analysis of this noted by Patrick Keifert is "an intense skepticism about the relationship between language and reality."[52] Narrative analysis can devolve into a formalism concerned only with the autonomous world of the text and can forsake any quest for those meanings behind of or in front of the text.

A *sixth* and related factor is the realization that biblical studies is in a new era often described as "postmodern." Conservatives and liberal exegetes, as well as theologians, have voiced fundamental doubts about historical criticism, viewing it as one of the surviving heirs of enlightenment rationalism. At a symposium in 1986 Albert Outler called for a "post liberal" hermeneutics, as did the more conservative Catholic scholar Denis Farkasfalvy.[53] In a wide-ranging comparison of movements in biblical studies with trends in the natural sciences James Martin called for "a post-critical paradigm," and Edgar McKnight summed up a decade of reflection on hermeneutics by outlining in 1988, a *Post Modern Use of the Bible.*[54] Despite individual differences this proliferation of "posts" shares similarities.

Postmodernism is a Protean term which is applied to culture, art, and literature.[55] It emerges in the twentieth century in reaction to a modernism which "put critical thinking on the throne of human consciousness."[56] In place of a split between the object and subject of knowledge, postmodernism questions pure objectivity in both science and literature, and stresses participatory knowledge, with emphasis on the reader and reading process rather than on the author or the referent of the text. There is a call for personal and cosmic wholeness. Postmodernism is religious but not ecclesiastical and, while suspicious of metaphysics, its hermeneutic offers a new appreciation of symbols as doors to extra-subjective meaning. (Contrast Bultmann's demythologizing with Ricoeur's statement that the symbol gives rise to thought).[57]

It seems that, with Vatican II, the Church no sooner faced the challenge of modernity than it was faced with its evolution into postmodernity. In assessing postmodernism, however, we should remember McKnight's caution that his proposal for postmodern criticism "will give no comfort, however, to those who want to avoid the challenge of historical and literary criticism, for the approach is not premodern or precritical."[58] A postmodern approach can exist only in dialogue with historical-critical, new critical, and structural assumptions and approaches.[59] Often a restorationist reading of Vatican II which arises from the encounter with postmodernism proposes as a solution the return to premodern worldviews.[60]

Reactions to the postmodern challenge vary. Sandra Schneiders has called for a hermeneutics which integrates Ricoeur's phenomenological reading of texts with Gadamer's stress on the interaction of text and reader whereby readers actualize the unvoiced richness of texts.[61] Similarly Edgar McKnight proposes "reader-oriented criticism."[62] Elizabeth Schüssler Fiorenza offers a pastoral paradigm which combines both critical distance from texts and personal engagement with them.[63] A significant number of exegetes are calling for "deconstruction" of biblical texts.[64] Advocates of narrative theology, especially those influenced by George Lindbeck, call for a return to the Bible as the Christian story which both forms and reflects the faith of the community.[65] By the mid-eighties many diverse paths opened before our pilgrim biblical scholar.

III. A Tentative Proposal

My proposal is an attempt to bridge the gap between the meaning of an ancient text, as discovered by historical criticism, and its enduring religious power. As a brief prelude to my own proposal I would note that one defect of the model of interpretation proposed by the Vatican Council and historical criticism in general is its inadequate understanding of the intricacy of communication in literature or art. Textual communication, as the studies of M. H. Abrams, Paul Hernadi, and Roman Jakobsen underscore, is extraordinarily complex, involving minimally an author or agent who communicates through a sign system to readers in a definite context.[66]

The prime rule of hermeneutics which has governed Catholic interpretation since *Divinio Afflante Spiritu* is to uncover the literal sense of the text, described by Raymond Brown as "the sense which the human author directly intended and which the written words conveyed."[67] While this has been both a liberating and fruitful hermeneutical principle, it focuses too narrowly on one element of the communication process, the intention of the author, which is often the sole determinant of the communicative sign, the text. Whether wittingly or unwittingly the language of the Council presented a "romantic" view of literary interpretation at the very time when this view was disappearing from secular literary criticism.[68]

Contemporary hermeneutical theories stress other aspects of the communication process, either the communication itself, the text, or the reader. Reader response criticism and reception theory, for example, cause us to look again at one of the major achievements of Vatican II.[69] The Council was rightly perceived by Catholic and Protestant observers alike as moving in the direction of *sola Scriptura*, Scripture rather than tradition as the *norma normans non normata*.[70] Biblical text rather than community interpretation was to be normative.

Today practitioners of reader response criticism would argue that a text has no fixed meaning. Stanley Fish, a pioneer and leading theorist of this movement argues that "interpretive communities" ultimately determine what a text means and how it is used.[71] (Rather ironically this view is close to that of the conservative minority at Vatican II who wanted to subordinate the text to the "interpretive community" of the Magisterium.) Insights on how texts achieve meaning in interpretive communities, however, could provide a rich resource for a theology of tradition, which commentators on Vatican II describe as "semantically elusive" and undeveloped theologically.[72]

Nonetheless, I would argue that neither a biblical interpretation based principally on the text-centered phenomenological hermeneutics of Ricoeur nor on the reader-centered perspective of reader response criticism or reception theory (Fish, Gadamer, McKnight) present an adequate paradigm for hermeneutics.

Logically and responsibly I should enter into critical dialogue with these two important methods.[73] Perhaps thankfully, neither space nor my own lack of expertise in all aspects of these approaches allow this.

Though agreeing with Sandra Schneiders's comment in the *New Jerome Biblical Commentary* that "the variety of literary-hermeneutical approaches. . . precludes any totalitarian claims for any one method,"[74] I propose that it is rhetorical criticism, especially as understood by the practitioners of the new rhetoric, which offers the most comprehensive resource for theological hermeneutics.[75] Two prenotes are necessary. First, following George A. Kennedy, I would describe rhetoric as that quality in the discourse by which a speaker or writer seeks to accomplish his [or her] purposes.[76] The "quality in the discourse" is wider than the traditional *topoi* considered in ancient rhetoric. Second, the New Testament books are fundamentally rhetorical documents.[77] Their original purpose was to move people to action or conviction, to challenge the proud or to console the weary, in short to move the audience to take a position envisioned by the authors.[78]

I do not claim originality for this proposal other than putting together insights drawn from other pilgrims on the way of biblical interpretation. Very important is the work of Wilhelm Wuellner, over the past twenty years, but especially his recently published comprehensive review of rhetoric since the Reformation entitled "Hermeneutics and Rhetoric."[79] Wuellner's fundamental thesis is that "rhetorical criticism of literature takes the exegetes of biblical literature beyond the study of the meanings of texts to something more inclusive than semantics and hermeneutics."[80] He concludes his survey with the following claim:

> It made a revolutionary difference to take the familiar notion, that human beings in general, and religious persons in particular, are *hermeneutically* constituted, and replace it with the ancient notion familiar to Jews and Greeks alike, that we are *rhetorically* constituted. We have not only the capacity to understand the content or propositions of human signs and symbols (= hermeneutics); we also have the capacity to respond and interact with them (= rhetorics).[81]

Similarly, writing on "Literary Theory, Philosophy of History and Exegesis," Francis Martin remarks, "The testimony of the Scriptures makes not only meaning claims, but truth claims."[82]

Equally important is the description of the task and method of rhetorical criticism as presented by Elisabeth Schüssler Fiorenza in a now published address to the 1987 meeting of the Society for the Study of the New Testament.[83] She describes four stages necessary to rhetorical criticism: (1) identification of the rhetorical interests and models of contemporary interpretation, (2) delineation of the rhetorical arrangement, interests, and modifications introduced by the author, (3) elucidation and establishment of the rhetorical situation of the document, and (4) reconstruction of the common historical situation and symbolic universe of the writer/speaker and the recipient/audience.[84] This description is similar but not identical with that offered by Wuellner:

> As rhetorical *critics* (rhetorics as part of literary theory) we face the obligation of critically examining the fateful interrelationships between (1) a text's rhetorical strategies, (2) the premises upon which these strategies operate (gender in patriarchy *or* matriarchy; race in social, political power structures), and (3) the *efficacy* of both, text *and* its interpretation (= truth claim, or validity); of both, exegetical practice *and* its theory (= method).[85]

The major difference in the two approaches is that Wuellner is less sanguine than Schüssler Fiorenza about the historian's ability to reconstruct the "common historical situation and symbolic universe of the writer/speaker and recipient/audience." Wuellner understands by rhetorical situation not simply the particularities of a specific situation, for example that in Corinth, but the change in religious consciousness of the audience on a more fundamental level than that dictated by a particular problem. He seeks the religious power of the text which enabled these texts originally addressed to a particular community to shape other communities, perhaps in Paul's own lifetime, but certainly subsequent to Paul.[86] It is to this issue of the power of religious texts that I now turn.

I draw principally on two contemporary theologians, David Tracy and Edward Schillebeeckx. After describing the New Testament as a text which embodies "the classic, paradigmatic and

normative witnesses" to the event-character of God's self-mani-
festation through Jesus Christ, Tracy then lists two criteria for
an interpretation which is adequate to the status of the New
Testament as a classic and *to the original event* (emphasis mine).[87]
They are simultaneously (1) an interpretation whose understanding honors in practice the kind of fundamental existential religious questions these texts address, and (2) an interpretation
which recognizes that the fundamental disclosure of the text—
the world in front of, not behind, all these texts—is the world
of religious event.[88] While Tracy's call for a recognition of the
world of religious event embodied in the New Testament texts
is more programmatic, the magisterial two-volume study of the
New Testament by Edward Schillebeeckx lays bare the religious
experiences emerging from the religious event which we call early
Christianity.[89]

At the risk of oversimplifying I would argue that Schillebeeckx's two volumes probe those fundamental experiences which
give power to the texts of the New Testament. His fundamental
perspective is that "Christianity is not a message which has to be
believed, but an experience of faith which becomes a message."[90]
Of prime importance is the experience of Jesus and its impact on
his disciples. Two elements of Jesus' earthly ministry are foundations of the continuity and of the whole subsequent development
of New Testament theology. Paramount is the *Abba* experience
of Jesus, his trusting and intimate sense of the caring presence
of the Father.[91] Second is Jesus' proclamation of the kingdom,
because of which he is remembered as the eschatological prophet,
the immediate precursor of the new age, who announces God's
definitive act of salvation and enacts it in his ministry, especially
to the outcasts. The offer of salvation and trusting access to God
experienced by Jesus' followers during his life is renewed through
the proclamation of the risen one.[92]

The second volume, *Christ*, continues to explore early Christian experience and its implication for faith today, in dialogue
with the Pauline epistles. Despite differences in expression and in
communities, Schillebeeckx describes a continuity in experience
between the Easter experience of the disciples and the experiences
behind the Pauline and Johannine writings.[93] Likewise there is a

critical correlation between the experience of early Christians and the situation facing believers today.[94]

I would argue that Schillebeeckx's hermeneutics can be described as an *analogy of experience*. Analogy is neither the identical reproduction of early Christian experience, nor is it mere similarity.[95] A true description of analogy involves all those elements necessary to reconstruct the rhetorical situation of a document. The relation of early Christians who hear or read the original message in their situation and in the manner in which they are challenged to respond is analogous, that is both simultaneously similar to and different from that of Christian believers of subsequent ages. Fundamentalism would affirm that the experience of believers today is identical or similar to that of the first audience. The process of *distanciation* recommended by Ricoeur as contemporary readers move from the first to the second naïvete is a prerequisite for the analogy of experience.[96]

Conclusion

By way of a summary of what might seem to be an overly complex program, I would argue that rhetorical criticism by giving due attention to the role of author, text, and recipient in a communication process offers the best model for understanding and appropriating biblical texts. When combined with an analogy of experience, rhetorical criticism may provide a way to bridge the gap between the first and subsequent centuries. Since texts from a different age and culture form its subject matter, all the tools of historical criticism are indispensable in the quest for meaning. However, since these texts are religious and, in both their original settings and contemporary use, make claims to truth and summon people to conversion and commitment, rhetorical criticism must be integrated with philosophical understandings of the human condition and theological reflection on the divine-human encounter. Biblical scholarship, which was given such impetus by the Second Vatican Council, in order to address ultimate questions posed by its own research must remain in dialogue with theology and with philosophy of religion. These latter disciplines must be conversant with the results of biblical scholarship if they wish to acknowledge the historical nature of divine revelation and its human formulation in the language and culture of a previous age.

NOTES

1. "Quid ergo Athenis et Hierosolymis? Quid academiae et ecclesiae," *De praescriptionibus adversus haereticos*, 7, in Migne, ed. *Patrologia Latina* 2.23.

2. A full history remains to be written. Excellent overviews are Raymond F. Collins, *Introduction to the New Testament* (Garden City, N.Y.: Doubleday, 1987), 356–386 and John S. Kselman and Ronald D. Witherup, "Modern New Testament Criticism," *New Jerome Biblical Commentary* [hereafter *NJBC*], ed. R. E. Brown, J. A. Fitzmyer, R. E. Murphy (Englewood Cliffs, N.J.: Prentice Hall, 1989), 1142–1145 (on Catholic critical scholarship); R. E. Brown and T. A. Collins, "Church Pronouncements," ibid., 1166–1174. For the United States see, Gerald P. Fogarty, *American Catholic Biblical Scholarship: A History from the Early Republic to Vatican II* (San Francisco: Harper and Row, 1989).

3. See Jean Steinmann, *Richard Simon et les origines de l'exégèse biblique* (Paris: Desclée de Brouwer, 1959).

4. Edgar Krentz, *The Historical-Critical Method* (Philadelphia: Fortress Press, 1975), 15. Krentz calls Simon "the direct founder" of the historical-critical method. Richard H. Popkin (*Isaac La Peyrère [1596–1676]: His Life, Work and Influence* [Leiden: E. J. Brill, 1987] 88) calls Simon "the greatest biblical scholar of his time," and notes the influence of Spinoza and La Peyrère on his thought

5. Collected in *Enchiridion Biblicum*, hereafter *EB* (Rome: Editiones A. Arnodo, 1956), esp. nos. 324–331 (on historicity of Genesis 1–3); 390–400 (Catholic scholars may discuss the Synoptic Problem, but not adopt the two-source theory). English translations in James J. Megivern, ed., *Official Catholic Teaching: Bible Interpretation* (Wilmington, N.C.: McGrath, 1978), 228–252. These decrees were substantially reinterpreted in 1955; see *Catholic Biblical Quarterly* 18 (1956): 23–29. For summary and discussion of these, see R. E. Brown and T. A. Collins, *NJBC*, 1171–1172.

6. Fogarty, *American Catholic Biblical Scholarship*, 198.

7. Text in *EB*, pp. 200–227; English translation in Megivern, *Bible Interpretation*, 316–342. For early reactions see, A. Bea, "*Divino*

Afflante Spiritu: De recentissimis Pii XII litteris encyclicis," *Biblica* 24 (1943): 313–322; F. Braun, *Les études bibliques d'apres l'encyclique de S.S. Pie XII "Divino Afflante Spiritu"* (Fribourg: Libraire de l'Universite, 1946); M. Grunthaner, "*Divino Afflante Spiritu*: The New Encyclical on Biblical Studies," *American Ecclesiastical Review* 110 (1944): 330–337; 111 (1944): 43–52, 119–123.

8. *EB*, no. 555; Megivern, *Bible Interpretation*, 331.

9. *EB*, no. 557; Megivern, *Bible Interpretation*, 331.

10. *EB*, nos. 552, 553; Megivern, *Bible Interpretation*, 328–329.

11. Among them were Raymond E. Brown, S.S. and Joseph A. Fitzmyer, S.J., two of the most renowned biblical scholars of the past twenty-five years.

12. For a chronicle of these attacks, see J. A. Fitzmyer, "A Recent Roman Scriptural Controversy," *Theological Studies* 22 (1961): 426–444; also R. E. Brown, "Church Pronouncements," *NJBC*, 1168.

13. The Council is customarily divided into four stages, (1) Ante-preparatory, January 25–February 16, 1960; (2) Preparatory, June 5, 1960–July 1962; (3) The Four Council Sessions (October 1962–December, 1965); (4) The promulgation of the decrees and implementation of other directives (e.g., the reform of Canon Law). See L. Pacomio, *Dei Verbum*: Genesi Della Costituzione Sulla Divina Rivelazione (Turin: Marietti, 1971), 10–11; Aram Berard, *Preparatory Reports: Second Vatican Council* (Philadelphia: Westminster Press, 1965), 22–23. The documentation for the ante-preparatory and preparatory phase are collected in the multivolume *Acta et Documenta Concilio Oecumenico Vaticano II Apparando*. Series I *(Ante-preparatoria)*, Series II *(Preparatoria)* (Rome: Polyglot Press, 1969–)

14. Aram Berard, *Preparatory Reports*, 22–23

15. See Richard T. Lawrence, "The Building of Consensus: The Conciliar Rules of Procedure and the Evolution of *Dei Verbum*," *The Jurist* 46 (1986): 480, "The personnel of the preliminary theological commission largely overlapped with that of the Holy Office."

16. For the chronological development of the Decree, see U. Betti, *La Costituzione Dogmatica Sulla Divina Rivelazione* (Turin: Elle Di Ci, 1967), 13–68, schematically summarized in Pacomio, *Dei Verbum*, 10–12 and J. Ratzinger, in *Commentary on the Documents of Vatican II*, ed. H. Vorgrimler (New York: Herder and Herder, 1969), III:155–166. For other commentaries on the Decree on Revelation, see L. Alonso Schökel, ed., *Concilio Vaticano II: Commentarios a la Constitución sobre la divina revelación* (Madrid: Biblioteca de Autores Cristianos, 1969); B. D. Dupuy, ed., *Vatican II: La Révélation Divine*, 2 vols. (Paris: Les Éditions du Cerf, 1968); C. Hampe, ed., *Die Autorität der*

Freiheit (Munich: Kosel Verlag, 1967), I:109–239; R. Latourelle, *Theology of Revelation* (Staten Island, N.Y.: Alba House, 1968), 453–488; O. Sammelroth and M. Zerwick, *Vaticanum II über das Wort Gottes*, Stuttgarter Bibelstudien, 16 (Stuttgart: Katholisches Bibelwerk, 1966); R. Schutz and M. Thurian, *Revelation: A Protestant View* (Westminster, Md.: Newman Press, 1966); E. Stakenmeier, *Die Konstitution über die gottliche Offenbarung* (Paderborn: Bonifatius Verlag, 1967).

17. For the Text of this schema and its subsequent discussion, "De Fontibus Revelationis," see *Acta et Documenta*, Ser. II 2/1 (1965), 523–563.

18. Ratzinger comments: "the working sub-commission remained largely autonomous and its members used the suggestions as they saw fit." In Vorgrimler, ed., *Commentary*, III:159.

19. The official acts of the Council are contained in *Acta Synodalia Sacrosancti Concilii Oecumenici Vaticani II* (Vatican City: Polyglot Press, 1970–80). For the November 10, 1961 schema on revelation see 1/3 (1971): 14–26; Pacomio, *Dei Verbum*, 22–31.

20. No. 4, Pacomio, *Dei Verbum*, 23. In its decree on Scripture the Council of Trent never used the phrase "two sources"; see H. Denzinger and A. Schönmetzer, eds. *Enchiridion Symbolorum Definitionum et Declarationum de Rebus Fidei et Morum* 32nd. ed. (Fribourg: Herder, 1963) nos. 1501–1505, English translation in Megivern, nos. 264–267. On the ambiguity of Trent, see Ratzinger, in *Commentary*, Vorgrimler ed., III:156–157.

21. No. 12, Latin text in Pacomio, *Dei Verbum*, 25–26.

22. No. 22, Latin text in Pacomio, *Dei Verbum*, 29. On Pope John XXIII's understanding of the Council, see his opening address, in Walter M. Abbott, ed., *The Documents of Vatican II* (New York: America Press, 1966), 716.

23. *Acta Synodolia* I/3, pp. 131–259 for speeches. For a description of these days and a summary of the speeches see Xavier Rynne, *Vatican Council II* (New York: Farrar, Straus and Giroux, 1968), 1.76–92 (4 volumes in one).

24. In Vorgrimler, ed. *Commentary*, III:160.

25. Ibid., original in *Acta Synodolia*, I/3, 184–185.

26. "The Reception of Vatican II," in G. Alberigo, J-P. Jossua, and J. A. Komonchak, eds. *The Reception of Vatican II* (Washington, D.C.: Catholic University of America Press, 1987), 9.

27. On Vatican I, see Denzinger and Schönmetzer, *Enchiridion*, no. 3004; on Vatican II, *Dei Verbum*, par. 2.

28. This tension of perspectives was perceived during the conciliar debates by Cardinal Emile Léger of Montreal who felt that the Council

did not submit tradition strongly enough to the authority of the word, and noted shortly after the Council by Abbot Christopher Butler, O.S.B., who wrote, "It is all very well for us to say and believe that the magisterium is subject to holy Scripture. But is there anybody who is in a position to tell the magisterium: Look you are not practicing your subjection to Scripture in your teaching," in J. J. Miller, ed., *Vatican II: An Interfaith Appraisal* (Notre Dame, Ind.: University of Notre Dame Press, 1966), 89.

29. This sentence which was introduced into the Council text during its final redaction is treated extensively by I. de la Potterie, "Interpretation of Holy Scripture in the Spirit in Which It Was Written (*Dei Verbum* 12c)," in H. Latourelle, ed., *Vatican II: Assessment and Perspectives Twenty Five Years After (1962–87)* (Mahwah, N.J.: Paulist, 1988), I, 220–266. While giving an interesting history of the phrase, de la Potterie attempts to make it the hermeneutical key to the whole decree, basing his argument on a forced chiastic structure of the final text. See also D. Farkasfalvy, "The Case for Spiritual Exegesis," *Communio* 10 (1983): 332–350.

30. See esp. H. J. Pottmeyer, "A New Phase in the Reception of Vatican II: Twenty Years of Interpretation of the Council," in Alberigo et al., *Reception of Vatican II*, 27–43.

31. Shortly after the Council, J. Ratzinger wrote: "Even now, after the Council, it is not possible to say that the question of the relation between critical and Church exegesis, historical research and dogmatic tradition has been settled. All that is certain is that from now on it will be impossible to ignore the critical historical method and that, precisely as such, it is in accordance with the aims of theology itself." In Vorgrimler, ed., *Commentary*, III:158.

32. Alberigo, "The Reception of Vatican II," 7–11; Pottmeyer, "New Phase," esp. 39–41.

33. See esp. R. E. Brown, "Historical Biblical Criticism and Ecumenical Discussion," in Richard J. Neuhaus, ed., *Biblical Interpretation in Crisis: The Ratzinger Conference on Bible and the Church* (Grand Rapids, Mich.: Eerdmans, 1989), 24–49.

34. Terrence Curtin, *Historical Criticism and Theological Interpretation of Scripture: The Catholic Discussion of a Biblical Hermeneutic: 1958–83* (Rome: Pontificia Universitas Gregoriana, 1987). See also R. B. Robinson, *Roman Catholic Exegesis Since Divino Afflante Spiritu: Hermeneutical Implications* (Atlanta, Ga.: Scholars Press, 1988).

35. For a summary of the importance and achievements of historical criticism, see J. A. Fitzmyer, "Historical Criticism: Its Role in Biblical Interpretation and Church Life" *Theological Studies* 50 (1989):

244–259. For an example of an ungrounded and unscholarly attack, see George A. Kelly, *The New Biblical Theorists: Raymond Brown and Beyond* (Ann Arbor, Mich.: Servant Books, 1983).

36. "Historical Criticism," 244.

37. Edgar Krentz, *The Historical Critical Method*, 6.

38. "Hermeneutics," *NJBC*, 1148.

39. "Historical Criticism," 254.

40. Ibid., 254–255.

41. I follow Curtin's summary in *Historical Criticism*, 299–309.

42. Curtin, *Historical Criticism* 301.

43. Ibid., 302.

44. Ibid., 304.

45. Ibid.

46. For an excellent description of these emerging methods, see Stephen Moore, *Literary Criticism and the Gospels: The Theoretical Challenge* (New Haven: Yale University Press, 1989) and Sandra Schneiders, *NJBC*, 1158–1160.

47. Jonathan Smith, "The Social Description of Early Christianity," *Religious Studies Review* 1 (1975): 19–25.

48. *New York Times*, Book Review (May 10, 1987), p. 10.

49. See esp. F. Dreyfus, "Exégèse en Sorbonne, exégèse en Église," *Revue Biblique* 82 (1976): 161–202 and "L'actualisation de l'Écriture. I: Du text à la vie," *Revue Biblique* 86 (1979): 5–58, 161–193; "L'actualisation de l'Écriture. II: L'action de l'Esprit," ibid. 161–193; F. Refoulé, "L'exégèse en question," *Vie Sprituelle, Supplement* 27 (1974): 391–423.

50. Curtin covers the following articles: Sandra M. Schneiders, "Faith, Hermeneutics, and the Literal Sense of Scripture," *Theological Studies* 39 (1978): 719–736; "From Exegesis to Hermeneutics: The Problem of the Contemporary Meaning of Scripture," *Horizons* 89 (1981): 23–39; "The Footwashing (Jn 13:1–20). An Experiment in Hermeneutics," *Catholic Biblical Quarterly* 43 (1981): 76–92; "The Paschal Imagination: Objectivity and Subjectivity in New Testament Interpretation," *Theological Studies* 43 (1982): 52–68. Schneiders' views are now available in *The Revelatory Text: Interpreting the New Testament as Sacred Scripture* (San Francisco: Harper and Row, 1991). For Elisabeth Schüssler Fiorenza, see *Bread Not Stone: The Challenge of Feminist Biblical Interpretation* (Boston: Beacon Press, 1984).

51. "Gospel Narrative and Critical Theory," *Biblical Theology Bulletin* 18 (1988): 131.

52. P. R. Keifert, "Interpretive Paradigms: A Proposal Concerning New Testament Christology," *Semeia* 30 (1985): 202.

53. A. C. Outler, "Toward a Postliberal Hermeneutics," *Theology Today* 42 (1985): 281–291; D. Farkasfalvy, "The Case for Spiritual Exegesis," *Communio* 10 (1983): 332–350. Paul Lakeland (*Theology and Critical Theory: The Discourse of the Church* [Nashville: Abingdon Press, 1990], 211–216) following Hal Foster (*The Anti-Aesthetic: Essays on Postmodern Culture* [Port Townsend, Wash.: Bay Press, 1983]) speaks of a "postmodernism of rejection," which perceives the recent past as a series of contemporary ills and urges return to a more idyllic past, and a "postmodernism of resistance," which rejects the "antihuman" strain of modernism. These two strains explain why both "liberal" and "conservative" theologians and exegetes invoked postmodernism to attack contemporary issues.

54. J. P. Martin, "Toward a Post-Critical Paradigm," *New Testament Studies* 33 (1987): 370–385; E. V. McKnight, *Post-Modern Use of the Bible: The Emergence of Reader-Oriented Criticism* (Nashville: Abingdon Press, 1988). Since the mid-1980s postmodernism has become a concern of biblical scholars. See esp. F. W. Burnett, "Postmodern Biblical Exegesis: The Eve of Historical Criticism," *Semeia* 51 (1990): 50–80; R. Fowler, "Postmodern Biblical Criticism," *Forum* 5 (1989): 3–30; and G. Phillips, "Exegesis as Critical Praxis: Reclaiming History and Text from a Postmodern Perspective," *Semeia* 51 (1990): 7–49.

55. See D. R. Griffin, ed., *Sacred Connections: Postmodern Spirituality, Political Economy and Art* (Albany, N.Y.: State University of New York Press, 1990).

56. See Ted Peters "Toward Postmodern Theology," *Dialog* 24 (1985): 221–226, 293–297, and his forthcoming, *God—The World's Future: Systematic Theology and Postmodern Consciousness* (Minneapolis, Minn.: Fortress Press, 1991).

57. Paul Ricoeur, *The Symbolism of Evil* (Boston: Beacon Press, 1976), 347–357.

58. McKnight, *Post-Modern Use*, 14.

59. Ibid.

60. David Tracy, "The Uneasy Alliance Reconceived: Catholic Theological Method, Modernity and Postmodernity," *Theological Studies* 50 (1989) 554–555. See also F. J. Moloney, "Whither Catholic Biblical Studies?" *The Australian Catholic Record* 66 (1989): 84: "Indeed there is every indication that the golden era of biblical enthusiasm in the Catholic Church is on the wane. There is a return to a new dogmatism."

61. See esp. her essay, "Does the Bible Have a Postmodern Message?" in Frederic B. Burnham, ed., *Postmodern Theology: Christian Faith in a Pluralist World* (San Francisco: Harper and Row, 1989) 56–73.

62. McKnight, *Post-Modern Use of the Bible*.

63. Schüssler Fiorenza, *Bread Not Stone*.

64. See esp. Stephen Moore, *Literary Criticism*, 143–149, 165–170. If historical criticism was the hallmark of "modern" interpretation of Scripture, various forms of literary criticism characterize the postmodern period.

65. First proposed in G. Lindbeck, *The Nature of Doctrine: Religion and Theology in a Postliberal Age* (Philadelphia: Westminster Press, 1984), esp. 112–138; see also, "The Story Shaped Church: Critical Exegesis and Theological Interpretation," in G. Green, ed., *Scriptural Authority and Narrative Interpretation* (Philadelphia: Fortress Press, 1987) and "Scripture, Consensus and Community," in Neuhaus, ed., *Biblical Interpretation in Crisis*, 74–101.

66. The seminal essay for a "communications model" is R. Jakobson, "Linguistics and Poetics," in T. A. Sebeok, ed., *Style in Narrative* (Cambridge, Mass.: M.I.T. Press, 1960), 350–377. A clear adaptation of this can be found in R. Scholes, *Semiotics and Interpretation* (New Haven: Yale University, 1982), 17–36. See also M. H. Abrams, *The Mirror and the Lamp: Romantic Theory and the Critical Tradition* (New York: W. W. Norton, 1958), esp. 3–29; Paul Hernadi, "Literary Theory: A Compass for Critics," *Critical Inquiry* 3 (1976): 369–386.

67. "Hermeneutics," *NJBC*, 1148; see *Dei Verbum*, art. 12.

68. On romantic interpretation, see esp. Abrams, *The Mirror and the Lamp*, 21–26.

69. For an overview, see E. V. McKnight, *The Bible and the Reader: An Introduction to Literary Criticism* (Philadelphia: Fortress Press, 1985), 75–82. A leading figure in this approach is W. Iser, *The Implied Reader* (Baltimore: Johns Hopkins University Press, 1974). See also the essays in J. P. Tompkins, ed., *Reader-Response Criticism: From Formalism to Post-Structuralism* (Baltimore: Johns Hopkins University Press, 1980).

70. For a Catholic view see Karl Rahner, "Scripture and Tradition," *Encyclopedia of Theology: The Concise Sacramentum Mundi* (New York: Seabury, 1975), 1550–1551; for two Protestant positions see, Oscar Cullmann, "The Bible in the Council," in G. Lindbeck, ed., *Dialog on the Way: Protestant Report From the Vatican Council* (Minneapolis: Augsburg, 1965) 129–144, esp. 133; and Paul Minear, "A Protestant Viewpoint," in Miller, ed., *Vatican II: An Interfaith Appraisal*, 68–88.

71. Stanley Fish, *Is There a Text in This Class? The Authority of Interpretive Communities* (Cambridge, Mass.: Harvard University Press, 1980), esp. 1–17, 147–180, 303–321; for a helpful summary of Fish, see

Fred C. Burnett, "Postmodern Biblical Criticism: The Eve of Historical Criticism," *Semeia* 51 (1990): 51–80.

72. See Cullmann "Bible in the Council," and Minear, "A Protestant Viewpoint."

73. For critical comments on Ricoeur's project, see esp. Hans W. Frei, "The 'Literal Reading' of Biblical Narrative in the Christian Tradition: Does it Stretch or Will It Break?" in F. McConnell, ed., *The Bible and the Narrative Tradition* (New York: Oxford University Press, 1986); and J. P. Martin, "Toward a Post-Critical Paradigm," *New Testament Studies* 33 (1987): 370–385. For strong criticisms of reception theory, see Terry Eagleton, *Literary Theory: An Introduction* (Minneapolis: University of Minnesota Press, 1983), 66–90, and Stephen Moore, "Doing Gospel/Criticism As/With A 'Reader' " *Biblical Theology Bulletin* 19 (1989): 85–91. For the challenge to theology from both approaches, see Werner G. Jeanrond, *Text and Interpretation as Categories of Theological Thinking* (New York: Crossroad, 1988).

74. "Hermeneutics," *NJBC*, 1160.

75. On the "new rhetoric," see T. Sloan and C. Perelman, "Rhetoric," *The New Encyclopedia Britannica*, 15th ed. (1987) vol. 26, 803–810, and C. Perelman and L. Olbrechts-Tyteca, *The New Rhetoric: A Treatise on Argumentation* (Notre Dame, Ind.: University of Notre Dame Press, 1969). Also, W. Wuellner, "Where is Rhetorical Criticism Taking Us?" *Catholic Biblical Quarterly* 49 (1987):448–463.

76. *New Testament Through Rhetorical Criticism* (Chapel Hill: University of North Carolina Press, 1984), 3.

77. See McKnight, *Postmodern Use*, 103, 107.

78. From the Apologists on, church authors have used the rhetorical in service of exegesis. Especially important is the *De Doctrina Christiana* of St. Augustine; see Raymond F. Collins, "Augustine of Hippo: Precursor of Modern Biblical Scholarship," *Louvain Studies* 12 (1987): 131–151. In the Middle Ages Abelard was a strong advocate of the use of rhetoric. He begins his commentary on Romans with the statement: "The intention of all divine Scripture is to teach or to move in the manner of a rhetorical speech" *Commentaria super S. Pauli: Epistolam ad Romanos*, Prologus (*PL* CLXXVIII, 783–784). Cited in R. McKeon, "Rhetoric in the Middle Ages," in *Rhetoric: Essays in Invention and Discovery*, Mark Backman, ed. (Woodbridge, Conn.: Oxbow Press, 1987), 149.

79. In *Scriptura: Journal of Bible and Theology in Southern Africa* 3 (1989): 1–54.

80. "Hermeneutics and Rhetoric," 1.

81. Ibid., 38.

82. *Thomist* 52 (1988): 577.

83. "Rhetorical Situation and Historical Reconstruction in 1 Corinthians," *New Testament Studies* 33 (1987): 386–403; also, "The Followers of the Lamb: Visionary Rhetoric and Social-Political Situation," in F. Segovia, ed., *Discipleship in the New Testament* (Philadelphia: Fortress Press, 1985), 144–165.

84. "Rhetorical Situation," 388–389.

85. "Hermeneutics and Rhetoric," 38.

86. Based on personal conversation with Professor Wuellner in discussion of his article.

87. David Tracy, *The Analogical Imagination: Christian Theology and the Culture of Pluralism* (New York: Crossroad, 1981), 259, 281.

88. Ibid., 259.

89. Edward Schillebeeckx, *Jesus: An Experiment in Christology* (New York: Seabury, 1980) and *Christ: The Experience of Jesus as Lord* (New York: Crossroad, 1983). For Schillebeeckx's more concise description of his project see, *Interim Report on the Books Jesus and Christ* (New York: Crossroad, 1981). I have described his work in more detail in "The Changing Shape of New Testament Theology," *Theological Studies* 50 (1989): 323–328. On the importance of "experience" in his theology, see L. Dupré, "Experience and Interpretation: A Philosophical Reflection on Schillebeeckx's, *Jesus* and *Christ*," *Theological Studies* 43 (1982): 30–51.

90. *Interim Report*, 50. Dupré ("Experience," 37) notes that "Schillebeeckx keeps a safe distance from a romantic concept of religion such as is found in Schleiermacher's *Discourses*."

91. See esp. *Jesus*, 256–271.

92. *Jesus*, 386–392.

93. *Christ*, 463.

94. *Interim Report*, 50–64; *Christ*, 71–79.

95. As stressed by Troeltsch, "the omnipotence of analogy" is the "key to criticism"; see M. Hengel, "Historical Methods and the Theological Interpretation of the New Testament," in *Acts and the History of Earliest Christianity* (Philadelphia: Fortress Press, 1980), 129.

96. See the helpful exposition of Ricouer by Lewis Mudge in Paul Ricoeur, *Essays on Biblical Interpretation* (Philadelphia: Fortress Press, 1980), 1–40.

Three-sided Scholarship: Comments on the Paper of John R. Donahue, S.J.

Bas C. van Fraassen

With respect to biblical studies I am not even an amateur; I know even less than Professors Dummett and van Inwagen. They said themselves, as you will recall, that they knew very little; and some other people agreed! The good part about my ignorance is that I had the delight of learning a great deal in this conference and particularly from Father Donahue's paper. Scriptural studies do indeed make their presence felt everywhere in religious literature today, so I did know some bits of the history he recounted. These bits are now placed in context through Father Donahue's overview, together with its fascinating look behind the scenes and at new currents in the field. The not-so-good part is that if I am to comment at all, it must be to give my reaction to his paper and to this conference, to what I found and understood here, without much to draw on of my own.

So I will give my impression of the field of scriptural studies, as evidenced here and as described by Father Donahue, and then I shall raise two questions. Both in those questions, and in my prolegomenon to them, I will try to speak as a philosopher looking at and discovering a sister discipline.

1. Interpretating Exegesis and Fact Finding

Scriptural studies, which draws on so many other disciplines, appears to me to have three main sides or aspects. The *first* is that now at least a scriptural scholar can also be at the very same time, and as part of his proper enterprise, a full-fledged participant in certain purely secular academic disciplines. He or she can be a contributor to history, archaeology, and philology, all scientifically pursued. As Father Donahue recounted, this was not always a real possibility for Catholic Bible scholars. It is, I suppose, not necessary for an effective scriptural scholar to also contribute to one of these disciplines, but it is a great and salutary development, which reveals a necessary unification of scholarly endeavors. The nearest parallel in my own area is found in philosophers of physics or biology, who also are physicists or biologists, contributing to the very field on which they draw and reflect in their philosophical work. Health of the discipline may not require so much; but the unity of disciplines which makes that possible is essential.

The *second* side which the discipline shows us is the closest to traditional exegesis, text interpretation, which now draws especially on developments in literary theory. To enhance our understanding of the texts, we need illumination, the uncovering and highlighting of mythical and metaphysical elements, of entwined and tangled themes within themes, of symbols and codes familiar to their original milieu but long since lost to us. That the discipline should draw on the literary theory arsenal of hermeneutics, reception aesthetics, reader response theory, speech act theory, and narrative structure analysis, as well as on deconstructionist, feminist, and Marxist approaches and new studies of rhetoric—all of that seems to me only natural and necessary. It is after all only the natural and necessary attempt to use the tools crafted elsewhere for a similar task.

Obviously, such tools and methods are not to be appropriated uncritically. Personally I have strong suspicions of elitism in reception aesthetics and of self-indulgence in, for example, Bloom's pretense to depth-psychology. I imagine that Father Donahue and others here could quickly add cautions of their own. But I know from my own experience with secular literature how much the new approaches to literary criticism can enhance understanding. My philosophical colleagues are not all of the same mind. To some even such a word as "deconstruction" is like a red flag to a bull already lost in a china shop. I think I know why: various quasi-philosophical battles among the literati tend to steal the limelight from the study of literature. It is our loss, however, if we let those distract us from the real value of the methods of literary criticism.[1]

Text exegesis, drawing for methods on literary criticism, finds its sources also in the secular disciplines I mentioned as side one. It draws on history, of the authors' and audiences' milieux as well as on history of their literature, on archaeological findings, on philological studies of adjacent literature and traditions, and so forth. It is easy enough to see parallels of this in secular studies. To give an example in my own experience: I needed to learn some art history before I could even see, let alone "read," the pervasive use of symbols in Renaissance paintings, which were of course like familiar words to their original viewers.

But it is the *third* side of the subject which seems to have disturbed philosophers, and which led to some controversy here in our conference. Scriptural studies has a subdiscipline, which is at the same time part of Bible studies and part of secular history, scientifically pursued. I will not try to give this subdiscipline a special name—it must be what van Inwagen called Critical Studies and what Adela Collins meant when she said that her enterprise was concerned with evidence and probabilities, not possibilities. I will characterize it as follows: it is the subdiscipline which (a) focuses on questions of a purely factual and empirically significant sort not different in kind from those addressed by secular historians, but (b) is concerned with events narrated in the Scriptures; and (c) uses only scientific methods, methods that are scientifically respectable and commonly used in secular historical research. As paradigm examples I can take Professors Davis's and Collin's discussions, in our conference, of the question "Was the tomb empty?" and of the more modest but no more easily settled "Did the Apostles believe, within a few days of Jesus' death, that the tomb was empty?" Such questions are not different in kind from those about the Herod's frantic family life or Flavius Josephus's beliefs about the destruction of the temple.

2. Is It Science, and Is It Secular?

This is my first question, and I mean to raise it solely about the subdiscipline which I have just characterized, and which I take to have been the special topic of concern of Dummett's and van

Inwagen's papers, as well as the part of scriptural studies practiced before our eyes by Davis and Collins.

You may think that I have already answered myself, because I said that the questions addressed in that subdiscipline are of a kind equally intelligible to a secular historian, and that the methods used are scientific. Nor shall I take back a word of that. I am not intent on disputing that the procedures and reasonings are scientific. But I want to show that this question is real, and remains nevertheless. As you will also see, I am not in a position to answer the question, though I can examine it with reference to the example we have been given here.

I will try to show that the question is a real one first of all by means of some simple examples. Philosophers tend to be generous with abrasive examples, and not always above choosing them with rhetorical intent. To show what could be wrong, I have to use examples of things that have something obviously wrong with them. I want to assure you beforehand that they are not meant to cast indirect slurs on the subject I am now discussing. They are not to be read as insinuating other analogies to Biblical studies—they are here only to highlight the nature of my question.

The first example is a potentially embarrassing one for my own institution. A few weeks before our conference, the *New York Times* ran an article on the Laboratory of Engineering Anomalies at Princeton, which studies psychic phenomena. I have no special inside knowledge of this work, and I try not to prejudge it. But the general reaction I have encountered everywhere, both inside and outside Princeton, is that almost no one is ready or willing to call it science. I can tell you something of the history and intent. J. B. Rhine's work on psychic phenomena at Duke University some thirty years ago was eventually discredited in part because the statistical methods he used, though correct in themselves, could not yield significant conclusions from his *relatively* small sets of data. Experiments using coin tosses, card dealings, and dice rolls to test for clairvoyance and telekinesis were limited by the stamina of the human subjects and the time needed for individual trials. This limitation can be overcome with new technology, which can generate chance events at an incredible rate. Statistical deviations from randomness in such large-scale samples should of course be taken more seriously.

No one I have talked to so far has held either that the Laboratory addresses ill-formulated questions about random sequences, or that the statistical methods differ from those in other engineering research. So is the embarrassed look just prejudice? I don't think so. I think what almost everyone surmises is a certain disparity: namely, that the level of evidence to be had is not commensurate with the questions asked. The questions about statistical deviations in the samples are perfectly good ones, but to even touch the questions about clairvoyance and psychokinesis (which are certainly conceivable) quite another order of evidence would be needed. Let me give a simpler but more blatant example. Suppose I wish to investigate the width of human hair. There is not likely to be any prejudice on this subject. But suppose all I have is an ordinary ruler, and I decide to go ahead anyway. I place the ruler beside a hair, squint at it, and write down "1/65 of an inch." I repeat the procedure a few thousand times, and get others to do the same. To the resulting data base I apply some sophisticated statistical analysis, and I publish the results. I have transgressed no methodological canon. But what I am doing is not science. From a scientific point of view it makes no sense at all. The reason is obviously that the level of evidence is not commensurate with the question.

Consider now the concrete example of a historical investigation we saw here, which addresses those questions about Jesus' tomb. The questions about what exactly the texts say, how much of the text could be attributed to redaction, and so forth, are certainly legitimate and manageable. But let me now try to imagine how would I react to the question whether Jesus' tomb was empty on the third day, were I a secular historian with a strictly scientific approach. First of all, what are the sources where we can expect to find evidence? The Gospels and the Epistles. These were written from at least fifteen to thirty years after Jesus' death, by authors who may not have been present there or even have known Jesus during his lifetime. The documents themselves do not exist except in later copies. In the wealth of historical source material about the Roman empire in the first century, the Jewish wars, and the administration of the territory, we find nothing to shed light on those important first fifty days of the Church, what happened in it, or what it believed then.

Secondly—I say, still in the persona of a secular historian broaching these questions—those documents themselves belong to a class of documents produced by adherents of cults and religious movements, of which we do have many examples in recent history. Think of the Book of Mormon, the writings of Elizabeth Clare Prophet—whose followers are amassing in Montana even now, as our conference proceeds, to await Armageddon. Think also of the revealing histories of such recent movements in which predictions concerning the end of the world were made, and promptly falsified—what beliefs they then developed and proclaimed. All this has been studied extensively by sociologists, and we must conclude that this class of documents taken as a whole is of negligible reliability with respect to the events it narrates, or even with respect to the beliefs which were held at the times of those events. "Negligible" is of course the scientist's polite word for "zero, or so near zero as is not worth mentioning." Were Professors Davis and Collins simply secular historians turning to this question, they would not have argued it—they would simply have said "Let's put it on the shelf for another hundred years and see if some new evidence is found."

I would like to add some remarks on methodology. For as one follows such discussions, there is often a sense of evidence building up. Of course that cannot really be happening without new evidential input. Perfectly good scientific reasoning includes steps that are not simply deductive; but uncertainty increases and probabilities go down. I think you are familiar with the patterns of reasoning I mean, like

> First we face hypotheses A versus B, and the evidence for A is 3% but for B it is only 2%, so let us go with A—we must now consider C versus D, but *in view of A*, C has a much higher probability than D. Next we look at that troublesome bit of evidence E that everyone has difficulties with, but it must be pointed out that of the five interpretations of E already in the literature, three are incompatible with the conjunction of A and C to which we agreed above. The remaining two ways in which E could be true split into sixteen subcases if we take into account that...

and so forth. It sounds like probability, or weight of evidence, or level of confirmation, or whatever it is, is going up—but it is going up only as conditioned on preceding conclusions, and the absolute probability of the scenario being constructed (A and C and...) is going down, down, down.

The most important point is perhaps just this: analysis of evidence doesn't increase evidential support if not accompanied by new evidential input. I don't know how often, in other examples, there is such new input, but Professors Collins and Davis were not bringing each other new bits of evidence. It is possible of course to demolish the arguments one's opponents give for their conclusions. While Professor Davis argued cogently, his arguments were cogently opposed by Professor Collins. Only, from a scientific point of view, she needn't have refuted any reasons for belief in the empty tomb—from a scientific point of view there wasn't any evidence to speak of in the first place. To be sure, neither could one support the opposite conclusion, that the tomb was not empty, solely by such refutations. Even for negative conclusions you need (negative) evidence.

If no new evidence comes from outside, then something else needs to come from outside—for example, what Bultmann so openly states, the prior probability that modern science is correct and applies to Jesus' body too. But the lengthy arguments about the texts affect those prior probabilities (whatever they are for an empty tomb) only negligibly.

So while I cannot say this of scriptural studies as a whole, of this particular example I say: *it is not science.* The discussion is of no secular scientific interest.

3. But Why Is It So Fascinating?

This is my second question, and I'm still raising it about the same subdiscipline. I *am* fascinated—I stayed fascinated throughout, even after I said to myself "This is not science." For one source of fascination we don't have far to look—it is the horizon of exegesis. Should we interpret St. Paul as implicitly asserting, or clearly not even mooting, that the tomb was empty? This at least is fascinating, for we have here before us scholars trying to gain religious insight and addressing religious issues important to Christian beliefs. It is clear that they are doing so courageously, even when the verdict about the scriptural sources threatens to contradict cherished Christian traditions or the traditional scriptural bases for deeply held convictions, whether of faith or of morals. This is not a presuppositionless enterprise—it bears out what Father Donahue echoed us from Joseph Fitzmyer: modern Catholic Bible scholars employ those secular tools and techniques with a theological perspective, "a plus or presupposition," that the Scriptures are "the Word of God couched in ancient human language."

But the Roman Curia were also fascinated, already in 1907 when they forbade this to Catholic scholars. Professors Dummett and van Inwagen are fascinated, to the extent of writing lengthy, closely argued papers to demonstrate that they can safely ignore the subject and feel secure that it has not undermined their beliefs. Reluctantly I have come to the conclusion that my own fascination too has a second source: the fascination of the rabbit mesmerized by the headlights of the onrushing car, an inescapable fascination with a threat—a spectre, a devastating possibility. For even if scriptural scholars have actually run ahead of the evidence, even if many of their conclusions have been drawn in part from assumptions we reject—even if all our beliefs so far are still standing today, what about tomorrow?

Imagine then your worst-case scenario. Imagine that historians find manuscripts written by three people in the first century A.D.—one who lived in Galilee, one a member of the Sanhedrin in Jerusalem, and a third in Antioch or Ephesus. Imagine these three writers to be as fluent and knowledgeable as Flavius Josephus, independent but mutually confirming, full of data that guide archaeologists to important new sites, and full of information about Jesus and the early Church. Please finish the worst-case scenario for yourself: these sources tell us . . . what? that of all those lives of Jesus written in the last hundred years, the one most abhorrent to you is true, or that the Apostles were a violent group of zealot radicals who became bourgeois as they aged and turned their cause into a lucrative cult . . . finish it yourself, if you have the heart to do it.

Do we really have to ask ourselves this question? We cannot foresee what history and archaeology will uncover. In addition, we believe about our own beliefs that they are true—and hence

compatible with whatever will truly turn up. Short of contra-
dicting ourselves, we can say nothing else. But even so, *how* we
would react if new evidence did come to refute our beliefs—not
something that hasn't happened before, after all—is *also* at least in
part constitutive of our faith. Imagine a marriage or relationship
in which the spectre appears of infidelity, or emotional rejection,
or divorce. Even if it has emerged only so far in one partner's
imagination or fear, it will hang there, destructive through its
very presence, powerful as long as it is not confronted directly.

So one long, sleepless night last week I struggled with this
question: what would I think then? how would I react? how would
I emerge from this? It was not at all easy to say what I do believe,
or to what degree—as St. Augustine said about what time is, I
know it as long as you do not ask me. But that some such scenario
would shatter a picture of reality that I cherish, that there once
was a carpenter in Whose footsteps we falteringly walk, that is
clear. A thousand details could fall individually without harm;
if they fell all at once, however, to be replaced by a grinning
nightmare, that would shatter what I have. But in the end, and
it was coming close to dawn, I found my answer. I said: God, I
would not hold it against you. . . .

If something like this happened to any of us, we wouldn't be
alone. Could we face it as Christians together if *that* scenario of
evidence about Christianity emerged? *I don't know.*

After this point I only have questions, and I can't even begin to suggest answers.[2] That we would have to redescribe our
experience in entirely different terms—that is clear. I have the
impression that some theologians today are already considering
such conclusions from the evidence so far. They are already at
work articulating the new understanding of ourselves in relation
to God, that we would all be forced to seek if the worst-case
scenario came true. We might call that *after the bomb theology.*
Is that what ought to be done? I don't know.

Think again of my earlier analogy of a marriage or relationship. I didn't mean to suggest that all there is to love, or the
main thing or even anything approaching that, is your attitude to
how you would react to unfaithfulness or emotional rejection if it
came. If such a spectre of possibilities arises it has to be faced. But

on the other hand, if you become morbidly preoccupied, if you obsessively work on your counterfactual plans for life and self-understanding after it comes about—then you will most surely be destroying the relationship just as well. This is exactly what Professor Dummett, and I think from discussion also Professor Plantinga, believe the new theologians to be doing. Is that right? I don't know.

If it is right, though, does that mean that a different theology is needed for everyone who differs reasonably on how much probability our historical evidence, plus evidence for the universal applicability of modern science, allows? A different theology for Adela Collins if indeed she has already concluded that the tomb was not empty and for Stephen Davis who believes that it was? Could we still concentrate on the faith we share? Think of people in different denominations, from Orthodox to Quaker. They seem to differ typically in their factual beliefs, in doctrines. We here at this conference believe (I think) that salvation is not to be found in our own denomination alone. Nor does God's saving work stop at the boundaries of Christendom. Does that not mean that people can share faith despite differing factual beliefs? And if so, could there be a theology that articulates just that shared faith? My ignorance is showing here, for I am sure this has been discussed a great deal—but I don't know.

Or is it perhaps true, as Bultmann seems to have been certain, that we are already beyond all this? Born into twentieth-century Western culture, in a time we did not choose but cannot escape, the life-world we enter at our mother's knee is already thoroughly conditioned by science. Perhaps it is pervaded through and through by a new belief structure so thoroughly different from the "three-story world" that even fundamentalists can only pretend to beliefs which they are no longer capable of having? It may be so. If this is the situation at least for some people, must we insist that grace for them can only consist in re-entering a conceptual world their families left behind a number of generations ago? It sounds like an impossible thing to ask. Or was Bultmann wrong? He thought of each generation as bewitched by the world picture of its own science. But was Bultmann himself bewitched by a deeply flawed philosophy—by *scientism* rather than by science? I don't know.[3]

NOTES

1. Analytic philosophy and literary theory are not nearly such distant strangers as is sometimes thought. For some efforts at the interface, see my (1991) and also e.g. Martha Nussbaum's (1988) and my (1988) in Rorty and McLaughlin.

2. Michael Dummett summed up what I took to be the major reaction to my comments by at least some of the philosophers at the conference: "Undoubtedly there are conceivable empirical discoveries that really would demonstrate the Christian religion to be false; but we need not bother about these, since our belief entails that no such discovery will be made." Here I am taking the liberty to quote from a letter, but I think that this passage only repeats what he and some others said explicitly at the conference. Our difference on this matter, which clearly relates also to my previous note, is probably one of general epistemology, rather than peculiarly about religious faith.

3. In reconstructing my notes for this commentary, after the conference, I benefitted from very helpful comments by Professors Dummett, Plantinga, Stump, Suppe, Swinburne, van Inwagen, and a number of others at the conference, and from comments on a draft by Scott Shalkowski and Eleonore Stump, as well as from discussion and correspondence with Gary Comstock.

BIBLIOGRAPHY

Nussbaum, Martha. 1988. "Love's Knowledge," pp. 487–514 in Rorty and McLaughlin.

Rorty, A. O., and B. McLaughlin, eds. 1988. *Perspectives on Self-Deception*. Berkeley: University of California Press.

van Fraassen, B. C. 1988. "The Peculiar Effects of Love and Desire," pp. 123–156 in Rorty and McLaughlin.

——— 1991. "Time in Physical and Narrative Structure," in J. Bender and D. E. Wellbery, eds., *Chronotypes: The Construction of Time*. Stanford: Stanford University Press.